CONCILIUM

Religion in the Eighties

CONCILIUM

Editorial Directors

Concilium 132 (2/1980): Liturgy

SYMBOL AND ART IN WORSHIP

Edited by

Luis Maldonado
and
David Power

English Language Editor
Marcus Lefébure

T. & T. CLARK
Edinburgh

THE SEABURY PRESS
New York

February 1980

T. & T. Clark Ltd., 36 George Street, Edinburgh EH2 2LQ
ISBN: 0 567 30012 9

The Seabury Press, 815 Second Avenue, New York, N.Y. 10017
ISBN: 0 8164 2274 5

Library of Congress Catalog Card No.: 80 50 423

Printed in Scotland by William Blackwood & Sons Ltd., Edinburgh

Concilium: Monthly except July and August.
Subscriptions 1980: All countries (except U.S.A. and Canada) £23·00 postage and handling included; U.S.A. and Canada $54.00 postage and handling included. (Second class postage licence pending at New York, N.Y.) Subscription distribution in U.S. by Expediters of the Printed Word Ltd., 527 Madison Avenue, Suite 1217, New York, N.Y. 10022.

CONTENTS

Editorial   vii

Part I
Articles

Art in the Liturgy
  LUIS MALDONADO   3

The Content of Eastern Iconography
  CONSTANTIN KALOKYRIS   9

Gestures, Symbols and Words in Present-day Western
Liturgy
  ADRIEN NOCENT   19

The Politics of Symbol and Art in Liturgical Expression
  AIDAN J. KAVANAGH   28

Christian Art of the Oppressed in Latin America
  ENRIQUE DUSSEL   40

Freedom of Bodily Expression in the African Liturgy
  BOKA DI MPASI LONDI   53

Part II
Bulletins

Symbols in Christian Worship: Food and Drink
  CYRILLE VOGEL   67

Unofficial Eucharistic Prayers: An Appraisal
  JEAN-PIERRE JOSSUA   74

v

What has Literature to say to Liturgy?
  MICHAEL PAUL GALLAGHER   84

Image, Culture, Liturgy
  CRISPINO VALENZIANO   91

Liturgical Music after the Second Vatican Council
  BERNARD HUIJBERS   101

The Rediscovery of the Role of Movement in the Liturgy
  A. RONALD SEQUEIRA   112

Contributors   120

Declaration of Concilium   123

Editorial

THE THEME of this issue of *Concilium* consists of two distinct but closely related subjects—liturgical expression and beauty or art in the liturgy. Since these subjects are so inter-related the dangers of false aestheticism, mere structuralism, empty formalism and a biased psycho-sociological understanding of the liturgy can be avoided.

From the outset, the great tradition of Eastern Christianity directs us towards a perception of beauty that is specifically based on the gospels (Kalokyris). What we are dealing with is the expression and experience of holiness, the transfiguration of Christ, and, through Christ, the trans-figuration of the whole of creation, without ignoring the actual moment of salvation history in which we live—our situation in the eschatological 'meantime'.

The practising Christian's concept of beauty which the liturgy tries to express comes to him by way of the cross and the resurrection. Perfect beauty is the beauty of God's face in man, the icon of the risen Christ which has already been the disfigured, reviled and wasted Face of the Servant of Yahweh, the Holy Face sketched by Isaiah; 'he had no form or comeliness that we should look at him' (Isa. 53:2).

The glory of the resurrection shines from a face which has achieved the highest perfection through suffering. St Cyril tells us that the temporal dimension of the incarnation and the passion gradually formed the beauty of the Son of God; the beauty of a bloodied but resurrected Face, which, through death, conquered death itself. Through His tears, and without beauty according to worldly standards, the Man of Sorrows reveals Him-self as the Transfigured Christ (O. Clement).

In this way, the apparent irreconciliability of art and Christian liturgy is overcome and to a certain extent resolved despite the dialectic intran-sigence of some who would maintain otherwise.

However, another practical approach towards overcoming any such irreconciliability is suggested by several of these articles—namely, the elimination of all élitism which creates privilege of any kind within the Church's worship.

History shows us that a certain Roman respect for privilege coupled with an endemic poverty of visual appeal has been the cause of the unfortunate dichotomy which appears so frequently in the Catholic West between an 'official' and a 'popular' liturgy (Nocent). The results of this dualism are well known; an ever-growing intransigence, an increasing abandonment of rubrics, a gradual deterioration of what is genuinely popular in favour of devotionalism and 'folklore' and an aggressive resentment towards established structures.

The Second Vatican Council's emphatic statements on the Church as the People of God, the priestly participation of the people in the Church's worship and the use of vernacular languages in the liturgy have brought about vast changes with consequences which we still cannot assess. Respect for privileged positions and the aesthetic tastes of a minority are increasingly being replaced by a liturgy which is 'popular' in the fullest meaning of the word; viz., not just in the theological but also in the sociological sense.

Art, expression and symbol can begin to reflect the struggles, incidental difficulties and the destitution of people, but, given the tensions that exist, it is very difficult to create unifying links of sensitivity, symbolism and aesthetics which reflect the faith of all—a faith which conquers divisions and at the same time looks forward eschatologically, and not 'ideal-istically' to reconciliation (Kavanagh).

Aesthetics cannot ignore ethics. There is an aesthetics of domination and an aesthetics of liberation and Christian aesthetics has no choice but to opt for the latter. There is an art that properly belongs to the oppressed—the popular art created by the working classes—and an art that belongs to the prophetic vanguard of Christianity. Both kinds belong to the category of art of liberation and find their privileged 'locus' in the celebration of the Eucharist (Dussel).

However, if the liturgy is to be really a successful and complete ex-pression of the faith, as its nature demands, it has to be already, here and now, a liberation *in actu* to the extent that through it man achieves personal harmony, is completed and is reconciled with himself, with God and with his neighbour. This integration, reconciliation and har-monisation at all levels of the human person, but especially of his body, soul and spirit, are features of other cultures and civilisations which the Roman liturgy has so far chosen to ignore, but which can make a sig-nificant contribution to its renovation.

A creative vitality, a feeling of bodily sharing and participation, dance as an expression of the depth and intensity of one's feelings as well as an expression of contact with mystery through the uninhibited and liberating use of one's body are sure manifestations of what constitutes liturgical expression (Boka Londi).

The liturgy makes use of words, symbols, images, songs and move-ments, and dancing can be a means of worshipping God (Sequeira). Song and music are essential elements in the liturgy's expressiveness (Huijbers).

Liturgical symbols are numerous and their use in the post-conciliar liturgy has to be increased—the most important of these is the sacred meal. Given the numerous contemporary experiments and attempts to give new life to the celebration of the Eucharist (both as a community and a festival celebration), it is important to realise once again both the relationship and the distinction between a satisfying meal, a sacred banquet and the celebration of the Eucharist (Vogel).

Along with symbols, corporal movements, song, etc., there is no doubt that the word is the fundamental means of expression in the Christian liturgy. The Council has made a very serious effort to re-direct the Church's liturgy towards becoming a more evangelical-prophetic liturgy. The value of this aspect of the liturgy cannot be argued away.

The word of prayer is the liturgical response to the word proclaimed and listened to by the community as the living revelation of the personal God who reveals himself in history. And since a very special form of the word of prayer is the Eucharist Prayer, it is specially important that the texts in use today should be carefully studied. Here, there arises the problem of the tensions between what is official and what is creative, between what is institutionalised and what is freely inspired. Creativity, however, is not the kind of improvisation that can follow a moment of enthusiastic euphoria, supposedly aroused by the Spirit. True creativity always follows subtler lines, like the threads of a cloth woven patiently by tradition; in this sense, true creativity has the character of *midrashic* or Targumic glosses, the results of a practical re-reading of ancient and venerable texts.

One thing that has to be considered above all is the form, literary value and poetic beauty of a liturgical text. To be truly beautiful and poetic a word has to be a faithful reflection of real life. It must not be in any way an imitation of literacy *clichés*—simplicity and constraint must be its hallmarks (Jossua).

Liturgical texts must avoid utilitarian, mediocre and trite language, and expressions which have been rendered trivial through over-use or propaganda. The literary style of liturgical texts must attempt to demand attention, readiness and receptivity at a deeply spiritual level. Every aesthetic experience tries to awaken the spirit of man and sustain his attention; the texts used in the worship of God must try to do the same.

The development of ideas and concepts within the liturgy, must be enriched by stories, parables, symbolism and imagery. Thus, narrative and evocative forms must take precedence over the purely conceptual forms of discourse. The flexibility and interplay of a variety of style and language can be of great benefit in a liturgical celebration which moves at varying rhythms and uses a wide variety of liturgical texts (Gallagher).

Contemporary popular culture makes use of literary images (the 'image' word), liturgical symbols and 'iconic' imagery and the inter-relationship of these creates many problems for their use in liturgical worship. One fundamental criterion for recognising and safeguarding the specific nature of the liturgical image (be it literary or plastic in the two-dimensional or three-dimensional sense) is that of communal participation. Anything that smacks of or creates passivity, inactivity or a lessening of one's personal transaction with the community is anti-liturgical or aliturgical (Valenziano).

LUIS MALDONADO
DAVID POWER

Translated by John A. Macdonald

PART I

Articles

Luis Maldonado

Art in the Liturgy
(A Theological Meditation in Response to an Ecumenical Essay by Olivier Clement)

THE REFORM of the Roman Liturgy by Vatican II has inspired many communities to try and create liturgical celebrations which are based on the gospel and also proclaim the Good News of salvation. Accordingly, this kind of liturgy would have to use the resources of the poverty recommended by the beatitudes and be creative to the extent that it would encourage spontaneity.

These good intentions have been fruitful, but have also created problems. Lack of vision, and inexperience of authentic evangelisation and creativity have brought into being a kind of mutilated liturgy; a liturgy which is devoid of true expressiveness because it lacks the most basic form which is artistic expression. Proclaiming and celebrating the faith in the liturgy can be ineffective if the liturgy itself does not touch the inner depths of man, and this can only be achieved through some form of aesthetic experience. Artistic expression is never the fruit of spontaneity but of genuine creativity which implies a long period of gestation and the search for adequate structures. Because creativity has often been confused with improvisation, an inadequate, impoverished and frustrating form of liturgy has come into being.

This issue of *Concilium* is intended to contribute towards clarifying some of these points. While it was in the process of preparation, *Le Visage intérieur* by Olivier Clement was published and this has been my 'book at bedtime' as I have been thinking over this subject.

When we turn to the Eastern Christian Churches and consider how they have dealt with these problems, we discover that their sensitivity to artistic expression and the way they deal with it in the liturgy have been very successful and is remarkably relevant to our situation in the West. It is well known that a variety of new liturgical experiments, by Catholics and Protestants alike (e.g., the Community of St Gervais in Paris and the accounts in *Seduction of the Spirit* by H. Cox respectively), find their inspiration in the Byzantine liturgy.

O. Clement's work, however, is not just the fruit of Eastern Orthodox inspiration but also derives from the very heart of Western European culture. This dual genesis of his thought creates a favourable atmosphere for ecumenical dialogue. A look at some of his observations, intuitions and conclusions will provide a suitable synthesis in which to consider the theme of this issue of *Concilium*.

A basic expressive ingredient of liturgical tradition is the spoken word and it has to be included in liturgical celebration in a totally artistic context as a way of preparing the senses for experiencing the beauty of the sacred. Moreover, the liturgy has always tried to use art to integrate time (through music and poetry) and space (through painting and architecture). And, in addition, all the material elements of a liturgical celebration, e.g., the smell of incense, shining lights, hymns, images, are symbols of heaven and earth united in the body of Christ through the Holy Spirit.

Through our bodily perceptions, the liturgy makes us spiritually receptive. Its beauty reaches beyond our normal perception of beauty because it comes to us through the cross and resurrection. Furthermore, it is full of silence and light.

A consideration of some of the artistically expressive elements in the liturgy will help us discover their significance for theology and for pneumatic-Christology in particular.

After the Conciliar reforms, there should be no doubt that the spoken word is the principal expressive element in the liturgy, and while it is much used it is also abused. Thus a balance has to be struck by restoring to the word its corresponding polarity of silence. Silence can be equally expressive if properly understood as the antithesis of the spoken word; thus, it is not merely the absence of speech but also expresses completeness, intensity and the brimming-over and ineffable nature of experience.

The binomial reality word-silence, as a dialectic of expression, is not a purely formal or psychological entity because, despite its merely formal appearance, it has a real foundation in theology and is rich in content. In the very depths of its being, the spoken word has its corresponding reality in the Word made flesh just as silence has its complement in the Spirit. Word and silence have their roots in the Trinitarian reality of the relationship between the Word and the Spirit. The Spirit is the breath of the One who bears the Word; it is the silence of the One in the heart of the Word.

The Holy Spirit has no proper name (qua relationship), and no feast-day or specific prayers. In the activity of the Trinity, *ad extra*, the Spirit hovers over the primeval waters as a bird rests over its brood to provide them with shelter and warmth; this is the 'cosmic Pentecost' which makes all things open to the influence of the Word of God who speaks to us in everything; his words are the *logoi spermatikoi*.

Faith, as a personal commitment to God's self-revelation of his hidden presence which allows us to participate in his sanctifying vitality and as an encounter of joy, of fire and of dazzling light is a kind of 'implosion' of silence. Man is rendered speechless and his silence becomes totally expressive; full of the joy of the Spirit, his experience evolves into a celebration.

The Fathers of the Church tell us that we have to 'breathe the Holy Spirit' and the breath of God, which is the Spirit, thus unites with our own physical breathing. The receptive silence which is the fruit of the Spirit's influence becomes fertile ground for meditation which is the natural complement to liturgical prayer. And it is this kind of meditation which the East is offering us today—a prayer in time with our breathing, the circulation of our blood and all the other natural rhythms of our bodies.

Accordingly, in some communities, liturgical celebrations are preceded by half an hour of silent meditation and even the nave of the church is left free so that prayer may be said in a variety of postures.

One special form of rhythmical and corporeal expression is dancing which once again is being used in the liturgy to complement the spoken word within terms of the pneumatology already mentioned. The psalmist says: 'Let them dance in praise of His name' (Ps. 149:3).

Silence saturates the word but does not absorb it just as the Spirit reposes in the Word eternally and acts in the incarnation and in the deifying transfiguration of Christ's humanity. Moreover, silence is neither anterior or posterior to the word itself but is its very essence.

In the liturgy, silence can also be present through poetry and music— aspects of the temporal dimension of art which forms part of the total and integral art of the liturgy. Liturgical singing can be especially important and useful in this sense as it disposes the word towards silence and directs it towards mystery.

The rhythm of singing and music breaks the autonomy of speech, reveals the mystery therein contained and is a catalyst for the silent music of the body; in this way, it reaches man's heart—'that other body in the very depths of our being'. It is precisely here, in this 'inwardness' of body, heart and silence, that symbols and images become meaningful to form the poetry that unites heaven and earth.

Music takes away the purely conceptual element from the words of a song and through sound makes them produce their own most fascinating and enchanting effects.

When the spoken word becomes liturgical song it creates a fusion of antinomy and symbol. I refer to the antinomy of inaccessible mystery and the divine 'philanthropy'; the antinomy of the infinite which allows itself to be limited and defined and that of the incomprehensible which wants to be understood.

The dynamism of this antinomy demands that the structure of songs be symbolic. This symbolism can represent the 'wonderful deeds' of God in salvation history or be the cosmic symbolism which reaches its fullest significance in the transfiguration. The burning bush then becomes an image of the mother of God, sign of the earth on which light has been cast—the land of those living in Christ and his Eucharist. Water becomes the water of death and resurrection. The three elements of fire, wind and living water represent the Spirit, which, in the Eucharist, gives life to the dead earth. Finally, the Cross, prefigured by the tree of Paradise, the ark of Noah, and Jacob's ladder, becomes the new tree of life which for ever unites what is created with what was not created.

This last point is more relevant to sacred song as a text and is specially applicable to liturgical poetry which is an important form of expression neglected at the moment in the liturgy. Apart from the psalms, there is a very serious lack of lyrical texts and hymns in the present Roman Missal, while there is a vast quantity of poetic texts which are used in the Byzantine liturgy especially when the office forms part of the celebration of the Eucharist.

An important source of material to meet this need could be the corpus of liturgical poetry created between A.D. 500 and 1000 not just in the East but also in the West, and which can still be of use today. The renewal of liturgical poetry which has just begun will be unsuccessful if it does not follow the living traditions initiated by the Fathers of the Church.

It is very significant that monasteries are the cradles of the best hymn composition and liturgical experiments in the West as well as in the East. Perhaps we could note that the traditional desert situation of the monastery has been replaced by the urban desert of our vast cities today. The most favourable environment for the creation of liturgical texts, especially the poetic ones, is that of long and patient prayer and regular meditation.

Within the spatial dimension of art which completes the context of total and integral art in liturgical celebration, pictorial art makes a special contribution towards uniting liturgical and aesthetic experience. Painting unveils the mystery of things in the scrutiny of light and it does so, not by creating 'another world' but by showing up the intensity of what is real, the density of things, that which makes them what they are; art expresses the truth of things and their peace in being. Art does not attempt to create an external similarity but to make known the secret nature of things, which manifests and hides itself in a continual process, this is the secret of appearance.

We can recall here the word used in Genesis to describe things when they were created: *tob*. It means real, beautiful, and good; and the same can be said of the biblical Greek word *kalos*. The painter sees and allows us to see that a particular thing is real, beautiful and good. He enters into things and causes things to reveal their true being. For their part, things open out to the artist so that the painter and the world have a kind of nuptial relationship.

The ancient Greek concept of the world of things corresponds to this process of pictorial art. The *physis* is what makes itself manifest in the mystery; it appears but never fully manifests itself. The earliest Byzantine aesthetics which inspired the builders of Sancta Sophia used the *techné* for a similar purpose. Artistic technique is a form of procreation, a bringing to life and a giving birth which reveal the secret beauty of things. Thanks to the artist, matter and the materials used become beautiful partners, and then fertile mothers who produce children of light.

The painter, and the plastic artist in general, knows how to live in silence till he experiences the world around him not just as a body of flesh but also as a clothing of light. He also discovers that his body is not limited by its 'tunic of skin' but is interwoven with the wind, the sun, the rocks and the clouds. The same perceptions can come to us if we enter into communion of contact with the artist's work. We feel that our bodies are made of light and can reach the furthest corners of the earth. Man, the prisoner of haste and eagerness, can only capture what is momentary and useful. The painter teaches us to see. And helping us to see is helping us to slow down and capture the present both as an instant of eternity and as a free gift. He helps us to perceive something which is beyond us, not in the sense of being 'of another world', but as being the revelation of being itself; the secret of things revealed in light.

In real terms, iconic art shows that the incarnation really took place in matter, that it has lightened up the secret depths of matter and restored to matter its fundamental sacramentality. In Christ, matter has become 'spiritual'; it has become impregnated with the 'powers' of the Spirit. Thus, the face of man becomes a sacrament of beauty. An icon tries to express 'the ineffable beauty of the luminous glory of the face of Christ', and the Spirit's participation in that light.

What constitutes the very essence of beauty is the light which is Christ; the Christ whom the Alexandrian theologians described as 'the light of light', 'enduring brilliance of the divine sun', 'splendour of the Father' and 'spreading glow of the lamp of the sun'. The Alexandrian theology of the fourth and fifth centuries symbolises the relationship of Christ with the Father by means of imagery of the sun's fertility.

B

Beauty is a divine attribute, a divine energy, one of the fundamental areas of God's presence in his creation, his 'ecstasy'. Through Christ, divine beauty restores human beauty in light. As one of the antiphons of the feast which celebrates the restored cult of the icon says: 'It has restored its original dignity to the image of God, and has united it to the divine beauty'. And Cyril of Alexandria comments: 'Through the beauty of the Son in time, men are brought to eternal beauty' (*Treasury* 559).

Today, more than ever, we have to rediscover the ultimate beauty which brings the breath and fire of the Spirit to us. The Spirit is the hypostasis of beauty. Absolute beauty is the beauty of the face of God in man, the icon of the risen Christ; and the beauty of the faces of men in God, the icons of the resurrected. On both the human and the divine level, on the level of the Spirit, this beauty is the 'burning bush' of the union of earth and heaven. Through the Spirit of beauty, God goes out of himself—beauty is the 'ecstasy' of God—and the earth becomes receptive, and heaven comes into being.

It has to be added that absolute beauty is inseparable from creative love. When man discovers the words of the Word made flesh in things ('The Bible of the World' or *logoi spermatikoi* of the Fathers) and when he sees the inalienable vocation of the icon in so many faces of those who have died for the faith, he becomes a person with a community dimension who takes part in the transfiguration of the earth.

Christian culture has always tried to discover and purify the mystery in things in order to free the world from its idols, magic and narcissistic illusions. And this kind of desacralisation of the world is only a step towards its transfiguration. Art, then, has to bear witness to the Spirit, imminent and becoming known in all things, for whom there is no sacred or profane but only the 'beauty of the world as an icon of God's Kingdom'; that is, the truth of things in light.

Within this transfiguring process the face becomes completely readable as the ancient aesthetes say; that is, totally and fully transparent; in addition, all things display the *splendor veri* of the definition which the ancients gave of beauty. In other words, mystery comes to the surface in the truth of all beings and things once they are freed from all opaqueness, banality and vagueness in the light whose inaccessible source is in the risen Christ.

Translated by Angus Macdonald

Constantin Kalokyris

The Content of
Eastern Iconography

1. ICONS IN EASTERN CHURCHES

FROM THE beginning, iconography in the Eastern Churches appeared as art not for its own sake, but for the Church. Thus, its content was determined directly by the needs and the profounder purposes of the Church. Faith in the spiritual reality, in the immortality of the soul and in the blessedness that is in God was primary. The believer had to be taught in every way possible that in his journey towards perfection in Christ he would have to struggle against the powers of darkness, against manifold evil, and even to reach martyrdom, as did the Saviour, the apostles, and the martyrs of the Faith. It was necessary for the Church to present these personages as examples to inspire, to guide, and to encourage the faithful. In the life of the Church there were also misinterpretations of the orthodox teaching that she followed, that is, heresies emerged. For this reason, the Church established her creed, her dogmas. For these and about these, the Church developed the higher theology. This theology was expounded and interpreted from the pulpit. But besides these dogmas, there was need (especially for the simpler folk) of other more empirical commentaries.[1]

For all these purposes, i.e., her needs and her aspirations, the Eastern Church sought the assistance of painting. So Orthodox icons of all periods answered these purposes completely. Thus, the content of the icons was interwoven with the life, the evolution, and the whole tradition of the Church.

Especially after the iconoclastic controversy and the victory of Orthodox belief regarding the icons and the official bond of Orthodoxy with iconography (the victory of the icons was regarded for this reason as a victory of Orthodoxy and it is as such that the Sunday of Orthodoxy has been named in commemoration), the painting was characterised as dogmatic, since its content dealt with the doctrinal truths. The Pantocreator in the dome depicts at once the Father and the Son—the expression of the dogma concerning consubstantiality. The dogma of the Virgin as ὄντως Θεοτόκος (truly mother of God), formulated by the Council of Ephesus (431), was expressed characteristically, after the iconoclastic controversy, by consistently portraying the mother of God and the child Jesus on her knees in the quarter-sphere of the niche canopy, in the sanctuary. The dogma of the first and second Coming of the Lord was expressed by presenting the Ἑτοιμασία (preparation of the Throne) with the empty Throne of Judgment and the instruments of the Passion of the Saviour in the vault before the apse of the sanctuary. Finally, from the Macedonian and Comnenian period (tenth-twelfth century), the development of the monastic spirit, the cultivation in it of ecclesiastical literature, and the study of the apocryphal writings, gave the content to the contemporary iconography, which, especially during the period of the Palaeologoi (thirteenth-fifteenth century), became a narrative art. The iconographic compositions, from this period on, became richer and contained many persons; psalms and hymns (such as the Akathistos hymn) as well as many scenes from the Apocrypha, were depicted in the churches.

But let us see these things more specifically. As we said, the faith of the Church in the reality beyond this world, that is, in the truth of the spiritual world, from the beginning defined the essential character of the content of Eastern iconography. She is primarily interested in the beauty of this spiritual world and, with the means which she possesses, the Orthodox Church seeks to be the interpreter of that world. Her transcendental content is not the physically beautiful or the naturally good; and for this reason does not seek to project natural good and beauty (τό κατά φύσιν καλόν). Those, therefore, who see and judge Byzantine iconography with the conceptions of classical antiquity regarding the beautiful, will only confuse things. The purpose and the ideal of ancient Greek art was the presentation of the natural good and the beautiful by nature in that well known undivided unity of καλόσ καγαϑός (beauty and virtue). On the contrary, the purpose and the ideal of Eastern iconography is the expression of holiness, which, of course, is not made sensate by the physically beautiful, that is to say, it is not by necessity united to this. In antiquity the ideal was shown by the formation of things according to the laws of the naturally good.[2]

On the contrary, in Christian Eastern art the beautiful is determined not by the natural formation of the objects, but by its sublime content, that is, by its power of serving the ideals of the Faith. This is characteristically confessed by St John Chrysostom: 'Οὕτω καί σκεῦος ἕκαστον λέγομεν καλόν καί ζῷου καί φυτόν οὐκ ἀπό τῆς διαπλάσεως, οὐδ'ἀπό τοῦ χρώματος, ἀλλ'ἀπό τῆς διακονίας'. (Thus, we say that each vessel, animal, and plant is good, not from its formation or from its colour, but from the service it renders.)[3] Thus, what concerns the Church is the sublime purpose, the content of a superior spiritual quality, so that it regards as good any work whose formation, colour, and form in general can express this content. And the Eastern art did not copy nature nor seek the form or the colour as an end, but, taking such technical and artistic elements as were necessary for the believers to become familiar with its spirit, succeeded in rendering the more sublime meanings of Orthodoxy by means of an exceptional abstraction.

2. THE USE OF ICONS IN THE EASTERN LITURGY

The position of the mystery of Holy Eucharist in the Church is known from the beginning as it constituted the centre and the essence of the liturgy, which is but a representation of the mystery of the divine economy. The fundamental significance of the Holy Eucharist is not only unequivocally stated by the Fathers, but also manifested by Christian art in its most ancient monuments. Believers assemble in church primarily in order to experience the represented work of salvation in Christ and to participate at the Τράπεζαν Κυρίου (Lord's Table), to which the prayers, the hymns, and the sermon are directed. The liturgical act of the priest is a repetition of the one done in heaven by Christ, the great high-priest.

Generally from the era of the Macedonian and Comnenian emperors, the representation of the 'Θεία Αειτουργία' (divine liturgy) was reserved for the niche in the sanctuary depicting the great high-priest, Christ, below a ciborium (permanent canopy over the Holy Table)—rarely only once, but more commonly twice: transmitting on one side his body and on the other side his blood to the Apostles who in order or, as later, in groups approach with awe. But later still the divine liturgy was represented in this space in the form of its ideal performance in heaven, so that the sacred gifts are carried in litany by the angels wearing the vestments of deacons and are presented to the great high-priest, the Lord, as we have it in that excellent wall-painting in the Perivleptos church of Mystra, Greece (fourteenth century). Below the divine liturgy are depicted the 'σεβίζοντες' (the venerating ones), great hierarchs (especially from the Palaeologian period) with their liturgical scrolls (they are the editors of the divine liturgy). These personages are inseparably linked to the depicted mystery, a fact which was made more emphatic from the twelfth century onwards by the presentation of the sacrificed Lamb upon the paten, which later became the Μελισμός, that is, the painting of the Lord as a child in this vessel (divided into pieces) and alluding to the sacrifice of the Lamb performed by the priest on the holy table.

The liturgical themes mentioned above determine especially the so-called liturgical inconographic cycle which, with the two other cycles (that is, the dogmatic and the cycle of feast days) dominate in the Eastern churches from the Byzantine period. Thus, the liturgical content is one of the principal characteristics of the essence of Eastern iconography.

When the Eastern Church calls us who 'τά χερουβίμ μυστικῶς εἰκονίζοντας' (mystically represent the cherubin) to 'πᾶσαν τήν βιωτικήν ἀποθώμεθα μέριμναν' (abandon every wordly concern) in order to receive the King of all who is invisibly escorted by angelic orders, Orthodox iconography comes to help more empirically in making this invitation as well as the whole purpose of the cherubic hymn more conscious. The ideal figures of the angels represented in the Eastern Churches, who approach with awe as they bear the gifts to the great hierarch Lord, and the Apostles, depicted in utter contrition and compunction, who come to receive communion from his immaculate hands, make perceptible the content of the hymn perceptible in the best manner and impose an understanding of it with their whole spiritual atmosphere. No other art, I think, ever succeeded in expressing what was expressed by the Orthodox art in Mystra (Greece). Here, in the famous wall-painting of the Perivleptos church, the fleshless figures of the angels in a magnificent rhythmic procession, bearing with fear and trembling the sacred gifts, and covering their eyes before the highest sacrifice, offer to the spectator, through the dematerialisation achieved, the impression of a vision from the other world and make incomparably perceptible the content of the liturgical hymn: 'Σιγησάτω πᾶσα σάρξ βροτεία καί στήτω μετά φόβον καί τρόμου καί μηδέν γήϊνον ἐν ἑαυτῇ λογιζέσθω . . .' (let every human being keep silence and stand with fear and trembling and think not of any earthly thing concerning himself). Truly, the technique and the style of the inspired iconographer succeeded in commenting excellently upon the magnificent hymn and in exalting the believers to its liturgical height.

What we have said should, I think, make apparent the significance of Orthodox iconography as a liturgical art, aiming to make understandable and conscious to the faithful the sublime content of the divine liturgy and especially the profounder liturgical act of the Holy Eucharist.

3. OTHER ELEMENTS OF EASTERN LITURGICAL ICONOGRAPHY

Eastern iconography is not simply a religious art, it is also theological. Its themes are not simply related to religious history, but are organised according to the high theology of the Orthodox Church. Roman Catholic churches are usually decorated with pictures of the Passion of Christ, which are related to the familiar 'stations' of the cross of the Roman Church. Thus, the whole church is filled with the Passion, emphasised in a sided and exclusive way, while on the doors of the churches, the Church receives her faithful with the fearful scene of the second Coming. Eastern Churches, on the contrary, are filled with the twelve scenes of the great feasts from the whole life of Christ, the familiar 'Δωδεκάορτον' (Twelve Great Feasts). Thus, it is not only the Passion that is emphasised, but the whole life of the Lord, including the main events in his life from his birth until his ascension. In other words, the high theology of the divine economy is represented, which is certainly not confined to the Passion.

Whatever is taught by the divine liturgy, by the hymns of the Church and the words from the pulpit, is excellently commented upon by the silence of iconography. The cross of the vaults in particular, which covers the Eastern Church and which depicts within its four sections the whole life of the Saviour, gives the faithful standing below the impression that they are dominated by that sacred symbol *par excellence*, that they are under the protection of the Κυριακοῦ σημείου (the Lord's sign),[4] which contains and expresses all Christian teaching.[5] At the entrance of the church, at the βασίλειον πύλην ('royal gate') the faithful are received by Jesus, τήν θύραν (the door),[6] that is, by the Lord as teacher.[7] Later on, in the dome which rises at the centre of the church and at the point where the vaults cross, the triumphant figure of the Pantocreator, the Lord ἐξομολόγησιν καί μεγαλοπρέπειαν ἐνδεδυμένος (clothed in praise and magnificence), dominates over the entire area and is illuminated by the abundant radiant light which enters from the windows in the drum of the dome. As the Pantocreator is projected from the depths of the dome, the centre of the cross formed by the vaults appears to be hollowed and extended by him to the infinite, as if to denote that this central point of the cross is the triumph of the Resurrection, that its essence and depth is the victor over death, the infinite Lord, who dwells in heaven καί τά ἐπί γῆς ἐφορῶν (and supervises the things of earth), the immortal King of all to whom πᾶν γόνυ κάμψῃ οὐρανίων καί ἐπιείων καί καταχθονίων (every knee shall bend in heaven and on earth and below the earth).[8] Actually the dome became for the Easterns the symbol of heaven, while the Pantocreator, as already noted, was more specifically ὁ Πατήρ ἅμα καί ὁ Υἱός (The Father and the Son together), the expression of the doctrine of their consubstantiality. More generally speaking, we must see three other attributes which the Byzantine Pantocreator expresses. He is the Creator, the Saviour, and the Judge. This triple theological significance is successfully conceived and excellently rendered by Eastern iconography. Thus, the Byzantine Pantocreator possesses the royal magnificence of the Creator, the expression of the active goodness of the Saviour, and the austerity of the impartial Judge. Even here the art, serving the ideals of the Church, created a work of great power which expresses a whole theology (Creation, Salvation, Judgment).

In the quarter-sphere of the niche in the sanctuary of Eastern Orthodox churches, the *theotokos* is usually depicted holding the child Jesus and escorted by two archangels. This quarter-sphere, with the rest of the niche, is the architectural section which unites the roof of the church with the floor; the upper (dome), symbolising the heavens where the Pantocreator is represented, is united with the lower, that is, the earth, the floor of the church, where the faithful are standing. Here, therefore, the *theotokos* stands between heaven and earth, as ἡ μεσιτεύ-σαοα τήν σωτηρίαν τοῦ γένους ἡμῶν (the intercessor of the salvation of our race) as ἡ κλῖμαξ ἡ ἐπουράνιος δι' ἧς κατέβη ὁ Θεός (the heavenly ladder by which God descended), as ἡ τά ἄνω τοῖς κάτω συνάψασα (the one who united the upper with the lower) by means of the divine child in her arms. (Akathistos hymn.)

The representation of the Lord as teacher at the entrance of the church, the Pantocreator in the dome, and the *theotokos* in the niche of the sanctuary determine the so-called dogmatic cycle of iconography in the Eastern Orthodox Church.

4. RELATIONS BETWEEN EASTERN AND WESTERN ICONOGRAPHY

Totally characteristic of the content of eastern iconography is its depth. It is evident that a spiritual, a liturgical, and a theological art, as we have seen, should have sought to express depth and profundity in the representation of its themes.

What this means is that the iconography is directed not only to the sentiments, but also, and primarily, to the spirit. It does not seek to make a momentary and passing impression, but to create a permanent and continuous influence upon the soul by means of the understanding and practice of its content by the faithful. Indeed one Western icon of the Lord, for example, the so-called 'Blond Nazarene' (sic), with hair parted in the middle of the head and falling to the shoulders in uniform waves, with blue eyes, with the musing or melancholy countenance of nineteenth-century romanticism, and the whole naturalistic rendering of the figure, is perhaps directed, through the passion for beauty, to the emotion of certain people. But the lack of expressive power of such pictures does not move those who seek spiritual satisfaction, that is, those who seek under the expressive figures the shattering and profound idea of the icon, just as happens with the Byzantine icons of Christ in which the exuberance of the characteristics (such as the large eyes and the searching spirit) and the whole vigorous expression render, in the best possible manner, the majestic and exalted spiritual mobility of the Lord's face.

What we are saying becomes clearer when we examine the icons of the Crucifixion in Western art in contrast to similar icons of Eastern iconography. Western art presents here the tragic drama of a man undergoing the ultimate agony of suffering. It is primarily directed to the emotions and seeks to move one by exalting human pain. And so Western artists compete to see whose work will be more dramatic. With the picture of the horror of a human corpse (cadaver) they seek the creation of 'sympathy' (*Einfühlung*)—in the artistic sense—in the spectator. Some examples of this, among many others, are the 'Crucifixion' of Cranach (1472-1553) in the gallery (Haus der Kunst) of Munich; the 'Crucifixion' of Fernandez (1566-1636) in the museum of Valladolid; the 'Crucifixion' of Goya (1746-1828) in Madrid (Prado), and especially the 'Crucifixion' of Grünewald (died 1530) in Isenheim, where the tragedy of the suffering Christ comes to a climax in the dying spasm displayed by the teeth projecting from the opened mouth and the foaming tongue.

By contrast to the above Crucifixions of Western art, in Orthodox Eastern art, the iconographers were concerned not only with the emotion but with the whole being of the believers. Thus, they created icons of the Crucifixion in which, in the face of the Lord, royal majesty (the majesty of controlled passion), calmness and serenity dominate and in this way express not so much the pain of martyrdom as the sublime theological significance of the completed sacrifice upon the Cross, which is condensed in Christ's world τετέλεσται . . . (It is finished, that is, his work is completed). Thus, while the Western painter, directing his work to the emotions, presented a human drama, the Orthodox iconographer, directing his work primarily to the spirit, expressed τήν ἐν στραυρῷ θείαν κένωσιν (the divine kenosis or emptying on the Cross) of the God-Man. Moreover, the Orthodox painter, believing with the Fathers and the hymn-writers of the Church that the flesh of the Lord did not suffer any decay whatsoever (ἡ γάρ σάρξ σου διαψθοράν οὐκ οἶδε δέσποτα 'for thy flesh, Lord, knew no decay'), represented the body of the Saviour without any change on account of death. The body of the Lord διά τόν ἐνοικήσαντα Λόγον ἄψθαρτον διέμεινε (remained incorruptible because of the indwelling Logos), according to St Athanasius the Great.[9] For this reason there are neither spasms of the mouth here nor effaced eyes; the colour of the body is not made greenish-yellow, nor distorted. The calm inclination of the head and the closed eyes are sufficient in great Eastern art.

Whatever is true regarding the difference between Western and Orthodox art in the presentations of the Crucifixion is also true in the representations of the Resurrection. In the Resurrection icon according to the impressive Latin type (created in the eleventh century in the West and made known through Giotto) the Lord is usually represented holding a banner of victory as he is raised in the air as if by a vigorous jump from a sacrophagus tomb, whose slate covering is raised by an angel, obviously to permit him to exit, while the guards are shown fallen upon the ground. But according to the Eastern type, the Resurrection, from the ninth century on,[10] is shown primarily by Christ's descent into Hades. This iconographic type represents the Lord in Hades surrounded by a radiant glory;[11] he is trampling upon the demolished gates of hell and bears in his left hand the Cross of the Resurrection, while with his right hand he raises from a sarcophagus Adam, who represents the human race. Often, below the broken gates, one can see stretched out and bound in chains the personification of death as an old man, whom the Saviour θανάτῳ πατήσας (defeated by death), while he Himself was resurrected.

In contrast to the Latin type, the Byzantine Resurrection clearly expresses a more profound spiritual content. It renders incomparably the profound significance of the victorious Hymn of Easter:

Χριστός ἀνέση ἐκ νεκρῶν, θανάτῳ θάνατον πατήσας
καί τοῖς ἐν τοῖς μνήμασι ζωήν χαρισάμενος,

(Christ was risen from the dead; He defeated death by death, and to those in the tombs he gifted life.) This hymn declares that Christ, through his descent into Hades, defeated him who has the power of death, that is, the devil,[12] and by his Resurrection he liberated and resurrected the dead of old and redeemed the entire human race—living in darkness and death—whose symbol is the forefather Adam. The Eastern type, therefore, expresses, like the Resurrection of Jesus Christ, a universal redemption, that is, the work of salvation completed through the descent into Hades and the resurrection following the victory over Hades. Thus, the Resurrection is not merely, as in the Latin type (exit from the grave), a visible declaration of that very instant in time only, when the event of rising from the grave took place.

The Western type showing Christ jumping out of the grave was imposed upon Orthodox iconography during the Turkish domination (especially from the seventeenth century), through the influence of the West. It practically became the prevalent icon of the Resurrection, when in essence it is a type not only untraditional but orthodox. It shows the Saviour rising from the grave after the angel has moved the large rock for this purpose. But the removal of the rock ἀπό τῆς θύρας τοῦ μνημείου (from the entrance to the tomb), which is mentioned as a known fact by all the evangelists (Matt. 28:2; Mark 16:4; Luke 24:2; John 20:2), was certainly not done so that the Almighty Lord could emerge from the grave, but precisely so that the myrrh-bearers and the Apostles could see the empty tomb and verify the Resurrection. According to the Church faith, the Lord was resurrected θεοπρεπεῖ δυνάμει καί ἐξουσίᾳ (by divine power and authority) while the tomb was still closed.[13] Moreover, οὐδέ κεκλεισμένον ἦν τι τῷ ποιητῇ (there was not anything shut to the creator),[14] as we are further reminded characteristically by the hymn-writers:

Κύριε, ὥσπερ ἐξῆλθες ἐσφραγισμένου τοῦ τάψου,
οὕτως εἰσῆλθες καί τῶν θυρῶν κεκλεισμένων πρός
τούς μαθητάς σου,

(Lord, as thou camest out from the sealed tomb, so also didst thou enter while the doors were shut to thy disciples.)[15]

John Chrysostom also taught that after the Resurrection the angel came . . . for the women. In order that they may believe that he arose, they see the tomb empty of the body. For this reason, did he remove the rock.[16]

From all that we have said above, one should not think that Eastern iconography, during its long process, ignored natural reality, that is, the so-called realistic element. This element of realism, however, was not used as in the West, nor even as we perhaps understand it today (being taught so by the Renaissance), but rather for a definite purpose and only after it had been assimilated and subordinated to the whole vigorous spiritual power of Eastern art. Whereas in Western art the element of realism constituted an end in itself, that is, it was sought as an artistic ideal, in Orthodox art, on the contrary, it served another purpose, that is, the need to subordinate the material element to the spiritual, our lower nature to our higher. Moreover, the manifest subordination of the material to the spiritual in these icons also shows the beauty of high quality which the first element comes to possess from the second, that is the beauty which the material element ἐνδύεται (puts on) when it is dominated by the life-giving and life-transforming power of the spirit of 1Christ.[17] Christ, μορψωθείς τό᾽ καθ ἡμᾶς, ἐθέωσε τό πρόσλημμα (being formed in likeness to us, deified what he received).[18] And it is this deification, this theosis of human nature that is made perceptible by the art of Eastern icons.

Notes

1. P. G. Migne *Patriarch Germanos* 98, 384.
2. Plato *Politeia* 401, B.f.
3. P. G. Migne *Homily 4 on I Timothy* 11, 253.
4. According to Clement of Alexandria *Stromates*, 11 in P. G. Migne 8.

5. Ο λόγος τοῦ Σταυροῦ (the word of the Cross), according to St Paul, I Cor. 1:18.

6. John 10:9 (I am the door; if any man enters through me, he shall be saved).

7. Matt. 23:8.

8. Phil. 2:10.

9. P. G. Migne 25, 112.

10. See C. Kalokyris *Byzantine Wall-Paintings*, p. 75, note 9.

11. According to the Apocrypha p. 328, and to the bishop of Caron, Theodore Aboukaras (eighth century) P. G. Migne 97, 1496.

12. Heb. 2:14.

13. P. G. Migne *Cyril of Alexandria* 76, 1165.

14. P. G. Migne *Athanasius the Great* 25, 140.

15. *Pentecostarion* (Venice edition) p. 130.

16. P. G. Migne *Homily on Matthew* 58, 783.

17. In regard to the 'formation' of Christ in us, as St Paul writes 'until Christ be formed in you', see Gal. 4:19.

18. *Menaion* of December 24, p. 183.

Adrien Nocent

Gestures, Symbols and Words in Present-day Western Liturgy

IF THERE is one thing that is clear about present-day European and American culture, it is that it has over the past few years become emphatically audio-visual. This new feeling for gesture and symbol links our culture up again with older civilisations and also with the civilisations of Asia and Africa. Films and television have accustomed us more and more to the presentation of images, and illustrated adventure and science-fiction stories are more and more widespread. This tendency could, of course, go too far and in that case would be the expression and signal of an alarming decline of culture. At the same time there is a real question as to whether an abstract intellectualism which makes no attempt to body itself forth in gestures is the best model of culture. Religious aspirations today also tend to want to express themselves by means of gestures. Charismatics show this in their meetings, for they instinctively make extensive use of bodily gestures, thereby exhibiting a marked contrast with the impassive serenity of those taking part in official liturgical assemblies. Karlheinz Stockhausen, the German musician, born in Cologne in 1928, in 1964 wrote *Inori* (Adoration) for soloist and orchestra. The piece is composed on the basis of a series of 13 pitches, 13 tempi, 13 intensities, to which correspond 13 gestures of prayer or *mudra*, borrowed from various traditions and performed by a dancer in the middle of a symphony orchestra of some 90 musicians. The dancer is referred to in German as 'Beter', a 'prayer', the one who prays. Gestures and music develop in perfect synchroncicity, so much so that the gestural part has its own score written for it. I can vouch personally for the fact that at every production of this work in the large towns I have been present at the audience took part in this danced prayer with great interior fervour. It

19

is impossible not to be aware of the contrast between the attitude evinced here and the distant and jaded behaviour of our congregations in many a place still.

This fact compels us to dwell on it now that fifteen years have elapsed since the renewal of the liturgy. And it would not be fair to criticise this recent reform without also criticising many of its applications with some severity. For it is strange that, in our audio-visual epoch where everybody talks about the need to adapt, we go to such lengths to refuse to allow even the most discreet symbolism and the most dignified gestures into our celebrations. This smacks of a fixed determination to prefer the ear to the eye. The fashion of the moment affects a sort of immobilism: the arms hang limply down the sides; any procession that might suggest a marching prayer on the way towards the altar, towards a meeting and dialogue with God, is suppressed as a piece of pompous formalism; a procession with the Book of the Gospels is proscribed as being a sort of relic of the middle ages—it is after all only a book like any other; the altar is primarily what it is rationally—a table; incense has been done away with since it belongs to another civilisation and has no symbolic relevance for us today; candles are only just tolerated, even though our present-day aesthetic sense of a banquet is incomplete without them.

1. KEEPING THE VISUAL AT A DISTANCE

This horror of gesture and symbol is pretty primitive and simplistic, but it seems to be rooted in a reaction against the clutter of accumulated riches piled pell-mell on top of each other and against the formalised and hollow performance of the liturgy that a misunderstanding of this clutter gave rise to. There is some excuse for repugnance to a liturgy based on 'court etiquette' and for the lack of enthusiasm for a romantic and mock-Cluniac reform. Such feelings are authentic enough and go with a certain ideal of poverty, but they do not justify certain colloquialisms that verge on the vulgar: the replacement of 'The Lord be with you' by 'Good morning, everybody', which is a paternalist adaptation if ever there was one, the work of clerics who are perpetual Peter Pans and children of the rich playing at having the common touch. And it is fair enough to be unhappy about a tendency to what has recently been called 'mis-erabilism'. This is certainly not what Vatican II wanted and these so-called applications cannot be laid at its door.

Is it not, however, the case that there has always been a suggestion of visual diffidence and aristocratic aloofness about our Roman liturgy? It, therefore, becomes important, if not indespensable, to try to analyse the attitude of the Roman liturgy down the ages. This is a delicate enterprise, in which absolute and over-simplified affirmations have to be avoided. Space here does not permit anything more than suggestions for more serious work.

An examination of the liturgical documents of the first three centuries yields only indirect descriptions of the unfolding of the liturgy in Rome. Thus, the description which St Justin gives us in the year 150 contains no allusion to any gesture or symbolism of any kind: it confines itself to the essential and to the functional. It is true that he is writing to an outsider.[1] We have to wait for St Cyprian to have the mingling of wine and water, mentioned by St Justin, enriched with symbolic explanation.[2] We must, however, realise that this symbolism is theological in inspiration and is applied conventionally to the water and the wine, whereas the Eastern interpretation derives from the blood and water that flowed from the side of Christ. The same reservation applies to the Apostolic Tradition of Hippolytus of Rome 65 years later. We do, it is true, find here a blessing of the lamp which relies for its meaning on the symbolism of light.[3] When neophytes share in communion for the first time, they receive not only bread and wine but also water, milk and honey; these are symbols of the promised land—but also conventional specifics for newly-born babies.[4] Apart from the rite of total immersion, the laying-on of hands for confirmation,[5] the laying-on of hands over the offerings by the concelebrants during the Eucharistic prayer[6] and the laying of hands on bishops and priests during their ordination,[7] and the laying-on of hands on the deacon by the bishop,[8] there is no insistence on gesture symbols.

After the peace of Constantine, the liturgies diversified. Western liturgy became remarkable for the scope of its creativity, but this was limited almost exclusively to the euchology, for its gestures and symbols remained very sober. Even when solemnities came to be created on the model of the development of the liturgy for Christmas in the context of the victory of the sun over the clouds, the liturgy did not develop a corresponding symbolism. The euchology and Roman canon might well contain such Constantinian and imperial expressions as *Honor, secundus meritus*; the Roman canon might well seem influenced by the central preoccupation of the pagan cult, namely, the offering, but the symbolism still did not come into the liturgy of Rome along with the terminology and literary forms. How is one to explain this apparently deliberate rejection of symbolism and gesture? Is it because of a conscious opposition to the practice of contemporary pagan religions? Or is it on account of the insistence on that spirituality of worship which distinguishes the Christian cult? Or is it a matter of prudence and the desire to avoid all confusion? It is St Ambrose of all people who seems to testify to this perplexing rejection of symbolism on Rome's part. The context is that of the washing of feet, which in Milan takes place as the neophytes emerge from the baptismal font. This is the way they are welcomed by the community. St Ambrose seems to feel the need to justify himself, and he writes: 'I desire to follow the Roman Church in every respect; at the same time we too have minds. That is why we preserve such customs as are observed elsewhere for better reasons and so have better reasons for doing so.'[9] In the whole of this passage of his treatise St Ambrose is trying to work out for himself why the Church of Rome did not preserve this symbolic gesture and he justifies himself by writing: 'It is the apostle Peter himself whom we are following, it is his fervour which we are embracing. What does the Church of Rome say to that? For it is indeed the apostle Peter himself who suggests this course of action to us, and he was bishop of the Church of Rome. It is Peter himself when he says: "Lord, not my feet only but also my hands and my head" (John 13:9).' So St Ambrose registers a lack of enthusiasm for symbolic gestures on the part of the Church of Rome, even when they are ones that the Lord himself performed and which he regarded as important. She seemed to confine herself to essential rites and sacramental signs. Not that the ancient Church as a whole was unacquainted with such things. Etheria, in the account of her pilgrimage to Palestine, recorded the expressive rites of Holy Week in Jerusalem,[10] and especially the ceremony of light, symbol of the resurrection. The Church in Rome enriched its celebrations only later, and then only by copying such symbolic presentations rather sparingly, as, for example, by importing the adoration of the Cross. Later still it accepted the customs of the Frankish Church.[11] Even so, these importations, copied from other liturgies, were not always well received, and St Jerome wrote a harsh letter accusing the *Exsultet* of frivolity.[12] This is why the papal liturgy knew this song rather late. When Lent began to develop through the rite of the catechumenate, the Church of Rome accepted the essential rites, like those of the laying-on of hands, the Ephpheta, the handing over of the symbol of the faith and of the Our Father, and of the gospels.[13] But Rome had no equivalent to the very expressive rite of renunciation known in the East: the candidate, bare-footed, and facing the West, the symbol of darkness, spits in this direction, and then turns towards the East, whence the light of Christ dawns from on high. We should also bear in mind that the most ancient basilicas in Rome were not oriented and that it was only later that Rome began to take note of orientation.

2. THE INFLUENCE OF OTHER LITURGIES

We should, however, note that Rome may have had little taste for symbolism but that it did not close itself to the influences of other liturgies, or even, surprisingly enough, to pagan symbolism, provided only that it did not lend itself to any confusion. This is why it provided for a celebration of the Eucharist that included the blessing of the wife,[14] and yet was quite content with the ordinary family ritual of marriage, and this right to the end of the eleventh century.[15]

Ordo Romanus I of the mass could have introduced some gestures into its description of the papal celebration, for instance, in connection with the use of Africa according to which the faithful brought their gifts to the altar. The ritual is, on the contrary, reduced to the minimum in that the pope and his assistants take the gifts themselves without a procession of the gifts.[16] It is only the prayer *super oblata* that gives the offertory its theological significance. The description of several other rites in this *Ordo*—such as that of the procession from the Lateran to the basilica of Santa Maria Maggiore by way of the Via Merulana[17]—might suggest a certain triumphalism on the part of the bishop of Rome. We must, however, be accurate and record a rite that is purely Roman in origin and is profoundly theological in function: the rite of *fermentum*. According to this rite, when certain priests have been deputed by the pope to celebrate the Eucharist for faithful who live too far away from where the pope is celebrating, then at the moment of the breaking of the bread, a fraction of the consecrated bread is sent to them so that they can place it in their chalice, as a sign of their unity with the local bishop, thus emphasising just that aspect of the theology of the Eucharist which was so dear to St Ignatius of Antioch.[18]

This ritual austerity was not accepted everywhere and in the ninth century France witnessed the birth of such eccentric symbolical explanations of the Eucharistic celebration as those of Amalarius of Metz.[19] This symbolism originated, of course, in a lopsided theology of the mass in so far as this was seen as a divine representation of Calvary, symbols of which were, therefore, to be found in the most minute gesture of the celebrant. And we know how Florus of Lyons combatted this luxuriant symbolism that verged on heresy.[20]

In Germany during the tenth century the monks of St Alban of Mainz were by dint of great ingenuity able to make even the Roman euchology more visual.[21] The Roman-German pontifical, therefore, marks a very important phase in the history of the development of the Roman liturgy, for this absorbed many usages of the German pontifical into its own pontifical in the twelfth century, thereby manifesting its desire to welcome certain forms of symbolism which it did not have the spark of genius to create for itself.[22] This did not, however, prevent Gregory VII from protesting that the Romano-Germanic pontifical spelled a destruction of the Roman liturgy.[23]

The Roman liturgy nevertheless continued to adopt symbolism which it found elsewhere. At the end of the thirteenth century it allowed itself to

C

be influenced by the pontifical of William Durandus of Mende and virtually made that its own, right down to the recent reform of Vatican II. Worthy of special note is the rite of reconciliation, which consists in a dramatisation of the rite of penance for the morning of Maundy Thursday. The Bishop of Mende had introduced into it some usages and antiphons that were theologically very rich.[24]

It is enough to open the collection of manuscripts copied by Edmond Martène in his *De Antiquis Ecclesiae Ritibus*[25] to see how much people outside Rome felt the need of symbolism that was only too often absent from the Roman liturgy.

3. INTELLECTUAL ARISTOCRACY?

This survey is unduly summary for its subject-matter but also unduly long for this article, and yet it can allow us to draw some very firm conclusions about Rome's attitude towards symbolism. This amounts not to repugnance—this would just not square with the way Rome often welcomed symbolism—but to reticence and even a notable indifference towards symbolism, or, more exactly, to an astonishing absence of possible creativity in this regard. Roman liturgy is undoubtedly very cerebral, very undemotic, and it is hardly surprising that what we nowadays call 'popular religiosity' should have been an instinctive reaction on the part of the Christian people who could not be satisified by celebrations that were first and foremost euchological.

It is here that we come to the heart of our subject: Could it not be that the recent reform of the liturgy, often inspired as it was by a return to the sobriety of the past and of antiquity, has not gone too far towards that intellectual aristocracy of spirit which characterises the genius of ancient Rome? A perusal of the rituals of the different sacraments, of the rite of the Eucharist, of the Christian year, discloses a patent desire for sobriety and for an often radical suppression of anything that is not functional. A look at the rite of Holy Week alone, compared with what it was before, shows this. The renewal of the liturgy certainly ensured the authenticity of the rite of light and of the Vigil by restoring it to the night of Easter in accordance with the historic data of the gospels. At the same time, it is clear that anything a little out of the ordinary in, say, the different offices of saints' days, or certain ommissions from the mass like the offertory and the Agnus Dei on Holy Saturday, was brought into line with ordinary practices at Matins, Lauds, etc.

It is this rather intellectual return to the past of the liturgy that could be the reason for a certain visual poverty which does not correspond to our needs today. We have already seen how very intellectual the liturgy was in ancient Rome. This is not easy to analyse even when we see it in its context. The very fact that the liturgy of Rome had this predominantly euchological and relatively unvisual character distanced if from its own surrounding culture, and the need for more visual celebration was being felt even then, though we need not attribute to the Romans of old the same need to be demonstrative that people feel today. Nevertheless the very text of certain liturgical celebrations betrays the attraction which some Christians and even some priests felt for the more spectacular and luxurious pagan celebrations such as the Lupercalia.[26] It is clear that the Roman liturgy did not satisfy the instinctive needs of many Christians and many fairly soon had recourse to supplementary devotions. This tendency became more and more pronounced as the centuries elapsed and especially when biblical culture began to disintegrate. This is the way in which a serious gap opened up between the official worship and celebrations that were more or less spontaneous or else allowed and even encouraged by the authorities, though they were parallel to the liturgy and even replaced it, so that devotion became more important than the essential rite. By the same token, there is cause to fear that a renewal which concentrates too much on the ear and leaves so little scope for the eye will open the door to similar parallel developments. The attempts made by the reform of Vatican II to restore the Word of God to the celebration will no doubt bear fruit, but will this restoration suffice to appease the visual needs we feel today?

4. THE POSSIBILITY OF THE VISUAL

It is here that we must pose some delicate but unavoidable questions. The renewal of the liturgy has proceeded by going back for the most part to antiquity in order to discover the essence of a celebration underneath successive symbolic layers coming from more or less everywhere. This has been a very useful service, and it would be unfair to deny this. But could we not say that precisely by giving us a framework cleaned and cleared of all extraneous matter the renewal itself offered us the possibility of introducing the visual wherever local and contemporary needs warranted it? This seems to emerge—tentatively, no doubt, but definitely—from several parts of the new rituals wherever conferences of bishops are given the discretion to allow such and such a gesture into the celebration. This applies to the case, for instance, of the rite of Christian initiation of adults and of the baptism of children. We must, however, admit that scope for such discretion to adapt remains very limited. On the other hand, it would be dangerous just to open all doors, for we cannot think of reintroducing the visual into our predominantly auditory liturgy without first undertaking objective research. And we can proceed with this only by stages.

The first stage in any such programme of research would consist in an objective study of the symbolism and gesture which our present liturgy already offers us. As I have already indicated at the beginning of this article, some people have jumped to the conclusion that what they happened to consider formal and unadapted is in fact so, whereas it may not be seen by the faithful in so inhibited a way. Only to often clericalism still prevails here in the form of projecting the clergy's own sentiments onto the faithful.

The second stage would consist in attempting to ascertain those moments of a celebration which demand symbolism and gestures. This clearly requires more study, because symbolism and gesture should not be introduced artificially. The necessity for technical study does not justify an artificial introduction. We must therefore study history and we must do so by studying it with the precision tools of anthropology.

The third stage is the most important one: What was done yesterday does not rigidly determine what we have to do today. It would, therefore, be a question of seeing how the symbols and gestures of the past in all the variety of their local adaptations, meet our needs today. At the same time, the replies to such interrogations of the past, whether affirmative or negative, cannot be the last word. For the fact that any particular symbol or gesture is esoteric cannot of itself close the question. The liturgy must indeed be incarnated because of the incarnation of Christ, and yet the adaptation involved must also take account of the fact that Christ became incarnate in a given historical culture, and one must therefore respect the visual dimension of this incarnation of Christ. There may, therefore, be symbols and gestures which are not immediately intelligible and which require catechesis. This is already the case for the inspired word, which is integrated into a culture that we must respect. At the same time, we have to study the possibility of introducing new gestures and new symbols. The work involved here is fraught with hazard, however necessary it is, and it supposes intelligent prudence and a clear awareness that the results of an anthropological inquiry cannot state the last word.

If the liturgy is life, it is hardly surprising that it should always be growing.

Translated by Iain McGonagle

Notes

1. See especially the description of the mass, chapters 65-67.
2. Cyprian *Epistola 63 ad Caecilium* ed. Bayard, Collection Budé (1925) II p. 208 (P.L. 4, 384).

3. Hippolytus of Rome *La Tradition apostolique* ed. B. Botte (Coll. Quellen und Forschungen, Münster, Westphalia) n. 25 p. 64.

4. *Ibid.* n. 21 p. 56.

5. *Ibid.* n. 21 pp. 48, 50, 52.

6. *Ibid.* n. 4 p. 10.

7. *Ibid.* n. 2 pp. 4-6; 7 p. 20.

8. *Ibid.* n. 8 p. 22.

9. *De Sacramentis. De Mysteriis* ed. B. Botte (Sources Chrétiennes 25 bis 1959) 3, 5 p. 95.

10. Etheria *Journal de voyage* ed. H. Pétré (Sources Chrétiennes 21) pp. 218-244.

11. For Palm Sunday, for example, see H. Graf *Palmenweihe und Palmenprozession in der lateinischen Liturgie* (Stelyer 1959).

12. Jérôme 'Lettre à Praesidius' ed. G. Morin *Bulletin de l'ancienne litterature et archéologie chrétienne 3* (1913) pp. 52-60.

13. *Sacrementaire Gélasien* ed. L. C. Mohlberg (Coll. Rerum Eccles. Documenta, Rome 1966) nn. 283-328.

14. *Sacrementaire de Vérone* ed. L. C. Mohlberg (Coll. Rerum Eccles. Documenta, Rome 1966) nn. 1105-1110; *Sacrementaire Gélasien* nn. 1443-1455.

15. K. Ritzer *Formen, Riten und religiöses Brauchtum der Eheschliessung* (Münster 1962).

16. 'Ordo Romanus I' ed. M. Andrieu in *Les Ordines Romani du haut moyen âge* (Coll. Spicilegium Sacrum Lovaniense, Louvain 1960) 2, p. 91 nn. 69-78.

17. *Ibid.* pp. 69-76 nn. 7-28.

18. *Ibid. Le fermentum* p. 61; *Ordo* II n. 6; *Ordo* IV n. 106 and p. 169.

19. Amalarius of Metz *Liber Officialis* (P. L. 105, 985-1242); *Amalari Episcopi Opera Liturgica Omnia* (Città del Vaticano 1948-1950), Coll. Studi e Testi 138-140.

20. A. Franz *Die Messe im deutschen Mittelalter* (Freiburg 1902) pp. 359, 394.

21. *Le Pontifical romano-germanique du Xième siècle* ed. C. Vogel and R. Elze (Città del Vaticano 1963) 1 and 2, (1972) 3, Coll. Studi e Testi 226, 227, 269.

22. *Le Pontifical romain du XII siècle* ed M. Andrieu in *Le Pontifical romain au moyen âge* (Città del Vaticano 1938) Coll. Studi e Testi 86.

23. M. Andrieu *Les Ordines Romani du haut moyen âge,* cited in note 16, 1 p. 519, 1.

24. 'Le Pontifical de Guillaume Durand' ed. M. Andrieu in *Le Pontifical romain au moyen âge* (Città del Vaticano 1940) 3, Coll. Studi e Testi 88.

25. Reference may be made much more reliably to this book since the publication by A. G. Martimort of *La Documentation liturgique de Dom Edmond Martène* (Città del Vaticano 1978) Coll. Studi e Testi 279.

26. This is proved by the protests introduced by Pope Gelasius into the very formularies of the mass. See *Gelase Ier. Lettre contre les Lupercales et 18 messes du sacrementaire léonien* ed. G. Pomarès (Sources Chrétiennes 65, 1959).

Aidan J. Kavanagh

The Politics of Symbol and Art in Liturgical Expression

WHEN ONE discusses symbolic and artistic expression in liturgical worship, there is an aspect which often is never mentioned. It is the political aspect, and it touches all phases of the issue.

1. THE NOTION OF 'POLITICS' EMPLOYED

The politics one refers to is not primarily that assumed by modern popular consciousness. It has little directly to do with concepts of the state, the governing process, or methods of liberation from oppression. Politics as it will be used here means simply the structure and quality of the relationships between members of a social group, including the elusive ways in which these relationships are sustained both by governance and by social contract, usually unwritten. Politics in this sense, it will be remembered, is a most liberal art, the breeding ground of symbol and the other arts.

Symbol and art are difficult enough to speak about, but their political roots are even more difficult to articulate. Perhaps for this reason most normal social groups seem less to analyse their symbols, art, and politics than to practise them. Learned papers on Zulu art and symbolism astonish no one more than the Zulus. The point being that living at normal depth within a society's functioning patterns of symbol and art seems to be an impediment to having a clear analytical grasp of their scope and function. Anthropologists therefore tend to study almost any culture so long as it is not their own. The methodology of critical analysis requires an objectivity that can be had only at a certain distance from the object studied, a distance that comes either from being an 'outsider' or from a crisis of alienating proportions within. This last instance suggests why those in political or cultural power usually find themselves at a disadvantage in defending a shifting *status quo* against revolutionaries. The latter, by definition to some extent alienated from the given order of things, specialise in analytical critique at the expense of the former, who often have no response except flight or coercive force. The successful revolutionary invariably must then overhaul not only the politics but also the symbolic and artistic patterns of the society. Symbol and art may cause political evolution, but political revolution makes drastic shifts in symbol and art a necessity, as the recent histories of Russia, China, and more lately Iran illustrate.

So too the recent history of Roman Catholicism, especially since the summoning of the Second Vatican Council in 1959. Whatever else the Council did, it sanctioned a political shift in the structure and quality of the relationships between Roman Catholics at every level, including the elusive ways in which these relationships are sustained both by governance and by unwritten social contract. The political breeding ground of symbol and the other arts therefore changed to a degree that is still not possible to fathom, much less to be clear about, since the results of the change have by no means yet run their course, pulling many of the other Western churches along with them. It cannot be forgetten that the perhaps more modest results of the political shift sanctioned by the Council of Trent took almost four centuries to run their's.

2. THE POLITICAL SHIFT OF THE VATICAN COUNCIL

While any analysis of the political shift sanctioned by the Second Vatican Council must be highly tentative due to one's close proximity to it in time, it may be possible to point out some results it seems to be having upon the worshipping assembly's symbols and art, especially as these regroup themselves within the reformed liturgy.

To be brief about it, the reformed liturgy simply assumes a participatory politics that is less aristocratic and élitist than that assumed by the liturgical settlement sanctioned by the Council of Trent. While one might often point out that the Roman liturgy originated in such a participatory politics, the roots of which reached back even to a supper in an upper room, and while one might also point out that even the Tridentine liturgy *could* be participated in actively by all (as in the *missa recitata*, the 'dialogue mass', or the German *Gebetsingmesse*), nonetheless its language and art forms made this difficult if not impossible to accomplish. Many parishes with few resources found the effort needed to teach congregations Latin and Gregorian chant greater than the positive pastoral results that were expected. The resulting silent masses led to the near displacement of the liturgy by a surrogate form of endeavour called sacramental confection. Generations of seminarians were taught not how to celebrate the Roman liturgy but how to confect a sacrament according to officially approved Roman texts. Thus the active cooperation of a congregation and other ministers was recommended but deemed unnecessary on the whole.

This is not the place to detail the results of centring so much on the priest's act of sacramental confection—how it largely rendered private not just the Eucharist but the whole of the Church's liturgical system, how it impacted sacramental theology, and how it made bringing *liturgical* data to bear on a whole range of theological and pastoral issues almost impossible. The liturgy sank nearly to the level of adiaphora where, paradoxically, many sixteenth-century Protestant reformers had said it ought to be.

It can be maintained that such a situation as this provides the only context which explains satisfactorily why by the mid-nineteenth century a liturgical ferment began to stir in Roman Catholicism and was addressed with increasing frequency by popes beginning with Leo XIII in 1902. It is estimated, indeed, that the next seventy-five years witnessed the issuance of at least 300 documents of all kinds on liturgy by the Roman See.[1] So formidable a body of official literature is not produced except in response to formidable problems: both are essential background for grasping the seismic political shift that was sanctioned by the Second Vatican Council. Against the conventional shrinkage of liturgy to sacramental confection centring on the priest's private low mass, the *Constitution of the Sacred Liturgy* reasserted the traditional norm of Eucharistic celebration. It is to be that of the bishop presiding within an event that concretely expresses the full involvement of the whole local church—people, presbyters, deacons, and other assistants.[2] The norm requires, even when it must be departed from for serious reason, that the Church be manifested in all its variety and diversity in all its sacramental deeds; but especially in the Eucharist, which is the mode in which the Church itself most regularly assembles.[3]

The contrast between this restored standard of Eucharistic celebration and the previously prevailing one of the individual priest's private low mass illustrates the dimension of the political shift sanctioned by the Second Vatican Council. Yet the participatory politics of the Council's standard for the Eucharist was hardly new in Roman tradition. Such a politics is evident in the earliest sources of Christian liturgical usage— sources which were being rediscovered, edited, and published during the scholarly phase of the liturgical movement from the sixteenth through the nineteenth centuries—sources which were the support of those conservative innovators of the pastoral phase of the same movement from Guéranger and Moehler in the nineteenth century to Beauduin, Pius X, and Pius XII in the twentieth. The shift was thus anything but sudden: it was the result of a long-term political process of recovery set in motion by many factors including the collapse of medieval Catholicism, the reforms of Trent, scholarly historiography, and three centuries of social revolution in the West.

As is the case with any long-term social process, some structures and attitudes changed more slowly than others. In the West, for example, changes in liturgical practice, which began to come with increasing frequency only after Pius X altered communion discipline in 1905 and 1910, were relatively easy to set in motion due to the liturgy's having been made a latter of law administered exclusively by the Holy See. A politics of aristocratic authoritarianism thus immeasurably aided Catholic liturgical reform during the half-century prior to 1959. Yet the substance of the reform, once it was sanctioned and given strategic scope for the Church universal by the Second Vatican Council, went far beyond mere rubrical changes, discreet alterations of policy, or indults given in specific instances. The liturgy was given back into the hands of the faithful, that fundamental *ordo* of the baptised which all orders of ministry are ordained to serve.

There can be no doubt that any future history of Roman Catholic worship in the several decades since the Second Vatican Council will have to discuss at length how both faithful and clergy found ways in which to cope with a situation of restored liturgical normality after so long a period of liturgical abnormality. Such a future history will perhaps be able to see more clearly than the present generation can do that the main liturgical problems after the Council were less those of rubrical changes and the proliferation of trial texts than those of working out ways of maintaining liturgical discipline and governance within a restored participatory politics. In this, both clergy and faithful are having to rediscover that tradition rather than canon law is the force that gives thrust to liturgical development. This is so because tradition is that continuity which gives shape to participatory politics, a continuity having nothing to do with the dead hand of the past but everything to do with the community's awareness of its present. Such an awareness, if it is to be both accurate and to some future purpose, can never be amnesiac about the past. For the past is where presents are made, and presents are the future's beginning.

Written histories of the Church covering the past four centuries unfortunately do not often give much help concerning how all this might be done. Such histories usually focus on the politics of the Church, especially at worship, as being aristocratic and élitist. So long as this politics survived, its liturgical manifestations still had access to the symbolic and artistic forms which that politics had produced—such as monastic chants of great monophonic beauty, composed masses and motets, towering plastic and architectural artifacts, and a body of literature as good in some ways as any which had preceded it. These monuments, which involved a certain style in symbol and art and which founded a whole piety, were largely produced by virtuosity made possible by benefaction intended to benefit the masses, who were expected to be reverential toward benefactor, virtuoso, and product together.

3. RESULTS OF THIS SHIFT

Three centuries of political upheavals both in Europe and the new world changed all this or at least rendered its underlying politics moribund, and the change finally penetrated the liturgy significantly in the 1960's. Liturgical scholars were no more prepared for the results, it seems, than anyone else. Many were alarmed when participation in the liturgy degenerated into a sort of egalitarian *camaraderie* whose novelty produced an elation that dwindled as the presumably solid artifacts of the aristocratic past either collapsed or sank beneath a whole new political climate in the worshipping assembly. More often than not, given a choice between a poorly performed 'folk mass' and a splendid high mass set to Gregorian chants and Palestrina, all the young and most of the old chose the first. The liturgy increasingly became talky, didactic, and prone to ideological manipulation. That the Eucharist, the sacrament of the Church's faith-communion in Christ, was perhaps more alien in an act of anti-war protest on the steps of the Pentagon in Washington than was a solemn concelebrated exorcism seems to have crossed the mind of no one except Mr Norman Mailer, the American author, who composed a splendid exorcism precisely for such use.

There is some initial evidence that the rush into liturgical egalitarianism has begun to moderate as the novelty of the shift into a more participatory politics as manifested in the reformed rites has begun to wane. One hopes that some hard lessons about aggressive egalitarianism have begun to be learned—that in liturgy as in politics, science, education, and family affairs it produces euphoric mediocrity at best and a hopeless tangling and flattening of due process at worst; that participatory politics and egalitarianism are by no means synonymous; that an élitism of career clergy and ecclesiastical princes is not significantly different from an élitism of experts, committees, and guidelines.

Concerning this last lesson, one's hope remains modest. For the reaction that seems to be gathering from our having begun to learn the first two lessons about egalitarianism (a reaction beginning to be called a 'new conservatism' in American seminaries) gives evidence of being tinged with an unhealthy sort of nostalgia for a liturgically aristocratic past and, paradoxically, with an even less healthy presumption that modern secular bureacracy can provide the categories (high degrees of professional specialisation and organisation) that will allow such an aristocracy to work. Bluntly stated, ordination is becoming 'academicalised' to the point that obtaining an academic certificate of specialised competency overshadows the sacrament of holy orders. One obtains one's academic certificate and then searches for a pastoral situation in which one can exercise one's specialty. The specialisation of ministry, not in itself a bad thing on the level of the diaconate and the lesser orders, becomes a mixed blessing when it is inserted into the presbyterate and episcopacy. It narrows these two orders to 'job descriptions' of an implicitly bureaucratic sort to the detriment of their primary sacramental, presidential, and ascetical nature. Furthermore, given the tendency of the presbyterate to become the paradigm for all ministry in the Western churches at least for the last thousand years, allocating a large repertoire of specialised competencies to it is a sure way to recreate it as a modern aristocracy of 'first-class citizens' by certification in the Church.

But the matter is complicated further. What such a recreation produces is a minister whose ability to preside comfortably within a tradition of worship as distinctive and rich as the Roman is significantly reduced. Such a one's presidency is often idiosyncratic in the extreme, due perhaps to its being a personally therapeutic event of secondary importance to one's real professional work, which lies elsewhere. Liturgical presidency thus shrinks to a matter of personal need for the minister. The assembly and its worship end by serving the minister, rather than he them.

That participatory politics is not mere egalitarianism seems to be increasingly clear to many. That it cannot be allowed to be swamped by therapeutic élitism for weary ministers will, one hopes, become equally clear. Participatory politics as the recent Council and tradition understand it does not arise or function in the Church along exclusively secular lines. The worshipping assembly does not recognise the origin of its internal political 'power' as lying with competencies, committees, or ideologies, but with Jesus Christ present and active in the Church, both universal and local. As an enacted icon of this, the liturgy draws its power not from the committee which controls the worship programme of the parish, or from the scrupulous idelogical fairness with which special ministers are approved, or from the pastor's tastes, but from the active presence by faith, word, and sacrament of Jesus Christ in the Church's midst. One does not become a Christian by being elected pope, ordained a presbyter, or appointed to a parish liturgical committee, but by being plunged into Christ's own death through baptism. One does not remain a

Christian by obtaining an academic degree, joining a charismatic prayer group, or by voting for or against this or that, but by participation in Christ's body broken and his blood poured out Sunday by Sunday. One is not initiated into Christian communion on the basis of what one thinks of liberation theology, the ordination of male or female, or the 'democratisation' of the Church, but in response to one's stated faith in Father, Son, and Holy Spirit.

4. THE POWER BY WHICH THE CHURCH LIVES

If to speak of politics necessitates speaking of power, then the foregoing truisms seem to need restatement over and over again, as John Paul II did for the whole Church in his remarks to the Peubla conference of Latin American bishops in 1979. And perhaps the main fact made clear by this Slavic pope's journey to Poland later that same year, a fact deserving much consideration by the churches west of the Iron Curtain, is the sheer power of Christ's active presence especially in faithful churches where parish schools are outlawed, clerical vocations restricted, and hierarchies shackled. One has the impression that *because* of state hostility and its repressive policies the Polish church has in its own way generated a participatory politics after the mind of tradition and the Council that is unsurpassed among churches further West and unequalled except in certain churches in Africa. Against the powerfully renewing lives of these churches—lives forced through suffering back to basics— the lives of 'first world' churches appear largely to be over-financed, over-educated, and over-organised, gradually losing their self-confidence in direct ratio to the secular state's withdrawal of its approval and support.

The Catholic Church in the United States, for example, gives evidence of becoming increasingly enervated by polarising debates on a series of issues that are essentially introverted and self-indulgent. The issues are supported by special interest groups who have learned from the civil rights and anti-war movements of the 1960's how to turn society's corporate life-thrust (for better or worse) to their own purposes—frustrating development, dispensing political power, and rendering a consensus by the slimmest majority of only one or two statistical points the best that can be hoped for. With this, a sense of communal identity begins to ebb, frustration rises, bishops become little more than mediators in endless disputes, and the liturgy becomes a battleground where vested interests collide not over accidentals but over essentials—such as whether the Eucharist even *can* be celebrated until all justice is attained, all the hungry fed, women ordained presbyters, all oppressive régimes toppled, and until the Church has taken the 'correct' stand on every issue sensationalised by the mass media.

The faithful community, afloat upon a sea of polarised permissiveness, is numbed by aggressive arguments that do not relativise its values so much as they atomise them into an incomprehensible state. Yet these are the values whose mutual communion produces art and symbol, major components in that complex symphony of artfully enacted meaning which the liturgy is. The liturgy celebrates nothing if it is not an agreed upon commonwealth of lived presumptions in faith: when this either collapses or becomes so intricate as to be arcane, the liturgy loses its ability to lift its participants to a level where the whole can be perceived simply and participated in directly by all. Then the liturgy dissolves into an educational set-piece or an arena for conflict, and the faithful go elsewhere for their 'images of survival'. For survival is what the liturgy is ultimately about—survival in Christ through his own passage from death to life in his Father. Christ is the fundamental image of survival, an image that causes what it signifies because it is its own content.

This is not only the definition of sacramental liturgy. It is at the same time the source from which all great Christian art has arisen and the foundation in power which holds the Church together. It is both the precondition and outcome of all Christian life. And its maintenance is not produced merely from a tentative encounter with Christ, but from that sustained mutuality of presences between Christ and his faithful ones tradition calls communion—a state of existence which Paul likened to the wedded union between man and woman, and which Aquinas termed the *res* of the Eucharist, the *unitas mystici corporis Christi*, the Church. Taken whole, it is not easy to be too firm about this fundamental principle of Catholic orthodoxy. To be mediocre about it is to trivialise it and thus to lapse gently into apostacy from it on many levels at once.

The political is one such level. Indeed, the theandric nature of the incarnation of Jesus Christ, together with the maintenance of that incarnate presence by faith, grace, and sacrament corporately in the Church, assured that politics would be a central issue in orthodox Christianity from the beginning.[4]

Church governance and the sustained relationship of the churches of God was anything but a tertiary consideration, as the Acts of the Apostles, the Didache, and the letters of Ignatius and Clement make clear even in the most primitive strata of Christian documents. Yet these sources and others like them never make the mistake of assuming that Church governance takes its beginning anywhere but from within. No other factor can account for the relative ease and self-confidence with which the Church of the first thousand years absorbed cultures, renewed them, and then both authored new ones and maintained its right to stand in judgment of them.

5. THE DANGERS EXPERIENCED

Historically, two dangers have arisen in this regard. The first is the danger of becoming rigoristic about this, with the consequence that the Church turns away from all possibility of political entanglement with the world of human affairs, introverting itself and becoming exclusivist. Certain forms of Christian spiritualism have always had an affinity for this sort of theological anarchism which often has ended in a degree of monophysitic emphasis on the divinity of Christ and the divine aspects of the Church or Christian experience to the detriment of the human in both. Orthodox tradition has been quick to diagnose such a shift, despite the benign appearance of its piety or the warmth of its devotionalism, as being a fundamental assault upon both the relation of creation to Creator and the theandric nature of the incarnation, seeing it thus as heterodox in nature and sectarian in effect. The tradition has reacted in a similar manner towards the opposite alternative, that of emphasising the human nature of Christ and the human aspects of the Church or Christian experience, as one finds in forms of arianism or pelagianism. While it is a risky generalisation, one might characterise the monophysitic temptation as typical of the pious Christian 'conservative' (Archbishop Lefèbvre and some modern charismatics), and the arian-pelagian temptation as typical of the socially radicalised Christian 'liberal' (as in the reductionisms of some liberation theologians). In the first, one detects a flight from politics: in the second, political excess. At their extremes, each is an assault on the gospel and all that flows from it.

A second danger is by far the more difficult to diagnose and counteract. For it issues not from clear and internally logical, if mistaken, apprehensions about Christ, the world, and the Church, but from a slothful and unresourceful muddling of sacred and secular, of gospel and world, of Church and state. On the American scene in particular, the religious roots of which derive mainly from influxes of Puritan, Catholic, and Jewish immigration from the seventeenth to the early twentieth century, one finds that perhaps the new thing produced by such commingling of traditions is not a renascence of Judaeo-Christianity but a religious syncretion of a peculiarly nineteenth century American sort seen in the Church of the Latter Day Saints (Mormons). In this group the American virtues of independent self-reliance, family-centredness, hard work, and stable middle-class values, together with the special American vices of a certain proness to religious humbug, a gentle xenophobia, and a taste for glitter and random display, are combined in a corporate empire of massive wealth and political influence that radiates out from Utah over the far-western United States in particular, extending even abroad by way of a highly disciplined evangelicalism aided by the latest techniques in public relations. Mormonism is the religious analogy of the large American business corporation, and each draws its strength from the same power-sources that lie deep in the American experience.

This experience supports a curious sort of secularised Christendom, and the United States may be the last country on earth where a Christendom of whatever kind can be said to be alive and functional, if not completely well. The supreme icon of this is a 'born-again' head of state who teaches Baptist Sunday-school and insists on being addressed in a diminutive form of his Christian name, a pure American type without guile. Which means that he is largely without political power because his sort of Christian commitment renders him incapable of engaging in the labyrinthine arts by which such power has always to be exercised. All he possesses, besides a real personal goodness, may be only the appearance of power conferred by the celebrity of his office.

A certain celebrity, at least the appearance of affluence (which is not the same thing as financial security, much less real wealth), and more lately a sense of personal well-adjustment seem to be the main virtues cherished in such a secularised Christendom. They are at least the images of survival most frequently endowed with greatest value by the mass media, which control the discourse in such a society and thus the quality of that context of meaning from which its symbols emerge. And it is worth a lot of thought how frequently a church released from an old discipline, but not yet arrived at a new one, has seemed thoughtlessly unable to resist absorbing such questionable values. This is particularly true of its clergy. The presbyterate becomes a sort of celebrity which must be conferred by right on whomever feels a desire for it; the appearance of affluence is sustained by clerics at the Eucharist who display expensive personal jewelry even as the elevate simple and inexpensive pottery chalices; and the liturgy, together with certificates of specialisation (such as degrees in theology or counselling), affirm to them their own successful well-adjustment in a society that values such abilities. Such clergy often conduct the liturgy as though it were a television talk-show or a group session in spirituality, social action, or personal therapy.

The images of survival cherished by a secularised Christendom thus enter into the very heart of Christian polity by the inadvertance typical of those who possess only uncritical good intentions. Once lodged there, these images seem so benign as to be almost impossible to dislodge. A bishop must think very hard indeed before he is so bold as to remove a bejewelled, well-liked, and 'relevant' cleric from pastoral office and liturgical function only because the cleric has nothing at all to say about the gospel of Jesus Christ. Yet Jesus Christ was notoriously without the appearance of affluence, oddly 'adjusted' to the religious relevances of his time, and finally deserted by those who were attracted to him only by the celebrity of his words and cures. He was too liberal for Pharisees and too conservative for Zealots, going too far for the first and not far enough for the second. He confused and scandalised all the apostles but one, who with his mother was alone with him as he finally redeemed the world, foregoing life that he might find it and give it without reserve to all. Catholic orthodoxy, which is first of all a liturgical criterion, has always arisen from this central mystery because this is all it has ever celebrated. Jesus Christ is the root-image of survival, an image that causes what it signifies because it is its own content.

6. CONCLUSIONS

From all this one might derive several conclusions.

First, it is idle to expect symbol and art to arise from a minimalist, a trivialised, or a merely educative or therapeutic liturgy. Such a liturgy will have to have symbol and art imported into it from elsewhere, an endeavour which in itself by no means assumes that the liturgy will escape either radical secularisation or becoming reduced to yet another facet of civil religion in countries of the 'first world'. While the liturgy does indeed make use of symbols and art drawn from the culture in which it exists, this is a secondary process of assimilation necessarily catalysed by the primary presence within it of Jesus Christ become, as Paul said, 'life-giving Spirit'. When this catalytic presence suffers any degree of restriction or dispersal in the worshiping assembly, it is inevitably restricted or dispersed in the assembly's liturgical act, which is *itself* the artfully enacted symbol or sacrament of that corporate presence in the worshipping assembly by faith and grace. The liturgy thus is said to 'use' symbols and art only to the extent that it is itself artful symbol in the first instance.

Second, artful symbolism in act need not be arcane, but it always demands high discipline. Rules, rubrics, laws, choreographies, or scores establish a stylistic floor beneath which performance may not fall without causing the given act to mutate into something different. Merely tapping out the rhythm of a Chopin sonata on a typewriter is not enough; reciting Prokofiev's *Romeo and Juliet* is an impossibility for there are no words; simply ignoring the Roman rubrics transmutes the Roman liturgy into whatever inept clergy may wish to make it. Yet neither does a merely wooden observance of rules automatically produce artful symbolic performance. Rules, scores, choreographies, and rubrics exist to be gone beyond, and here the even higher discipline of the tradition of performance must be entered into. Laws do not maintain style, but tradition does. Liturgically, rubrics must be insisted upon, but tradition must be well known, its levels discriminated, and its agents both diversified and elegantly controlled.[5]

Third, egalitarianism breeds comradeship; élites breed style. The problem lies not in choosing between one or the other but in how best to use each in a coordinated service of the liturgical tradition—without reducing comradeship to the level of an alienated proletarianism or raising style to the level of a gnostic secret. A robust and self-confident church order seems to be the only general context within which such a balance can be achieved and sustained.

Fourth, and finally, there is much contemporary need for firm criticism, both positive and negative, of actual liturgical acts as they occur. This criticism must be constructive, and it should come from all quarters in the worshipping assembly, representing a variety of points in view. In particular, bishops who are moderators of worship in local churches can best serve a critical function not merely by being sensitive to a narrow range of rubrical neuroses, but by regularly presiding at excellent liturgies in their own cathedral churches. Good quality has a way of communicating itself by drawing the attention of all. Also, people who are exceptionally knowledgeable in liturgical matters bear a special responsibility to speak not only in general but to specific instances of correct and incorrect liturgical usage. For the artful symbolism which is the liturgy is never secured in the abstract or in general. It is accomplished in specific acts done by people in certain places at given times. Literary critics must know how to think clearly and to craft a good sentence, as an architect must know how to pour a good foundation and fit a door. No less must a person who loves the Church's worship be able to distinguish not good liturgy from bad so much as correct liturgical procedure from incorrect; and to tell why. For on this good or bad liturgy rests—as politics rests upon relationships, art upon craft, and symbol upon meaning.

Notes

1. See *Worship and Liturgy. Official Catholic Teachings* ed. James J. McGivern (Wilmington, North Carolina 1978).

2. Paragraph 41-42.

3. See Aidan Kavanagh *The Shape of Baptism. The Rite of Christian Initiation* (New York 1978) pp. 106-109.

4. See Frederick D. Willhelmsen *Christianity and Political Philosophy* (Athens, Georgia 1978).

5. See Constitution on the Sacred Liturgy *Sacrosanctum Concilium*, para. 26-32. Also the useful commentary of Thomas Richstatter *Liturgical Law Today. New Style, New Spirit* (Chicago 1977) pp. 61-87.

D

Enrique Dussel

Christian Art of the
Oppressed in Latin America
(Towards an aesthetics of liberation)

THIS ARTICLE is an introduction to a subject of crucial importance, a theological aesthetics of liberation, and an outline of the problem.

1. 'ECONOMIC' STATUS OF THE EUCHARIST

In the Catholic liturgy the priest at the Offertory says the following prayer: 'Lord, we offer you this *bread* which has come from *working the earth.*' The bread which the celebrant holds up is not just symbolic, it is *real*. The work which produced it and the earth whose fruit it is are not symbolic, they are real. We must return to the reality which has often been hidden behind the symbol. It is the reality and not just the symbol 'which makes us think' (in Kant's or Ricouer's phrase).

The relationship between human beings and nature is work (*habodah* in Hebrew). Work is the intelligent effort by human beings to transform mere nature (the 'earth') and produce a 'fruit'. In the Bible the fruit of our labour *par excellence* is 'bread'—which is made from the Mediterranean crop, wheat. Thus the Eucharist presupposes *materially* the existence of 'bread' but its true status is *economic*. The economic relationship, as we understand it, is a 'practical-productive' relationship. The 'practical' relationship is that between two persons (me and you, man and God). The 'productive' relationship, as we have said, is the relationship between man and nature. The Eucharist is a relationship between two persons via the product of labour (and hence an economic relationship):

40

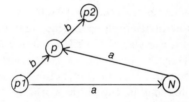

Work (arrow *a*) upon nature (*N*) results in a product (*p*) which is the condition for the possibility of the service of the cult (arrow *b*) man (*p1*) offers to God (*p2*). This cult or service (in Hebrew the same word is used as for work: *habodah*) paid to God is the offering of the product of labour. The cult is the *theologal economy*, the ultimate proof of Christian life. On the cross Christ made his body the cult 'object' and offered himself to the Father as a sacrificial victim. The victim (the dove, the ox or the martyr's own body) is the product of work and history consecrated to God. But even in Israel God made known his will. The best service of God is to give food to the hungry: 'I want mercy and not sacrifices' (Hos. 6:6). God is the absolute *Other*. The poor person is the absolute *other* in the system of domination. Giving the poor the real and *material* product of one's labour is to offer the absolute Other one's life and the product of life for the reproduction and growth of life. The condition of a Eucharist acceptable to God is that the poor should *materially* eat. Thus justice in historical economic systems is the preliminary requirement for the celebration of the liturgy, because the Eucharist is the celebration in history of the perfect, Utopian economy. It is the banquet which requires that all who share it have satisfied their *material* hunger through historical justice. The Eucharist is a reminder of justice, it celebrates justice and foreshadows the justice of the Kingdom (by justice we mean also salvation and liberation). Thus the Eucharist is the critical yardstick against which every historical system of economic injustice must be measured.

2. A THEOLOGY OF PRODUCTION?

The theology of liberation, like all Christian theology possible today depends totally on a preliminary 'theology of production' (i.e., productive *creation*). From ancient times philosophy—and theology too— have discussed the 'work of art'—as Heidegger did for example in his *Der Ursprung des Kunstwerkes*.[1] The ruling class always paid attention to the works of artists and to art in general, from the Greeks (with their *techné*) and the Middle Ages (*ars*) to the aesthetics of Baumgarten. From his bourgeois standpoint Kant expressed it thus: 'The art of man is also distinguished from science as the practical faculty from the theoretical, the technical from the theoretical. . . . Art is also distinguished from craft (*Handwerke*). Art is called liberal, whereas craft is paid. Art thinks of itself as a game . . . whereas craft thinks of itself as work (*Arbeit*), that is to say as an occupation in itself disagreeable, and irksome whose only attraction is its effect, the wage.' (*Kritik der Urteilskraft* 43, A 171).

Continuing via Hegel's *Aesthetik* to Heidegger, we find that the 'aesthetic' is the *clean* part of production, belonging to the ruling class and the geniuses, and leaving in the dark world of the irrational, contemptible, irksome and economic, the paid work of the worker under capitalism, whence however, the oppressed produce the *real* and *material* bread of the Eucharist (whereas the bourgeois artists build the fine churches, the stained glass windows, the statues of the saints, and publishers make fat profits with aesthetic missals etc.). On July 25 1976 the bishops of Gautemala wrote after the earthquake that destroyed the city and many great works of colonial art: 'From the historical point of view the cultural and artistic loss is irreparable. However all this was not the chief or only wealth of the Church. The Church does not get its strength or its true wealth from churches or from works of art collected through the centuries.'[2] We are not despising 'sacred art' but we want to put it in its place within a 'theologal economy' in which the aesthetic is not of primary importance in the 'theology of production'. First comes the daily work of the labourer. The most important thing is productive work for the essentials of life: food, clothes, housing (see Matt. 25:35) and only after this comes everything that improves the *quality* of life: enjoyment, delight, admiration. The million and a half human beings who are hungry and almost naked living in the satellite city of Nezahualcoyotl in Mexico and in the Indian towns, need life first (right to work, eat, basic necessities) and aesthetics later.

A 'theology of production' should think of the universe and nature as a 'product' of the divine vitality and God's creative act as an expression of himself as love. And it should think of man as a 'productive subject' (not an *ego cogito* but an *ego laboro*) who in producing the goods required for the *basic necessities* of human life creates the conditions for the celebration of the Eucharist: 'Take, *eat*, this is my body' (Matt. 26:26).

Need (unfulfilled negativity) is a tension towards the joy of satisfaction and fulfilment, and if this satisfaction is *just*, it is a foretaste of the kingdom of heaven.

A 'theology of production' is the *matter* (Christian materialism has nothing to do with Engels' 'cosmological' materialism, which in any case contradicts 'historical' materialism) of a theology of the sacrament.

3. PRODUCTION, ART AND SOCIAL CLASSES

It is well known that the 'Frankfurt School's' break with Heideggerian thought was, among other things, on aesthetics. Although the *Kritische Theorie* never emerges from a certain aestheticism into the broad field of human production in general, that is to say, to the point of valuing work highly enough,[3] Theodor Adorno at least reached the point of saying: 'Music—one of the arts—is not a manifestation of the truth (as Heidegger thinks) but it is in a real sense an ideology.'[4] If art is 'ideology', this means it is *one* aspect of the total productivity of a social class.

In fact a social class is defined essentially by its material *substratum*: a certain type of work. The type of work determines (but not absolutely) the customs and culture of a human group. If it is true that there is a 'technical division' of work (for example between engineer and labourer) this means that the worker is situated in an historico-social division. In post-feudal European society, for example, the social classes are determined by the fact that some sell their productive labour and others hold the private property of capital. Among productive human actions of all kinds, 'artistic production' has a special place. An artistic action always remains connected (not absolutely) to the social class of the artist that performs it. Likewise the ideal of beauty or fidelity is closely linked to the aesthetic value system of different social classes. For example Latin American neo-classicism (which began to appear from the beginning of the nineteenth century in the struggle against Spain) represents the irruption of a bourgeois oligarchy simultaneous with the expansion of Anglo-Saxon capitalism in Latin America. The baroque, on the other hand, corresponded to Spanish mercantile and pre-industrial capitalism. That is to say that there are not only *periods* in art, but in these periods there is a *contradiction* between the art of the ruling class and the art of the oppressed classes. It is obvious that triumphant, hegemonic, dominant art is the art of the class in political, economic, ideological and therefore artistic power.[5] Thus through its objective content, art is 'in a real sense an ideology'. Expression in objects (words, images, sculpture, buildings etc.) manifests, justifies or criticises the given structures of a society. Art occupies a central place in the ideological struggle in the system (as *dominative art* when it reproduces and supports the system, as *liberation art* when it expresses the oppressed classes and offers models of the new and still utopian world). As one aesthetician put it: 'If the future revolution is planned only for economic reasons and not also from the rise of a new sensibility which seeks new objectives and priorities, it will not be a revolution, and the artist is very important to an authentic revolution.'[6]

4. RELIGIOUS ART AND OPPRESSED CLASSES IN LATIN AMERICA

In general the history of art in Latin America well into the nineteenth century is fundamentally the history of religious art. At the same time it is the stage of a real 'struggle between the arts' of domination and of the oppressed.

The symbolic and mythical 'production' of the people, as Hugo Assmann pointed out, is the central moment in artistic production, secondary to the production of *bread*, but central in regard to other aesthetic productions (songs, poems, images, churches etc.). We shall take an example to illustrate the problem of the struggle between dominators and dominated in the three periods of Latin American religious art (pre-Hispanic, Spanish colonial and the period of dependence of Anglo-Saxon capitalism, until its defeat).

(a) 'Quezalcoatl-Tonantzin' as symbols of the oppressed classes

In the ninth and tenth centuries A.D. a barbarous people of the Pima-Nahuas group invaded the high culture zones of Mexico. These were the Toltecas. Their second king, a young priest, Quezalcoatl-Topilzin, reigned in Colhuacan. He was full of wisdom, patience and holiness. He was obliged to abandon Tula and go north, promising to return from the east and, according to tradition, changing into the evening star (Venus):

'The Toltecas were wise thanks to Quezalcoatl,
the Toltecoyotl (all the arts combined) was his wisdom,
everything came from Quezalcoatl,
the Toltecas were very rich and happy.'[8]

When the Aztecs conquered, the Toltecas became an oppressed class, like the Greeks in the Roman Empire. But the Aztecs (like the Romans) had a guilt complex and feared the return of Quezalcoatl—who was particularly honoured in Cholula, the land of the Tlaxcaltecas, the first allies of Hernan Cortes. Quezalcoatl became the expression of the messianic hope of the oppressed in the Valley of Mexico. When the Spaniards came from the east, Moctezuma the Aztec Emperor himself trembled with fear—the hope of the poor was being fulfilled: 'It truly must be certain,' wrote Bernal Diaz in his *Historia Verdadera de la conquista de la Nueva Espana*, 'that we are they whom their predecessors long ago said would come from the sunrise . . .'[9]

Likewise the farmers of the Valley were dominated by the Aztec nomads and warriors. Every year the oppressed farmers made a pilgrimage to the great sanctuary of the Earth Mother, the mother of the gods: 'The first of these goddesses,' says Sahagun OFM in his *Historia General de las cosas de Nueva Espana*, 'was called Cihuacoatl, which means Serpent's Wife (*sic*) and she was called Tonantzin which means our mother.'[10]

To which he adds in another place: 'One of these cult places is here in Mexico, where the hill called Tepeyac stands . . . here there was a temple dedicated to the mother of the gods who was called Tonantzin . . .'[11]

Quezalcoatl-Tonantzin was a 'fundamental pair in the Mexican pantheon, whose Creole avatars are inseparable. From the pre-Colombian past they are linked together as the two faces, male and female, of the creator first principle'.[12]

(b) St Thomas, apostle and the Virgin of Guadelupe as symbols of the liberation of the oppressed Creoles

On April 15 1549, Manuel de Nobrega related in Brazil that 'a trustworthy person told me that the cassava with which they make the bread in this country was a gift of St Thomas'.[13] The same Jesuit relates having seen the apostle's footprints imprinted on a rock. ('Not far from here there are footprints imprinted on a boulder.')[14] In Patagonia another Jesuit found other footprints of the apostle. In Mexico Quezalcoatl means 'twin' (the 'dual' origin of the universe), just as Thomas does in Greek (dual, divided, twin). Moreover the Toltecan god had a 'cross' on his pointed hat (because he was the god of the winds from the 'four' cardinal points. This cross and its relation to the Great Flood and 'so many other signs' made Fr Diego Duran, OP, think that the Toltecan priest and king—and thus god—was the apostle Thomas, no less, who went to India from Palestine (it was known that there were 'Christians of St Thomas' in Mylapore), and thence had come to Mexico: 'God sent his holy apostles all over the world to preach the Gospel to every creature . . . and it was Topiltzin who came to this land, and according to the story told about him, he was a stonemason who sculpted stone images with curious workmanship, and we also read this about the glorious St Thomas.'[15]

This story deprived the Spaniards of their justification for the conquest of America: the Christian Gospel had been preached there before they came. This tradition, referred to constantly by the 'Creoles' (people born in America) became the ideological banner against the 'Gachupines' (Spaniards born in Spain). Tovar, Acosta, Torquemada and others are aware of this tradition. However, Gregorio Garcia wrote the crucial work: *Predicacion del Evangelio en el Nuevo Mundo viviendo los apostoles* (Baeza, 1625). If this was true, it gave the 'Creoles' the theological (ideological) right to fight colonialism from the beginning of the seventeenth century. Belief in St Thomas-Quezalcoatl was the first affirmation of national consciousness by the American Creoles, a class oppressed by Spanish bureaucracy. The apostle Thomas rose up against the apostle James, the saint venerated by the Spaniards in their struggle for liberation from the Arabs from the eighth century onwards. Thus Hernan Cortes took as his war cry against the natives: 'St James against them! . . . After the battle they were afraid of our horses and shots and swords and crossbows and our brave fighting and above all the great mercy of God.'[16]

With good reason, St James was thought of by the natives as the god of war and the horse of St James—as represented in the popular art of the Reconquest—was venerated more than the horseman himself.

In the 'Sad Night'—as history called it, when the Aztecs were on the point of defeating the invaders—Cortes prayed to the Virgin of Remedies, always the protector of the Spaniards, conquerors, rulers, white. And just as the Creole Thomas rose against the Spanish St James, so the Virgin of Guadalupe rose against the Virgin of Remedies. Everything began thus: 'Wanting to repair this great damage, our first religious (Franciscans) decided to place a church in Tonantzin, near Mexico, to the Most Holy Virgin who is our Lady and Mother.'[17]

An image of the Virgin of Guadalupe—who liberated Spain of the Reconquest and guarded the warriors who fought the Moors—rapidly gained the homage of the natives. They came to Tonantzin by tradition, and continued to venerate the mother of God. On the Virgin's shoulders shone the rays of the sun (the Sun, Huitzilopochtli, was the supreme god of the Aztecs); the blue of her cloak was the sacred colour of the gods, the sky (*teotl*); the moon indicated maternity and the earth; she was a mother like Tonantzin; she conquered the serpent (like Tonantzin who conquered over a cactus like the eagle the serpent) . . . in fact she could be clearly decoded by pre-Hispanic codes (but of course with different meaning than for the Christians or the Spaniards).

The Virgin of Guadalupe of Tepeya was thus the protector of oppressed native class, she especially helped in the frequent floodings of the Valley and in the terrible plagues which decimated the Indian population.

But it was not until 1648 that the 'Creole' Bachelor of Theology, Miguel Sanchez, a Mexican and therefore oppressed by the Spaniards, wrote his *Imagen de la Virgen Maria Madre de Dios de Guadalupe milagrosamente aparecida en Mexico* (printed by Calderon, Mexico, 1648). The author held that from all eternity God had ordained the appearance of the Virgin in *Mexico*, as could be clearly seen from chapter 12 of *Revelation*. In fact the text reads: 'A great portent appeared in heaven, a woman clothed with the sun' (Rev. 12:1). For the author this was precisely the Virgin of Guadalupe clothed in the rays of the sun. 'But the woman was given the wings of the great eagle that she might fly' (12:14), meant the 'Aztec eagle' the imperial sign of the Nahuas. 'The serpent poured water like a river out of his mouth after the woman, to sweep her away with the flood' (12:15), meant Lake Texcoco, where Mexico City was situated. In the end the woman conquers the serpent (who had been the 'sign' for the Nahuas to found Mexico City in the middle of the lake) etc. Miguel Sanchez even said that the Guadalupe image was 'native to this country and the first *Creole* woman' (p. 195). 'God fulfilled his admirable plan in this land of Mexico, conquered for such noble ends' (p. 49). Creole national consciousness, of the oppressed against their oppressors, depended much more on this tradition than on the reading of the authors of the Enlightenment. Patriots were imprisoned by the Holy Inquisition for their devotion to the Virgin of Guadalupe, like Fray Servando de Mier in the eighteenth century. Even in 1800 a subversive group of Creoles armed against the Spaniards called themselves the *Guadalupes*. When the parish priest Miguel Hidalgo, the liberator and founder of Mexico, sought a flag for the popular armies, which he led against the Spaniards in 1810 in Michoacan, by common consent they adopted the standard of the Virgin of Guadalupe, which was used in processions. And the priest Morelos, the leader who succeeded Hidalgo told his soldiers fighting for liberation to wear in their hats 'a device of ribbon, tape, linen or paper declaring their devotion to the most holy image of Guadalupe'.[18]

Even in the Mexican revolution of 1910 the peasant leader Emiliano Zapata, who destroyed churches, took as his banner when he was occupying Cuernavaca, the Virgin of Guadalupe. The leader of the agricultural unions in California, Cesar Chavez (of the UFWOC) also took the Virgin of Guadalupe as the insignia of his union.

Thus St Thomas versus St James, the Virgin of Guadalupe against the Virgin of Remedies was a struggle between religious symbols, a class struggle, a contradictory art in which the poor and oppressed produced their own forms and used them against the dominators.

5. SOME EXAMPLES OF THE RELIGIOUS ART OF THE OPPRESSED

It is a difficult task to find works of art which are 'the religious art of the oppressed', because, since they are oppressed, their works are easily destroyed, because of the materials used, their lack of significance for the ruling aesthetic system, because they are in out of the way places etc. However, there are clear signs of the presence of this art throughout the Church's life.

Think, for example, of the famous Latin American Christs, which some ascribe to popular *tremendism* (the grotesque). These Christs have deep wounds, enormous clots of blood, infinite sadness in their big eyes, great thorns, and a realism which is shocking in the pain portrayed. There is the 'Lord of Patience' in Santiago de Xicotengo,[19] who is sitting down, defeated, with his head resting in his hands and his arm on his knee. How different from the triumphant risen Christ with great wide-open peaceful eyes, the *Pantokrator* of the Byzantine mosaics. In Byzantium he is the Christ-emperor of the ruling classes, in Latin America he is the suffering Christ of the oppressed classes. 'Christs representing the established power and Christs representing the impotence of the oppressed are the two faces of the Christologies.'[20]

These suffering, *tremendist* Christs are the brilliant and authentic expression of an oppressed people, *identified* with Christ crucified and not yet risen, defeated by the Power of this World . . . and the hope of liberation. Francisco Goitia in his work *Tata Jesucristo*[21] shows in the praying faces of the natives the infinite pain and deep hope in their prayers addressed to the suffering Latin American Christ.

It is known by art restorers that frequently, when they treat sculptures of Christ crucified made of maize flour and beautifully painted, their internal vertebral structure is a stone icon of a pre-Hispanic deity. Thus the popular religious sculptor thinks of Christ crucified as the sublimation of his ancient gods, who were conquered by a Christ who was also conquered. In this double defeat, which is not just morbid masochism, they affirm the hope always deferred, but stronger than life itself, for liberation.

In the great colonial churches—which include some of the best expressions of the baroque, such as the splendid Jesuit churches of Tepozotlan in Mexico and in Quito with its marvellous Creole art—the natives introduced innovations into the decoration which became works unique of their kind, like the interior of the Church of St Mary of Tonantzintla in Cholula,[22] where the plaster decorated in the native style is truly amazing. In other cases the native artists introduced modifications into the specifications of the architects, as in the Church of San Ignacio Mini, of the Jesuit settlements in Paraguay, which was finished in 1717. This church has 'such decorative richness that it covers the tympanum, cornices, counterpilasters with stylised leaves, eggs, ribbons, pearls and other motifs used with complete disregard for the order and harmony in classical architecture'.[23] Thus the artistic work of the oppressed is present in the works of the Christian oppressors. As well as visual art there is a vast field of popular art of the oppressed in music. There are carols in all rhythms (South American, Brazilian, Central America, Caribbean), 'Creole Masses' now stylised (like those of Ariel Ramirez) or the 'Mariachis' Mass of Cuernavaca Cathedral, among many others. Popular religious songs also express the sad and painful reality of the oppressed classes. Some display a tragic resignation, others are simply the artistic religious expression of the reality:

> Friends, men are born
> to suffer,
> till death comes
> and beats them down.[24]

Death is ever present in these popular religious songs. But this death is lived with, even joked at, although it is treated with respect. It is called 'St Death' in Paraguay, and in Mexico he is 'conquered' on the Day of the Dead when each child receives a present of a skull made of sweet bread with his name on it, which they play with and then eat with delight. This 'skull' is not frightening. For those who live the life of the oppressed, death is not so terrible. As a Sandinista guerrilla recently expressed it:

Death come secretly,
don't tell me when
so the pleasure of dying
won't bring me to life again.[25]

Clearly great artists can give these popular expressions unexpected brilliance, as in the case of Ernesto Cardenal—the artistic vanguard of an oppressed people: 'I believe that the contemplative, the monk and even the hermit, is really a revolutionary. He is also bringing about social change. And he also bears witness that as well as social and political changes there is a transcendent reality, beyond death. I believe it is important that there should also be people to remind mankind that the revolution goes on also after death.'[26] Likewise the great José Gaudalupe Posada uses the theme of death on the Day of the Dead and the peasants' death-in-life to formulate a political critical art of the 'skulls'.[27] Social, religious and eschatological criticism. And great Mexican muralists like Diego Rivera, José Clemente Orozco, David Sigueiros and Bufino Tamayo, who are anti-Catholic but non the less 'religious' in their chosen themes, give organic expression to popular art with the revolutionary techniques they use in their magnificent works.

Inside their homes, in peasants' cottages and the tin huts in the wretched shanty towns of the big cities, beside the image of the Virgin of Copacabana in regions which belonged to the Inca Empire or the Virgin of Lujan in the South, or many others, there are photos of relations (who, when they are remembered, protect from 'evil spirits'), and the lighted candle signifies the presence of the family. The 'family altar' is an art of the oppressed which expresses the longing for security and justice in an intimacy not violated by the capitalist system outside.

The numerous processions to popular sanctuaries—which the oligarchy does not join in—where special saints are implored with interminable prayers, movements of body, head and lips and offerings, for daily bread, health, work, safety . . . which the ruling system has denied the oppressed.

This art of the oppressed is an expression of bitter need, but it is also a protest and hope of liberation. . . . Within popular Latin American messianism (particularly characteristic of the Brazilian *sertao* with its saints, prophets and messiahs . . . persecuted and killed by the police and even by parish priests at one time) there exists an authentic creative *productive* power, which reveals the historical liberating force of the poor.

6. AESTHETICS OF THE OPPRESSED AS LIBERATION ART

It is important not to confuse three kinds of Christian artistic expression:

(*a*) *The art of the ruling classes* or 'aesthetics of domination' (which includes the art of the *masses* or what Arnold Hauser called *popular* art, as opposed to the authentic art *of the people*.[28] This art is triumphant and can be seen in the restored German churches (glass doors, bronze decorations, perfect lighting, organs with wonderful acoustics etc.).

(*b*) *The art of the oppressed classes* or 'popular art produced by the working class, *liberation art*' as Nestor Garcia Canclini[29] describes it, an art which needs to be discovered and valued. Of course the art of the oppressed at a certain period (for example the Latin American *Creole* art of the eighteenth century) can be transformed into ruling class art (of the natives and workers in the nineteenth and twentieth centuries).

(*c*) *The art of the prophetic Christian vanguard* which is an integral part of the people's struggle. Among others we find here Ariel Ramirez in music, Ernesto Cardenal in poetry, the muralists in numerous parishes, centres and popular Christian meeting places etc. Both the art of the oppressed class and of its artistic vanguard are *liberation art*, which in Latin America today is revolutionary,[30] and supplies the essential requirement for the celebration of the Eucharist.

The 'theology of production' as part of the theology of liberation and which includes the aesthetic theology of liberation, should first investigate the economic conditions for the production of *bread* to satisfy the basic needs of the people—and only then can the Eucharist be celebrated. Secondly, it should study the *aesthetic* production of works of art which express in their 'fidelity' to the face of the oppressed (the bleeding Christs of popular Latin American *tremendism*) critical, prophetic and eschatological 'beauty'. This *fidelity* of expression of the poor, of Christ tortured and crucified, criticises the governing dominant 'beauty' of the system.

Christian *liberation art* of the oppressed classes, like the people in *Exodus* who expressed themselves in the simplicity and poverty of the nomad Tabernacle rather than in the splendour of the Temple in Jerusalem (criticised by Christ: Luke 19:46; 21:6), makes the *economy* the foundation of *symbols*. In developed capitalist countries there appears to be *freedom, bread* and *art* to celebrate the Eucharist, even though some think that really 'it is sacrificing the son to his father to take from the poor to offer sacrifice' (Ecclus. 34:20). The *bread* stolen from the Third World cries to heaven. In developed socialist countries in Eastern Europe, like Poland, the people have *bread*—which is important—and some are asking for *freedom* to celebrate the Eucharist. In Latin America the people have no *bread* to celebrate the Eucharist, because they are hungry, and only those in power have *freedom*. The oppressed people do not have the freedom to create the new world they need (bread and works of art) and which the Eucharist requires as a *preliminary condition* for its celebration. Only the oppressed people and a heroic prophetic vanguard risk even their lives, to create the new . . . as in Nicaragua today (June 1979), making their own bodies (the 'flesh' of the sacrifice) the living 'symbol', manifestation and witness (*martyrs*) of the kingdom: the new *bread* of the future Eucharist.

Translated by Dinah Livingstone

Notes

1. Klostermann *Holzwege* (Frankfurt 1963) pp. 7-68.

2. Pastoral letter of the Episcopal Conference 'United in hope' in *Praxis de los padres de America Latina* (Bogota 1978) p. 791.

3. As does, for example, Georg Lukacs, not so much in his *Eigenart des Aesthetischen* (Berlin 1963) but more particularly in his *Zur Ontologie des Gesellschaftlichen Seins,* XIII(XIV 'Die Arbeit' (Berlin 1973).

4. *Einleitung in die Musiksoziologie* (Frankfurt 1962), beginning of chapter 4. Herbert Marcuse in his recent work *The Aesthetic Dimension* shows how art cannot be reduced purely to the 'ideological' dimension, because it has a certain 'autonomy' and selfhood, but this autonomy, being 'relative' does not deny art's material conditioning. In this article we have concentrated more on the 'relative' than the 'autonomous' in art. See Theodor Adorno *Aethetische Theorie* (Frankfurt 1970).

5. See Nicos Hadjinicolau *Histoire de l'art et lutte des classes* (Paris 1973). The author confines art unilaterally to ideology, and this reduction describes the 'relative' in art well but neglects the 'autonomous'—(although this autonomy is of course also relative). We discussed these questions in our *Filisofia de la poiesis* (Mexico 1978). It is worth pointing out that Hegel's *Aesthetics* is the best description of the aesthetics of the ruling classes: 'In the forms (*Gestalten*) it uses, art selects one stratum in preference to others, the stratum of the princes (*Fürsten*) . . . Perfect freedom of will and production (*Hervorbringens*) cannot be achieved except in the representation of principality (*Fürstlichkeit*).' *Vorlesungen über die Aesthetik*, I, III, b, II, I, a; *Theorie Werkausgabe* (Frankfurt 1970) XIII p. 251.

6. Marta Traba *Dos decadas vulnerables en las artes plasticas latinoamericanas, 1950-1970* (Siglo XXI, Mexico 1973) p. 179.

7. 'El cristianismo, su plus valia ideologica' in *Theologia desde la praxis de liberacion* (Salamanca 1973) pp. 171-202, especially 'La operacionalidad de los universos miticos y simbolicos' pp. 103-195.

8. *Codice matritense de la Real Academia de la Historia*, Sahacun, sheet 176, reverse side.

9. (Mexico 1955) Book I chap. 89 p. 266.

10. ed. Garihay (Mexico 1956) Book I chap. 6 I p. 40.

11. *Ibid.*, Book XI, Appendix 7-; III p. 352.

12. J. Lafaye 'Quetzalcoatl y Guadalupe' Fondo de Cultura Economica (Mexico 1977) p. 299.

13. *Monumenta Brasiliae Societatis Jesu* I (1538-1553) p. 117.

14. *Ibid.*

15. *Historia de las Indias de Nueva España*, chap. 79 (Mexico 1880) II p. 73.

16. Bernal Diaz del Castillo, *Historia Verdedera*, chaps. 52 and 63.

17. Torquemada *La Monarquia Indiana* (Mexico 1723) II Book X, chap. 7 pp. 245b-246a.

18. 'Sentimiento de la Nacion' (1814 copy) in *Poletin del Archivo General de la Nacion,* 2nd series, IV, p. 3 (1963).

19. M. E. Ciancas *El arte en las Iglesias de Cholula* (Mexico 1974) p. 164.

20. Hugo Assmann 'The power of Christ' in *Frontiers of the Theology in Latin America* (New York 1979) pp. 149-150.

21. Oil painting hanging in the Palacio de Bellas Artes, Mexico, dated 1927. See Justino Fernandez *A guide to Mexican Art* (Chicago 1973) p. 375. Consider the 'horrible' suffering expressed by the 'Cristo de la Columna' in the Church of Santa Prisca (Taxco, Mexico). Cf. Leopoldo Castedo *A History of Latin American Art* (New York 1969) p. 134.

22. L. Castedo *ibid.* p. 131.

23. Romualdo Brughetti *Historia del arte en la Argentina* (Buenos Aires 1970) pp. 133ff.

24. Hose Hernandez *Martin Pierro,* verses 1688-1692.

25. J. A. Carrizo *El tema de la invocacion de la muerte* p. 720. See my *El catolicismo popular en Argentina* (Buenos Aires 1970) pp. 133ff.

26. *Santidad de la Revolucion* (Salamanca 1976) p. 21. The artist and prophet takes the people's *contempt* for death and gives it its radical sense.

27. See L. Castedo in the book cited in note 21, at p. 357.

28. *Philosophie der Kunstgeschichte,* chap. 5.

29. *Arte popular y sociedad en America latina* (Mexico 1977) p. 74. Here 'popular art' is the same as Hauser's 'art of the people'.

30. David Siqueiros says 'Criticism must be complete so that useful lessons can be drawn from it with the aim of making a real "*revolutionary art*" ('El camino contrarevolucionario de Rivera' in *Documentos sobre el arte mexicano* (FCE, Mexico 1974) p. 54.

Boka di Mpasi Londi

Freedom of Bodily Expression in the African Liturgy

I HAVE only one aim in this article and that is to bring to light the fundamentally sacred and communicative nature of bodily expression, and particularly, in Africa, of festive dancing,[1] and, on this basis, to examine the merits of its claim for an integrated place in the liturgy. In African culture especially, dancing would seem to be the primordial and the most sacred of all man's forms of artistic expression and indeed the rite *par excellence*. If this is so, would it not be depriving the liturgy of its essential mode of expression if dancing were eliminated from it? In Africa, an encounter with the living God in communion with his people through dancing is a worthy and legitimate way of celebrating the incarnation of the Word and the presence of Emmanuel—God-with-us by justifying that incarnate presence. It is not difficult to understand the almost prophetic statement made by the late Cardinal Daniélou: 'I simply do not know how the black people could praise God without dancing because dancing is so deeply embedded in their whole being that it forms an integral part of their civilisation. In them we rediscover the liturgical meaning of the sacred dance. . . . They need an incarnation of Christianity which is different and which is in accordance with their instincts and their whole being'.[2]

The Constitution on the Liturgy, *Sacrosanctum Concilium,* the first publication of the Second Vatican Council (4 December 1963) gave back to the human body its freedom to praise its creator in many different ways: 'By way of promoting active participation, the people should be encouraged to take part by means of acclamations, responses, psalmody, antiphons and songs, as well as by acclamations, gestures and bodily attitudes. And at the proper times all should observe a reverent silence.'

A little later in the same document, we read that allowance should be made 'for legitimate variations and adaptations to different groups, regions and peoples, especially in mission lands'.[3] Statements such as these could only have a liberating and very stimulating effect. It should not be forgotten, however, that Vatican II, far from being the point of departure here, was the summit of a long and difficult movement marked by several important signposts: Pius XI's *Divini Cultus* (1929) and several of Pius XII's encyclicals: *Mystici Corporis* (1943), which formed a solid basis of theology for the later *Mediator Dei* (1947) and *Evangelii Praecones* (1951).

1. THE BREAK BETWEEN THE PRECONCILIAR LITURGY AND THE LOCAL CULTURE

The paths leading to the emergence of a new African liturgy at Ndzon-Melen (Cameroon) and a new Mass in the Zairian rite (Zaire) have been discussed at some length,[4] with the result that we do not have to retrace in detail the developments in liturgical studies before the Second Vatican Council. All that we need to do here is to point out, in broad outline, the main movements in the liturgy from which the Constitution on the Liturgy has released us.

In considering the psychological reactions to this liturgical behaviour, seen here in the socio-cultural context, it is, I think, important to note, on the one hand, the embarrassment caused by what may be rough physical initiation and, on the other, the unease and feeling of cultural oppression experienced as the result of a rough break between liturgy and life in the concrete.[5] This break is in fact a radical one—on the one hand there is a frozen, encaged and inhibiting liturgy, imported with its apparatus of sacred signs from the distant north and, on the other, the local traditional cultural pattern, with its exuberant symbolism and its quickly communicated vitality, excluded from the liturgy.

This radical break between liturgy and life has had three important consequences. The first is that the liturgy became an isolated action, necessarily confined within narrow limits of a given space and time. This time is one hour per week, per month, per term or even per year, depending on the place. It is, of course, negligible in comparison with the rest of the time—not consecrated because it is not adopted—that passes outside the action of the liturgy. The space is, of course, a church, which is a very minute and enclosed space in comparison with the great world within which day to day life is spent. Then there is the cultural separation of the liturgy from life. Most of the official symbols used—words, gestures and attitudes—were, in the past at least, not always readily understood. To make them more open to understanding, various commentaries and transpositions were used. Many of these changes of position were necessary because of local customs. It was, for example, regarded in Africa as a crude, even obscene gesture and an insult when the priest bowed low with his back to the congregation in the earlier liturgy, as he did, for example, during the *Confiteor*.[6]

So many aspects of African life and thought which are so precious to us have, moreover, been absent from the action of the liturgy. These include the African's ancestral sense of his environment, his vision of the world and his total conception of man, in whom he sees no separation between body and soul, between the individual and the community and between the community and the cosmos. In this vision, the African is conscious of no division between the visible reality and the reality that he cannot see, in other words, between the profane and the sacred. Yet all this cultural inheritance was lacking, so it seemed to Africans, in the liturgy.

The opportunity was therefore missed to make the liturgy the special place where structures could be baptised and values evangelised and where both could be traced back to their Christian sources. Liturgy might have been able to act like leaven in the lump and have an influence on the spread of Christianity within the African culture. This influence, however, was impeded by division between the sphere of liturgy and the environment of ordinary life. The Christian felt frustrated because he had to tear himself away from his own world in order to enter, for an hour, a space that was regarded as sacred and where a ceremony that was a spectacle took place. What generally happened was that the believer was present at the action of the priest, who was always busy. He was not able to take part himself. He was forced to be a spectator and was not a committed actor or participant. This accounts for the strong recommendation of the Council: 'Christ's faithful, when present at this mystery of faith, should not be there as strangers or silent spectators. On the contrary, through a proper appreciation of the rites and prayers they should participate knowingly, devoutly and actively.'[7]

When we heard the Second Vatican Council say that the liturgical renewal was to be based on 'full, conscious and active participation',[8] it was like hearing the hour of our deliverance sounding, the hour when, in the freedom of the restored children of God, we too are invited to restore the inalienable traditional African values by integrating them into our faith through our living liturgy. It is significant that words like 'restoration', 'renewal', 'progress' and so on, on the one hand and 'participation', referring the whole people of God on the other, are used so frequently in the conciliar document on the liturgy and that the need to make an effort is equally stressed.[9]

2. THE PLACE AND FUNCTION OF THE BODY IN THE AFRICAN VIEW OF MAN

In stressing the need for the whole people of God to participate in the liturgy, Vatican II came very close to the most profound and precious

E

desires of African Christianity. It would take too long for me to discuss even briefly the many studies that have dealt with the African understanding of what is meant by 'participation'.[10] I can only mention two here: *La Philosophie bantoue* by Fr. P. Tempels and *Le Visage africain du christianisme* by Fr. V. Mulago.[11] The first author stresses the living force of the African people and the second emphasises their living communion. Both, in fact, deal with the idea of relationship and participation.

This participation forms the basis of the community's cohesion and at the same time justifies the solidarity that follows from it as well as all the connected African values praised by Paul VI in his message *Africae terrarum*.[12] It is not difficult to guess that the liturgical renewal urged by the Council's document was welcomed by African Christians as an initiative giving them freedom of bodily expression in the liturgy. In accordance with our distinctively African way of speaking, we speak of the liberation of the whole man or of man as such. We do not, generally speaking, think of man as consisting of two almost separate parts, body and soul. We think of him as a *muntu*, as a personal living whole or as a capacity of communion. The human body is not seen as a simple wrapping, like the bark of a tree, but as the essential place, the inherent place of life and its expression. It is eminently the mediation of communion.

It is through the body that the person is in communion with the surrounding material world. It is in communion with the air, for example, by breathing, with the vegetable and animal world by eating and drinking and with the world of human beings by what is expressed, for example, in the words sensitivity, sympathy, welcome, hospitality, compassion, understanding, solidarity and, in a word, love. It is also through the body that the human person feels himself to be in communion with the spiritual world.

This spiritual world includes the supreme being, God, and the intermediate spirits, both benevolent and malevolent, who live in solidarity with the ancestors of men. It is their relationships with the world that brings into being an entire network of spiritual influences between 'souls', unequally strengthened from above, some, in other words, being more powerful than others. Finally, it is through the human body that the *muntu*, the whole human person, is in communion[13]. It is hardly surprising, then, that God became flesh in order to be intimately and totally in communion with man. In this sense, then, existence is 'being with' and living is being in communion with. Following Aristotle, Thomas Aquinas saw life as consisting of movement. The African, on the other hand, sees it as consisting of communion or inter-relationship.

This is the vision which prevails even now, more, of course, in African villages than in the towns. It is a view of the world, of man and of the human body which is inculcated into children by the traditional form of education in riddles, stories of various kinds and rhythmical games which shape the children's way of thinking and assure that this way of thinking will continue to be handed down. By virtue of their structure, these stories, games and conundrums combine to produce in the child an experience of communion with the environment in which he lives so that he thinks of himself, especially in adolescence, as a universe in miniature. What takes place in him is the development of a consciousness of being, in and through his body, in a permanent relationship with an immense world that is not in any sense limited to objects and phenomena that can be perceived by the senses, but goes far beyond this.

Riddles and conundrums are the most effective way of inculcating this consciousness. It is not difficult to recognise from a few current examples of such traditional formulae taken from the Bakongo ethnic group (widespread in Angola, Congo and Zaire) how this way of thinking, in which the creator, God, is placed in the centre of the whole of creation, penetrates imperceptibly into the child's mind and how, in this way of thinking, the body as it were sums up the whole of the surrounding universe and brings the whole of the surrounding universe and brings the whole of man into communion with it. In these conundrums, the universe is explored in reference to God who is its creator and in reference to the human body who sums it up in miniature. Man is, for example, in his body a field created by God where nothing grows (the palm of the hand). Or he is a forest created by God which is always being stripped of trees that grow again and again (the hairs of the head). Or he is two trees planted by God; they grow on each side of the house, but never see each other and never meet (the ears).[14]

3. THE SPIRITUAL AND MYSTICAL SIGNIFICANCE OF THE DANCE

Rhythmical movement and especially dancing are the specific ways in which contact with the spiritual world is expressed in the human body, which, as we have seen, is thought in Africa to be the place *par excellence* of communion with man's environment. It has been observed that the African baby makes little rhythmical movements and graceful gestures at a very early age. He also grows up in an environment that is full of rocking rhythms and melodious airs. From the moment that he makes his first steps, he shows how astonishingly sensitive he is to the slightest appeal made by rhythmical sounds. Such sounds make him move eagerly up and down or from side to side quite spontaneously and wave or beat his hands, smiling contentedly and displaying obvious satisfaction. There are three main ways in which the growing child is surrounded by an environment of rhythmical song, movement and dance in Africa—games, fables and palavers. Since the structure of the palaver or African conference sums up that of the other two, we shall confine our discussion to that.

The Palaver as a Model of Community Ceremony

At the level of the local community of the village or clan, the so-called palaver in fact takes the place of liturgy. The conferences known as palavers are really plenary assemblies, often with a predominantly legal character and with the emphasis on oratory. Their procedure is highly complex and their aim is not always easy to define. At the same time they frequently resemble fairs and act as an entertainment, a relaxation within the community, an artistic show or an educational and socio-cultural manifestation. The educational aspects in particular make the palaver a kind of summary of the clan's traditional wisdom and everyone takes part in it, as though it were a kind of re-education in ethnical knowledge.

Let us consider, for example, the case of a meeting called to settle a difference between two villages or two clans about landed property. Food and drink are prepared for the occasion and the day of the meeting is arranged. The palaver may last, in fact, for three days, a week or even two weeks. During this time, all ordinary activities cease and the families concerned in the dispute come together. The assembly includes the chiefs, orators, judges, counsellors, witnesses and other members of the families together with a crowd of curious neighbours and their orchestras.

The situation is discussed in detail and, in particular, the whole history of the land in question is retraced, including the various movements of clans and changes in occupation up to the present. Each orator stands and questions the other side in a series of proverbial formulae that evoke a lively response from the others. He then reconstructs the sequence of events step by step. Each stage in the story is concluded with a proverb or a series of proverbs. This conclusion takes the form of lively chant sung by all those present. From time to time, too, the orator, acting as the animator of his community, makes the outline of a dance movement which is at once taken up by those of his own side and developed more fully.[15] Even from this very brief description, then, it can be seen that the orchestra or choir of people, the proverbial sayings, the chanting or singing and the dancing—and, of course, the dress—all play a very important part in the palaver. There are three constitutive elements of active participation on the part of the whole people in the African palaver which could be used with great benefit in the liturgical renewal. These are the dialogue (which has an obvious place in the homily), local rhythmical chanting or singing and the rhythmical movement accompanied by gestures of the dance.

Dancing has a very special function in a shared action carried out by the whole assembly under the guidance of an animator. On the one hand, it bears witness to the intimacy, intensity and depth of the participants' feelings. On the other hand, it symbolises their contact with the sphere of mystery. This idea can be expressed differently in the following way. Dancing testifies to a special density of feeling that cannot, in the normal course of events, be exteriorised in any other way. The intensity of feeling united vertically with what lies beyond this world has repercussions in the horizontal communion through the fact that it is shared with the community in dancing. The dance therefore marks the summit of communication between beings.

4. THE REPERTORY OF DANCES

There are, of course, many different kinds of dance in Africa. They are not all of the same quality, nor do they all have the same aim. They cannot therefore all be praised without distinction, adopted with equal enthusiasm or condemned without careful consideration. It is worth while looking very briefly here at a few special forms of dance currently practised in Africa. If we are to assess the value of a dance, we must, of course, refer to the context within which it takes place and we shall therefore examine this context first. There are certain circumstances which normally call for dancing as an integral part of the situation.

1. *The Context within which Dancing takes place*

(*a*) Birth, especially of twins, which is regarded as an unusual event, implying an exceptional intervention from on high and seen as a gift of special kindness on the part of the ancestors; it is therefore inevitably connected with the sacred sphere of life and has to be welcomed and indeed 'consecrated' by a special ceremony of dancing.

(*b*) Reception of the mother after childbirth: After spending two or so weeks in 'retreat' after childbirth, the mother 'comes out' into the fresh air and 'shows' the newly-born child to the sun. In districts where there is a high rate of infant mortality, a baby who has overcome the test of the first two weeks of life bears witness to the fact that he is especially favoured by the ancestors. The event is closely connected with the sacred sphere and calls for a ceremony of thanksgiving when new favours are at the same time sought. Dancing forms an essential and necessary part of this ceremony.

(*c*) Initiation rites of many different kinds, of different length and importance, according to the ethnic group, the region and the aim. There can, for example, be rites to initiate people into a trade or an association or to initiate adolescents into adulthood (with or without circumcision). Dancing plays such an important part in these rites that some (see (*d*), (*e*) and (f) under 'Special Dances' below) are employed exclusively in initiation, with the result that to use them in a different context would be regarded as offensive and abnormal. Some dances are learnt, for example, only during the initiation to prepare young men and women for their social, procreative function and consist of simulating, in a way that may sometimes not even be known to the dancers themselves, and by means of ritual gestures which do not have a lewd meaning, but rather point to the games of conjugality. Where life itself is concerned in any of its forms and aspects, dancing is normally involved, because, as Roger Garaudy has pointed out, 'dancing is a way of living' and, where there is feasting, the dance reigns as queen.[16]

(d) Other events with a clearly vital and sacred character also take place within the framework of the dance. These include, for example, exorcisms and healings,[17] incantations said or chanted with the aim of curing, marriage, funeral and ceremonies marking the end of mourning and propitiatory or expiatory prayers chanted at the burial ground as well as feasts of enthronement or reconciliation.

A festive or sacred occasion in Africa without dancing is, we may conclude, like a body without life in which there is no communion with the world. To quote Garaudy again, 'dancing is experiencing and expressing with the maximum intensity man's relationship with nature, society, the future and his gods'.[18]

2. Special Dances

Because of the great diversity of contexts within which dancing takes place in Africa, there is a very rich and varied repertory of African dances. Apart from the many general dances that are often used for recreation, there are also many special dances that are sometimes set aside for certain persons or functions. In this section and the following one on dances used for recreation and amusement, we shall discuss very briefly some of the main types—

(a) The chief's dance: On certain special occasions when a parade takes place, the chief, with a solemn gesture, rocks backwards and forwards, waving the insignia of authority and gently moves his legs.

(b) The head dance: In this dance, the head is swayed from right to left and sometimes moved in all directions, either with or without rocking the whole body.

(c) The shoulder dance is performed by rocking the shoulders from top to bottom and turning them, sometimes both together and sometimes alternately; this dance is often performed by the chief alone or for him.

(d) The belly dance, in which the belly is made to ripple with the navel uncovered.

(e) The hip dance is basically a skilful combination of swayings and twistings of the waist and hips.

(f) The buttock dance is a quivering, waving motion of the buttocks.[19]

3. Recreational Dances

(g) The face to face dance: the dancers are in two rows; in a continuous movement backwards and forwards, they come close to each other, facing each other, but without touching each other (in the traditional form of this dance, there is no dancing body to body in pairs); withdrawing together, the dancers gently move their legs and beat their hands together.

(h) The ronde: formed up one behind the other, the dancers move around a drummer who animates their dancing, determining the pace and the movement.

(i) The solo dance, in which the dancer moves in front of the tom-tom player, swaying and rocking in various esoteric ways.

(j) The fray: this is almost a mass dance. Following the rhythm set by the tom-tom, everyone moves in every direction, hopping, twisting and swinging almost at random.

This great range of dance techniques has, in addition to the aim of creating communion with life or living union, several other main purposes: the full exploration of the human body and each of its parts so that it can be used in a controlled way, exercised and freed from inhibitions.

Combining the chief's dance (a) and the head dance (b) has resulted in an excellent complex of swaying movements in the Mass of the Zairian rite for the procession of entrance, offering and leaving the church and for the incensing of the altar. In the cathedral church of Idiofa in Zaire, the priest-in-charge has succeeded in using the shoulder dance (c) very effectively around the altar. In the church of Notre Dame de Kimwenza in Zaire, a little group of girls mime the offering and the creed extremely well.

Dancing has preserved its character as a primordial rite and as a living expression of communion. One small fact is worth mentioning in this context. When Mgr B. Gantin was created a cardinal two years ago, a party was arranged in his honour by the fathers of the African Missionary Society in Rome. Many guests came from many different countries and I was curious to see what the party might have to offer that was distinctively African in style.

Towards the end of the party, a group from Benin City suddenly came together in front of the cardinal, apparently quite spontaneously. One of them made a movement with his shoulders and soon the whole group was dancing with the upper parts of their bodies, a typical African dance. The leader who had initiated the dance was the cardinal's brother and the dance represented the family's sanction and the ancestral consecration of the event. On the other hand, it also symbolised the exultation of the group, the desire to bring down God's blessing on the cardinal and the honour given to him. It also expressed for him certain wishes, which could be translates as: *Proficiat, vivat ad multos annos.* This dance was a fitting and necessary conclusion to the evening and without it the Africans present would not have felt fulfilled. It was for them the expression of the sacred sphere of life. The African feels in the depths of his being that dancing is a summary of many ways of expressing communion with that sacred sphere. He also feels that it restores to the body its spiritual value of living mediation and universal communion.

5. CONCLUSION

What we have integrated into our liturgy is not one or other category of dance in the form in which it already exists, nor one or other dance that is peculiar to one ethnic group or another. What we have tried to do is to integrate the fundamental value of African dancing, the value or philosophy that does not divide man into two or regard the body as created by the devil or as the prison of the soul, but teaches that it is the place of universal mediation. The dance symbolises for us contact with what lies beyond this life and communion with the cosmos. It also puts an end to the division of man into soul and body and restores harmony to that unity of soul and body in the individual, the unity between the individual and the community and the unity between the material and the spiritual world, all within the one universe. The beauty of the dance reflects the harmony that exists between the one who dies and the one who remains behind and in that way marks the end of all solitude.

In this harmony and rhythm formed by human voices, musical instruments and dancing, the traditional communities of Africa take on a festive air. The festival is an explosion of joy, and upsurge of life and emotion born in man's encounter with his fellow-man. It is the birth of freedom. Even more, man's encounter in Christ with the Quite Other one, his Father, is an even more powerful source of this feeling of festival and freedom. In this sense, then, the Eucharist is the festival *par excellence*. If Christ sets us free, then he must also set free what is valuable in life in the eyes of his Father, the Creator. According to the Fathers of the Church, Christ saves only what he takes up. The African is strengthened and heartened by the integration of what he values in life—his gestures, rituals, rhythms, melodies and symbols—into the liturgy and is anxious to purify his techniques in dancing so that these too can be used.

In the form in which it is accepted in our churches, that is, at our present stage of research and experimentation, dancing consists mainly of rhythmical, controlled and recollected movements of the whole body (and not simply of one part of the body). These liturgical dances are carried out either by everyone present in the church (during the processions at the entrance, the offering and the leaving after Mass, for example), or by the choir alone (during certain chants or hymns) or by the priest and his assistants (during the incensing). Especially when they are accompanied by graceful gestures, which are symbolic and often stylised,[20] the harmonious swaying of the people and the sound of local musical instruments and full-throated, melodious singing irresistably call to mind the omnipotence of God echoed in the community of his children. It is this life of the Spirit of the Father and the Son, the breath of the community of brothers and sisters, which gives the liturgy of Africa its air of festivity and true celebration, in which the human environment is a reflection of the divine environment and indeed of the heart of the Father, in whom all his sons are brothers. It is right for our bodies to move in dancing rhythms!

In the future, when there is an original African theology, it will perhaps be called a theology of 'inculturation', because it will have been preceded by this festive liturgy in which a living communion with the love of the Father, the Son and the Holy Spirit—the living God made flesh—is celebrated by the bodily expression of the dance.

Translated by David Smith

Notes

1. My article is based mainly on my experience in Cameroon and especially in Zaire. Despite the heterogeneity of its populations, there is, however, a fundamental cultural unity in Black Africa. See, for example, C. A. Diop *L'Unité culturelle de l'Afrique Noire* (Presses Africaines 1959) p. 7.

2. J. Daniélou *Le Mystère du salut des nations* (Paris) p. 55.

3. Constitution on the Liturgy *Sacrosanctum Concilium* 30 and 38.

4. A. Abega 'Ndzon-melen, Une expérience liturgique' *Telema* 4 (1978) 41-50; 1 (1978) 69-70; Sambu Mbinda 'Kiezila ki Khieza' *Telema* 4 (1976) 27-29; see also *Telema* 2 (1978) 91.

5. See the other questions pointed out by A. Abega and Sambu Mbinda in the articles cited in the previous note.

6. See other comments by A. Abega and Sambu Mbinda in the same articles.

7. Constitution on the Liturgy, 48.

8. *Ibid.,* 14.

9. The word 'restoration' and related words occur twenty times and 'participation' occurs thirty times in the Constitution on the Liturgy.

10. One has to be wary of the use of the word 'participation' in the sense in which it is employed by L. Lévy-Bruhl, tied as it was to his theory of prelogism; see *Les Fonctions mentales dans les sociétés inférieures* (Paris 1910). This was in any case later withdrawn by the author; see *Carnets* (Paris 1949) pp. 60, 73.

11. Presses Africaines 1948 and 1962 respectively. See also H. Maurier *Philosophie de l'Afrique Noire* (Anthropos 1976); F. Boulaga Eboussi *La Crise du Muntu* (Presses Africaines 1977); D. Nothomb *Un Humanisme africain* (Lumen Vitae 1965).

12. *Documentation Catholique* (November 1967) 1505 Col. 1941-1943.

13. See certain other approaches to the concept of 'muntu': J. Hahn, *Muntu* (Paris 1958) pp. 110-116; A. Kagame *La Philosophie banturwandaise de l'être* (Brussels 1956) p. 267; P. Tempels *La Philosophie bantoue* (Presses Africaines 1948) p. 28.

14. Boka di Mpasi Londi 'A propos des religions populaires d'Afrique sub-saharienne' *Telema* 2 (1979) 23-24.

15. The interruptions made in the story by the proverbs, questions, chants and dances break the monotony of the proceedings and make it easier for those present to absorb what is going on, with the result that the sessions can continue for a much longer period. The Zairian Mass modelled on this structure lasts for two and a half hours and no one finds it tiring—not even children and old people.

16. R. Garaudy *Danser sa vie* (Paris 1973) p 13.

17. See the formulae described by M. Hebga *Croyance et guérison* (Yaoundé 1973) pp. 9, 21; E. de Rosny *Ndimsi* (Yaoundé 1974) pp. 242-243ff.

18. R. Garaudy *Danser sa vie* p. 14.

19. Other types of dance can also be added to this list—the war dance, for example. If they are interpreted outside their original context and the philosophical framework and ethical structure within which they have developed, these dances can easily be incorrectly assessed and disparaged. They have above all to be judged within their own objective context.

20. Everybody seems to be caught up in the effort to invent new gestures, even in convents of sisters. See for example 'Expression corporelle et parole de Dieu' *Telema* 2 (1976) 29-34.

PART II

Bulletins

Cyrille Vogel

Symbols in Christian Worship: Food and Drink

SYMBOLS—means of recognition and signifiants[1] attempt to give tangible form to that which in intangible. In this sense, all human activity is symbolic: gestures, words, language, social interaction, theological debate, liturgical celebration. More specifically, the liturgical symbol can be analysed as follows:

1. It is necessary to assume a common ground of knowledge and understanding. This implies the existence of a group of initiates; otherwise particular gestures and utterances would be incomprehensible. Some familiarity with an object or event is necessary for any act of recognition; we see this at Emmaus (Luke 24:35: '. . . they recognised him in the breaking of the bread.'

2. There is no room for the arbitrary: the symbol must be understood by all the members of the community and accepted on these terms. Otherwise, gestures and utterances would become meaningless.

3. The tension and polarity between the signifiant and the referent must be kept constant. Should the one be identified with the other in any way, the result would be a 'reification' or recourse to an act of magic. The *Verona Fragments* provide an example: 'gratias agat panem quidem in *exemplum*, quod dicit graecus antitypum, corporis Christi; calicem vino mixtum propter antitypum, quod dicit graecus *similitudinem*, sanguinis quod effusum est.' Destruction of the symbol would amount to the creation of an idol. Conversely, neither the choice of signifiants and symbols, nor their possible modification (bread, wine, rice and the breaking and consumption of the same), will affect the referent in any way. Thus, Thomas Aquinas, in the hymn *Lauda Sion,* states: 'Nulla rei fit

scissura/*Signi* tantum fit fractura/Qua nec status nec statura/*Signati* minuitur.'

The gestures and utterances which constitute the act of worship *represent* the intangible, they do not define it merely in terms of concepts and images; they have the effect of making the intangible present and indeed of anticipating it, thereby ensuring a level of understanding which is more profound and more direct than that afforded in ordinary speech; this is especially true of the Eastern liturgy.

1. SACRED FOODS

The types of food and drink which Christians have held sacred are very few in number, showing little variety; meat and vegetables have never been included amongst them.[2]

1. *Bread, wine and water*

These three elements are variously presented:

(*a*) As a trinomial: bread, wine and water. This is attested by Justin Martyr, *1 Apol. 65*: 'Finally, (at the baptismal eucharist), bread, a cup of diluted wine and a cup of water are brought to the president. ... Those ministers whom we call deacons distribute the consecrated bread, wine and water to all those present.'

(*b*) As a binomial (first combination): bread and wine. These two elements figure in the so-called institution narratives (or Last Supper narratives) and vary in presentation:

  (i) According to Mark 14:22-25 and Matt. 26:26-29, the rites of the bread and the cup, juxtaposed directly with no time lapse between the two, take place during a full meal (it is not clear whether at the beginning, in the middle, or at the end).

 (ii) According to 1 Cor. 11:23-26, the rite of the bread takes place at the beginning of the meal, whereas that of the cup is at the end.

(iii) According to Luke 22:17-19a, the rite of the cup and that of the bread (in that order, with the cup preceding) take place before the full meal.[3]

There is no longer any room for discussion as regards the origin of the two rights: Jesus availed himself of the Jewish Kiddusch at the time of the last supper (whether or not we consider this latter to have been paschal).

(*c*) As a binomial (second combination): bread and water. In certain places, for various reasons, the wine was replaced by a cup of water. In connection with this, see Cyprian *Epistle 63 to Caecilius of Biltha* (relating to the Aquarian controversy).[4]

(*d*) In singular form:

(i) The cup alone: the obvious alterations in the narrative of the institution given in Luke 22:17-20 do not destroy the hypothesis that the Eucharist might have been celebrated with the cup alone.

(ii) The bread alone: there are many texts documenting the celebration of the Eucharist with bread alone, in the form of *fractio panis*.[5] Thus: Luke 24:30-35; Acts 2:42, 46; Acts 20:7 (Troas); Acts 27:35 (the storm); 1 Cor. 10:17. The second Eucharistic narrative in the *Didache* gives only the breaking of bread at the dominical Eucharist. *Didache* XIV, 1: 'When you come together on the Lord's Day, break bread and give thanks'.

In addition to the documentation of the official Church, it is useful to look at evidence from dissenting congregations: the *Acta Thomae* cc. 27, 29, 46, 48 (Lipsius-Bonnet *AAA* II, 2 pp. 143, 146, 164) and the *Acta Iohannis* cc. 109, 110 (Lipsius-Bonnet *AAA* II, 1 p. 207).

2. *Milk and dairy products*

Milk and dairy products are consumed either separately or in conjunction with bread or honey (or water); this was the case for the Artotyrites: *Passio Perpetuae et Felicitatis* c. 4.[6] Milk mixed with honey and water forms part of the baptismal Eucharist, together with the binomial of bread and wine. The *Hauler Fragments* give clear evidence of this.[7]

3. *Oil or olives*

Oil or olives are consumed either separately or in conjunction with the consecrated bread and wine, or even with cheese. The *Hauler Fragments* do not distinguish between the blessing of the bread and the wine on the one hand, and that of the oil, the olives and the cheese on the other.[8]

4. *Salt (sacramentum salis)*

Salt has never, strictly speaking, formed part of a sacred meal. As far as we can tell, it was used in the rite of baptism as a symbol of fidelity and protection, but not as a theophagous symbol.

5. *Obscene foods*

Let us also mention those obscene foods (*sperma, menstruum*) used in certain Gnostic groups; information about these is given in the *Pistis Sophia* p. 147 and by Epiphanius *Haer* 26, for example.

6. *Fish*

In pre-Christian cultures, fish had long been eaten as a sacred food. In the ancient world, it was a symbol of virile strength (*ichthyphalles*);[9] in Judaism, it heralds the messianic age. Christians took it up for its eschatological significance. In the context of a meal, fish does appear in singular form, but most frequently in a trinomial (bread, fish and cup).

2. SACRED MEALS

Sacred food is tantamount to a sacred meal, yet it is nevertheless necessary for us to define our terms. A sacred meal is one which, by the intermediary of ingested food and drink, brings those who participate in it into a relationship with the divinity; in the act of eating, the participants communicate with the divinity. Therefore, the sacred meal aspires to theophagy, with a view to union with the deity or to participation in the divine life (usually bliss in the after-life). Thus:

1. The sacred meal is not merely an oblation of gifts to the deity, in honour of whom they will be eaten. Due to the existence of a symbolic relationship between the gift and the god, oblation merges with immolation (the suffering and dying god) and consumption: *ipse offerens, ipse et oblatus* [or *oblatio*].

2. The sacred meal differs from, indeed, is set in opposition to an ordinary full meal. It is always a 'stylised' meal, which never becomes identified with a meal eaten to appease hunger, even if the sacred act takes place in the context of an ordinary feast.

3. The sacred meal is not merely a dinner, even one set in a context of prayer or within a religious framework, such as the monastic meal, *agape* or caritative meal.

4. The sacred meal must be consumed in the place of consecration, the items of food and drink may not be taken from the place of worship (whether it be a private house or a building specifically intended for worship). This we find in Graeco-Roman religions: Cato *De Agricultura* 83: *Ubi res divina facta erit, statim ibi consummito*; *CIL* VI, 1 p. 576: *Extra hoc limen aliquid de sacro Silvani* [temple of Silvanus] *effere fas non est*.

Similar examples within Judaism can be found in: (Passover) Exod. 12:10; Num. 9:12; Deut. 16:14; (outside the Passover) Exod. 24:31-34; Lev. 7:9, 19; Num. 18:10; Lev. 22:30; 24:9,[10] and within Christianity: Innocent I *Letter to Decentius of Gubbio* (416): 'Nec longe portanda sunt sacramenta [here the *fermentum*, that is, a fragment of the consecrated bread]'.

5. The sacred meal is eaten in secret, that is, amongst initiates alone, excluding outsiders, thereby creating a privileged bond between those eating together.

3. PRIMARY EUCHARIST

The term 'primary Eucharist' is used here to designate any sacred meal where the sign or signifiant (bread, wine, water; either alone or in combination) is placed in a direct relationship with the body and blood of Christ as referents. As early as the middle of the second century, bread and wine established themselves as the dominant elements, and remain to the present day in the celebration of the Eucharist, the only sacred meal still current in Christian worship (in Eastern and Western churches and post-Reformation churches).

4. MEALS INCLUDING FISH

1. The narratives dealing with the institution of meals including fish (bread and fish) are:

(a) The feeding of the five thousand with bread and fish. (Mark 6:30-44; Matt. 14:13-21; Luke 9:10-17).
(b) The feeding of the four thousand with bread and fish. (Mark 8:1-10; Matt. 15:32-39).

Let us take Mark 6:39-44 as an example: 'Then he commanded them all to sit down by companies upon the green grass. And taking the five *loaves* and the two *fish* he looked up to heaven, and *blessed,* and *broke* the loaves and *gave* them to the disciples to set out before the people; and he *divided* the two *fish* among them all. And they all ate and were satisfied. And they took up twelve baskets full of broken pieces and of the fish.'

2. Other New Testament accounts apart from the institutionary narratives (bread, fish, honey).

(a) The appearance of Christ at Jersualem after the resurrection, recounted at the end of Luke, chapter 24:41-43: 'And while they disbelieved for joy, and wondered, he said to them, "Have you anything to eat?" They gave him a piece of broiled fish and a honeycomb. And he took it, and ate before them.'[11]

(b) The appearance of Christ on the shore of lake Tiberias, according to the appendix to John's Gospel, chapter 21:9-13: 'When they got out on land, they saw a charcoal fire there, with fish lying on it, and bread. Jesus said to them, "Bring some of the fish that you have just caught." . . . Jesus said to them, "Come and have breakfast." Now none of the disciples dared to ask him, "Who are you?" They knew it was the Lord. Jesus came and took the bread and gave it to them, and so with the fish.' Such sacred meals with fish are not recorded after the third century. They did survive beyond that date in the form of a funerary meal (*refrigerium*), including, it seems, the eating of fish (because of the eschatological significance of the

F

Ichthys). The funerary feast is always held directly beside the tomb, the deceased is assumed to be present (a votive *cathedra* is reserved for him) and to experience some comfort in the precariousness of his existence in the after-life.[12] As no relationship is established between the fish (plus bread and cup) and the body and blood of Christ, the *Ichthys* meal does not constitute primary Eucharist.

Translated by Christine Halek

Notes

1. The French original of this article employs the words *signifiant* and *signifié*, linguistic terms introduced by Ferdinand de Saussure. Although the obvious grammatical and semantic relationship between these words can be brought out in the Romance languages without any difficulty (as in Latin *signum—signatum*), this is not possible in the context of the Germanic languages. It has therefore been decided to translate them here using the corresponding linguistic terms current in English, that is, as 'signifiant' (a direct borrowing) and 'referent' respectively. (Translator's note.)

2. There is an extensive bibliography relating to food and sacred meals in Christianity. In order to avoid overburdening this article, we would refer the reader for a *status quaestionis* to C. Vogel *Symboles cultuels chrétiens. Les aliments sacrés: Poisson et refrigeria (banquets funéraires chrétiens* (Spoleto 1976) pp. 197-265.

3. Luke 22:17-20 is open to a three-fold interpretation justified, in each case, by the manuscript tradition: (*a*) Luke 22:17-19a (the version given above in the text of the article); (*b*) Luke 22:17-20: the first cup and the bread *before* the full meal; the second cup *after* the meal, that is, a sacred meal with two cups; (*c*) Luke 22:19b-20: a single cup at the end of the main meal.

4. For information relating to the Aquarians, see Filastrius *Haer.* 96; to the Ebionites, see Irenaeus *Haer.* V:1:3; to the Marcionites, see Epiphanius *Haer.* 42:3; to Tatian, see Epiphanius *Haer.* 46:3; to the Encratites, see Clement of Alexandria *Paed.* 3:2:32; *Strom* I:19:96; to the Judeo-Christian Gnostics, see Epiphanius *Haer.* 30:16; to the Apotactics, see Epiphanius *Haer.* 61:1; *Martyrium Pionii* 3 (sanctum panem et aquam degustare); see also the *Actus Petri cum Simone* 2 and the *Acta Thomae* 158 and 126. See G. Gentz 'Aquarii' in *Reallexicon für Antike und Christentum* (1950) I pp. 574-575.

5. A. Harnack 'Brod und Wasser' in *Texte und Untersuchungen* (Leipzig 1891) VIII p. 2; A. Schweiwiler 'Die Elemente der Eucharistie' *Forschungen zur christlichen Literatur und Dogmengeschichte* III: 4 (Mainz 1903); H. Lietzmann *Messe und Herrenmahl* (Bonn 1926). (The existence of a *fractio panis* without any cup whatever is independent of the theological conclusion which the author believes may be consequent upon it.)

6. *Passio Perpetuae et Felicitatis* 4: 'I saw [the vision of Perpetua] a large garden in the centre of which a tall, white-haired man was seated, dressed in shepherd's clothing, milking his ewes; around him were thousands of men dressed in white. Lifting his head, the man saw me and said, "Welcome, my child". He called me to him and he gave me a mouthful of the milk [dairy produce]. I took it in my clasped hands and I ate it [*sic.*]. All those present said "Amen". I woke up whilst still eating something indescribably sweet and soft.'

7. The *Hauler Fragments* (Latin version of the *Apostolic Tradition*) (Tidner p. 131): 'Frangens autem *panem* singulas partes porrigens dicat: Panis caelestis in Christo Iesu. Qui autem accipit respondeat: Amen. Praesbyteri vero si non fuerint sufficientes, teneant calices et diacones . . . primus qui tenet aquam, secundus qui *lac,* tertius qui *vinum.* Et gustent qui percipient de singulis . . .' The baptismal Eucharist involves five consecrated elements: bread, wine, water, and milk and honey mixed together.

8. The *Hauler Fragments* (Tidner p. 127): 'Si quis oleum offert, secundum panis oblationem et vini [in the episcopal Eucharist] et non ad sermonem sed *simili virtute* gratias referat . . . Similiter si quis caseum et olivas offeret . . .'

9. We reproduce the author's thought and word, but there seems to be a confusion. Both the *Shorter Oxford English Dictionary* and Jung himself in *Memories, Dreams, Reflections* (London 1963) know only *Ithyphallus,* not *Ichthyphalles,* i.e., *ithus,* erect, rather than *ichthus,* fish. (Editor's note.)

10. Exod. 12:9-10: 'Do not eat any of it raw or boiled with water, but roasted, its head with its legs and its inner parts. And you shall let none of it remain until the morning, anything that remains until the morning you shall burn.' Exod. 29:34: 'And if any of the flesh for the ordination, or of the bread, remain until the morning, then you shall burn the remainder with fire; it shall not be eaten, because it is holy.'

11. The accuracy of the reading 'honeycomb' which has disappeared in certain modern translations is excellently attested; see Nestlé (in a note) and H. J. Vogels *Novum Testamentum graece* (in the Greek text). The reading is retained in all the Latin translations. It is known that honey is an important element in Jewish funerary feasts and ritual usages.

12. Basic documentation relating to Christian funerary feasts is given by F. J. Dölger (1922), Th. Klauser (1928), A. M. Schneider (1928), A. Parrot (1937), A. Stuiber (1957), F. Cumont (1949), R. Marichal (1962), J. Doignon (1969) and J. Engemann (1969). It is impossible within the limits of a short article to enumerate the literary, epigraphical and iconographical material relating to the subject and the work which these have occasioned. We attempt to give an account of the state of the question in C. Vogel *Symboles cultuels chrétiens. Les aliments sacrés* (the work cited in note 2) pp. 233-247; *Le Repas sacré au poisson chez les chrétiens* (Paris 1970) pp. 83-116; *Le Banquet funéraire paléochrétiens, une fête du défunt et des survivants* (Paris 1976) pp. 61-78; *L'Environnement cultuel du défunt durant la période paléochrétienne* (Rome 1975) pp. 381-413.

Jean-Pierre Jossua

Unofficial Eucharistic Prayers:
An Appraisal

I HAVE been asked to produce some aesthetic evaluation of modern public prayer. For more than a decade this production of non-official public prayer has flourished in the field of what the new missal calls 'the Eucharistic prayer' and used to be called the 'canon of the Mass', and so I thought it best to limit myself to this field.

But when one has to produce an aesthetic criticism of an artistic creation which is meant to express the belief which Christians incorporate in their prayer, it is impossible to dissociate the aesthetic aspect from the theological one. In this case, indeed, it is not simply a matter of producing a more or less successful verbal composition as a garland with which to decorate some thought or prayer which could equally well do without this. It is much more a matter of creating something which expresses both the religious content and its beauty, and therefore of finding the best possible words to convey what is crying out to be conveyed to God or to one's fellow men. Any judgment of such a text must therefore take the composition as a whole. We have to consider not only the aesthetic quality of the text but also the question whether it can take up, and at the same time renew, a traditional religious experience which is already structured and, lastly, where the liturgy is concerned, the question whether such a prayer lends itself easily to actual use by the Christian community. It may well be that a text which is thought to have this kind of evocative power may one day be used for other purposes by other readers and at other times: how many 'sacred' words do we not use today in a purely 'secular' way? Nevertheless, since the text is meant for us as Christians and we have to consider its value, we have to judge its aesthetic quality according to whether it helps us to develop and revive our own prayer.[1]

1. WHAT HAS LED TO THE DEVELOPMENT OF UNOFFICIAL EUCHARISTIC PRAYERS?

I have no intention of analysing here the clerical power-system which has led the supreme authority to reserve jealously to itself the right to approve any Eucharistic prayer and to reject others. Nor am I here concerned with the 'safety-first' obsession which is supposed to justify this attitude. This obsession seems to go hand in hand with an evident Malthusianism: Christian folk cannot be associated with establishing what should be the very core of their prayer. Here I only want to indicate the reasons why people are no longer happy with the official or approved canons which, in spite of repeated prohibitions, have led to the creation of other canons, once the taboo of having only one canon in one sacred language had been broken.[2]

The first weakness of the official canons is their anachronistic and hieratic language, the cultural distance of which has become paradoxically obvious in our living languages. This defect has become even more obvious, especially in the prefaces, by the emphasis and a certain triumphalism which derive particularly from the misuse of texts taken from the Old Testament. This cultural shift not only prevents believers from praying in a language with which they are familiar and in which they have expressed their experience as Christians and as human beings since their childhood, but also from developing the poetic potential of their language. These texts, imprisoned in the style and liturgical language used by the Fathers, led to formulae in which people can see neither the meaning they could have for them nor the faith which they were supposed to express, just as they do not leave any room for the imagination they were supposed to inspire.[3]

To 'pray that your angel may take this sacrifice to your altar in heaven' (Eucharistic Prayer I); to say that 'He (Christ) opened his arms on the cross to put an end to death' (II); to call to people's minds the 'countless hosts of angels that stand before God to do his will, look upon God's splendour and praise him day and night' (IV); to call the Spirit 'God's first gift to those who believe' (IV); to ask God to give us the body of Christ 'so that we may become good Christians' and 'to let the dead be close to him in heaven' (Germany, in a liturgy for children); to make schoolboys say 'we offer you the holy victim' (Switzerland), and, to finish this litany, to strike up a powerful and exciting hymn with 'The towns and the countryside, ordinary people and those in power, the living and the dead already sense your presence and cry out to you' (Holland)—all this is using a large amount of imposing words to convey very little to people today.

There is no room to deal with the scruples which beset a number of ordained or lay celebrants as a result of using certain theological formulae that are hardly convincing,[4]—this simply helps to weaken the authority with which the present forms of the Eucharistic Prayer have been invested.

There is a much more serious problem which has to be tackled, and this is that formally fixed formulae of prayer seem to be incapable of connecting with people's actual life. Christian worship, which implies the total spiritual dedication of a person's life and which at the same time is supposed to be the force leading to conversion and to an increasingly meaningful life, makes no sense if it does lose contact with life as it is. How can those petrified, antiquated and never varying texts possibly express and produce a relevant and committed faith in this or that community or situation?

Only people who know little of the tradition of the Eucharist will object that this is not what the canon is supposed to do, but rather the business of general prayer or the sermon. These canons are in perfect harmony with the anonymous, passive, and wholly uncommitted character of our typical parochial gatherings. So, why should we be astonished that there actually are some committed Christian communities which are determined to integrate their prayer and interpersonal communion with their actual existence and their witness, and because of this want to make their Eucharistic prayer fit in with their need? Hence the creation of their own Eucharistic prayers.

Here we are touching the heart of the matter. The main weakness of the Christian liturgy does not lie so much in its anachronism or its abstract nature—these things can be remedied. It is much more its rigid uniformity of meaning and expression. Every particular event demands its own way of celebrating. There are parish masses, Eucharistic celebrations for groups of young people, Eucharists celebrated at home, Eucharists celebrated for vast gatherings, Eucharists for annual or exceptional festivities. It should be possible to reconcile the need for reliable texts which safeguard a given tradition with the need to build up a Eucharistic prayer composed by and for our present contemporaries in a way which is both more beautiful and closer to their personal existence. It should not be too difficult to reassure those who need objectivity and security, and at the same time to allow others, sensible enough to accept advice and to be discerning, the freedom to compose Eucharistic prayers their own way. In any case people are beginning to do exactly that—but unfortunately sometimes in a way which rejects all norms and is often not very responsible. In actual fact, people are creating their own canons of the Mass, whether we like it or not, and they are doing it all over the place.

But, do they really achieve what they are crying out for, aesthetically, theologically, liturgically, and existentially? That is the issue.

2. WHY DO THE COLLECTIONS OF FREELY COMPOSED CANONS FAIL TO SATISFY?

Most of the freely composed texts that go the rounds inevitably pro-
voke severe criticism when a reader is wholly ignorant of the circumstances which produced them. It would be wrong, in my opinion, to
extend this criticism to the liturgical event from which they originated.
But while backward-looking ecclesiastical reactions lack a sense of
perspective, the spread of freely composed canons very often lacks a
sense of proportion or is the result of satisfying some childish need. As a
result the reader is liable to see in them only the glibness, the clumsiness,
the theological weakness and the literary mediocrity of a prayer which, at
a given time and in a given gathering, may well have conveyed exactly and
even felicitously the life they lived and the celebration of their most
profound religious conviction.

So the first thing I would like to say is that we must very carefully
distinguish in most cases between liturgical effectiveness and aesthetic
value discernible by hindsight. So we should discourage the spread of new
canons, particularly since printing adds significantly to the weight of
'careful research' already attributed freely to its productions by a Church
now addicted to duplicating. At the same time one would like to suggest
that people do not judge what such a text meant actually on the occasion
for which it was composed, simply by *reading* the text: it would deprive it
of its context.

There are two collections of canons which were indeed worth publishing[5] and deserve looking at more closely.

The first has the title: *A la recherche de prières eucharistiques pour
notre tems* (*Coll. Vivante Liturgie*, 90, Paris 1977). It comes from the
abbey of St Andrew (Bruges) and shows great luturgical maturity. As
one reads these canons one feels that all of them achieve a high
level of authenticity and some of them (e.g., VIII and XXI) are quite
remarkable. They presuppose a high degree of culture—particularly religious culture—among the participants, but, granted that
feature, these participants must have found them well within their
reach.

There are, however, a few flaws which are rather obvious. For instance,
in places where the people are expected to join in, the texts are too
complicated and literary to lend themselves to being spoken in chorus.
The introduction of a new canon in the Eucharist presupposes either that
there is only one celebrant (in any case, the claim, whether clerical or lay,
to 'recite the whole lot' makes no liturgical sense at all) or that there are
parts in the text which are easy to speak by the whole congregation. To
reserve the canon exclusively to the ordained ministers is in no way
demanded by theology as is sometimes maintained: the whole con-

gregation is sacramentally active—though this does not mean that they have to assert this all the way through.

Another drawback is the frequent use of the Syrian canon. Because this canon recapitulates the thanksgiving, it has the advantage of enabling the narrative of the institution to be inserted into the flow of the evocation of benefits and thus avoids the usual abrupt introduction of the narrative without having to suppress the Sanctus. But this leads to Eucharistic prayers which put considerable strain on our modern patience. This is particularly true when the author is a great liturgist, such as H. Dufrasne, but not a great poet.

This leads to another weakness in this collection: the literary quality is of an unfortunately low calibre. The images and similes are sometimes awkward ('may this space of depth and communion/take shape in silence', I), often trite ('life has run out like a handful of sand', II, or 'the bread of hard work/the wine of our timid joys', VII, or 'looking at the growing grass or the blue sky', XIV), and sometimes as antiquated as those used in our official canons ('You gather us in the light of the luminary bodies/under the heavenly tent which your hands have erected', V).

The real problem, however, lies elsewhere. Practically none of these prayers can be used for another group without appearing rather phoney. The only way of understanding the themes and the vocabulary which are rather enigmatic is to put them back in their context, and this, fortunately, is made possible by the detailed explanations which accompany these canons. For instance, canon I originated in a cultured religious seminar after doing a great deal of work in groups on the Jewis roots of Christian prayers; canon II was worked out by a group of persons who were going through a very difficult phase in their life, but all were fairly well acquainted with the Bible; canon XII came from a semi-parochial community which had been discussing their social responsibilities.

The second lesson to learn from this study is therefore that even a high-quality collection is not easy to make use of in other circumstances.

Frankly, I do not even see how such a collection would be educationally useful for those who would like to make up their own canons, except for the critical observations which, as far as I know, only this collection provides. The reader may draw his own conclusions on this after reading about the collection Saint-Bernard.

This collection bears the horrible title: *L'Ombre du silence* ('The Shadow of the Silence', Paris 1977) and has been edited by members of the Saint-Bernard community. In a somewhat pretentious and rather fumbling way it tries to play on two registers at one and the same time and contains not only canons but also religious poems and prayers which can be used privately.

From the strictly literary point of view it is far more effective than the

Belgian collection but often moves considerably away from the Eucharistic tradition. In general, it reveals a fine and profound religious intuition which is sustained throughout the canon. On the other hand, the text is much more difficult to grasp since the composition comes close to modern poetry and so the language is rather less articulate, more disjointed. Must all serious attempts at renewing the language of religion necessarily be as esoteric as modern poetry?

These canons, then, are certainly more evocative, but this evocative quality implies a cultured public in a somewhat exclusive context, and this makes them once again difficult to use outside their context. And while there are some texts (e.g., 9 and 54) which stand out for their simplicity, they are at the same time rather trite. Some others are wholly centred on one passage of the gospel, such as the parable of the seed (28), and could therefore well be used in a congregation or group which has been meditating on this passage, but then again, is it wise to compose a whole canon on such a clearly dominant theme?

Then there is the theological criticism which such publications have to face when they present themselves as models. At its root every Eucharistic tradition must contain a number of basic values: the proclamation of the word, the commemoration of Jesus Christ, thanksgiving, the offering of oneself in the faith, the communion with Christ and one's fellow believers in the meal, the belief in the action of the Spirit, and so on. A theologian will assess liturgical publications according to the presence of these values in the texts before him. From this point of view a very large number of the canons are found wanting. Here the French collection has no doubt achieved a higher standard than many others, particularly where the offering and the epiclesis are concerned.

Should one blame those collections for this? The answer will be 'yes' if one judges them as models for repeated celebrations. But can one maintain that everything must be mentioned explicitly in every single canon? If a creative group maintains an on-going renewal, surely, the whole of the Eucharistic tradition will find itself expressed in the whole of the group's productions? Is it then, once again, a matter of publishing or not? The problem seems to be rather one of freezing something that makes sense only as one moment in the flow of a common search or that met the needs of an extreme situation which it would be absurd to think of as representative.

So the third lesson we ought to draw from this investigation is that it would be wrong to want to turn the result of some hesitant research or something which fitted a particular occasion into an inscription on marble. A celebration is but one act, and therefore transitory—and by the same token not really dangerous. Some other time, in some other place, one produces something else, and bit by bit we shall come closer to the ideal of a liturgy which is perfectly traditional and perfectly significant in its actual performance. . . .

Should we record and publish an improvised liturgy? My own opinion is that these freely composed canons should be taken as improvisations put down on paper beforehand in order to bolster psychological confidence—just as one writes down a sermon—but not as liturgical productions meant for regular use. They only replace the kind of improvisation which the early Christians practised and the re-birth of which would meet our present needs. They would take the same chances as any lyrical or epic creation which becomes a success.

3. HOW CAN WE ENCOURAGE AN IMPROVISATION WHICH IS BOTH BEAUTIFUL AND RESPONSIBLE?

If the composition of canons is prohibited, the very idea of improvising one must produce a real sense of horror in some church authorities. Moreover, the whole training of the clergy points in the opposite direction and makes them incapable of improvising in any way whatever. So they are not merely inhibited but will be legitimately afraid of the danger to which they might expose the liturgical heritage which is entrusted to us. This danger, in fact, exists because people have had so little training (leaving aside the whole matter of gifts) in improvisation that the theological lacunae and the feeble aesthetic sense of so many canons are nothing compared with those that beset most of the rare improvisations which it has been my luck to witness.

Now, this situation is in total contrast to the improvisation, which was universally practised, as we know, in the old liturgical tradition, slowed down afterwards, and practically disappeared completely in the fifth century. This was the result of the over-sacralisation of communion and the lowering of the quality of those who presided over the Eucharist. But the decisive factor doubtless was the prevailing mentality of fighting heresies and saving the confession of faith which was embodied in the canon.

It is important, however, to remember that this improvisation was not inspired by some 'enthusiasm' or the urge to create something totally new every time with regard to a canon which is attested as 'traditional' in the New Testament from the beginning and by the underlying influence of the liturgical Jewish heritage. We are ill-informed about how this guided improvisation proceeded. Perhaps we would not be too far out if we imagined a definite framework which had to be filled in, an accepted and extending canvas, and an alternation of literally fixed prayers and improvised ones. Without wanting to bring back a far-off past, it is not hard to understand that a practice which was universal at some time may well be legitimate. We should also realise that not everything in a liturgical tradition is of the same importance. The renewal brought about by the Council showed this, but only in rather belated measures.[6] Thus disappeared an absolutism which led to attributing equal value to everything passed on by history. Consequently, either it is sacrilege to touch anything whatever, or the 'transgressors' do not know where to stop.

It is true that a Eucharistic tradition comprises a certain amount of basic and precious elements which were listed above and described as *values*. These constitute its real foundation, indispensable for the authenticity of the celebration as well as for the faith of the Church which they express and engender.

This tradition also comprises a certain amount of time-honoured *forms* which vary as varying traditions spring from the old root. These forms express the 'values' mentioned in the preceding paragraph in particular rites: prayers, prefaces (thanksgiving), canons consisting of such parts as an epiclesis, an anamnesis, doxologies, intercessory prayers, etc.

Finally, everyone of these traditions goes through a linguistic experience born of the test of practice, and in this way produces a liturgical *language*, a transmission of texts, formulae and specific, meaningful gestures. It should be obvious that such varying ingredients cannot all be treated in the same way when it comes to the question what should be integrally transmitted and what can be handled more freely and therefore lend itself to some measure of improvisation.

I have frequently improvised myself, but not until I had gradually been introduced to this phenomenon, had seen the remarkable effect on the congregation as a help to the understanding of the richness of a traditional prayer and as a way of making people feel the poetic flavour which simple words can have when they are carefully adapted to the group and the situation. And so I am convinced that one not only can, but must improvise to bring the liturgy to life.

What is absolutely required is to do this only according to what the congregation can really take and according to the degree in which they have assimilated the tradition. In one case one will add or change some words or gestures to help people to accept traditionally given prayers in a personal way, with understanding, and so that these prayers become actually relevant. In another context one improvises on the basis of the whole body of inherited forms, in the manner of one or other of the great traditions. Finally, one or other community may well be sufficiently mature to re-structure completely the whole celebration for some particular occasion, and so to give new life to the basic values which are the substance of the Eucharistic heritage.

It would seem obvious that the diffusion of this sort of liturgical initiative requires some appropriate training. It is only by trying out improvisation very gradually (in the way in which one learns to preach and not in the way in which one is initiated into the exact reproduction of what the rubrics say), by accepting criticism, and even by undertaking, with others, a strenuous analysis of what one is doing from the point of view of theology, liturgy and the aesthetic rendering of it all, that we may turn improvisation into an opportunity instead of a catastrophe where the life of prayer of our communities is concerned. The availability of the tape-recorder nowadays should make this critical study easier than the practice of being able and having to submit beforehand the texts of the canons which have been made up. In any case, only some initial training is not enough. If the present circulation of freely composed canons does not prepare people for improvisation any better than the official monopoly, how could we help those who, in the spirit of the ancient tradition, would like to have a go at it? At present I can only make one suggestion. This is to produce clear schemes which would set out a twofold sequence of (a) liturgical forms and (b) of the themes contained in those forms, linked either with the annual liturgical cycle or with particular situations.

There remains a last point. When does a prayer strike us as beautiful and evocative? It would seem to me that a word will find an echo within us if it springs from a genuine human experience. It will touch some serious facet of our human experience, some real sharing in the life of the community, and will be recognised as something truly derived from spiritual experience. Its effect will no doubt be more powerful according to the simplicity of its expression: so-called 'poetic' clichés are useless. Let him or her who is gifted this way have the chance of really creating something, something that rings true. But any word which is personal and really meaningful will also be beautiful if it bears the mark of modesty. On the other hand, words blazing with poetic genius will only be useful in the liturgy if they fit in with the reality of the situation.

It is impossible to produce something that could serve as example in this area of improvisation. And so, to conclude, I refer to an exceptional collection of Eucharistic prayers, namely, that of Huub Oosterhuis.[7] In spite of one or two weak points, its theology is sound. A fair number of these canons manages to be actually relevant and usable in other circumstances, modern without being esoteric or affected, and often genuinely beautiful and moving. This may have been the fruit of a powerful Christian experience which has integrated the confused and complex human experience with that sense of respect and infinite distance which should mark any approach to God. This success may also be due—and this is the marvel of creative art—to the fact that the words are genuinely poetic and so can catch the simple beauty of everyday life in words, the loving search of a heart looking for God, and the vibrant hope of a people that cannot do without God. So it would seem to be possible to produce a canon which is beautiful, new, and charged with tradition, all at once.

Translated by T. L. Westow

Notes

1. A fair number of Eucharistic prayers, hand-written, typed or printed, has come my way. So I have been able to devote several seminars to analysing them. But in an international periodical one cannot limit oneself to examining the style of canons written in one or other particular language. It is therefore hoped that the reader will accept the somewhat general nature of my observations.

2. Apart from the four canons, approved for the universal Church, there is a collection of canons which have been approved in various localities: *Eucharisties de tous pays*, published by the C.N.P.L. (Paris, 1975).

3. Fortunately, the official canon 1 for a group of children—which could be used for adults just as well on condition of some modification in the dialogue— and the Philippine canon for children ('prohibited' today!) are happily free from such shortcomings.

4. The acceptance of the late formula *vel qui tibi offerunt* of the Roman canon, as if the *offerimus* applied only to the ministers, is one thing, but to relapse into mentioning the pope and the bishops before instead of after and in the midst of the Christian people is too much. What does one think of the dead being saved because 'God knows their righteousness'? Why use a harsh Augustinian formula like 'as he had lost your friendship by turning away from you, you did not abandon him to the power of death'? Why continue an equivocal statement about an effect of salvation that is proper to the sacrifice of the Mass by saying: 'the sacrifice which is worthy of you and redeems the world'? Why use the comparative to express the relations between God and the world: 'Lord, you are better than anything that exists' (Australia)!? etc. . . .

5. Some of these collections show a distressing mediocrity. From among those available in book-shops, I mention the two referred to in the text because the St Andrew's collection shows a literary quality far superior to the average, and contains a remarkable critical analysis, while the Saint-Bernard collection is one of those where the Eucharistic character of certain prayers is rather discretely suggested than explicitly stated.

6. See A. P. C. Hanson 'The liberty of the bishop to improvise prayer in the Eucharist' *Vigiliae Christianae* 15 (1961) 173-176; P. de Clercx 'Improvisations et livres liturgiques: leçons d'une histoire' *Communautés et liturgies* 2 (1978) 109-126.

7. Huub Oosterhuis *Autor de la table* (Paris 1974, translated from the Dutch). The 'spiritual sacrifice' is often concealed and the role of the epiclesis is arguable. Some canons (e.g., 1, 2 and 3) show the classical formula. Others are more provocative but also more interesting, such as no. 12 (in spite of some expressions which would have been better positively stated rather than put in question-form); no. 14 (which re-introduces the narrative of the institution and inserts an epiclesis aimed at communion); no. 17 (for the marriage ceremony—rather long, in my opinion), and no. 18 (bereavement).

Michael Paul Gallagher

What has Literature to say to Liturgy?

We are in a state of radical distraction. . . . To possess your soul in peace for a few minutes you need the help of medical technology. . . . Is reading possible for a people with its mind in this state?

Saul Bellow

To pray is to pay attention to something or someone other than oneself. Whenever a man so concentrates his attention—on a landscape, a poem, a geometrical problem, an idol, or the True God—that he completely forgets his own ego and desires, he is praying.

W. H. Auden

IT SEEMS appropriate to open these few reflections on the lessons literature can offer to liturgy with quotations from a novelist and a poet who were both, in different ways, aware of the contemplative dimension of their art. The last few decades have witnessed many efforts to establish links between imaginative literature and theology, but some of these have seemed misguided: in so far as they approached literature as principally a source of religious insight, they neglected the unique power of literature, the fact that its value lies on the level of experience rather than of message. Similarly, this essay would propose that liturgy can be inspired by literature more in terms of a level of communication than in terms of contents.

Indeed there may be a particular relevance in this perspective today: the values of literature could highlight a serious impoverishment of post-Conciliar liturgy in the Catholic Church. One hears on many sides that the new liturgy, as normally enacted, lacks a sense of mystery, that it has become levelled down to one mode, that it has become strangely inflexible and unable to answer the pastoral needs of a pluralist world, that it is often interpreted in an excessively horizontal manner, stressing human togetherness at the expense of mystical dimensions. In short, thinness and banality have sometimes resulted where relevance was intended, and a symbolic richness is lost which has not been compensated for by the intelligibility and participation potentials of the new rites.

Literature, by contrast, has often assumed the functions of worship or at least of spirituality for many readers of today. Almost exactly a century ago Matthew Arnold predicted such a role for imagination: 'More and more mankind will discover that we have to turn to poetry to interpret life for us, to console us, to sustain us', and he went on to claim that 'most of what now passes with us for religion and philosophy' would be replaced by literature. Setting aside the more secularist assumptions of his prophecy, Arnold's words have proved alarmingly accurate in some respects. In the contemporary culture of the West, many people approach the value-laden arts of fiction, film and theatre with something akin to worship and religious hunger. Artists such as Hermann Hesse, William Faulkner, Patrick White, Solzhenitsyn, Samuel Beckett or Ingmar Bergman have become cult figures in a time of frustrated religiousness. Where the Church mediations of mystery have failed to speak, the world of story and metaphor has become a substitute scripture and revelation and liturgy.

A paradoxical situation surely. Although the majority of modern authors have been far from any religious orthodoxy, they seem to have formed almost a conspiracy of hidden theology and secret spirituality. What T. S. Eliot (himself a most orthodox Christian) wrote about Hawthorne and Henry James might be applied to many of their successors in this century—they exemplified 'indifference to religious dogma and at the same time exceptional awareness of spiritual reality'. On another occasion Eliot offered a related and crucial distinction:[1]

> Much has been said everywhere about the decline of religious belief; not so much notice has been taken of the decline of religious sensibility. The trouble of the modern age is not merely the inability to believe certain things about God and man which our forefathers believed, but the inability to *feel* towards God and man as they did. A belief in which you no longer believe is something which to some extent you can still understand; but when religious feeling disappears, the words in which men have struggled to express it become meaningless.

In this light it could be asked whether liturgy today is not suffering a crisis of religious feeling and whether this might not be more central than the more evident crises of creed and culture. If so, the reform of liturgical externals urgently need completion by a renewal of internals also. And it is here that the world of literature could be of special service in reminding us of three areas of possible malnutrition in modern liturgy: (a) the level of spiritual receptivity of a congregation; (b) the medium of symbols and words as revelatory of mystery; (c) the various levels of communication possible within a celebration.

The area of pre-evangelisation or preparedness for worship

Both liturgy and literature require a certain level of receptivity if their richness is not to remain unattainable in experience. David Martin has analysed the convergence between aesthetic and religious consciousness in terms of the conditions needed for a genuine 'participative experience'.[2] For readers of this journal, it may be more helpful to draw together some ideas of Karl Rahner on the theme of poetry and imaginative writing as relevant to faith. An essay of 1959 put the emphasis on the 'greatest threat to religion' as lying 'in its *human* dimension', and on literature as a 'pre-religious' liberation of human potentials, capable of 'mediating the indispensable pre-requisites of Christianity'. In the course of Rahner's *Theological Investigations* at least five individual pieces expand on this basic insight.[3] A 'receptive capacity for the poetic word' is described as 'a presupposition of hearing the word of God', because in both man needs openness to mystery and hearing from the heart. But in fact the 'religious element' today is in danger of being out of tune with 'man's genuine experience', when it should be expressing that experience better and more deeply than he is able to himself; and this warning is extended to some overly enthusiastic uses of Scripture, as if it communicated automatically to man today. Thus, the preacher of God's word can be helped by being something of a poet, with a poet's gift of telling 'man his ambiguity in such a way that he perceives it'; and this is attained by means of *Urworte*, language that transcends utility and the shallow clarity of appealing to the mind alone. In this respect creative writers are viewed as capable of saving us from the banal, from being smothered by 'the forces of all that is average'.

Even from this rough summary, it should be evident that these themes in Rahner are relevant for our discussion of liturgy. Does liturgy need to regain the courage to be special and sacred? Has it too easily assumed that involvement means inner participation? (cf. *Sacrosanctum Concilium* 19) More particularly, has it neglected the dimension of interiority in the course of its valid and exciting reforms of rites? These are some of the questions that the literary world would put to liturgy today, in the hope that liturgy would find new means to create wonder and silence, to evoke something of the attentiveness of the aesthetic experience in a context of worship. The success of literature as a kind of private spiritual liturgy for many people today is a reminder of the quality of experience required. Thus the world of literature would join forces with Eastern spirituality in encouraging liturgy to be more slow, silent and solemn. In Hamlet's words, 'the readiness is all'. Preparedness for prayer is our first crisis area raised by thinking about liturgy in the light of the aesthetic-contemplative experience of literature.

The Verbalist versus the Parabolic

In recent years there seems to be a new danger of disobedience to the counsel of Christ that one should not use many words in prayer; and the liturgist does not have to wait for the literary man to point this out: at least two recent surveys of the state of liturgy diagnosed an 'excessive verbosity' or 'verbal inflation' in contemporary worship.[4] Paradoxically, literature which is rooted in the verbal is also a reminder of the perils of verbalism—of thinking that an accumulation of words means an accumulation of significance. An internationally successful drama such as *Equus* is a classic example of fraudulent verbalism in recent writing: although superficially impressive, it mistook cleverness for wisdom and mystification for mystery; its audiences were excited with powerful verbiage but the taste turned sour on reflection, on looking for human reality. The lesson for liturgy is obvious: if words in drama belong within the eloquence of a human situation, words in worship must be held suspect unless situated in faith and in the actions of a believing community. 'Words alone are certain good' was the chorus of Yeats's first collected poem, but it is a dangerous motto for dramatist or liturgist. It forgets, to cite a rather different line of Eliot's, that 'words after speech reach into the silence'.

If the previous section dealt with the pre-verbal area of receptivity, this section asks rather about the role of words in a basically dramatic medium. Aristotle put *lexis* third in his list of the elements of tragedy, and with a sure instinct gave precedence to *mythos* and *ethos*, the realms of story and of human values. Some contemporary drama has witnessed a radical subverbalism as exemplified in the works of Beckett. Here the focus is on the tragedy and the comedy of man's inability to live without words even though they are only empty counters filling in the time; and in his more recent work Beckett embodies man's essential poverty in gestures of silence. Once again a possible warning emerges for liturgy against giving language the centre of the stage.

And this warning is all the more necessary if the language in question is doctrinal in a conceptual manner; in fact this would constitute a second infidelity to the example of Christ who never spoke to the crowds except in parables (Matt. 13:34; Mark 4:34). Not only from literature but also

G

from the scriptural emphasis on the parabolic the liturgist can relearn the simple truth that man is a story-loving animal, and that this has a relevance beyond any mere improvement of communications. The parable is not simply a tool of rhetoric, a means of attracting interest in the congregation. If imagination is not valued as a 'form of thought', then faith, theology and liturgy 'will only use the images of literature . . . in a secondary and unimportant way'. For the Cartesian tradition of clear ideas, parables were for didacticism, useful vehicles of moral messages. In the Coleridgean tradition, where symbol is not so automatically reduced to allegory, the parable is more an extended metaphor, a trap for echoing wonderment.[5] If so, our preaching should be more parabolic and less rationalist; it should create echoes rather than offer explanations. Such at least would be the advice of Robert Frost, one of the masters of parable and indirection in modern poetry: allow hints to set up reverberations within consciousness, to arouse 'the pleasure of ulteriority'. Or, finally, on this point, one may recall a celebrated saying by another American poet, Wallace Stevens: 'poetry must resist the intelligence almost successfully.'

The conclusion emerging here is that liturgy becomes dreary when it limits itself to the language of concepts, when it overloads itself with explanations for the mind, when it forgets the symbol as the most appropriate medium for mystery. The vast success of modern literature as a vehicle of spiritual quest gives testimony to this power of symbol and of story in embodying human complexity and in reaching human hearts.

Flexibility of Styles

One of the great moments in the patristic theory of Christian communication involves the revolution brought about by St Augustine in the history of rhetoric. Having been professionally occupied with this discipline for some twenty years before his conversion, his *De Doctrina Christiana* shows his way of rethinking his old skill in the light of his new faith. His insight was that now he would love the truth in words rather than words themselves (*in verbis verum amare, non verba*), and his innovation is to break down the strictly separate divisions of style in classical rhetoric.[6] The Christian sublimity of subject-matter was to join with a simplicity of eloquence in a way unheard of in antiquity, and even the plain style is allowed to become exalted, not by ornament but by power of feeling. This example—of introducing new flexibility into an older decorum—may seem far-fetched here, but it is a way of suggesting a flexibility in modes of communication that modern liturgy may have lost. One of the greatest spiritual poems of this century offers a parallel example: Eliot's *Four Quartets* deliberately exploits high and low styles in contrast with one another, setting passages of rich density side by side with passages of stark colloquialism, and thus miming something of the flux of spiritual states.

Would it be against the split of the new liturgy to encourage a similar and quite marked difference of wavelength between the liturgy of the word and the liturgy of the eucharist? Just as literature communicates at varying levels of intensity, even within one work, so too liturgy may need a conscious variety of levels of action. It needs to be able to range, even within one celebration, from direct human contact through communal inwardness to solemnity.

The limitations of the literary perspective

One should note that in many ways literature is an unsuitable partner for dialogue with liturgy. Apart from drama, the literature of the last few centuries has assumed a very privatised world of isolated consciousness; increasingly, what is termed 'literary' has been the product of an alienated and élitist minority. From this point of view it has serious limitations in any convergence with liturgy as a community action involving many kinds of people.[7] As approached here, literature has been seen as a stimulus for one dimension of liturgy, the sometimes forgotten dimension of depth and the indirect modes of discourse that awaken that depth more truly than the language of the head.

To put the proposals here in larger perspective, one can suggest that there are four dimensions that enter into maturity of faith, and that if liturgy is to reflect and cultivate maturity of faith, it will need to do justice to all four aspects. The first is the element of the Church as tradition and community of faith. The second is the realm of revelation, of encounter with Christ and personal conversion. The third is the changed life-style that results from the surrender of faith, the whole area of social commitment and love. The fourth is the inward or contemplative dimension, the realm of interiority, of man's searching in various ways to find himself and to be found by God. Post-conciliar discourse on liturgy has focussed on community, on evangelisation, and on linking worship with engagement in the world—the first three elements. The fourth element of interiority has tended to be not so much forgotten in theory as left impotent in practice. It is the element that literature thrives upon, even to the extent of becoming a gnostic wisdom forgetful of community, revelation and commitment. Modern literature has been intensely religious in its mood and its questions even when it is largely agnostic in its matter and its answers. Liturgy by contrast cannot assume that the religious question is alive or that the religious awareness is alert in a congregation. Hence modes of preparation become vital and a broader ambitiousness on the spiritual level seems essential. Without this dimension the stress on community becomes cosy, the good news becomes unhearable at any depth, and the urgency of social commitments become unrooted and in danger of the withering spoken of in the parable of the sower. From listening to literature, liturgy will not solve all its problems, but it will receive a healthy challenge and a reminder that it needs more than intelligibility to do justice to the mystery of God and of man.

Notes

1. 'The Social Function of Poetry' in *On Poetry and Poets* (London 1957) p. 25.

2. F. David Martin *Art and the Religious Experience: The 'Language' of the Sacred* (Lewisburg 1972) chap. 2 *passim*.

3. The quotations in this paragraph are from various essays of Karl Rahner (these references being to the English editions): *Mission and Grace,* III 119-122 ('On the theology of books'); and the following from *Theological Investigations:* 'Poetry and Christian' IV pp. 357-363; 'The Future of the Religious Book' VIII pp. 252-253; 'Priest and Poet' III pp. 296, 313; 'Prayer for Creative Writers' VIII p. 131. See also in the same volume 'The Task of the Writer in Relation to Christian Living'.

4. James Hitchcock 'La Voix du silence' in *Communio* 3 No. 6 (1978) 71; Joseph Gelineau *The Liturgy today and tomorrow* (London 1978) p. 77.

5. The quotation in this paragraph is from William Lynch 'The Life of Faith and Imagination' *The Month* (January 1979) 8. On the parabolic see Sallie McFague TeSelle *Speaking in Parables: A Study in Metaphor and Theology* (Fortress Press 1975).

6. 'De Doctrina Christiana' *Patrologia Latina,* ed. Migne 34, 1845. On these points see Christine Mohrmann *Etudes sur le Latin des Chrétiens* (Rome 1958) 1 360, and Erich Auerbach *Literary Language and its Public* (London 1965) on the *sermo humilis*.

7. The Canadian cultural journal *Mosaic* announced a special issue on 'Liturgy and Literature', for 1979, but it had not appeared by the time of writing this article.

Crispino Valenziano

Image, Culture, Liturgy

1. IMAGE, ANTHROPOLOGY AND THEOLOGY

THE atomic bomb on Hiroshima of the 6th of August 1945 seems to me a symbol, almost a trope of the transfiguration sung the wrong way round for the unconfessed loss of sight in the face of man. Ever since Clement of Alexandria, we Christians have repeated that man resembles God because God resembles man, and since Gregory of Nyssa that man is the human face of God. Additionally, both within the contexts of Christian cultures and outside them, anyone looking at man characterises him with qualities assessed on the premise 'to the image and likeness': intelligence, freedom, capacity to plan . . ., divine essence, divine race, impotent god, god-man. From Aratus and Cleanthes or from Heidegger to Feuerbach the names suggest, however crazily, the true reality.

But it would be inaccurate and unjust to see man, the man of our time, as calcified on the 6th of August at Hiroshima. The incident seems to me symbolic as a threshold between two civilisations, between the tragic end of the second millennium and a laborious beginning to the third millennium. One should listen again to the passage on 'prophets of misfortune' in the speech by John XXIII at Vatican Council II on the 11th of October 1962, and to the passage on 'humanism that becomes eccentric Christianity' in the speech by Paul VI at Vatican Council II on 7 December 1965. They contain an interpretation of the signs of the times, of anthropology and theology, which are useful and necessary to the present theme.

In our epoch man has reached the threshold-point through the evolution of his inner conscience, and human cultures have fulfilled their actual dynamic stages, achieving them, admittedly at great acceleration, consistently all together and in polarity. Everywhere today man is carefully attentive to his own totality, meaningfully outstretched towards more

91

complete and more intensely correlated new cultures. Rarely in history have convergences been as favourable to the perception of Christian themes concerned with the 'iconic' approach of anthropology and with Christian models concerned with the 'sacramental' standpoint of theology. It would be counter-productive alienation not to realise this but to insist on interpretations and activity based on enlightened *a priori* logic. It would be a senseless subterfuge to deprecate further the 'civilisation of the image' as a civilisation identified with neo-positivism and materialism. Since in fact it is the phenomenological event that established the synchronism, there is no great daring in establishing in Christian cultures structural equivalences between the depreciation of the person, the secularisation of society, the juridicalism of ecclesiology, the formalism of liturgy, the atypicism of spirituality, the non-mystagogy of catechism, the praxicism of pastorality, the intellectualism of theology and the eclipse of the image—any eclipse, from physical and mental insignificance to metaphysical and artistic disfiguration, with all the burden and implication involved. Whatever the connotations of the first members of these pairs, the image remains in an anthropological and theological circle, negative and positive, in relation to each of them and to all of them together: from man to Church, from the Bible to faith, from experience to testimony.

I am fundamentally in agreement with the affirmation that Hellenism in comparison with Hebraism is visual culture as against auditory culture, even if G. Kittel in *Die Religiongeschichte und das Urchristentum* observes that in the messianic biblical texts 'Hear O Israel' yields to 'Lift up thine eyes and see'; and P. Evdokimov in *L'Art de l'icône* reads Job 42:5, 'I had heard of Thee by the hearing of the ear: *but* now my eye sees Thee'. It is a question of intensity, not of exclusion. It would be crude, however, to accept the 'Hellenic' Christian cultures for their iconological components and the 'Hebrew' Christian cultures for their biblical components; as if the teaching of John and Paul and the New Testament in general did not remain the fount of all Christian cultures within the whole arc ranging from hearing to seeing.

One absolute hypothesis is the postulation that man, and so much more the Christian, could not do without beauty without diminishing himself, even losing himself. According to Gregory of Nyssa man made to the image of God strives to become that image because his own likeness to God is a manifestation, an epiphany of the beauty of God. In the same sense John Climacus tells of the saint who, looking at the beauty of a woman, cried for joy and sang to God. The civilisation of the image emerges in cultures which are each in their own way sensitive to beauty. And even if the beauty of human vision is ambiguous, such sensitivity must not condemn that civilisation: it is an ambiguity that subtracts nothing from the progressive Christ-like transfiguration of the universe; rather it defines the obligation of the Christian in the world and nourishes it to augment its quantity and quality.

Do I identify beauty only with the visual image? Not precisely. But the fact is that beauty always espouses light, since light and life are one. *Christus Pantocreator* opens his gospel at the passage John 8:12; and there is a widespread myth in many cultures of the ray of light that penetrates the darkness of the oyster and generates the pearl. . . . And there is another that the eye is the most privileged organ and sight the most privileged sense because it is patient of metaphor and symbol of the most comprehensive kind, not excluding the divine. Every artist, painter, sculptor, architect, musician or poet *sees* nothing 'ugly' and offers his eyes to let them bring him vision of everything 'beautiful'. The Holy Spirit, 'the finger of God's right hand', who 'renews the face of the earth' directs 'illumination' and 'illuminates' those whom the Spirit has made reborn from the water. We should also listen again to our Lord in Matthew 6:22-23. The metaphor to be taken in both an allegorical and anagogical sense, in the context that from Origen to the pseudo-Denys the Areopagite and beyond hands on the doctrine of the 'spiritual senses', underlines unifying perspectives from which man emerges, as Macarius would say, as 'the only eye'.

It is not materialism of the spiritual nor aestheticism of the divine; it is the 'divinisation of man'. But by the same token, it is the human realisation of the artist and of anyone else that purifies the 'lucency of the eyes'.

At this point I expand on the subject of the symbol and of symbolism.

Let us follow the deliberations of the second Council of Nicea. (It is better if we read it in collation with the Synod of the Blachernae and with the *Libri Carolini*.) All the problems considered gravitate around symbolism, since the symbol is a sign which is a factor of *presence,* not a pointing index finger, which is a sign which implies absence. And the iconological question is a question of the typology of presences: Is the icon a symbol or an index? Up to which point is it one or the other, up to which point one *and* the other? Under what conditions is it the only symbol of the Christ-mystery? With regard to the relationship between image and word delineated at Nicea II, their equal potential was confirmed and emphasis was laid on the dynamics of visual beauty; colour and substance point to the possibilities of transcendence; the circumscribability of Christ is attributable to the real incarnation of the Word; the consistency of the painted nave is identified with the prototype of the image named; the Eucharist is distinct from the icon—and this hints at a typology within the specific symbolic presence.

Let us jump a millennium and come to the problems of 'new art'. 'To present, not things, but their meaning'—'Modern art is subjectivist presentation': these are the extremes of the debate. Now symbolism, approximately defined, refers to the typologies of generic significant presence which, although extending eventually to true symbolic presence, limits its interest to the general comprehensiveness of what is significant and what is signified. In so doing it skips over the most important nuances in the whole spectrum of images extending from analogous 'images' to the visual 'prime analogate' image. The axioms previously stated hold equally whether relative to visual language or auditory language; while the real relevant symbolic question concerns the completely original visual sign and, for example, the *poetic* verbal sign, but excludes from its ambit the *didactic* word equally with the comparatively rare *facsimile* image. Now the aesthetic presentation offered to us by modern art can be sad because it is significant-image devastated in its expression and significance-image inadequate in its communication, but then it is an image of a meaning that is *itself* devastated and inadequate: need one confirm that the presentation is in itself a real symbol of an impoverished reality? If expressionists, cubists, magicorealists, surrealists and abstract artists have proclaimed the importance of presenting 'the interior essence of things', 'images of being', not to be visibly registered by the naked eye, they are nevertheless fatally Luciferian in relation to God and they are Docetists in relation to his Christ. Perhaps Matisse depicts an authentic transcendence, Chagall outlines religious forms, Rousseau sees an evangelical infancy, Rouault celebrates the Christian mystery. The enchantment of many works of Klee is certainly begotten by the wonder which the inexplicable inspires in him; so that the enigma of his 'carpets' approached the 'liturgical toccatas' of Roman cosmati work. Is it irrationality?—may they correspond to the Arabic equations solved in the 'liturgical fantasies' of the Norman-Sicilian mural slabs? And as in the images of such people, so in the images of the subconscious of Goya, of the occultism of Bosch, of the overturning of Liepchitz, of the transsubstantiality of Moore, or in the diagonals of Malévitch and the right angles of Mondrian. With all these artists we are left with cultural experiences no less dramatic than iconoclasm and its complex pattern; we come back to the question of the symbol as presence. Sartre said that the yellow of the Crucifixion of Tintoretto *does not represent* dismay and anguish, *it is* dismay and anguish.

All this talk about beauty and perception brings us back to the relationship between image and presence. To separate the image from the presence-in-symbol is to imprison it within the confines of being visible to the naked eye, within the confines of the didactic word and its analogies. These are images which have their place in intellectual theory and human action but they are not the matrixes of a true, authentic 'civilisation of the image'. If, on the other hand, the image is significant of mysterious meaning, then to separate it from the presence-in-symbol is to deprive it of any true theological significance. The images which Gregory the Great sketches for the instruction of the ignorant are images of this type; and if the Carolingian culture were not wrong in believing that the identity of image, symbol and presence was absurd, the *Libri Carolini* would be right in everything.

We must add two observations:

The first is that the symbolisation of the image is not a question of technique: or rather, it is not a question of technique alone, and eventually it is a question of technique as a secondary issue. From the time of the second Council of Nicea 'rules' were established whereby the iconographer became 'hagiographer'; but even though starting in the 'sacred art' of the third dimension and of perspective, of chiaroscuro and the optical illusion, it originated the separation of the mystery-image from the presence-in-symbol. I would not be so sure that the theological insignificance of too much of the corpus of sacred art derives directly from such 'irregularities' as to believe that the Franciscan Giotto is at the root of western iconological disasters, or that Fra Angelico lost himself and went astray in his Dominican preaching. As long as the presence-in-symbol does not decline! As a proof of this, the suggestion of Athenagoras I on the urgency of the renewal of Byzantine iconography occurs to me (see the entire chapter 'Leitourghia' in O. Clément, *Dialogues avec le patriarche Athénagoros*). It could constitute an ecumenical encounter: Western 'subjectivity' or 'realism' meeting Eastern 'theology' and 'liturgy', Eastern 'traditionalism' *vis-à-vis* Western 'creativity' (the coining of that term from the verbal form 'creare' is by Athenagoras himself).

The second observation is that a reform of the space-time 'norms', such as the image-symbol is, produces a realisation of man which is simplified in unity. Perception is, then, truly a 'field' in which circulates all that is lived, experimented, learned, all that is codified, precomprehended, awaited . . .; and therefore what is seen goes beyond the 'objective'. Already an ordinary objective spectator is unreal, as alleged scientific objectivity is unreal: positivism is bankruptcy up to that point, the point of imagining the subject involved and enwrapped in symbolic communion!

We have, then, to recall as never before what was reflected in the seventeenth century and what Bergson underlined beyond Vico: perception rooted in an embracing corporality and in memory that is also imagination, has a duration of its own into which enters all the freedom which, in truth, the spirit shares with nature. In the communication which

is a circularity of presences there is established a reciprocity of consciousness which is an anthropogenetic circle between symbol and subject, and vice versa.

2. IMAGE, ASSEMBLY AND CELEBRATION

It is within this setting that the renewal of image becomes part of our
liturgy; not as within a frame, but as a determining and qualifying component. In fact the 'ritual' image is a cultural constant which lies between
the constitution of the 'sacred universe' that every culture conceives and
the constitution of *homo liturgicus* which happens in every culture, both
being members in symbiosis. The constitution of the 'sacred universe' of
Christian cultures is a mystery and is bestowed; the constitution of the
Christian *homo liturgicus* is sacramental and is a grace; but this does not
alter the fact that Christian cultures form an otherwise symbolic perspective of the mystery and the sacrament, with consequently different ritual
anthropogeny. Furthermore the rite is constantly 'symbolic realism' and
the ritual image participates in the same realism. In our case it is a matter
of the realism of mystery and sacrament, but this does not deny the fact
that our images risk being symbolically realistic merely in a conventional
or even magic perspective according to the different ways in which the
symbolism of mystery and sacrament is arranged. Every ritual image
tends to be called 'acherotypical' (not made by human hands) and
'miraculous': whoever executes it or gives it the denominative touch, it is
not the hand of the iconographer and its execution is *always a marvel to the
eye*; one should study again the numerous myths, Christian or otherwise,
so charged with presence, expressed in paintings, sculptures and architecture. But the Christian ritual image is an expression in the vocative case
and not simply a nominative verbal description, it is a verb of action in the
imperative mood and not simply indicative. It is an interrupting, interpersonal mark of interpellation: evocation not as a recollection, invocation not as a request, but a true and dignified anamnesic epiclesis. This
contains the marvel of the works which are *mirabilia Dei* and the dox-
ology of man *doxa Dei*.

One used to speak of 'renewal' of the image in our liturgy. It is not
difficult for anyone, and it proves our thesis, to go back to the synchrony
(we repeat this now in the positive) between such a phenomenon and
renewals in the anthropological aspect, in social sacredness, in the sacraments of the Church, in the mysteries of the liturgy, in the typification
of spirituality, in catechetical mystagogy, in pastoral neo-praxicism, in the
pneumatics of theology.

At this point the thesis considers the typologies of image in liturgy.

1. *Image of the assembly—image in the assembly*

Our image-civilisation has established itself through the explosion of the instruments of visual transmission. This has a double reaction in our case: as transmission of projected images at the liturgical assembly, and as transmission of the images of liturgical celebration to receivers outside the assembly congregated *hic et nunc.* We do not at the moment consider the first side of the duality, but the second—what we call the 'image of the assembly'. We are in the semiotic sphere of communication and the situation to which we are addressing ourselves is the possibility of an assembly meeting beyond the limitations of *hic et nunc.* It does not seem to me that adaptations of the 'physical' and 'moral' presence at the television phenomenon or the televisual potentiality of a category of 'visual' presence in psycho-sociological intensity are acts that resolve this dilemma. In my view one cannot disregard a resort beyond the generic category of 'participation' exemplified by the specific liturgical participation which is 'ministerial communion': the assembly which meets *ad Patrem per Filium in Spiritu* is the Church in a state of permanent edification and in the temporal reality of supreme edification. The state of *sine dominico non possumus,* taken also in the *hic et nunc* sense of the liturgical gathering, is the condition governing the ministerial exercise of the participants. (Obviously our remarks do not reflect on the rights of the disabled, nor the obligation of information, nor the duties of precepts and observance.) At this point however I should observe that ministerial communion seems to me to be adequately served by direct closed circuit in the same assembly (one thinks of St Peter's, one thinks of St Peter's Square . . .). The same can be said of unrepeatable celebrations in other actual assemblies, assemblies which *celebrate* the Mass of the Chrism, receiving into their cathedral church from the actual celebration the liturgy of the Word and continuing 'their' eucharistic liturgy. Would one not *exalt* the true tone of that Mass (which certainly does not diminish the status of the ordained priesthood)? Would one not succeed in this way in translating into visual symbolisation (from the progressive culture of the image) the Latin invention of *fermentum* of the Byzantine invention of the *antiminsion?* However, these are cases of mixed typology: the image *of* the assembly *to* the assembly.

2. *Real image—projected image*

The image at the assembly for the celebration is 'real' and not 'projected' if the executant does not impose a controlling expression on his own representation of the assembly. Again we are in the semiotic sphere of the representation and the expression, because we are concerned with the symbolism and the symbolic realism of the liturgical image. With a simple television dolly-shot of this nature from a static or wheeled camera we do not succeed in touching the horizon of real liturgical images and of their ritual synergy, except by indications, hints, allusions: the images of *time*, Sunday as an icon of the Resurrection, the morning as an icon of the Incarnation, the evening as an icon of Creation, the ritual year with its psychological, social and cultural iconology; the images of *space*, the altar icon of Christ, the pulpit icon of the Garden and of the empty Tomb, the iconic assembly edifice of universal celebration, architecture and its anthropological iconography; the images of the *human body*, its movement and its plasticising, fluid in shape and clad in colour; the images of *humanised objects,* furnishings and the like, the iconology of the 'sacred universe'; the images ordinarily intended as such, in sculpture and painting. Sculpture has its facile tendency to idolatrous seduction based on the powerful suggestion of an all-round comprehension: even if, as Cellini says, one has never seen a beautiful figure from every side there are eight basic points of view and at least twenty-four secondary angles from which—we are still quoting Cellini—the perambulating spectator can take in the work; therefore, from the status of 'intermediate art' between architecture and painting, sculpture can alternate and swing up to the height of an autonomous icon; and therefore it can be elevated to levels of ritual animation; and therefore one must commission the sculptor to carve directly onto the medium, since by that method the production is slower and more reflexive, and one must invite the liturgical spectators to purify the eye into virginity and indulge the other senses in this regard, since contemplation is less equivocal and more keenly symbolical.

Painting, whether in fresco on damp plaster, burnt in encaustically, as mosaic, glass or enamel, in oil or in miniature, marked out in niello or other media or coloured as embroidery or in textiles—all these have a wider physical scope and therefore a greater aesthetic freedom in all their forms. Consequently they are more liberating, their forms and their syntheses are more ductile and their symbolism is more faithful. For this reason painting refines the colours of mundane memory, purifies the enslaved eye of the prosaic, enables us to see beyond the trivial systems of the day more and better than any other art. Therefore one must envy the artist-painter, and not impose on him any further schematic systems. One must invite him in particular to become the hagiographer, and one must then invite the liturgical spectators to 'let themselves be captured' by the symbolic colour.

3. *Image of reality—image of the scene*

The projective image at the assembly in the celebration takes us rigorously back to the semiotic sphere of the language in which it is being conveyed, because our object is to surpass the language of information. Now the projective image is an image where its executant does not impose a controlling expression on his own representation; but for this reason it is not a strictly informative image. A photographer is a person who 'writes with light'. There are two consequences. On the one hand he consistently intervenes in the registration: one must remember the sophisticated and mutually influential skills of focussing and squaring up, of cinematic artifices and effects, the editing, the determination of sequences. On the other hand, the viewer must decipher a product which is continuously mechanical: one needs to recall the intrusions and domestic accretions which materialise as parasites to the message. The fact is that in this present thesis the symbol is culturally connotative (not denotative) in putting through an average of considerable quality. Yet one succeds ritually, in my opinion, where one records reality, not scene. We may call 'scene' a fact or situation already essentially put across by artifices of various kinds. We may call 'reality' a fact conveyed only by iconic artifice.

Always, in my opinion, the recording of the scene is informative even if transmitted directly, whilst the recording of reality succeeds in being performative, being a matter of living reality transmitted in normal psycho-sociological conditions only if it is put out directly.

Everything that has been dealt with in this thesis, therefore, should be read synchronically.

Translated by Joyce Andrews

Bibliography

I give a brief bibliographical selection of general orientation. I allow myself to refer to my *Prospetto per una trattazione antropologica del simbolo nelle nostre culture cristiane* in *Symbolisme et Théologie* (Studia anslemiana 64. Sacramentum 2) (Roma 1974) 29-44, towards an eventual integration of the context (and of the connected bibliography).

AA. VV., *La comunicazione audiovisiva* (Roma 1972).

AA. VV., *Liturgia e strumenti di comunicazione sociale* (Quaderni di 'Il nostro cinema', 2), Roma s.d.

Barthes, R., *Rhétorique de l'image*, 'Communications' 4, (1964) 40-51.

Berenson, R., *Vedere e sapere,* (Milano-Firenze 1951).

id., Estetica, etica e storia nelle arti della rappresentazione visiva (Milano-Firenze 1953).

Cassirer, E., *Philosophie der symbolischen Forman* (Berlin 1923) ss.

id., An Essay on Man (New Haven 1944).

Fast, J., *Il linguaggio del corpo* (Milano 1972).

Francastel, P., *Peinture et société* (Paris 1951).

Itten, J., *Art de la couleur. Approche subjective et description objective de l'art* (Paris 1973).

Keim, J. A., *La photographie et l'homme. Sociologie et psycologie de la photographie* (Tournai 1971).

Kepes, G., *Language of vision* (Chicago 1944).

Libague, P., and Speri, G., *L'immagine come liberazione. Spunti per una cultura alternativa* (Firenze 1972).

Mercier, G., *L'art abstrait dans l'art sacré* (Paris 1964).

Merleau and Ponty, M., *Le visible et l'invisible* (Paris 1964).

id., L'oeil et l'esprit (Paris 1964).

Metz, C., *Au-delà de l'analogie, l'image* 'Communications' 15 (1970) 1-10.

Mounin, G., *Pour une sémiologie de l'image* 'Communication et langages' 22 (1974) 48-55.

Munari, B., *Design e comunicazione visiva* (Bari 1968).

Panofsky, E., *Die Perspktive als symbolische Form* (Leipzig-Berlin 1927).

id., Meaning in the Visual Arts (New York 1955).

Pierce, J. R., *Symbols Signals and Noise* (London 1962).

Thibault-Laulan, A. M., *L'image dans la société contemporaine* (Paris 1971).

id., Le langage de l'image (Paris 1971).

Bernard Huijbers

Liturgical Music after the Second Vatican Council

SO much new material has been published and even more is still in the throes of development and transition, that it is hardly possible to give an adequate account of the present state of liturgical music. However, it is possible to draw up an inventory of prevalent ideas with the help of available experiences, in particular those provided by the regular meetings of Universa Laus, an international group of people engaged in liturgical music.

Words such as 'new' and 'development' are hardly appropriate in this context and should be replaced by 'making up lost ground'. What is now called 'new' was already growing during the Reformation, also in the field of music, and led already long ago to musical climaxes in the works of composers like Schütz, Bextehude and Bach. The uncompromising attitude of the Counter-Reformation could result only in violent reverberations within the Roman Catholic Church. It caused a great deal of damage but, strangely enough, it was the means whereby some spectacular leaps ahead were made.

Music is an integral and constituent part of the liturgy and there is a close correlation between the two. I intend to describe this interaction in three phases, progressing from the obvious to the deeper causes lying within. These phases cannot be clearly separated. The distinction is more a methodical device and the sequence is phenomenological and diplomatic rather than logical.

1. *Interaction between music and other elements of the liturgy.* Here the question 'What?' will be asked, dealing with the repertoire in relation to the text, action and order of service. Dance and architecture will not be discussed.

2. *Interaction between the congregation celebrating the liturgy and the congregation performing the music.* Here the question 'Who?' is posed, concerning the proceedings.

3. *Interaction between the contents of the liturgical and the musical elements.* This raises the questions 'Why?' and 'To what purpose?' in other words, the ideology of the occurrence.

Phases 1 and 2 are followed by short intermezzi dealing with confrontations between old and new. These confrontations form part of the present musical situation and are not only caused by but also the cause of what is happening today.

1. MUSIC AND OTHER ELEMENTS OF THE LITURGY

(a) *Music and text*

The text *repertoire* (the texts of the musical repertoire) is in the course of radical change. Before the Second Vatican Council there was an absolute domination of composed texts from the Ordinary over a disappearing minority of motet-like texts. The music for texts of the Proper, intonations by the celebrant, melodies of lessons and vesper psalms, etc., were seldom or never composed, but borrowed from Gregorian chant. Since the Second Vatican Council this situation has been reversed. This, in itself, has caused an enormous rise in the *number* of compositions, as there are thousands of texts of the Proper and only five texts of the Ordinary. This total can then be multiplied not only by the many different languages but also by the number of groups within the parishes (young-old, popular-classical). The result is an abundance of compositions throughout the world, difficult to identify and not interchangeable, unlike the compositions of the Latin Ordinary of the olden days.

The *character* of the compositions appears to have changed. Before the Second Vatican Council, compositions, with some exceptions, used to be subjective, lyrical expressions arising from texts which were very often interpreted in a rather primitive way. Since the Second Vatican Council there has been a better understanding of texts, due in no small measure to the use of the mother tongue. The text is becoming more *dominant* in relation to the music because of a clearer theological perception of the liturgy. More attention is being paid to (1) the construction, (2) the style and (3) the function of the text. At the same time the *quality* of texts (e.g., in translations of psalms for use in the liturgy, of the Ordinary and of prefaces), the *choice* of texts (e.g., psalm responsories) and the *structure* of texts (e.g., when writing a text for different performers) are now also dependent on the feasibility of musical composition.

(1) More attention is being paid to the *construction* of the text, as can be seen by the use of old forms such as the two-line psalm verse or the versification of a hymn, and by the use of new forms such as the strophic composition of hymns for choir with a refrain sung by the congregation, the sung Eucharistic prayers and the texts for rounds.

(2) More attention is being paid to the *style* of the text used. There are old types such as acclamations, the oratorical style in the recitation of lessons and prayers, the less restricted style of antiphons and the more restricted style of hymns. Then there are the new types such as free verse in chanson-like compositions which are comparable to the ancient type-melodies, otherwise called nomos-melodies or tone patterns. It is probably true to say that really new literary and musical styles are hardly conceivable.

(3) More attention is being paid to the *function* of the text. The text may be a lesson which nowadays is less often intoned on a recitative than formerly, except on certain occasions (e.g., the sung passion). The text may be used as a prayer which is now also sung less frequently than in the olden days, except in the case of litanies or the sung eucharistic prayer. The text may be an invocation, more often used nowadays than previously, e.g., in acclamations. The text may be applied as a response or a meditation, as, e.g., in responsorial psalmody which is now an ever growing repertoire. The text may be used as an accompaniment to an action, as in antiphonal psalmody or processional chant. In all these cases the function of the text is predominantly determining the music. Is such an interaction between text and music not an anachronism? Which poet still writes hymn texts? Which prose writer still pays attention to the use of recitatives? How many tradesmen still sing the praises of their wares? On the other hand the question may be asked: Who can prove that types cannot be revived if they acquire a new function and if there is a need for them?

1 (b) *Music and action*

The response of 'Yes' by bride and bridegroom, the response of 'Amen' by a congregation . . . Both are a kind of action, the literary meaning being less important than the act of speaking. Specific actions—a better word for them might be 'gestures'—are quite common in the liturgy.

The music is involved with these gestures. The distribution of psalms or the distribution of holy communion may seem to last a long time without music. Music shortens the time, because it is, by definition, a musical passage of time, and gives it sense or fills it with emotion. Music can also express this sense and this emotion in a sung text. The liturgical renewal has acknowledged the importance of such actions or gestures. They have

H

been given a new lease of life. The congregation is invited to participate in many of them, and both vocal and instrumental music are used, partly in an old role and partly in a new role. Regarding vocal music, much has been drawn from the Gregorian past and from ancient forms still in use in the Eastern-Orthodox Churches. Joseph Gelineau broke new ground in this field (as he did in the whole manner of approach to liturgical music), and thanks to him everyone nowadays knows what is meant by *processional psalmody*. Many communion antiphons have been constructed on this pattern, even though they may not consist of psalm texts.

But above all, the *hymn sung by the people,* particularly in the beginning and at the end of the service, has now firmly established itself. I believe the reason for this is that the opening (or closing) of the service is now experienced more as a collective event (the congregation starting or closing the celebration) rather than as an hierarchical ritual (the entrance and exit of the officiating minister). A hymn is very appropriate to express this collective character. However, hymns are sometimes used too frequently, especially if one is not sufficiently familiar with other musical styles, which does the liturgy little good.

One can argue about the fact whether a *litany* is more an action than a literary affair. Characteristic of it is the lengthy and continuous repetition. In some cases composers have successfully found a musical form appropriate to solve this problem. Here, too, there is an interaction. Without music there would be no litany and without a litany that kind of music would not exist.

1 (c) Music and order of service

'Order of service' means the sequence of constituent elements. This sequence in itself is also a component, but the *ordo* is a kind of underlying framework and is not the service itself.

1. That there is an interaction between music and order of service is obvious, particularly from the antithesis between musical and liturgical structures which was so characteristic of the liturgy before the Second Vatican Council.

The liturgical sequence was completely smothered by musical forms, although still recognisable in spite of a multitude of additions on the one hand and the erosion and contraction of some parts on the other. This occurred when the Gregorian Gradual was sung during rather than between the lessons, when the Sanctus ran into the Canon or the Agnus Dei was not sung during the breaking of the host.

This became worse when, in classical Church music, the chants of the Ordinary began to show a closer musical relation to each other, an *ordo* of their own which, because of importance and length, acquired its own focal point in the so-called Mass of the catechumens. The chants of the Proper, usually in a Gregorian setting, were gradually overshadowed, not to mention the mixture of styles and times. The compositions of the Ordinary even acquired the title of 'missa', despite the fact that those parts of the text are least important and least liturgical compared with the parts of the Proper which vary continuously and are adapted to circumstances.

2. The hegemony of the Ordinary is now on the decline. However, influenced by history and because of other reasons, mostly musical, composers still tend to organise separate musical elements into one musical whole which looks similar to a cantata or an oratorio. I, personally, have experienced that tendency resulting in the composition of 'liturgies'. Joseph Gelineau tried to integrate all parts from the introductory rite to the communion rite into one whole.

I began to doubt if this were the solution. The principle of arranging musical elements seldom coincides with that of liturgical ones, which, of necessity, creates an inconsistency. Moreover, the components cannot so easily be used in another context, for another celebration. This leads to a special, fixed programme for each celebration which is contrary to the flexibility demanded from the liturgy now and in the future. It is a different matter where the *Eucharistic Prayer* is concerned, which is usually composed as one whole. It is a complete liturgical unit, and this fact is particularly obvious in the hundreds of experimental canons used, *praeter legem or contra legem,* in a great part of the world. The congregation as a whole often partakes in it, thus giving rise to new musical expressions and forms.

Intermezzo 1

Composition before and after the Second Vatican Council.

In general, Church musicians appeared to be badly prepared for the advent of the new liturgy. Movements to renew Church music were directed more towards the restoration of Gregorian chant and polyphony and the recognition of modern music than towards liturgical integration. In 1963 liturgists and Church musicians had not yet come to a full understanding of each other. Perhaps this was because the liturgical movement consisted primarily of *clerics* who were pastorally and theologically orientated, and the Church music movement consisted primarily of *laymen*, theologically and pastorally less well endowed. Using their best endeavours and sacrificing financial interests they aimed at the highest form of art 'for the honour and glory of God', but I believe they fell victims of prevailing aesthetics promulgating absolute music to be the highest form of art and relegating functional music to second place. Most musicians appeared to be blind to the fact that their Latin music failed liturgically within the congregation. They had been used to the lack of understanding of real art on the part of the 'common people', which, in the eyes of the romantics, was even considered to be proof of the quality of the music. And so it did not really affect them.

The *ignorance* of many Church musicians concerned:

1. Criticism being levelled against the prevailing concept of the Ordinary;
2. The musical scope offered by closely following style and function of the text. Intonations for the priest or recitatives for the reading of the lessons had not been composed for centuries;
3. The possibilities presented by the musical accompaniment of liturgical actions. We had forgotten what processional psalmody meant. Litanies had been composed only 'for the glory of Our Lady'. They had become completely alien to us as supplications.

This ignorance developed into a lack of understanding, a growing feeling of not being understood, hardening into estrangement, frustration, unwillingness, hostility and opposition. As more professional composers retired from the scene, more and more semi- or non-professional musicians occupied their places, which resulted in a lowering of the artistic level of new compositions. So Church composers became the cause of what they themselves dreaded so much. This disastrous, vicious circle has not yet been broken, although the signs are hopeful.

2. THE PERFORMERS

The musical proceedings have been changed by new liturgical celebrations. Here, too, there is interaction:

(a) The *liturgical* celebration has changed musically because of the (different) music.
(b) The *musical* element has been changed by the renewed liturgy.

2 (a) Before the Second Vatican Council there were low and sung masses. An intermediate form did not exist, with the exception of some prototypes of the liturgy to come (e.g., *Bet-Sing-Messe* and *Deutsches Hochamt*), quasi-liturgical functions such as Benediction, and para-liturgical ceremonies such as Stations of the Cross. The rules for low mass prohibited *any* part of it from being sung. If sung mass was celebrated, the whole mass had to be sung. The celebrant, for example, was to intone the Gloria and to recite the Preface, even though he were unable to sing a note. Only the lessons were allowed to be read in the absence of 'ordained' lecturers.

This 'all-or-nothing' situation has now changed. During most celebrations one or other part is usually sung. Which part this is depends very much on the circumstances. The Instruction *Musicam Sacram* contained an official, graduated list of preferences.

This change is not just a minor affair but is of essential importance. From now on text and action are being examined as to the meaning and function, and it has become clear that music is more or less *indispensable*. The active participation of the congregation as a whole is also a substantial element which has made the congregation an essential, rather than *ad libitum*, co-performer of the music, sometimes becoming even the main performer.

In that way liturgy with music has become the rule and liturgy without music the exception. Music has received a more important role *as a consequence* of the liturgical renewal, but was also the *cause* of it. Music gives a meaning and a function to texts and lends significance to actions (e.g., procession or litany). It forges people into a congregation, it creates the possibility of group expression which is more than the sum total of all individual expressions. It can evoke emotions and makes the expression of shared emotions possible, it offers the opportunity to contribute one's personal feelings emanating from one's innermost experiences. In short, music brings about communication, making the congregation into a real congregation.

Accordingly, music which fails to bring about communication should be called *bad* music, and musicians who (*salva erronea conscientia*) are unsuccessful in bringing about communication or, worse, oppose it, are in the same category.

2 (*b*) The congregation takes part in the singing. Choir and priest are no longer the sole performers. Choirs tend to change or to break up, new ones are formed. Instruments such as piano, flute, percussion and guitars are coming into their own.

Music making itself has changed. The importance of the meaning and the liturgical function of texts and actions cause some types of music and some types of performance to disappear, and others, of which only traces were left, to come back into existence again. Such ancient types which have been revived have already been mentioned, e.g.:

—acclamations (sometimes in the form of a refrain or litany) by the people or the officiating clergy;
—recitatives by readers, ministers or precentors;
—antiphons sung by the choir or the schola;
—hymns sung by the people, with or without choir;
—the singing of rounds by the people, with or without choir.

Each of these types of music is connected preferably with a certain group of performers.

The change of style or rather the diversification of *styles* of liturgical music is even more drastic. I am using the term 'style' for what is indicated by words as 'folk', 'popular', 'beat', 'guitar', 'rhythmic', 'youth', and, in contrast to these, 'classical'. This terminology is perhaps somewhat vague (as is the word 'style'), but the reader will know what is meant by it. Liturgical music is apparently in the course of becoming '*class-music*'. As different classes and groups of society speak a different language (Oxford English, dialect, slang, vulgar, jargon, group language), so they also have their own musical jargon in which they communicate with each other, recognise each other and make themselves understood to each other.

It is not the liturgy which causes the differences. The liturgy adapts to them as the various groups become of age as congregations and in turn start to contribute their own language and culture. Since only a minority of them is familiar with classical music, increasing numbers adopt the popular style (although what is called 'popular' in Amsterdam will still be very different from what is called 'popular' in, e.g., Kinshasa). This is much to the chagrin of professional church musicians who are nearly all of classical descent. For many years now there has been an unbridgeable gap between popular and classical.

This is not due to the present liturgy. It may, however, be due to the liturgy of the olden days. In support of this notion I can only refer you to my booklet *The Performing Audience* (North American Liturgy Resources, Phoenix, Ariz., 1973[2] *passim*). Briefly, my argument is that the liturgical choir music pre-1960 has been one of the strongest influences determining all music, even the later so-called classical music in the West. However, it should be realised that the liturgical music of before 1600 was the product of a split-situation. On one side we encounter imported Christianity, the Latin language, Gregorian chant and clerical liturgy, and on the other the people, looking on, listening, 'hearing mass'. The logical consequence of this was a dichotomy in the western music *tout court*.

Perhaps the new liturgy offers the opportunity of bridging that gap, because the various 'classes' meet together in the congregation (in as far as the Church has not lost the intellectuals and the workers). Might it not be possible for Church music to be the means of solving not only a class problem within the congregation but, via the congregation, also the class problem in the world? This would be too good to be true.

The solution is not to be found in the quantitative domination of one class over another (I estimate that 80 per cent of all celebrations in the United States are 'guitar masses'), but in the quality of both popular and classical music. In this respect I have drawn attention to Carl Orff's concept of 'elementary music'.

Intermezzo 2

Performance before and after the Second Vatican Council.

Musicians automatically think in terms of performers and audience. It is the result of the present arrangement in the concert hall, which is the bourgeois version of what took place at court. This arrangement can probably be traced back to the centuries-old liturgical ceremony performed by a choir, part-singing in Latin, and a clergy, speaking in Latin, and in between them a congregation, either passively 'hearing mass' or not 'hearing mass' at all.

The performing audience virtually did not exist. Even today compositions of the Ordinary are still performed in concert halls without the incongruity of it being realised. In the case of the Missa Solemnis by Beethoven or the Requiem by Verdi it is not quite so absurd, but it becomes a different matter when a mass by Palestrina, a passion by Schütz or choral preludes by Bach are involved.

The liturgical repertoire, especially Gregorian chant, contains many master-pieces which are totally integrated with the text and/or the liturgical situation, and which can only be performed with the assistance of the congregation. In the new repertoire this is the rule. Many choirs, conductors and organists were apparently unprepared for this. They were adapted to a 'concert situation'. The disappearance of this meant for them a lowering of artistic standards.

The fear of it caused exactly that which they dreaded so much. Many of them could not continue to give their loyal and creative co-operation, and the result was the emergence of many new choirs, instrumental groups, temporary conductors, temporary organists, all equally helpless in the new situation. At the same time many old choirs with their conductors and organists were responsible for the continuation of many Latin high masses, often badly attended, even in those place where the situation clamoured for the use of the mother tongue. It created a tragic conflict which could have been avoided, had there been better information and guidance. Or were they interested only in performing music—whether 'for the honour and glory of God' or not—rather than in contributing to the best possible celebration of the liturgy for the sake of the people, clearly a case of the 'first' commandment without the 'second'?

3. THE CONTENTS

What appears to motivate people is also part of the picture. Anybody who chooses to ignore it and pays attention only to the result or the process understands little of what is happening, has happened or will happen.

It is not easy to find out what appears to motivate people. It is a secret process within one, sometimes even without one's being aware of it. Another person can only surmise, discover some connections and then put forward an acceptable assumption. But he cannot offer absolute certainty.

Such questions seem to be outside the scope of an article about music. They appear to be more concerned with the text or the order of service. However, what is sung in the churches and the manner in which it is sung give a good indication of what the people believe, of what motivates them. Old hymn texts expressing the vertical relationship with God are characterised by their melodies (although the reverse is not necessarily the case, because old melodies have sometimes been used for new texts). Orthodoxy and religiosity often show in the choice and types of hymns. A visitor to a church can conclude much from what he hears. He will become aware of a baffling variety of music and texts some of which may seem to be even incongruous and incompatible with each other. But he will soon realise that, fundamentally, they all have one factor in common. He will discover that the liturgy in the mother tongue has gone through one and the same process everywhere, i.e., the *democratisation* of language and rite. The purpose of it can have been no other than to democratise the contents. But this democratisation has hardly yet been realised. Where, in the olden days, liturgy was not much more than religion, there can still be found an emphasis on typically religious modes, such as obedience, a lack of biblical spirit, and a great deal of moralism. Obedience: Just as little was done before the renewal of the liturgy (most churches did not ask for the use of the mother tongue), so now the new *Ordo* of 1969 is accepted without any original contribution on the part of those accepting it, and uncritical composers follow in these footsteps. This is clearly shown by the act of penance, the greeting, the reverence for the bible readings, the official Eucharistic prayers (with a solemn 'Amen' of doubtful artistic quality), the texts used during the communion rite and the dominating role of the officiating celebrant. A lack of biblical spirit: In spite of the respect for the Book, many hymns are just repetitions, paraphrases in verse form. There is little personal understanding, individual assimilation or application of the Bible text. Moralism: These churches resound with the authoritarian 'you shall' or with the use of the royal 'we', but seldom with the personalised 'I am', 'I feel', 'I want', 'I know'.

Groups which forged ahead before or during the Second Vatican Council have seen their initiatives and ideas being incorporated into the new liturgy. To them we owe, e.g., new canon texts, the canon in the mother tongue, communion in the hand. They are still 'way ahead of others', if they have not been orphaned by the marriage of their leaders. Much of what they are doing is not given much publicity, often purposely for fear of possible repercussions. Development stagnates, because 'it is not allowed by the bishop'. I know of cases in which responsible priests have been moved or dismissed. Active groups, known to me, have problems with the authorities in The Netherlands, Flanders, England, Germany and the United States. They use appropriate translations of the psalms and in their hymns they sing of humanity:

—loneliness, companionship, friendship and marriage,
—fears, suffering, death,
—justice, protests against injustice,
—power, helplessness, impotence,

often in a social and political context. Their religious character is marked by a *prophetical* Jewish-Christian criticism of religion. If they are familiar with transcendence, it is natural rather than supernatural. The more prophetic and Jewish (Christian), the more the text dominates the music. It then becomes critical what one says and equally critical is the manner in which it is said so that it is understood. Then the honour and glory of God become of less importance than the message of the text to the people.

Translated by W. M. P. Kruyssen

A. Ronald Sequeira

The Rediscovery of the Role of Movement[1] in the Liturgy

AS long as sixty years ago Romano Guardini surmised that a renewal of the liturgy that was concerned exclusively with reshaping the words (by introducing new texts, more understandable language, etc.) or with reshaping the music (by using contemporary settings, expanding the instrumental resources used, etc.) or with both would never achieve a definitive break-through if at the same time it did not concern itself with the renewal of a third dimension, one that from many points of view is more important: the dimension of movement, of liturgical gesture, of symbolic dance (often misleadingly labelled 'body language', as if word and music did not also involve the body).

For Guardini the way to liturgical life led 'above all through action. . . . Action is something elemental in which the whole human being with all his or her creative powers has to be involved; it has to be an accomplishment that is alive; a living experience, perception, vision'.[2] In keeping with this he attempted in his short book on sacred symbols to breathe new life into the surviving remnants of the old liturgical language of gesture. But he was aware that what was basically involved was a fundamental renewal of worship: 'The man who is moved by emotion will kneel, bow, clasp his hands or impose them, stretch forth his arms, strike his breast, make an offering of something, and so on. These elementary gestures are capable of richer development and expansion, or else of amalgamation. . . . Finally, a whole series of such movements may be co-ordinated. This gives rise to religious action . . .'[3]

If one reflects that the various movements for renewal were under way by the latest from the time of the Malines Congress of 1909, the question can be asked why in the 1920s Guardini was arguing for consideration to

112

be given to the dimension of movement. The reason that suggests itself to the author of this article is that the first waves of renewal were concerned exclusively with word and music, with the introduction of the vernacular, for example, and the introduction of chants and hymns to be sung by the congregation, but 'at the start people had no criterion and no norm for how the faithful's share in action and prayer, apart from mere verbal responses, should be more properly organised. In many cases everything was simply prayed through. . . .'[4] To Guardini it was manifestly clear that, if the liturgy were the accomplishment of an action expressing the faith of the 'whole man', the customary manner of joining in with words and music ('mere verbal responses') was not enough. Liturgy is rather a combination of movement and action, an experience and at the same time an expression of the senses, an act of being present that involves the whole person.

It can hardly be claimed that this proposal of Guardini's fell at first on fruitful soil. From the historical point of view there had been a tradition of church dance right up to and including the Middle Ages, but this was followed by a period of stagnation which historians of the liturgy have called the age of rubricism (1614-1903). It was this reduction of the liturgy to a matter of rubrics that Guardini was attacking. But where would one be able to obtain more up-to-date liturgical gestures more in keeping with the modern world? A gulf had long since developed between the language of liturgical gesture and secular arts involving movement—at least as far as the West was concerned. What would have been necessary was a new language of gesture which was based on the basic gestures of the liturgy (which after all are quite simply the most elementary human gestures) and which helped the congregation to join in the liturgy in a living way. But for this the right kind of 'liturgical method'[5] was lacking. During the period before the Second World War what was emphasised was the role of word and music in the liturgy. It was the period of the *Betsingmesse*, the form the celebration of Mass took in German-speaking countries under the impulse of the liturgical movement, with hymns in German replacing Latin chants and with German used for much of what was said out loud: even today this can be described as the chief form of community prayer in the German-speaking world. In this there was only one opportunity for genuine movement on the part of the congregation: at the procession, a survival of the oldest form of man's religious expression.

It is only after the Second World War that we can speak of a rediscovery of the dimension of movement in the liturgy. Since the shape of Christian liturgies has for the most part been moulded by western forms of expression, this rediscovery is to be understood against the background of the recent cultural history of the western nations and their relations to other parts of the world. In general, however, it can be said that the first half of the twentieth century was the period in which Western man rediscovered his bodily nature. As a result, among other things, of developments in the field of the social sciences, for example in depth psychology, the Church's deep-rooted hostility to the body was called into question. As early as 1932 Gerardus van der Leeuw wrote in the first edition of his book *Wegen en Grenzen*: 'The movement of the body often expresses more of the totality and the background of life than words or sounds are able to do.'[6] Soon after the war, Thomas Ohm published the work he had completed in 1944 on Christianity and gestures used in prayer (*Die Gebetsgebärden der Völker und das Christentum*, Leiden 1948), and in the same year (1948) Hugo Rahner, at an Eranos conference, argued for man at play, a Church at play, a liturgy at play.[7]

At first the *Betsingmesse* and processions were enough. The first years of reconstruction after the war—and the business of coming to grips with the recent past—left little room for the significant experimentation without which it would hardly be possible to make the liturgy an experience of celebration and play. It was only about ten years after the end of the Second World War that a turning-point seems to have been reached.

A whole series of factors were responsible for this, and we need mention only the most important. First of all we must observe that Christian theologians had rediscovered man. There was an increasing emphasis on the anthropological dimension of faith. At the same time, as is well known, all the Christian churches were going through a process of self-renewal, a process which as far as the Catholic Church is concerned reached its first culmination in the Second Vatican Council.

In this the first place was taken by the renewal of the liturgy. It cannot be claimed today that the Council's constitution on the liturgy was a downright revolutionary document with regard to the aspect of movement. But it had the effect of focusing attention: one had to look for forms of expression better adapted to the contemporary world.

The fact that interest in movement and in the language of the body first gained significance in the 1960s can be understood from the cultural developments in the period after the war. As far as the liturgy is concerned two factors need to be mentioned: first, the awakening of the 'young' churches of Asia, Africa and South America; and secondly the fact that in the West there had come to maturity a new generation which was itself engaged in the search for its own identity. Let us start by looking at the first of these developments.

The process of political decolonisation led to the emergence of local churches outside Europe which understandably were looking for a Christian identity of their own. There was everywhere the desire for a Christianity of a non-European mould, for genuine native local churches. Thus it came about that as early as the start of the 1960s there was a relatively large number of small groups in various countries outside Europe which were occupied with the search for native forms of liturgical expression. These could hardly be overlooked at the Eucharistic Congresses held at Munich in 1960 and at Bombay in 1964. One unmistakable fact was that for non-Europeans it was the most obvious and natural thing in the world to make use of the dimension of movement, in other words gestures and the dance. Many non-European cultures enjoy not merely a rich verbal and musical tradition but also a long tradition of movement and dance. Many of these attempts degenerated into a self-conscious folksiness, and thus were unable to exert any decisive influence on the liturgy. But the message to the West was clear: for non-Europeans the dimension of movement and the language of the body belonged to the expression of faith in action.

The question arises whether western Christians are really any different. Is not bodiliness, the fact and awareness of being embodied, constitutive for human self-realisation? As early as the end of the 1950s there grew up a generation, one-sidedly called the beat generation, which distinguished itself above all by its forms of expression, with the combination of music and movement uniquely personified in Elvis Presley. Western man's bodily nature seemed suddenly to be breaking free of the chains that had held it bound for centuries. An entire generation acquired what in the truest sense was a new feeling for movement and for their own bodies. (The question arises here to what extent what has been termed the 'sexual revolution' played a part in this.) The Christian churches could not ignore this phenomenon but had to come to grips with it and ask themselves whether there now existed a possibility of renewal.

Understandably it was the American churches that were in the van of this process of rediscovery. One of many indications of this that could be mentioned was the enormous popularity of Sydney Carter's song 'Lord of the Dance' which took up a primitive Christian biblical theme, Christ as 'Lord of the Dance':

> Dance, then, wherever you may be,
> I am the Lord of the Dance, said he,
> And I'll lead you all, wherever you may be,
> And I'll lead you all in the Dance, said he.

It was in the first place the student Christian movements of America and Europe that in the 1960s not merely discovered but actually introduced the dimension of movement into their forms of worship. These services were often the expression of a genuine commitment with regard to both Church and world. The liturgy had not merely to be contemporary but to be relevant too. People could not just sit there and mutter their way through the prayers: what was wanted was a mature participation, activity, the liturgy as an experience involving the entire human being.

In addition, the North Americans started with the advantage of having had for some generations in the black churches a tradition of movement united to worship. Gospel spirituals, such as 'He's got the whole world in his hands', are hardly conceivable or performable without movement. Well known, too, are the numerous smaller bodies—revivalist churches, Pentecostalists, among others—whose use of movement in worship even today characterises their image.

From the 1960s onwards the dimension of play and movement in the celebration of the liturgy was powerfully promoted in the churches of North America. The Harvard theologian Harvey Cox tackled the subject in his well-known book *The Feast of Fools* (Cambridge, Mass., 1969) and contributed to a revaluation of the liturgy throughout the world as a community celebration. An Episcopalian pastor in New York even rebuilt his church in the form of a theatre in order to enable his congregation, consisting largely of people engaged in that profession and in the arts generally, to feel more at home. As far as the Catholic Church is concerned, joy in experimentation with the dimension of movement is somewhat more subdued, especially when the official form of worship is involved. Nevertheless the liturgical gestures used by the charismatic movement, such as the stretching out of the hands or the raising of the eyes to heaven, show that ordinary Christians are capable of appreciating a greater share in this dimension of movement.

The greatest willingness to experiment is undoubtedly shown by the various 'underground' parishes and communities which are able to allow themselves a greater liturgical freedom.

As far as European countries are concerned, a certain openness towards the dimension of movement is first of all to be noted in the case of the Anglican Church. If progress in this country is somewhat laborious, this is in the first place to be ascribed to the fact that the existing forms of Anglo-Saxon dance culture, for example the ballet, can be not very helpful. 'Already the "ballet", as such, is a form of dance which has freed itself from its roots; a game, "no longer in the service of God and of nature, but of princes",' was the opinion of Gerardus van der Leeuw.[9]

It is only possible to speak of a genuine breakthrough in the dimension of movement when we consider the most recent developments within the German Evangelical Church in the Federal Republic. Within the context of a liturgical vigil at the Düsseldorf Kirchentag of 1973 it was able to mount a splendid attempt to bring the dimension of movement into the centre of the liturgy.[10] Thousands danced to songs like 'He's got the whole world in his hands' and to a setting of the Our Father that used calypso rhythms. Among those present at this event was the general secretary of the World Council of Churches, Dr Philip Potter. This celebration was the signal for numerous congregations throughout the country to stage their own liturgical vigils. The development gained ground. At Kirchentage above all the introduction of elements of play into services of worship has become something taken completely for granted.

While the Catholic Church is in theory completely open to liturgical creativity, in practice it is more reserved and cautious. Nevertheless an openness to the playful dimension of the liturgy has slowly come about, even though still far distant from what Hugo Rahner had in mind, as for example at the most recent Katholikentage.

The Catholic Church of the Netherlands is among those in Europe that takes the greatest delight in expression. Here one can gain the impression that what other countries approve in theory is put into practice. In Antwerp in 1971 the journal *Tijdschrift voor Liturgie* organised, with substantial Dutch participation, the only liturgical congress to concern itself exclusively with the question of the bodily dimension of the liturgy and the role of movement in it.[11]

Finally we should recall the forms of liturgical expression adopted by the many small groups and communities that over the past fifteen years have sprung up everywhere in Europe. Many of these have been inspired by the liturgy of the Taizé community, and every year hundreds of young people (though not young people alone) make their way from all over Europe to this village in Burgundy. While various opinions are possible about the significance of such gatherings, what is clear is that without music and movement the experience of community is hardly conceivable and that without community the Church is hardly possible. At Taizé what emerges most clearly is that movement is a fundamental expression of a praying community as well as of worship. The wealth of ideas generated by small groups shows how general and widespread is the need of the individual Christian for a living form of worship.

What is the significance of the rediscovery of the dimension of movement for the Christian liturgy of today and for the future? Like Guardini, liturgical manuals point out that the liturgy possesses a number of traditional gestures of prayer that bear a 'symbolic' character. The movement of renewal has so far only one as far as breathing new life into these signs and symbols and making them understandable once more. Such attempts will always remain an effort, since most of these gestures do not provide a suitable expression of the feelings of the praying community. At most the sign of the cross can be regarded as in general use. The question arises whether people today and the world of today do not need other and newer symbols of prayer and also of gesture. The extent to which the dimension of movement has up till now been neglected is shown by the fact that the search for new hymns and new texts has become something taken for granted.

At least as far as the churches outside Europe are concerned, the search for symbolic gestures that are more in keeping with the times has become an urgent necessity. In view of the unmistakable Western shape of the liturgy, it is only slowly that Asiatic and African churches in particular are able to discover new forms. Beyond the fact that in these countries the clergy have received a fundamentally Western training, what are lacking are the necessary research and investigations in the fields of the history of culture and of comparative philosophy and theology. These are the presupposition for significant experimentation. The introduction of new liturgical symbols is not, after all, something that can take place over-night. A lot of painstaking detailed work is needed to discover and develop them. In this respect the Indian sub-continent may form an exception, since it already enjoys a highly developed artistic system of gesture.[12] What is important in all these efforts is that the people play their part in the process of discovery. Outside as well as inside Europe, liturgy is no longer something that can be imposed from above.

In a certain sense this whole problem is more difficult for the Churches of Europe and North America. The appearance of the liturgy unequivo-cally shows the centuries of suppression of movement and of liturgical dance. Unlike the case of the Churches of Asia and Africa, there is no continuing tradition of religious dance which could possibly be drawn on to provide new gestures for Christian prayer. But in our view the need is even greater. The beat generation has in the meantime given way to the disco generation, but there is no slackening of the pressing need for movement. It is continually becoming richer in ideas, even if often more chaotic. Nevertheless any visitor to a modern discothèque can confirm that the need for gestures suitable for worship is more urgent today than ever before in the history of Christianity.

The question arises both for liturgical experts and for the study of liturgy whether the liturgy is in itself capable of development. Here it is less a matter of a particular understanding of liturgy as the manner in which this is to be expressed. Every understanding of the liturgy, after all, takes as its starting point the idea that God is calling his entire people and that the entire people answer him. How are they to do this except by means of word, music and gesture?

If the liturgy is capable of development, then the consequence must be drawn that a systematic search for new forms in keeping with the times—experimentation in the best sense of the word—must be actively encour-aged. Liturgical institutes should be centres of creativity and not just serve historical research exclusively. The liturgy must enter into a dia-logue with the world of today and with contemporary man if it wishes to be and remain the relevant sign of Christ's act of redemption. Church music and liturgical language have both for a long time been in the foreground of renewal. Perhaps the dimension of movement has now reached the point where the liturgy can really become a complete expression of the faith of the whole human being.

Translated by Robert Nowell

Notes

1. In connection with the whole complex of questions dealt with here the author will, it is hoped, be allowed to draw attention to the fruit of many years' work he has devoted to this field: *Spielende Liturgie—Bewegung neben Wort und Ton im Gottesdienst am Beispiel des Vaterunsers* (Freiburg/Basle/Vienna 1977). This includes a full bibliography of the subject.

2. *Von heiligen Zeichen* (Mainz 1927: 1963 edition) p. 8.

3. *The Spirit of the Liturgy* (in one volume, preceded by *The Church and the Catholic*) (London 1935) p. 168.

4. J. A. Jungmann *Liturgische Erneuerung—Rückblick und Ausblick* (Kevelaer 1962) p. 17.

5. See *Spielende Liturgie* pp. 117-135, especially pp. 118-120.

6. Gerardus van der Leeuw *Sacred and Profane Beauty: The Holy in Art* (London 1963) p. 66.

7. *Eranos-Jahrbuch* 1948 (Zürich 1948), XVI pp. 11-87.

8. Cf. J. G. Davies (ed.), *Worship and Dance* (Birmingham 1975) pp. 22-28.

9. *Sacred and Profane Beauty,* quoted in note 6, at p. 53.

10. A full report is to be found in *Liturgische Nacht—ein Werkbuch Jugenddienst,* edited by the *Arbeitskreis für Gottesdienst und Kommunikation* (Wuppertal 1974).

11. *Tijdschrift voor Liturgie* 56 (1972).

12. See A. R. Sequeira *Klassische indische Tanzkunst und christliche Verkündigung* (Munich dissertation 1970) (*Freiburger Theologische Studien* 109) (Freiburg/Basle/Vienna 1978).

Contributors

ENRIQUE DUSSEL was born in 1934 in Mendoza (Argentina). He has a degree in theology and doctorates in philosophy and history. He is professor at the Free University of Mexico and in the Department of Religious Sciences in the Ibero-American University. He is also president of the Commission of Studies of the Church in Latin America (CEHILA). He took part in the Ecumenical Dialogue of Third World theologians in Dar-es-Salaam, Accra and Sri Lanka. His recent works include the following: *Desintegracion de la cristiandad y liberacion* (Salamanca 1978); *Filosofia de la liberacion* (Mexico 1977); *History of the Church in Latin America* (Grand Rapids 1979); *Ethics and Theology of Liberation* (New York 1978); *Los obispos latinoamericanos y la liberacion del pobre (1504-1620)* (Mexico 1979); *De Medellin a Puebla (1968-1979)* (Mexico 1979).

MICHAEL PAUL GALLAGHER, SJ, was born in 1939, and entered the Jesuits in 1961. He is lecturer in Modern English and American Literature, University College, Dublin (National University of Ireland). He has written literary criticism mainly in the area of contemporary fiction. He is also film critic for *Studies*. He was recently allowed a sabbatical year in order to study developments in the theology of atheism and to link these with modern literature.

BERNARD M. HUIJBERS, composer of Dutch liturgical music, was born in Rotterdam in 1922. After studying philosophy, theology and music he became a teacher of music and choir master at the Ignatius College in Amsterdam. He was later appointed teacher of liturgy at the Conservatory in Amsterdam and at the School for Church Music in Utrecht. One of the founders of the study group Universa Laus, he has lectured and published in many countries.

JEAN-PIERRE JOSSUA, OP, was born in 1930 in Paris, obtained a doctorate in theology in 1968, was professor at Le Saulchoir, and since 1971 he has been professor at the Institut catholique of Paris. His publications include: *Journal théologique* I (1976) and II (1978); *Un Homme cherche Dieu* (1979).

CONSTANTIN KALOKYRIS, full professor of Byzantine Archaeology at the Theological Faculty of the University of Salonica, was born in Crete, Greece. He studied theology, philology and Christian and Byzantine archaeology at the universities of Athens, Paris, Erlangen and München and started his career as curator in the archaeological service in Crete and chief of the same service in Piraeus and Islands. He has lectured in universities in USA, Russia, Italy, Germany, Austria, Lebanon, Syria, Australia and other places. Prof. Kalokyris has carried out excavations and undertook restoration work in Crete and in the Aegean Islands. His publications include: *Mt. Athos, Themes of archaeology and art* (Athens 1963); *Introduction to Christian and byzantine archaeology* (Salonica 1970); *The Essence of Orthodox Iconography* (in English) (Brookline, Mass. 1971); *The painting in Orthodoxy* (Salonica 1972); *Church Buildings and Modern Art* (Salonica 1978).

AIDAN KAVANAGH, OSB, is a monk of St Meinrad Archabbey in Indiana, USA, and a graduate of the University of Ottawa, Canada, and the Theologische Fakultät, Trier, West Germany. For eight years he was director of the Graduate Programme in Liturgical Studies at the University of Notre Dame before becoming Professor of Liturgies, the Divinity School, Yale University. An associate editor of *Worship* and *Studia Liturgica,* he is author of: *The Concept of Eucharistic Memorial in the Canon Revisions of Thomas Cranmer* (1963) and *The Shape of Baptism: The Rite of Christian Initiation* (1978), together with numerous essays in many journals.

BOKA DI MPASI LONDI, SJ, was born in Zaire and studied theology at Louvain and at the Gregorian University, Rome. He teaches at Mayidi Seminary in Zaire, is a spiritual director at the Propaganda in Rome and is editor-in-chief of the Christian review *Telema* ('Get up and Walk'). He is also a visiting professor at Lumen Vitae in Brussels. He is the author and composer of the national anthems of the Congo (1960) and of Zaire (1971) and has translated two hundred and fifty hymns of the Kimbanguist Church from Kikongo into French, published in Kinshasa in 1960. He has also written articles in *Orientierung, Stimmen der Zeit, Lumen Vitae* and *Telema.*

LUIS MALDONADO was born in Madrid in 1930, and was ordained priest for the Archdiocese of Madrid in 1954. He is now lecturer in Pastoral Liturgy at the Pontifical University of Salamanca and Director of the Higher Institute of Pastoral Theology at the same university.

ADRIEN NOCENT, OSB, is a monk of the abbey of Maredsous, Belgium. Born in 1913, he has done special studies at the Institut de Liturgie in Paris, has been professor for ten years at the catechetical institute of Lumen Vitae in Brussels, and has been professor at the Pontifical Institute of Liturgy, San Anselmo, Rome, since its foundation in 1961. He has published numerous articles above all in liturgical reviews and has contributed to such joint works as *L'Eglise en prière*. His own books include *The Liturgical Year* (4 vols.).

A. RONALD SEQUEIRA was born in Bombay, India, in 1937. He was lecturer in the social sciences, Bombay University between 1962-64. He gained doctorate at Munich University under Karl Rahner (1970) with a dissertation on the classical Indian dance and Christian proclamation. He has lectured on eastern religions and liturgy at Heerlen theological college, Netherlands, 1969-72, and on history of religion at the Protestant theological faculty, Bochum University, West Germany, 1974-75. At the moment he is lecturer in comparative cultural studies at Maastricht and in the history of religion at Eindhoven, both in the Netherlands. His publications include: *Spielende Liturgie—Bewegung neben Wort und Ton im Gottesdienst am Beispiel des Vaterunsers* (1977) and *Klassische indische Tanzkunst und christliche Verkündigung* (1970).

CRISPINO VALENZIANO, born in Cefalù, Sicily, in 1932 and ordained in 1954, is a Doctor of Philosophy in the Gregorian University of Rome and the state university of Genoa and has specialised in anthropology at the Facult of Catholic Theology in Strasbourg and the Sorbonne in Paris. After ten years' university teaching of philosophy and anthropology he became in 1976 Dean of the St John the Evangelist Theological Institute at Palermo. Among many extra-mural appointments he works at ecumenical exchanges between the churches of Sicily and the Greek church. Editor since 1974 of *Ho Theologos: Cultura Cristiana di Sicilia,* he contributes articles on anthropology and theology to various reviews and has among his publications: *Limiti della cristologia kierkegaardiana* (1965); *Religiosità popolare e pastorale liturgica* (1978); *L'ambone, icone della Risurrezione* (1978); *La basilica cattedrale di Cefalù nel periodo normanno* (1979) (also translated into French); *Sacramenta* (1980).

CYRILLE VOGEL, is a lecturer at the *Université des Sciences Humaines,* Strasbourg. His recent publications include: *Introduction aux sources de l'histoire du culte chrétien au moyen âge* (2nd ed. Turin 1975); *Ordinations inconsistantes et caractère inadmissible* (Turin 1978); *Les 'libri paenitentiales'* (Turnhout, Belgium).

DECLARATION OF CONCILIUM

We, directors of the international review of theology *Concilium,* do not see any well-founded reason not to consider our colleague Hans Küng as a Catholic theologian.

We shall, therefore, press to have the judgment reconsidered.

In addition we ask with emphasis that the ecclesiastical procedure in religious matters will respect the commonly established rules of human rights.

Professor Jürgen Moltmann of Tübingen has indicated that he wishes to be associated with the fuller statement of the editorial directors published in our issue No. 10 1979.

Praise for Jeffrey Siger

Island of Secrets
(First Published as *The Mykonos Mob*)
The Tenth Chief Inspector Andreas Kaldis Mystery

"A perfect setting and first-rate storytelling."
—Ragnar Jónasson, bestselling author
of the Dark Iceland series

An Aegean April
The Ninth Chief Inspector Andreas Kaldis Mystery

Best Books of 2018 in Crime Fiction by *Library Journal*

"The great man behind Greece's crime mysteries."
—*Greek City Times*

"Vivid local color, agreeable central characters, and exciting action scenes make this a winner."
—*Publishers Weekly*

"The ninth case for Siger's Greek detective, brimming with suspense and a distinct sense of place, continues to deepen the backstory of its band of heroes."
—*Kirkus Reviews*

"Siger's ninth atmospheric mystery vividly depicts the political and economic issues involved in the European refugee crisis. VERDICT: Fans of Adrian McKinty's Sean Duffy books and other police procedurals that handle violence and political issues with black humor will welcome this outstanding crime novel."

—*Library Journal*, Starred Review

"This latest outing also offers a perspective on the Balkan Peninsula and the thorny issue of asylum seekers. A fast-paced international series."

—*Booklist*

Santorini Caesars
The Eighth Chief Inspector Andreas Kaldis Mystery

"[This is a] novel that's both a rock-solid mystery and comments incisively about so many issues besetting Europe and the world today."

—*Huffington Post*

"The eighth case for Siger's police hero has a timely plot and a handful of engaging back stories about its detective team."

—*Kirkus Reviews*

"As always, Siger provides readers with an action-packed plot, well-developed characters with lots of attitude, breathtaking Greek scenery, and a perceptive take on the current political and economic problems affecting Greece. International-crime fans need to be reading this consistently strong series."

—*Booklist*

Devil of Delphi
The Seventh Chief Inspector Andreas Kaldis Mystery

2016 Barry Awards nominee for Best Novel

"Siger brings Chief Inspector Andreas Kaldis some very big challenges in his seventh mystery set in troubled contemporary Greece… The final plot twist proves well worth the wait, but it won't take readers long to get there as they will be turning pages at a ferocious clip."

—*Booklist*, Starred Review

"Though the reader is always several steps ahead of the police here, Siger's sublimely malevolent villains make the book a page-turner."

—*Kirkus Reviews*

"A killer named Kharon (for the mythological ferryman who transports the dead across the River Styx) and bomba, or counterfeit wine, complicate the lives of Chief Inspector Kaldis and his team. The seventh book in Siger's Greek procedural series features a strong sense of place and a devious plot."

—*Library Journal*

Sons of Sparta
The Sixth Chief Inspector Andreas Kaldis Mystery

"Siger paints travelogue-worthy pictures of a breathtakingly beautiful—if politically corrupt—Greece."

—*Publishers Weekly*, Starred Review

"Kaldis's sixth case offers a lively, gritty plot, an abundance of local color, and two righteous heroes."

—*Kirkus Reviews*

"Filled with local color, action, and humor, this story will give readers a taste of modern Greek culture and its ancient roots."

—*Booklist*

Mykonos After Midnight
The Fifth Chief Inspector Andreas Kaldis Mystery

2014 Left Coast Crime Awards nominee for Best Mystery in a Foreign Setting

"Vibrant with the frenzied nightlife of Mykonos and the predators who feed on it. A twisty page-turner."

—Michael Stanley, award-winning author
of the Detective Kubu mysteries

"The investigation that follows—highlighted by political interference and the piecing together of a complicated international plot that threatens to disrupt the easygoing, anything-goes life that Mykonos is famous for—keeps the reader engaged, even as it makes obvious that in Greece, it really matters whom you know. The emergence of a shadowy master criminal bodes well for future adventures."

—*Publishers Weekly*

"Gorgeous Mykonos once again becomes a character when conflicting forces battle for the resort island's future in Siger's fifth series entry. Greece's financial vulnerabilities play a key role as Chief Inspector Kaldis digs in."

—*Library Journal*

"From the easy banter of its three cops to its clutch of unpredictable villains, Kaldis's fifth reads more like an Elmore Leonard caper than a whodunit."

—*Kirkus Reviews*

"Acclaimed (particularly by Greek commentators) for their realistic portrayal of Greek life and culture, the Kaldis novels are very well constructed, and this one is no exception: not only is the mystery solid but the larger story, revolving around the political machinations of the shadowy global organization, is clever and intriguing. Fans of the previous Kaldis novels would do well to seek this one out."

—*Booklist*

Target: Tinos
The Fourth Chief Inspector Andreas Kaldis Mystery

"Thrilling, thought-provoking, and impossible to put down."
—Timothy Hallinan, award-winning author
of the Poke Rafferty thrillers

"Nobody writes Greece better than Jeffrey Siger."
—Leighton Gage, author of the Chief
Inspector Mario Silva Investigations

"*Target: Tinos* is another of Jeffrey Siger's thoughtful police procedurals set in picturesque but not untroubled Greek locales."

—*New York Times*

"A likable, compassionate lead; appealing Greek atmosphere; and a well-crafted plot help make this a winner."

—*Publishers Weekly*, Starred Review

"An interesting and highly entertaining police procedural for those who wish to read their way around the globe and especially for those inclined to move away from some of the 'chilly' Scandinavian thrillers and into warmer climes."

—*Library Journal*

"The fourth case for a sleuth who doesn't suffer fools gladly pairs a crisp style with a complex portrait of contemporary Greece to bolster another solid whodunit."

—*Kirkus Reviews*

"Siger's latest Inspector Kaldis Mystery throbs with the pulse of Greek culture... Make sure to suggest this engaging series to fans of Leighton Gage's Mario Silva series, set in Brazil but very similar in terms of mood and feel."

—*Booklist*

Prey on Patmos
The Third Chief Inspector Andreas Kaldis Mystery

"A suspenseful trip through the rarely seen darker strata of complex, contemporary Greece."

—*Publishers Weekly*

"Using the Greek Orthodox Church as the linchpin for his story, Siger proves that Greece is fertile new ground for the mystery genre. Sure to appeal to fans of mysteries with exotic locations."

—*Library Journal*

"The third case for the appealing Andreas will immerse readers in a fascinating culture."

—*Kirkus Reviews*

Assassins of Athens
The Second Chief Inspector Andreas Kaldis Mystery

"Jeffrey Siger's *Assassins of Athens* is a teasingly complex and suspenseful thriller... Siger and his protagonist, Chief Inspector Andreas Kaldis, are getting sharper and surer with each case."

—Thomas Perry, bestselling author

"Siger is a superb writer... Best of all, he creates the atmosphere of modern Greece in vivid, believable detail, from the magnificence of its antiquities to the decadence of its power bearers and the squalor of its slums."

—*Pittsburgh Post-Gazette*

"This is international police procedural writing at its best and should be recommended, in particular, to readers who enjoy Leighton Gage's Brazilian police stories or Hakan Nesser's Swedish inspector Van Veeteren."

—*Booklist*, Starred Review

"With few mysteries set in Greece, the author, a longtime resident of Mykonos, vividly captures this unfamiliar terrain's people and culture. Mystery fans who like their police procedurals in exotic locales will welcome this one."

—Library Journal

Murder in Mykonos
The First Chief Inspector Andreas Kaldis Mystery

"Siger's intimate knowledge of Mykonos adds color and interest to his serviceable prose and his simple premise. The result is a surprisingly effective debut novel."

—Kirkus Reviews

"Siger's view of Mykonos (where he lives part-time) is nicely nuanced, as is the mystery's ambiguous resolution. Kaldis's feisty personality and complex backstory are appealing as well. Solid foundations for a projected series."

—Publishers Weekly

"Siger...captures the rare beauty of the Greek islands in this series debut."

—Library Journal

"Siger's Mykonos seems an unrelievedly hedonistic place, especially given the community's religious orthodoxy, but suspense builds nicely as the story alternates between the perspectives of the captive woman, the twisted kidnapper, and the cop on whose shoulders the investigation falls. In the end, Andreas finds more than he bargained for, and readers will be well pleased."

—Booklist

Also by Jeffrey Siger

The Chief Inspector Andreas Kaldis Mysteries
Murder in Mykonos
Assassins of Athens
Prey on Patmos
Target: Tinos
Mykonos After Midnight
Sons of Sparta
Devil of Delphi
Santorini Caesars
An Aegean April
Island of Secrets (First Published as *The Mykonos Mob*)

A DEADLY
TWIST

A DEADLY TWIST

A CHIEF INSPECTOR ANDREAS KALDIS MYSTERY

JEFFREY SIGER

Poisoned Pen
PRESS

Published by Poisoned Pen Press, an imprint of Sourcebooks
P.O. Box 4410, Naperville, Illinois 60567-4410
(630) 961-3900
sourcebooks.com

Library of Congress Cataloging-in-Publication Data

Names: Siger, Jeffrey, author.
Title: A deadly twist / Jeffrey Siger.
Description: Naperville, Illinois : Poisoned Pen Press, [2021] | Series: A
    Chief Inspector Andreas Kaldis mystery
Identifiers: LCCN 2020021161 (hardcover) | (trade paperback) | (epub)
Classification: LCC PS3619.I45 D43 2021 (print) | LCC PS3619.I45 (ebook)
    | DDC 813/.6--dc23
LC record available at https://lccn.loc.gov/2020021161
LC ebook record available at https://lccn.loc.gov/2020021162

Printed and bound in the United States of America.
SB 10 9 8 7 6 5 4 3 2 1

To Barbara G. Peters and Robert Rosenwald
I owe it all to you.

"Happy is the man, I thought, who, before dying, has the good fortune to sail the Aegean Sea."
—Nikos Kazantzakis

Naxos Island

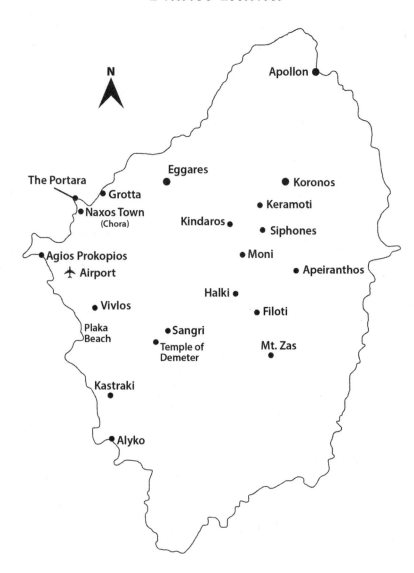

N

Apollon ●

The Portara
● Grotta
● Naxos Town
(Chora)

Eggares ●

Koronos ●

Keramoti ●

Kindaros ●

Siphones ●

● Agios Prokopios
✈ Airport

Moni ●

Apeiranthos ●

Halki ●

● Vivlos

Filoti ●

Plaka
Beach

● Sangri
● Temple of
Demeter

Mt. Zas
●

Kastraki
●

● Alyko

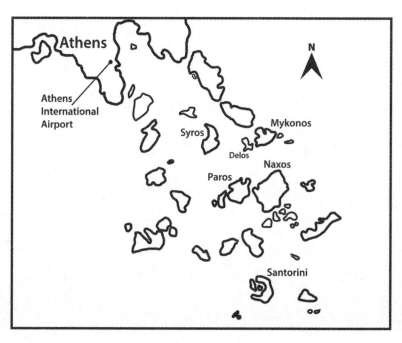

Cycladic Islands

Chapter One

"The key to getting away with what I do is lacking any possible motive. Motive's the first thing cops look for. Which is why I've never taken a job that could tie me to a target, no matter how tenuous the link or big the payday. I'm a conservative businessman, and if my work has taught me anything, it's that fast money comes with excessive risk. It's the gradual accumulation of wealth that makes a person secure in old age, and that's what I'm aiming for."

Chief Inspector Andreas Kaldis sat in his office in Greece's Central Police Headquarters in Athens (better known as GADA) reading and rereading a front-page newspaper article that opened with that paragraph.

A reporter named Nikoletta Elia claimed to have landed an exclusive interview with "the computer underground's most successful hacker" while on holiday on the Greek island of Naxos. Andreas took it to be a made-up story, likely pieced together by a seriously hungover reporter following an all-night booze session with some braggart trying to impress his bar mates with tales of international intrigue.

Strangers admit to weird things late at night in island bars, but this confession made no sense. It was inconceivable to Andreas that a "conservative" computer hacker who wanted to make it to "old age" would be stupid enough to open up about his business to anyone, let alone a reporter, about how he used his elite hacking skills on behalf of clients to ravage businesses, steal state secrets, and mask murders behind accidental equipment malfunctions.

Still, the article was in today's issue of Athens's most respected daily newspaper, and Andreas expected it would kick the city's many conspiracy theorists into overdrive. *What does the hacker's presence in Greece mean? And why are the police doing nothing about it?* As head of Greece's Special Crimes Unit, charged with investigating matters of national concern or potential corruption, Andreas expected his phone would soon light up with calls from members of Parliament looking to show their constituents that they cared about who visited their country.

Andreas looked at his watch. It wasn't yet eight a.m., too early for MPs to be calling. His administrative assistant, Maggie, would be at her desk any minute. He'd tell her to take messages. He didn't have the patience to be diplomatic with politicians this morning. He'd spent most of last night listening to his kindergarten son and toddler daughter coughing. Their colds had kept him awake longer than they had the kids.

I guess that's what it means to be a parent.

A compact, five-foot-three, redheaded ball of energy poked her head in through the doorway. "Morning, Chief."

"Morning, Maggie."

"So, what fresh hells do you have for me today?"

"Just your routine international bad guy on holiday looking for publicity blowback day."

"That should do wonders for Naxos tourism."

"You saw the article?"

"Who didn't? It's a front-page story by a crime reporter with a big following."

"But it makes no sense. Don't people realize it has to be phony?"

"Since when did being phony keep a story off the front page? At least this one's entertaining."

"Good, then keep entertaining yourself by taking messages on any calls for me about it."

"I'll need to requisition a few more message pads."

Andreas and Maggie had been doing their variation on a vaudeville routine since he'd returned to GADA from a brief stint as the chief of police on Mykonos. The luck of the draw had landed him with Maggie, GADA's mother superior and source of all wisdom about its many secret ways.

Ring, ring.

Maggie headed for her desk to answer the phone. "Let the games begin."

Andreas drew in and let out a deep breath. *It's gonna be a long day.* He picked up the newspaper and stared at the byline. "Nikoletta Elia, there must be more to this story than you're telling us."

Another line rang. He looked up. *A very long day.*

———

Despite a lifetime of reporting the news, Nikoletta Elia had never expected to write that story, nor had she anticipated the surge of international attention it received. Her editor had sent her to Naxos for a few days to do a piece on the simmering conflict between the island's traditional agrarian population and its growing cadre of tourism advocates.

She'd been surprised by the assignment and wondered what she'd done to draw the ire of her editor. After all, it wasn't the kind of hard-hitting reporting on which she'd built her byline. Breaking new ground on the crime and corruption beat was her forte, not rehashing the age-old debate about the pros and cons of tourism.

"Give it to a business or features writer," she'd argued to her editor.

"Don't be so negative. After all, it is an island steeped in myth, poised on the cusp of modernity."

"Get a travel writer, then. You know it's not my thing."

"Try it, you might learn something. Besides, you could use a break from chasing cops and robbers."

Nikoletta crossed her arms and scowled. "I couldn't care less that Naxos is where Zeus was raised, Ares took refuge, or Dionysius called home."

He feigned a smile. "Okay, point made; you know your mythology."

"Oh, that's just the start. Theseus, Ariadne, blah blah blah." She raised a hand to stop him from interrupting. "I also know that Cycladic life began on Naxos before Minoan Crete and Mycenaean Greece. Oh, and let's not forget that Naxos flourished as a society through most of antiquity up until the Persians ended its long independent run. Then came the Athenians, the Spartans, and a string of other Greeks, followed by the Romans, Venetians, Turks, and a touch of Russians, though the most lasting influence is clearly Venetian."

The editor chewed at his lip.

She waggled a finger at him. "I don't do historical pieces because I *prefer* running around with cops and robbers."

He held up his hands. "Fine, so write about modern-day conquerors—tourists and real estate developers. Do the piece however you like, but I want you over there and writing it *now*."

Nikoletta shut her eyes and silently counted to ten. She needed this job. Greece was still deep in financial crisis and, besides, she liked what she did. At least most of the time. She opened her eyes, smiled, curtsied dramatically, and headed for the door.

"Send me a story," he yelled after her.

She didn't stop but shot a hand above her head and flashed him the middle finger.

———

Nikoletta's assignment was getting lousier by the minute. The newspaper refused to pay for a plane ticket that would have had her on the island in less than forty minutes. Instead, it paid for a boat that took four hours. That she wasn't forced to take a ferry, which would have made it a six-hour trip at best, did nothing to improve her mood.

Her boat sailed into Naxos harbor past the massive marble Portara, the 2,500-year-old gateway to a never-completed grand temple to Apollo and the modern-day symbol of Naxos. Beyond the harbor the old town spread out and rose along a hillside covered in low whitewashed buildings. Flagstone lanes beneath soaring stone archways led up to a thirteenth-century Venetian castle that still dominated the town. The Castle, or Kastro area, constituted the upper part of the old town, distinguishing it in topography and social standing from the old town's lower Bourgos section.

Nikoletta barely glanced at any of that, choosing instead to maneuver to where she could grab her bag from the luggage storage area and disembark as quickly as possible.

She'd packed lightly, hoping to spend no more than a couple of days, and had arranged to stay in the island's main town of Naxos, also known as Chora, as every island's namesake town is called.

She'd picked Chora because it sat on the island's west coast, virtually equidistant from its northern, southern, and eastern edges. She also assumed that, because it was the island's capital and largest town by far, it would give her the best chance of ferreting out interviews with island officials and tourism advocates. Locating the island's agrarian defenders in the rural parts of the island would prove more logistically challenging, but she'd worry about that later.

She walked along the pier past a phalanx of waiting empty taxis and through a gauntlet of locals hawking places to stay and stopped by a driver holding a small placard with her name written in bold letters. He took her bag and led her to a van bearing the name of the hotel. After five minutes of winding through a maze of one-way streets, they arrived at a bright-white stucco-and-glass hotel just north of the harbor and perched atop a steep bluff overlooking the Portara.

Now free from her four-hour internment on the boat, caressed by gentle winds rolling in off the sea and catching the scent of wildflowers, she thought that a few days away from the madness of Athens might not be so bad after all. She shut her eyes, drew in a deep breath of sea air, and stood quietly for a moment. She opened her eyes, exhaled, and stared out to sea.

Yes, not bad at all.

Nikoletta checked into the hotel, put away her few things, and decided to stroll into town to catch the sunset at a harborside café. Unfamiliar with Chora, she asked the receptionist for the best walking route into town. The receptionist pointed toward the sea, and said the most direct way was to follow a rock-and-dirt path running down along the edge of the bluff through a field of gorse, maquis, stonecrop, and smother weed.

Nikoletta hesitated at first, but the route did offer spectacular views of the Portara set against its islet of Palatia, plus a shimmering orange sun and a deep-blue sea. Besides, it was still daytime, and despite a sign at the top of the path marked BEWARE DANGER, many were walking along the same path. Returning in the dark would be a different story, especially since she was intent on finding a bar in which to drown her sorrows at her lousy assignment.

She easily made it down from the bluff, across a not so busy road, and into a lane opening on to a square in front of the island's eighteenth-century Greek Orthodox cathedral. It was built on the remains of ancient temples and faced the ancient city's agora, or meeting place, but she did not pause, and two minutes later she was at the north end of the harbor.

She strolled by what seemed an endless line of tavernas, bars, and tourist shops, many trying to look more modern and chic than the next but not quite pulling it off. If they were examples of the sort of modern development tourism advocates had in mind for the rest of the island, she could understand why the island's traditionalists were so adamantly opposed.

She paused beside a wide marble harbor-front square and watched as local children rode their bikes and scooters helter-skelter among the passing tourists. It was as if all the world were their playground. She smiled. This was Nikoletta's idea of a Greek island experience.

Her eye caught a flagstone stairway tucked away between a jewelry shop and a *kafenio*, and she headed straight for it. A sign above the stairs read TO THE CASTLE & THE MUSEUM.

She wound her way up the hill along archway-covered lanes lined with stone and stucco buildings, all plainly laid out without any plan other than to confuse marauding pirates. She kept climbing through a residential area randomly trimmed in geraniums and bougainvillea, determined to make it to where signs promised she'd find the Kastro and the seventeenth-century Naxos Archaeological Museum.

As expected, given the hour, the museum was closed.

Nikoletta stood in front of the museum, looking back on to the square, and wondered what to do now. To her right sat a well-tended garden of oleander, geraniums, bougainvillea, and a host of flowers she could not identify; to her left stood the Naxos Cultural Center. She sat on the wall outside the cultural center and watched an amber-colored queen lead her onyx and amber kittens scampering into the garden. This seemed to be the right place to contemplate the direction of her life. After all, she now sat before what once had been the Ursuline School for Girls, representing seventeenth- and eighteenth-century efforts at educating them.

She shut her eyes and listened to children playing nearby. She imagined what life must have been like here so many centuries before and wondered whether the sounds of children at play would have been any different back then.

Amid this unexpected tranquility, Nikoletta decided her editor had been right in asking her to do a piece on tradition versus tourism. She'd made her reputation reporting on the basest of human propensities, stories in which brute force was the currency of choice. It was time to write about humankind's better nature, how those of goodwill could battle over a contentious issue without violence and reach a balanced result acceptable to all sides. Or so she'd like to believe.

She didn't move from her perch until well past sunset, listening all the while to the birds and children. She felt at ease as she backtracked down the hill, but before the harbor a waiter called out to her to please come try his tiny bar. She hadn't noticed the place on the way up, but it had a certain charm reminiscent of the sort of Bohemian café you'd expect to find on a Paris backstreet.

Why not? she thought and made her way to an empty table

by an open window, ordered a glass of red wine, and sat staring out at people passing by.

She didn't notice the tall, fit man until he stood next to her table. He wore the stylized haircut and week-old black beard of men in their late twenties but struck her as considerably older. At first she thought he was another waiter.

"Excuse me, miss, are you Nikoletta Elia?"

She stared at him. "Do I know you?"

"May I sit down?"

"Not until you tell me who you are."

"Someone with a story to tell that I know you'll be interested in hearing."

He'd said the magic words.

She nodded for him to sit. "This better be good."

"I'm a big fan of your work. We must have arrived on the same boat, because I saw a man holding up a sign with your name on it. I waited to see what you looked like but didn't want to bother you. Later, I saw you walking along the harbor front and decided to follow in hopes of getting the chance to speak with you."

"If you've been following me, how come I didn't notice you up in the Kastro? I was virtually alone up there."

He smiled. "Precisely. Which is why when you went into the Kastro, I waited until you came out. I didn't want to spook you."

"How did you know I'd come out the same way I went in?"

He smiled again. "I see you're not familiar with the town. There are only two gates into the Kastro, the Paraporti to the south, and the Trani to the north. You went in through Trani, and I guessed you'd come out the same way."

She stared at him. "Okay, so you guessed right, and now you have your chance to tell me your story. So, tell me."

"If I expect you to believe me, I first better demonstrate my bona fides." He waved to a waiter. "Bring us a bottle of whatever the lady's drinking and a glass for me. Then leave us alone unless I call for you." He turned to Nikoletta. "The wine's on me, and I'm pretty sure that what I have to say will take at least a bottle."

Whatever's on his mind, he has a unique way of getting to the point.

"I'm going to tell you facts about stories you've covered that I could only know if I'm who you'll think I am after you've heard me out."

"Uh, okay?" She picked up her wineglass and leaned back in her chair. "I'm listening."

Over hours of conversation, and just as many bottles of wine, he delved into a half dozen sophisticated ransomware attacks, three embarrassing government document dumps, and two mysterious deaths officially recorded as accidents, all reported on by Nikoletta. He did not object when she pulled a notebook out of her bag and started taking notes but warned her not to record his voice or take his photo.

She pressed him with questions, and he answered with details she already knew, plus many she did not but that were consistent with her long-held suspicions. Details that only someone intimately aware of the ransomware and documents involved, and how the victims' deaths were made to look like accidents, would know.

"It's easier than you can imagine to interfere with a computer that controls a vehicle's antilock brakes, and if you do that on a twisting mountain road, investigators will just chalk it up to another tragic accident."

Nikoletta stared at him. "You do realize how nonchalant you sound in talking about the harm you've done to so many."

He shrugged. "All I want to know is have I told you enough to establish my credibility?"

"I assume you won't tell me your name."

He smiled. "Next question."

"What about your online nickname?"

He smiled again, saying nothing.

"Why are you telling me all this? You're implicating yourself in major crimes, including murder."

"I don't view them that way. I think of myself as employed to make computer systems do what my clients want. It's an intellectual challenge. I'm a black hat hacker, battling the white hats trying to keep me out of their systems."

Her eyes narrowed. "This is not a video game. What you're doing literally destroys lives. You can't seriously believe that's just an *intellectual challenge.*"

He leaned in. "My bottom line is that however you wish to characterize my past, I'm giving up that life. I no longer feel the rush I once did on achieving what others had thought impossible. It is time for me to leave the game and, having made that decision, I want to set the record straight."

"Some might say this is all hubris on your part, a desire to see your exploits glorified in the press."

He smiled. "They can say what they like, but that's not in keeping with how I've lived my life." He picked up his nearly empty wine glass. "My reason for this conversation is simple. The world should know that there are people out there like me. Plain, seemingly ordinary folk, paid to do very bad things for calculated purposes without leaving a trace of guilt or motive. We thrive in places where officials are quick to embrace innocent excuses for anything bad that happens on their watch—and where the media are reluctant to question authority."

He slugged down the rest of his wine and leaned forward. "In other words, I mean this conversation as a warning to you and your readers. Beware: we are among you."

He called for the check. "I think you should leave now, Nikoletta. I'll take care of paying. You just take care of yourself."

———

Nikoletta couldn't believe her good fortune at the widespread attention generated by her story. Magazine and TV crews tracked her down on Naxos for interviews, and her editor told her to forget about writing the tourism piece. He wanted her back in Athens, where he'd assigned two reporters to assist her on follow-up stories tied to her mysterious interviewee.

She told him she wanted to write the Naxos article. When he asked why, she said fate had sent her to Naxos for a reason, perhaps an even bigger one than meeting with the hacker. She'd only know for sure once she completed the piece.

Her editor pointed out that it was he, not fate, who'd sent her to Naxos, and now *he* wanted her back in Athens ASAP. They argued back and forth and compromised on her returning in Athens in four days' time.

"But I can't promise you that the police won't be hounding you before then," he told her. "They keep screaming for access to you, and I don't know how much longer I can stall them."

"I'm sure you'll do your best, as you always do."

"Stop with the BS and just make sure you're back here in four days."

"You mean on the fifth day."

"First thing in the morning. Bye."

As soon as they hung up, Nikoletta set off in search of sources for her other story. With her newfound celebrity, she had little trouble getting politicians to talk, but they spoke only in platitudes reflecting the interests of their particular constituencies. Representatives of the tourist industry were also readily available and eagerly expressed their polished, politically correct views on each topic she raised. She completed those interviews in one day, all without leaving Chora.

Her next three days had her trekking across rural Naxos, trudging from one remote location to another, following one introduction to the next, charming and cajoling opinions out of largely taciturn farmers and herders. Most interviews were frustrating, teeth-pulling exercises, but every so often she came across a tiger anxious to devour a perceived adversary with sharp-toothed rhetoric.

It was a grueling four days, but she got what she wanted for her story, and more.

Nikoletta returned to her hotel in Chora exhausted. It was well after dark, but also her last night on the island, and she'd promised a group of locals who'd helped her with her story that she'd celebrate with them at a bar in town.

She made it to the bar by eleven with the intention of putting in a quick appearance and heading back to her hotel. But her friends had brought along homemade food and a bouzouki band. She had to stay—and didn't escape until after two in the morning.

Alone and a bit tipsy, she stumbled in the direction of the hotel. At the base of the path leading up along the bluff, she paused, wondering if she dared risk going that way. As she was about to take the longer, safer route, she noticed fireflies moving along the bluff path.

Fireflies? she thought, shaking her head. It couldn't be fireflies. Then it hit her, and she laughed. They weren't fireflies but folks like her, hiking along the path with light from their mobile phones to guide them. She dismissed her earlier pangs of anxiety, lit up the flashlight on her mobile, and struck out on the path.

The wind had come up, and she could hear the sea crashing on the rocks below. It was a bit trickier a walk than she'd imagined, but somewhere up ahead, others were headed the same way, and from the sounds she heard coming toward her, likely even more intoxicated than she. In a matter of minutes, she'd be safely in her bed. She had nothing to fear.

———

Ring, ring.

The phone rang four more times.

A grasping hand knocked a book off the nightstand before finding the mobile phone.

"Hello."

"Nikoletta, I must see you right away."

She looked at the time. "It's four o'clock in the morning. Who is this?"

"The storyteller who bought you several bottles of wine a few nights ago."

She sat up in bed. "What do you want?"

"Trust me, it's important. *Very* important. Meet me outside the lobby of your hotel in ten minutes. *Don't be late.*"

He hung up before she could say another word.

How did he know I was in this hotel? How did he get my mobile number? Did I tell him? Those were the first questions running through her mind. *But... he was a skilled professional.* She pulled on her jeans, a sweatshirt, and sneakers; grabbed her room key; and hurried down to the lobby.

"The game's afoot" is what Sherlock Holmes would say at a moment like this, she thought.

Ah, the joys of the reporting life... even at four in the morning.

Chapter Two

Conventional wisdom holds early summer in Greece to be a beautiful time of year. The water is warm, the winds are mild, and the tourists are better behaved. But as far as Andreas Kaldis's workload was concerned, he saw little difference from season to season. The nation's criminal underbelly never seemed to go on holiday.

Ring, ring.

Nor do the phones.

He waited for Maggie to answer.

"It's the managing editor of your favorite newspaper," Maggie bellowed in from her desk outside Andreas's open office door. "And he's in his usual foul mood."

"Great, just what I need to make my day." Andreas picked up the phone. "Hi, Gio—"

"Kaldis, it's Pappas here."

Andreas wondered if Giorgos Pappas had purposely patterned his abrupt telephone style after the curmudgeonly stereotypes popularized in film and TV. Though it could be grating, Andreas viewed it as an act—like the cowardly lion in *The Wizard of Oz*—and liked the newspaperman.

"What a pleasant surprise, Giorgos. To what do I owe the honor of this call?"

"I need you to find my reporter."

"I beg your pardon? What reporter?"

"Nikoletta Elia. She should have been in my office hours ago, but isn't."

Andreas wanted to ask Pappas if he'd been drinking but decided to play along for a bit longer. "Do you think something's happened to her?"

"Of course I do. Otherwise why would I be calling you to find one of my reporters?"

"What do you think happened?"

"Damn it, man. If I knew, I wouldn't be calling you."

Andreas counted to three. "Giorgos. If you want my help, *back off.*" He paused for Pappas's response. None came, so he continued. "Why do you think her being a few hours late for work involves something that would interest the police?"

"Five days ago, we published a story she wrote about a mysterious computer pro operating on the Dark Web. It sent cops all over Europe scouring through their closed files, looking for clues to who he might be."

"Yes, I recognized her name. But what makes you think something's happened to her?"

"We agreed that she'd stay on Naxos until today to finish up a story on the push to expand tourism there. When she didn't show up in the office this morning, I tried calling her, but my calls kept going into voicemail." He paused. "So, I called her hotel to see if she'd left yet. I was told she'd not checked out, and when I asked to be put through to her room, again there was no answer. I convinced the manager to check if she was there. He said she wasn't, but her things were."

"Please excuse the indelicacy of this question, but perhaps she spent the night elsewhere?"

"I thought the same thing, but her mobile was next to her bed, and she'd never go anywhere without it."

"I'd like to help you out, but frankly, this still doesn't sound like a police matter."

"I'm not done yet. I haven't told you about the body?"

Andreas sat up in his chair. "What body?"

"The hotel sits on a bluff high above the sea. According to the manager, a body was found early this morning on the rocks just below the hotel. Police have been there all morning looking for evidence."

"I take it the body was not your reporter's."

"Correct. Police haven't identified him yet, but their thinking is he was a tourist unfamiliar with the terrain who lost his footing in the stiff winds that came through there late last night."

"Sounds plausible."

"Yeah, just like Nikoletta's hacker made his handiwork look like accidents."

"Are you suggesting that the body somehow ties into your missing reporter?"

"According to the manager, a hotel security guard saw Nikoletta leave the hotel a little after four in the morning to meet someone over by the edge of the bluff."

"And was that someone the body they found?"

"The security guy never saw who she met, but she never returned."

Andreas picked up a pencil and began drumming its eraser on his desktop. "So, what do you think happened to her?"

"Not a clue. But I'm worried her disappearance is somehow tied into the hacker."

"If you're suggesting he had second thoughts about talking to her, or was worried that she could identify him, I'd think *she'd* be the body they found on the rocks."

"That's why you're the detective, and I'm just the hysterical editor."

"There's another obvious angle," said Andreas, "but it, too, doesn't explain why a tourist ended up dead instead of your reporter. Nikoletta must have alarmed anyone who'd ever hired her hacker. Even though the cat's out of the bag for those exposed in her article, his other clients could be worried about follow-up articles covering other activities pointing back at them."

Andreas heard a deep swallow on the other end of the line.

"Um, we do have an investigative series planned to look into other incidents potentially linked to him."

"Who beyond you knew of those plans?"

"My publisher and the two reporters I assigned to work with Nikoletta." He gave Andreas the names of the two reporters. "But anyone familiar with the newspaper business could guess that's what we'd do. I mean, that's how you sell papers."

Andreas leaned back in his chair. "Okay, you've piqued my interest. I'll send someone over to Naxos to look into this. Just one promise I need from you."

"What is it?"

"Don't publish anything about your concerns for your reporter—or my unit's involvement in this. If she's been abducted and is still alive, the last thing she needs is for her captor to think we're onto what happened and closing in."

Silence.

"Well, do we have a deal?" asked Andreas.

"I had to tell my publisher what happened. He went ballistic at the possibility of someone kidnapping one of his reporters. No telling what he might do."

"Just tell him what I said. Publicity at this time will only endanger her more. And keep your fingers crossed that he listens."

"Following directions is not a customary strong point among publishers."

"I'll take that as a yes, you'll try."

"Let me know as soon as you hear anything."

"That's a two-way street," said Andreas.

"Understood."

"Great. Now let me get back to work."

"Thanks, Andreas."

Andreas stared at his dead phone. That was the first time Giorgos had ever called him by his given name.

He's worried.

———

Detective Yianni Kouros looked forward to spending the coming weekend in Athens with his girlfriend, Toni, something her job playing piano in a Mykonos bar rarely permitted. This weekend, though, the bar was closed for a wedding, giving Toni the opportunity to visit him, and Yianni a break from his weekend ferryboat commute to Mykonos.

He planned on showing his American-born girlfriend the *real* Athens, not the heavily promoted version sold to tourists. But that was still two days away, and at the moment he had a message to see his boss "as soon as you get in."

Yianni had been Andreas's right-hand man since their days together on Mykonos, when Andreas was the island's police chief and Yianni a brash young bull of a rookie cop. He stuck his head through the open doorway to Andreas's office.

Andreas was talking on the phone but waved Yianni toward a chair in front of his desk. "Yes, Minister, I understand the importance of protecting members of our free press from violence." He rolled his eyes. "Yes, we are not Turkey."

Andreas put his hand over the mouthpiece, "It's our Public Order and Citizen Protection Minister grandstanding for a publisher demanding that we find his missing reporter."

"What missing reporter?" whispered Yianni.

Andreas took his hand off the mouthpiece. "Of course I'm listening. I was just telling my best detective to clear his desk to take charge of this matter." Andreas rolled his eyes again. "Absolutely. I'll let you know as soon as we learn anything more." Andreas nodded. "Yes, the best to you and your wife too. Bye." He hung up the phone, sighed, and looked at Yianni.

"Every day I thank the Fates that I gave up that position as Minister of Public Order and returned here to the relative calm of chasing bad guys." Andreas pointed at the phone. "The gyrations he has to go through to satisfy all the interests demanding his attention is enough to drive a person mad. In order to keep the jackals constantly nipping at his heels from getting a clear shot at his throat, he has to keep his constituents thinking only he can be relied upon to make things happen. This time he had to put on an act for a publisher who'd burst into his office venting about us failing to find a reporter I just learned *might* be missing."

Yianni leaned forward. "I get all that political stuff, so let's get to the part about me clearing my desk."

"The reporter who broke that story on the mysterious hacker has gone missing, or so her editor thinks." Andreas told Yianni of his conversation with the editor and his request the paper not run a story about her disappearance until Andreas had a better handle on what happened. "At this point, we don't know if she disappeared willingly or unwillingly. She might just be out somewhere partying." Andreas leaned back in his chair. "Then again, with so much of our world facing lethal attacks on the media, we do have to consider the worst as a possibility."

"I take that to mean the worst is about to happen to *me*."

"Hey, don't complain. It's why you get paid the big money."

Yianni waved off the teasing. "I've got plans with Toni for the weekend."

"You've got a couple of days before then, and besides, Naxos is only an hour from Mykonos."

"But our plans are for Athens."

Andreas nodded. "Well, let's see what you can turn up by Friday, and we'll take it from there."

"I'm not happy."

"Understood. I'll find some way to make it up to you."

"Your bigger challenge will be finding a way to make it up to Toni. After all, she's become best friends with your wife."

Andreas nodded. "Neither of whom is shy about speaking her mind to me. I guess that means you should be on your way ASAP. The sooner you get a handle on things, the better our chance of salvaging your weekend." He paused. "And my domestic bliss."

"Where do you suggest I begin?"

"I spoke to the Naxos police chief and told him to keep Nikoletta's hotel room sealed off until you get there. She apparently left in a hurry, taking nothing with her. I'd say that's the place to start."

"I'll get going." Yianni stood. "Can you get me a list from Nikoletta's editor of everyone she met with on Naxos?"

"I'll get Maggie on it."

"Thanks."

"It's the least I can do for you."

Yianni headed for the door. "You mean the *very* least."

———

Yianni caught a flight from Athens that had him to Naxos in about the same time as it took to fly to its neighboring island of Mykonos, two islands different in practically every way imaginable. Shaped like a broad granite and marble arrowhead pointing north, Naxos was four times the size of Mykonos, and the largest island in the Cyclades. It also boasted the Cyclades's two tallest mountains, Zas and Koronos. Naxos had long ago been deforested but was still green, agriculturally blessed, and since antiquity, famous for its marble and emery mines. Though Mykonos had its barite mines and grain windmills, it was a dry, arid, and rocky place, with modest agriculture that in no way rivaled Naxos's natural riches and virtual self-sufficiency.

But times had changed, and today Mykonos possessed a high-end tourism reputation that was the envy of every Greek island seeking to maximize its own tourist potential. Yianni wondered how long it would be before Naxos embraced the same tourism fervor so many of its island neighbors had.

He stared out the window as the light plane approached Naxos Island National Airport. A relatively modest facility, it stood approximately two and a half miles southwest of Chora, east of a massive salt pond, and surrounded by a patchwork of chocolate, beige, and green open fields. Its short runway kept big international jetliners away, an obvious check on tourism expansion. Yianni wondered if that was intentional and, if so, who wanted it that way.

As Yianni walked across the tarmac toward the tiny terminal building, the final scene from *Casablanca* popped into his mind—Humphrey Bogart and Claude Rains strolling through the fog along a lonely stretch of airstrip on their way to neither knew where.

Naxos's local police chief stood waiting for Yianni at the gate. They knew each other from Yianni's time as a cop on Mykonos. Back then, they'd worked together at catching thieves who'd milk one Cycladic island until things got too hot for them there, then jump to another.

"You haven't changed a bit, Dimitri," said Yianni, hugging the chief and exchanging cheek kisses.

"Too bad I can't say the same for you," smiled Dimitri. "But in your case, you look better than ever."

"Puh, puh, puh. That's all I need, you giving me the evil eye with bullshit compliments." He slapped Dimitri on the back.

"How's your chief doing?"

"Andreas? Great. You know he's married now with two kids."

"I've heard, to the only daughter of one of Greece's wealthiest old-line families."

"Yeah, that's what gets played up in cop gossip, but she's a down-to-earth, no-bullshit lady. In fact, she and my girlfriend created a program to mentor vulnerable young girls."

"Sounds impressive."

"It is, but I want to hear all about your family."

As they made their way to Dimitri's car, he filled Yianni in on the expanding size of his family and listened to Yianni go on about the state of his own love life.

"Your friend sounds like an interesting woman."

"She is, but this case is threatening to wreck our plans for the weekend."

The chief shrugged. "Have her come over. You can stay with us."

"That's kind of you, but I was hoping to show her Athens."

"Well, the offer's open." Dimitri pressed a button on his key fob to unlock the doors to his cruiser. "I assume the first thing you'll want is to see the reporter's hotel room."

"Yes," said Yianni as he slid into the passenger seat, "then the people she talked to."

"I'll arrange to have one of my local Naxos cops drive you around the island. Trust me when I say that'll be a hell of a lot easier than turning you loose with a GPS, a map, and a car. The island's too big, and the places and people you'll want to see way too difficult for you to find on your own."

"Thanks, but how do you know who exactly I'll want to see?"

"I don't." Dimitri pulled out of the airport onto the main road leading back to the heart of Chora. "But from what I've heard, your reporter was all over the island, speaking to some of its most *interesting* characters."

"What's that supposed to mean?"

"This island is filled with strong opinions, rooted in a deep pride in Naxos's historically independent ways. Some show it in words, some in dress, some in actions. I expect every one of them will have an opinion on what happened to her."

"Are you saying word's out that she's missing?"

"We're trying to keep it quiet and officially have said nothing, but there's no way this sort of thing stays out of the local gossip mill for long. After all, the story she wrote about meeting up with that cyber guy attracted international attention in a way that gave the island a bit of celebrity. People know who she is. When word gets out that she disappeared the same night that tourist died"—Dimitri waved his right hand in a small circle—"I can only imagine the theories that will be circulating. Each one undoubtedly aimed at implicating someone the teller of the tale despises."

"Why would locals want to spread that sort of bullshit? It seems sort of self-destructive for the island."

"The answer to that question, my friend, has been a mystery haunting Greeks for centuries. For example, our illustrious mayor made it clear to me this morning that he's prepared to turn this into a political issue aimed directly at me. To quote him, 'Unanswered questions surrounding a dead tourist and missing journalist cannot be allowed to hang over our island.'"

"I take it you two don't get along."

"That's putting it mildly. We have serious disagreements over what he and I see as legally permissible behavior on the part of his political cronies."

"Hmm." Yianni changed subjects. "Any evidence of the tourist's cause of death?"

"Yes, a header off the top of a cliff onto the rocks below."

"What else do you know about him?"

"No ID yet, but we know his physical description." Dimitri described him.

"That's it?"

"No signs of foul play, no drugs or alcohol in his system."

"Then what the hell was he doing out there in the middle of the night?"

"That's what half the island wants to know, and the other half doesn't care because it's already convinced he was murdered."

"I can see you're feeling the pressure. Any leads?"

"That would be too much to expect. A lot of accusations are being lobbed back and forth between rival interest groups, and of course, a rash of conspiracy theories abound. All, at least so far, unsupported by evidence."

"In other words, business as usual."

"Yes, but I've compiled a list of everyone preaching me theories." Dimitri handed Yianni an envelope. "Take it for what it's worth. It just might give you a place to start."

"And give your harassers the sense that you took their opinions seriously enough to pass them on to me." Yianni smiled.

Dimitri grinned. "One must keep one's public happy."

They fell back to talking about old times and how much the world had changed in so few years.

Yianni paid little attention to the neighborhoods they passed through on the two-lane road into Chora. To him, the modern areas that developed around the outskirts of virtually every town of sizable population, be it an island or mainland town, looked the same. The perennial favorite choice of construction remained two- and three-story buildings thrown up for the rents they generated, from street-level commercial space to residential apartments above. Gas stations, hardware stores, and electronics shops mixed in among supermarkets, pharmacies, bakeries, butchers, and banks. Doctors, lawyers, and accountants worked in offices next to fast-food shops, nail salons, hairdressers, and lotto sellers, plus the ubiquitous *kafenia* and tavernas.

Dimitri wove though Chora's maze of one-way streets to a tiny parking area wedged between the edge of a cliff and the hotel.

"Here we are. I've taken the liberty of arranging for the security guy to be here for you to interview. He's our only witness to whatever happened. I figured you'd like to speak to him first."

Yianni followed Dimitri into a reception area decorated in pale grays and whites. Walls of glass enclosed two sides of the adjoining bar and restaurant area, affording sweeping views of the Aegean, Portara, and Chora.

Dimitri introduced Yianni to the hotel's owner, a tall, slim man with the practiced, welcoming smile of a hotelier. He showed the two cops into his office. A squat, swarthy man wearing blue jeans, a Grateful Dead T-shirt, and a scruffy, Jerry Garcia–style gray beard, slouched in one of two taverna chairs in front of a simple wooden desk.

"Anargyros, these are the policemen who want to speak with you," said the owner. He pointed to the upholstered office chair behind the desk. "Please, Detective, feel free to take my chair."

"Thank you, but Dimitri can sit there. I'll take this one." Yianni sat in the chair next to Anargyros and turned his head to face the hotel owner. "You've been most kind. We'll let you know as soon as we're finished with the interview."

The hotel owner looked disappointed at being subtly told to leave but nodded and left the office, shutting the door behind him.

Yianni smiled at Anargyros. "First of all, thank you for seeing us at a time when I assume you're normally asleep. My name is

Detective Yianni Kouros, and I have some questions that you may have already been asked by others."

Anargyros shrugged.

"I'd like you to tell us everything that happened last night conceivably having anything to do with Nikoletta Elia."

Anargyros shut his eyes and rocked his head from side to side. "Do you mind if I smoke?"

"No."

Anargyros reached into his jeans, pulled out a small sack of tobacco and rolling papers, and began making himself a cigarette.

Yianni shot a where-the-hell-is-this-headed look at Dimitri.

"Anargyros," said Dimitri, "this isn't one of your group therapy, addiction support sessions. We need answers *now*."

Anargyros stared at Dimitri and kept quietly rolling his cigarette.

"Do you want to keep this job or not? Just answer the detective's questions and you can be on your way. Otherwise..."

Yianni jumped in as the good cop. "We really don't want to take up any more of your time than necessary, but we do need your cooperation."

"Or else I'll drag your ass down to the station and keep you there until you answer his questions," added Dimitri.

Anargyros finished rolling his cigarette, pulled a plastic lighter from another pocket, lit the cigarette, and drew in a puff. "She came into reception at about three a.m." He exhaled. "Pretty close to shitfaced when she did."

"Did she say anything to you?" asked Yianni.

"Just took her room key and said good night." He took another draw on the cigarette. "About an hour later she burst into reception, wearing blue jeans and a gray sweatshirt and asking if someone was looking for her. I said no, and she went running off into the breakfast room and bar area."

"What did you do?" said Yianni.

Exhaling a cloud of pungent smoke, he said, "I got up from behind the reception desk to see what she was doing. Considering how drunk she'd been an hour before, I didn't want her grabbing anything from behind the bar. My job would be on the line if I'd let her."

"What was she doing in there?"

"I never got to see—she came out before I had the chance. She seemed panicked. Then she asked if anyone had been in reception since she'd come back to the hotel at three. I said no. I also suggested she calm down and go back to bed."

"What did she say to that?"

"She never answered, just pointed to one of the windows looking out toward the bluff and yelled, 'There he is.'"

"Did you see who she was pointing at?"

"It was so dark I couldn't see if a tall, short, thin, or fat he, she, or it was out there. Whoever it was stood beyond the hotel's lights."

"Then how do you know someone was out there?"

He took another drag. "Because when I turned to see what she was looking at, I saw a blinking light coming at us from the dark."

"How do you know it was aimed at you?"

"Aimed at her." He exhaled. "When I turned to her, she was running for the front door. I looked back at the light and it stopped blinking right after I heard the wind slam the front door shut."

"And she never came back?"

"Correct." He let the smoke drift out of his nose.

"Didn't that seem odd to you?"

Anargyros stared at Yianni. "Are you serious? This is a holiday island. A woman staggers back to the hotel at three in the morning after too much to drink, and an hour later comes down from her room looking to hook up with some guy who'd just called her, and you expect me to wonder why she didn't come back before my shift was over at seven?"

Yianni nodded, "Good point. But how do you know someone had just called her?"

"I don't. I just assumed it."

"Could the call have come through the switchboard?"

He shrugged. "I'd have had to put it through, and none came in for her."

"Are you sure?"

"Calls at four in the morning are rare. And if one came in, the caller would have had to convince me to put it through. There were no calls."

Over the next hour, Yianni and Dimitri plumbed Anargyros's memory for every detail of Nikoletta's appearance, words, and behavior that night, but his story and recollections remained the same.

"Well, what do you think?" said Yianni to Dimitri after they'd sent Anargyros on his way.

"I think he's telling the truth. He's a bright guy seduced by a bad meth habit, but he's done a pretty good job of kicking it. I don't see an angle in this for him."

"Well, let's take a look at her room," said Yianni. "There's got to be a clue somewhere."

"You always were an optimist."

———

Nikoletta's room reflected the new minimalist trend in beach accommodations. Tastefully done in pale-gray and white, with marble floors and light-oak wooden shelving and furniture, it perfectly stated what it was: a modern place for a holiday stay.

Yianni stood in the doorway, studying the room before stepping inside. "Have your guys gone through this?"

"Every millimeter, but they left things right where they found them."

"What did they turn up?"

"Fingerprints, likely from housekeepers, workmen, and past guests."

"Anything else relevant to us?"

Dimitri pointed to a pile of notebooks on the nightstand. "Four of them contain the reporter's notes on interviews for her tourism story. The fifth covers her interview with the mysterious cybercriminal."

"What about the mobile phone?"

"It's locked. We assume it's hers."

"Did you try opening it?"

"I thought about asking my five-year-old son to take a crack at it. He always seems to know how to get into my phone, but I decided to leave that challenge to your tech wizzes back in Athens."

"Good decision," said Yianni. "Let's get it couriered to Athens right away."

He carefully made his way over to the nightstand. "I assume the notebooks have been examined for fingerprints?"

"Yes. Only hers turned up."

Yianni sat on the edge of the bed, picked up the top notebook, and opened it. On the first page was a notation handwritten in Greek and English.

IF FOUND, PLEASE RETURN TO NIKOLETTA ELIA, followed by a Greek mobile telephone number and the word REWARD underlined and circled.

On the next page was a neatly printed name, location, date, and beginning and ending time, followed by pages of notes and long bodies of text, presumably recording the words of the subject of her interview. Sections were arranged similarly for each person she'd interviewed.

Yianni looked up at Dimitri standing by the bed. "Have you read these?"

"Not carefully. I glanced at them, but as you can see there's a lot to read."

Yianni held the notebook open to the page he'd been looking at. "Who's the person named here?"

Dimitri leaned in to read the name. "That would be our mayor. I understand he was the first person she interviewed for her story."

"I'll need your help in identifying who she met with. The list my office received from her editor isn't complete."

"No problem."

"She had five notebooks?"

"That's all we found."

"That's a lot to read."

Dimitri nodded. "And steps to retrace."

Yianni shut his eyes and sighed. "No way I'll be able to complete all of this by the weekend."

"Like I said, the offer of a place for you and Toni to stay remains open."

"Thanks." Yianni slapped his free hand on his thigh and stood up. "Well, let's get started. First thing I need is a place to read these notebooks cover-to-cover, undisturbed. I want to finish reading them by tonight so that I can begin retracing her steps first thing in the morning."

"I know the perfect place for you."

"Not the police station. I'll be inundated with gossipers who won't take no for an answer."

"Don't worry, no one will disturb you where I have in mind."

"Good."

"There's only one hitch."

"Being?"

"Do you believe in ghosts?"

Chapter Three

Yianni called Andreas to report on what he'd found, or rather not found, and said he'd call again after he'd read through the reporter's notebooks. He pondered whether to call Toni, but she might be sleeping. Her job as a piano player in one of Mykonos's iconic clubs kept her up until four in the morning. She rarely stirred before noon, and then it was off to her day job playing finder of stolen goods for tourists and locals preyed upon by opportunistic thieves. Her late afternoon nap was sacrosanct, but he decided to risk leaving a message on her mobile.

He leaned against a wall as he patiently waited for the sixth ring to send him into voicemail. "Hi, my love. I'm just calling to let you know I'm on Naxos and will be incommunicado for the rest of the day and likely much of the night, reading documents. I didn't want you wondering why you hadn't heard from me, and—"

Ring, ring.

Yianni looked at his phone. It was Toni. He switched over to take her call. "You're awake?"

"Phones ringing six times have a habit of doing that to me."

"I didn't expect you to leave it on."

"When I sleep alone, I leave it on vibrate. And don't bother to ask why unless you're prepared to handle the answer."

Yianni laughed. "I miss you."

"I miss you too. Can't wait until the weekend."

Yianni swallowed. "Me too. I was just leaving you a message that I'll be tied up into the night reading documents."

"What sort of a case has you cloistered away reading documents? I thought all you big-time cops did was break heads and beat confessions out of bad guys."

Yianni grinned. "That's the fun part, but we can't beat on them until we find them. Which is what has me standing outside a monster medieval mansion atop old town Naxos."

"Sounds wonderful."

"It is. The local police chief arranged for me to have a key to the place so that I could do my reading undisturbed. But now I'm all alone, about to be surrounded by antiquities dating back to the fifth millennium B.C.E., and who knows what ancient spirits, so I decided to call you for company."

"Is it someone's home?"

"No, it used to be the School of Commerce for Boys, but now it's the Naxos Archaeological Museum."

"I think I'm supposed to respond, 'How sweet of you to think of me,' though my instinct is to say, 'You sound horny.'"

"So much for the moment."

Toni chuckled. "I've never been to Naxos. I hear it's wonderful. Maybe we could go there together someday."

Yianni bit at his lip. "Yeah, why not?"

"Well, try not to have too much fun among the artifacts while I labor on among the sinners."

"One man's sin is another's wished-for prayer."

"You sound more like a philosopher than a cop."

Yianni laughed. "On that note, I'll say goodbye, get to work on my reading, and let you get back to sleep."

"Little chance of that now, my love, but bye-bye." She signed off with a kiss.

Yianni lingered for a moment, holding the phone to his ear. Toni was unlike any woman he'd ever known. She could read a bar audience with wildly different musical tastes and come up with the perfect tune to please them all.

He wondered if that same intuitive gift had her somehow sensing that their weekend plans were in jeopardy. By suggesting they "someday" visit Naxos, did she want him to know that she was okay with that? Yianni shook his head and smiled, put his phone away, and stepped inside the museum.

He put the notebooks down on a small table just inside the entrance, picked up a brochure from the same table, and wandered for ten minutes through the museum's warren of rooms, halls, terraces, and staircases. According to the brochure, one of Yianni's favorite authors, Nikos Kazantzakis of *Zorba the Greek* fame, had attended the school that once inhabited this building. Yianni also read that an upper floor of the school had once housed a library full of artifacts and other valuable treasures, but occupying German and Italian forces destroyed them in World War II.

Yianni could easily spend a day in here wandering among antiquities. He decided the best place for him to do his reading would be as far away as possible from those distractions. So, he planted himself and Nikoletta's notebooks at the desk where visitors stood in line to buy their tickets.

Yianni drew in and let out a deep breath, picked up the notebook containing the reporter's earliest entries, and muttered to himself, "In the beginning…"

———

Toni turned onto her left side and stared at a blank wall next to the lone window in her bedroom. There was nothing there for her to see, but she wasn't looking, she was concentrating her thoughts. Since their last weekend together, all Yianni had talked about were his plans for them in Athens. What they'd see, what they'd do, who they'd meet. Now, not a peep.

Something's happened. I hope it's only work.

She rolled onto her back, stretching and yawning as she did. She lived in a hotel close by the sea. It was more of a big house with bedrooms, but its owner called it a hotel and the Tourist Board allowed him to do so, thereby entitling him to charge higher rates for his rooms. Toni had no complaint about the price because as a year-round resident she had a special deal. More importantly, the owner and his wife treated her like family. That meant a lot to Toni, because her mother had died a few years back, and her father's subsequent depression led him to give up his overseas position with the U.S. State Department and move back to New York City, the place of their marriage and Toni's birth.

She'd grown up as a diplomat's child, bouncing from one foreign American school to another. Music was her only constant during those early expat years. Straight out of high school, she skipped college and took off on her own, bumming around Europe, dreaming of setting the world on fire with her music. Ultimately, she landed on Mykonos.

She swung her legs out of bed, faced the bathroom doorway, and shifted her eyes to the mirror to its right. "Good evening, Toni, how nice to see you looking so fine and chipper. Another late night in store for you, I presume? Now don't start complaining, Dearie. After all, you're the one who wanted to be a piano player. In other words, get your ass out of bed."

Toni shut her eyes and shook her head. "I must be crazy talking to a mirror."

She looked back at the mirror. "No, Dearie, you just miss your boyfriend."

—

The more of the reporter's notebooks Yianni read, the more certain he was that his weekend plans were toast. As unhappy as that made him, he saw no alternative. From what Nikoletta had written, there could be any number of reasons why she'd disappeared, several of them fatal.

Her notes of her conversation with the hacker went into details not revealed in the newspaper article. Details pointing fingers at mobsters, private citizens, and government officials he claimed had retained him to target competitors, enemies, colleagues, and spouses. If true, every one of his clients had a reason to want Nikoletta silenced.

But her other notebooks suggested a different sort of suspect, one unrelated to him or his kills, yet with a definite motive for keeping her from publishing her second story. The players ranged from big-money developers to activists to uncompromising fanatics. Nikoletta's plans for laying bare the bad intentions and hidden agendas she saw as stoking a looming, pitched battle over the island's future would not endear her to many.

But enough to kill her?

Yianni leaned back in his chair and stretched. With all the crazies in this world, he wasn't about to play psychiatrist and eliminate any potential suspect. He'd simply assume the worst and say a prayer that it wasn't too late for Nikoletta.

On that thought, he looked at his watch. It was nearly one in the morning. He hadn't eaten a thing since a quick bite with Dimitri on their way up to the museum. He thought to call Andreas and report on what he'd read since they'd spoken shortly before midnight, but it was late and he'd didn't have much more to say than he'd already told him. Too many suspects, too many divergent motives. He'd call first thing in the morning. Tomorrow would be a busy day. Make that, *today* will be a busy day. He should get to bed, but before retracing Nikoletta's every step, he needed something to eat.

———

The path from the museum down to the harbor was a mix of stone steps and inclines, but all well lighted. There was life on the old town's winding streets, not surprising what with it being tourist season. Yianni had no trouble finding the bar where Nikoletta had held her interview, and though its kitchen was closed, a man Yianni took to be the owner offered to microwave a frozen pizza.

Yianni sat sipping a beer when the owner returned with the pizza in one hand and a fresh-made Greek salad in the other. "I thought, what kind of a host would I be if I didn't at least offer you a salad?"

Yianni smiled. "You're too kind. I never expected this."

"You don't like salad?"

"No, I meant this is very generous of you. Thank you."

"I always try remembering that hospitality shows respect not just for my customers but for what I do every day of my life to earn my living. That was a lesson passed on to me by my father." He crossed himself.

Yianni studied the man, who looked fit, in his late forties, taller than Yianni, but wiry, with a broad round face, a three-day beard, uncombed more than tousled hair, and the sort of close-set, dark eyes that suggested feral intensity.

Yianni extended his right hand. "My name is Yianni."

The man shook it. "Stelios. Welcome to this little bit of heaven."

"It's a lovely setting. You must get a lot of business."

The man nodded. "Yes, business has been very good. *Puh, puh, puh.*"

Yianni picked up a piece of pizza and took a bite.

Stelios started to turn away. "I'll leave you to eat in peace."

"No, please. Join me." Yianni pointed to the chair across from him. "No reason for me to eat alone, assuming you don't need to be doing something else."

Stelios sat. "No, the bartender has everything under control. The few customers remaining are just sipping drinks and basking in the notoriety of the place."

Yianni saw his opening. "Notoriety?"

"You didn't know?"

"Know what?" Yianni feigned ignorance.

"That reporter, the one who wrote a story about a mysterious computer guy she met in a bar, she met him here."

"Really?"

"Yes, they were sitting at that table behind you, in the window."

Yianni turned and looked at the table, then turned back to face Stelios. "How long were they here?"

"Two, three hours."

Yianni turned around to look at the table again. "What were they like?"

"He talked; she took notes. And before you ask, I never heard a word they said."

"Why do you think I would ask?"

"Because everyone asks me that."

"I guess that's only natural, but I'd also think it only natural for you not to admit you'd overheard anything, even if you had."

Stelios smiled. "Considering what the newspaper said they talked about, I think you're right."

Yianni nodded. "So, what did he look like?"

"I'm not good at remembering faces."

"Another wise trait. Though probably not a good one for a bar owner."

Stelios smiled again. "Don't worry, I'll remember yours. So, what has you over here on Naxos? Are you on holiday?"

Yianni reached into the front of his shirt and pulled out his ID on a lanyard around his neck. "Nope, I'm a detective with Greece's Special Crimes Unit." He took another bite of the pizza.

Stelios's face blanched. "I guess I've already said too much."

Yianni gave a quick upward jerk of his head. "Not at all." He took a taste of the Greek salad. "This is terrific. I particularly like the touch of oregano."

Stelios's face constricted, and he bit at his lip.

Yianni took another bite. "Tasty."

Stelios started to stand. "I've really got some work I should be doing."

Yianni nodded "no" again. "Stay. I like your company."

Stelios slunk into the chair. "Honest, I heard not a word."

"So, what did he look like?"

"I told you, I—"

"Would you like a piece of pizza?"

"No, I—"

"How about at least a bit of feta?"

"No, I—"

"Then how about a bit of truth serum?" Yianni slid his beer across the table to Stelios.

"He was a tall man, slim, with dark hair, but it could have been a wig. His eyes were intense. My guess is he's from one of those Scandinavian countries, maybe Iceland, but from the little I heard him say, he spoke perfect Greek without any trace of an accent."

"Anything else?"

"A big smile, I mean a really big smile."

"You said he was tall. How tall?"

"A little taller than I."

"When did he come into the bar?"

"Right after the woman sat down at the table."

"Did they know each other?"

"He knew her, but she didn't know him. I watched to make sure he wasn't going to harass her. I protect my customers from that sort of thing."

Yianni nodded. "I'm sure. So, what did you hear?"

"Basically, the things she wrote in the article. I heard him say he had some interesting things to tell her. Once she told him to sit, I lost interest in their conversation. I had no idea who he or she was and didn't have to hear another seduction routine. I think I've heard them all at one time or another. Besides, we were busy, and I had other customers to sit with."

"Did they leave together?"

"I don't remember. And I've never seen either of them again."

"I assume that's another question you get asked."

Stelios nodded.

Yianni extended his hand. "Thanks, for everything."

Stelios quickly stood and shook Yianni's hand. "May I go now?"

"Sure."

Stelios turned to walk away but paused and looked back at Yianni. "You're not so bad for a cop. Your dinner's on me."

"No, I insist on respecting your business by paying for it."

Stelios touched his chest with his hand. "Thank you. But only for the pizza. The beer and salad are on me."

Yianni returned the gesture. "Deal."

Yianni devoured the pizza and salad and ordered a second beer for which he insisted on paying. As he was about to leave,

Stelios came over with a plate of fresh fruit. He placed the fruit on the table and sat down across from Yianni.

"Something else occurred to me. I'm not sure it's important, but just in case it is, I wanted you to know."

"I'm listening."

"Someone else came into the bar at about the same time as the man and the woman. I can't be certain when he arrived, but he sat at the bar sipping beers with his eyes glued to the mirror behind the bar."

"Could he see their table in the mirror."

Stelios nodded.

"Did he speak to either of them?"

"No."

"When did he leave?"

"Right after the woman left."

"Why didn't you tell anyone this before?"

"I didn't even think about it until you asked me whether she and the hacker guy left together. That's when I remembered the fellow at the bar. He could have been her driver waiting for her to leave, but I don't recall her saying a word to him, even when she left."

"Have you ever seen him before?"

"No, or after."

"What did he look like?"

"Your height, a bit stocky, ruddy complexion, dark, normal-length hair, dark eyes, in his thirties."

"His ethnicity?"

"No idea, I never heard him speak. He could have been Eastern European, American, or even Greek. I've no way of telling."

That fits the description of the guy who did a header onto the rocks below Nikoletta's hotel.

"What about the bartender who waited on him. Where can I find him?"

"You mean her. I wish I knew. The staff in this place turns over before I can even learn their names. They move on as soon as they find a better job, whether here or on another island. I'm just happy if they give me notice."

"Do you have a name for that bartender?"

"Uh, that's a bit complicated."

"No working papers? So no legitimate name." Yianni shook his head.

"Hey, I was trying to help you out. Now you're going to burn me?"

"Don't worry, I'm not going to turn you in. Just promise not to do it again."

"Sure. Promise."

Good chance of that one being kept.

"Thanks," said Stelios, hurrying off as if afraid to test his luck with further conversation.

As Yianni walked back to the hotel, he put his conversation with the bar owner out of his mind to focus on his next challenge: telling Toni that their weekend plans were canceled.

———

"Hello."

"Sorry to bother you at work, but I know you take a break fifteen minutes before every hour."

Toni looked at her phone. "It's a quarter to three, and there's no one on the phone except you and me, so what's the story you have to tell?"

"One that I hope won't dampen your sense of humor."

"Try me."

"The case that has me on Naxos is going to keep me here through the weekend."

"Whew, I thought it might be something serious, what with this being so far past your bedtime. We'll do Athens another time. After all, it's not going anywhere."

"I'm sorry."

"Well, I can't say I'm not disappointed. I was looking forward to seeing you."

"Me too." Yianni paused. "You could come over here. I'll still have to work, but at least we could be together part of the time."

"Does Naxos have beaches, bars, and restaurants?"

"Great ones."

"Fine, then count me in. I'll find some way to keep myself occupied while you're busy elsewhere."

"I'm not sure I like that proposal."

Toni laughed. "It's no different than the sort of life I live over here on Mykonos without you. Need I remind you that I'm the experienced partier in this relationship? So, what is it, big boy, Naxos or *nyet*?"

"If Greece had you negotiating its bailout with the European Union, we wouldn't be in the mess we're in today."

"That's not an answer. I'll give you until tomorrow to make up your mind."

"You mean today."

"Whatever day is Friday. I can catch the first boat to Naxos Saturday morning."

"Excellent. Just let me know the boat's name so I can arrange for you to be picked up by the hotel if I can't be there."

"Works for me. Time for you to get to bed, and me to get back to work."

"Miss you."

"Miss you too. Kisses."

The EU wouldn't have stood a chance against her.

Chapter Four

Andreas couldn't remember the last time he'd slept past dawn. With two young children, one of them always found a way to serve as his wake-up call. Lila and he had live-in help who could tend to the children, but Andreas looked upon these early-morning moments as his only guaranteed time with his children, because his evenings far too often belonged to the vagaries of what awaited him each day in his office.

Lila never interfered with her husband's first thirty minutes of daybreak playtime, but then she'd show up and impose order on the chaos her husband seemed ingenious at creating. After all, Tassaki had to get ready for kindergarten, and Sofia needed some semblance of a schedule. All of which meant that by eight each morning, Andreas was out the door and on his way to GADA.

This morning he arrived in his office to find three voicemails from Nikoletta's editor, each a bit more frantic than the one before.

There was also a message from Yianni describing what he'd learned from the bar owner and promising to call in at nine. Andreas dialed the number left by the editor.

The phone had barely rung once when Andreas heard, "It's about time you called back."

"Morning, Giorgos. You should be honored. I'm actually calling before my first cup of coffee. So, what has you so riled up?"

"MY REPORTER IS STILL MISSING!"

"I know that. It's why I have my best detective working around the clock on Naxos to find her."

"Well, get more people over there."

Andreas drew in and let out a quick breath. "There must be another reason why you left three messages for me in less than an hour, other than to bust my balls over how I assign my overworked, underpaid staff."

"He left me a message."

"Who did?"

"The hacker, or at least someone acting as if he's the hacker."

Andreas's voice tightened. "When did you receive it, how did you get it, and what did it say?"

"I found it on my voicemail when I got up this morning. The voice sounded like it had been through a scrambler, and he told me not to worry, Nikoletta was safe, and he was protecting her from those who might wish to do her harm. He said he knew the police were looking for her on Naxos, but they would never find her unless she wanted them to."

"*Unless she wanted them to?* Did he actually use those words?"

"Those precise words."

"Sounds like someone is trying to slow down the search by suggesting all's fine. But it's a rather bizarre way to do it, since it suggests a Stockholm-syndrome situation in the making."

"My feelings exactly."

"Then again, the call could've been a phony," said Andreas.

"Could be. There are a lot of crank callers out there. I'll send over a copy of the voicemail to your office for analysis."

"Better yet, bring us your phone. Our lab might be able to pick up more from it than off a copy of the message."

Giorgos's voice tensed. "I've got a lot of other things on that phone. Confidential things."

"I'm sure. It's why I suggested *you* bring it over. Watching what the lab guys do to your phone might give you peace of mind."

"I'm expecting nothing of the sort until Nikoletta's found, safe and sound."

Andreas paused. "On that point, I've reconsidered your request to assign more people to look for her."

"How many more?"

"Just one. For now."

"One? You think that's going to make a difference?"

"My wife thinks the world of him."

"Your wife? What—" Giorgos chuckled. "Okay, wiseass, when do you leave for Naxos?"

"ASAP."

"I really appreciate that."

"Understood."

"Have you found anything helpful in her notebooks?"

"Just a lot of possibilities to follow up on."

"Any chance of an ID on the hacker from her sketchbook?"

Andreas sat up straight in his chair. "What sketchbook?"

"She always carries a sketchbook with her to draw images of the people she met and places she visited. Interviewees don't always care for cameras, so she sketches them later from memory. We don't put them in her articles, but she saves them in case a source later denies giving her the interview."

"Where did she keep her sketchbook?"

"Usually in the back pocket of her jeans. It's about the size of a thin paperback with a simple brown leather cover. She never goes anywhere without it."

"What are the chances it contains a drawing of whoever called you?"

"If she interviewed him, I'd say it's a given."

"My detective didn't find it in her room. That's too bad. It'd be helpful to know what our kidnapper looks like."

"You think she was kidnapped?"

"She disappeared, no one's heard from her, and you receive a call from a stranger telling you not to worry, she's safe, because he's protecting her. If not a crank call, it sure sounds like a kidnapping to me. Which makes it all the more important that you—and your publisher—don't let the story get out to your media colleagues."

"But the caller didn't ask for ransom."

"All that means is money isn't why he took her."

"Shit."

"And that he's likely a psycho." Andreas's other phone line rang. "Gotta run, it's my detective calling from Naxos. Let me know the moment you hear anything more from Nikoletta's *protector*."

Andreas hung up on Giorgos and answered the other line with a grunted "Yes?"

"That's a cheery greeting to hear first thing in the morning."

"It's not the first thing in the morning, and I'm not in a cheery mood. I made the mistake of answering my phone before having my first cup of coffee and haven't been able to get one yet."

"At least you had the chance to wake up. I may need to glue my eyelids open. I haven't slept. I tried, but my mind kept running through all the things Nikoletta wrote about the people she interviewed. The interviews are blending one into another, and I've got to talk to the mayor in an hour."

"I'm sure you'll handle it fine, but just in case you'd like to slow down, take a nap, or maybe even spend some time at the beach, don't worry, everything's under control."

"Uh-oh. What bad news are you about to drop on me?"

"Nikoletta's editor just received a voicemail from her potential kidnapper telling us not to worry, he's protecting her."

"What?"

Andreas filled him in on his conversation.

"I never saw a sketchbook," said Yianni, "and I searched her room thoroughly."

"I know, but when you have the chance, take another look at it from the perspective of someone looking for a hiding place."

"I'll do it as soon as I get off the phone."

"Don't run off just yet. Have you told Dimitri that the bar owner's description of a stranger hanging out in his place the night Nikoletta met the hacker matches the dead tourist?"

"Not yet. I plan on telling him when he picks me up this morning. That should spice up his morning almost as much as you've done mine."

"I have some good news for you too. I'm coming to Naxos tomorrow to help with the investigation."

"Terrific. I can definitely use the help running down suspects."

"Maybe you'll get lucky in your meeting with the mayor."

"Who knows, but it should be interesting. I hear he plans on turning it into a PR event to announce the disappearance of the reporter and claim the local police chief isn't competent to handle the investigation—as evidenced by the fact that Athens sent me here."

"I was afraid of something like that. Why avoid taking a swipe for political gain, even if it risks a woman's life? Does the mayor know you're friends with the chief?"

"Dimitri's the one who told me, so I doubt it."

"Sounds like you're in for a hell of a morning."

"The good thing is, it'll at least wake me up."

"Some folk like to get their morning jolt from a cup of strong coffee, others opt for bare-knuckles conflict. I guess you fall into the latter category."

"Frankly, I prefer sex, but since that's currently unavailable, I think I'll have to settle for doing my best at screwing the mayor."

"On that, I think I'll say goodbye and leave you to your good times."

———

Dimitri had left a note for Yianni with the hotel receptionist apologizing for not arranging to pick him up for his meeting with the mayor, but since the mayor hadn't invited Dimitri to attend, it seemed best that Yianni not show up with a police escort. Instead, he left Yianni the keys to an unmarked motorbike parked outside the hotel.

Greeks and their intrigues. They never end.

Yianni's drive to Naxos's town hall took considerably longer than he anticipated. From a map, he'd estimated five minutes, but a gnarled web of one-way streets filled with tavernas, shops, hotels, and tourists anxious to get to the beach made it seem as though he'd never get there. After twice finding himself caught in a loop taking him away from town hall, he decided to make up a route of his own. He made a U-turn and headed due south along the harbor front aimed directly for town hall, ignoring a host of ONE WAY and DO NOT ENTER signs along the way—not to mention a flurry of honking horns and salty gestures from oncoming drivers.

Town hall overlooked the southern end of the harbor and served the Naxos and Small Cyclades Municipality governing Naxos and its neighboring smaller islands of Iraklia, Schinoussa, Koufonissia, and Donoussa, among others. Of Naxos's 18,400 residents, 13,000 lived in Chora and its environs, which meant approximately seventy percent of the population lived within roughly thirty percent of the island's territory. The balance lived in the sparsely populated but much larger rural territory north, east, and south of Chora. Police divided coverage responsibilities between headquarters in

Chora and an auxiliary office at the center of the island in Naxos's second largest village, Filoti.

Yianni parked directly in front of the town hall in a spot overlooking a smaller replica of the massive marble *Sphinx of Naxos* donated nearly 2,600 years ago by the people of Naxos to the Temple of Apollo at Delphi. Town hall's modern-day version of that ancient guardian stared straight out to sea, ever vigilant for any sign of danger headed its island's way.

The relatively new, two-decade-old town hall bore no resemblance to any ancient architectural style associated with the sphinx, and little to the old town's distinctly thirteenth-century Venetian influence. Still, its neoclassical design, ecru stucco front, and parallel rows of turquoise windows framed in white marble sublimely complemented the Kastro's three-hundred-year-old former School for Girls—perched high atop the old town in the ideal spot for looking down upon her much younger brother.

The town hall's main entrance stood between a pair of Doric columns supporting a second-story marble balustrade and terrace fronting a set of French doors. From his experience with other town halls, Yianni assumed the French doors and Il Duce–style balcony opened into the mayor's office.

Yianni stepped into the vestibule leading to the main entrance and reached for the door handle, but there was none. He tried pushing against the door, but it wouldn't budge. He could see people inside, but no one stepped forward to open the door. As obvious a grand entrance as it was, this wasn't the way in.

He turned around, looked left, looked right, went left, and made another left at the end of the building. There he found an open door leading into a short hallway lined with offices.

He smiled. His superstitious aunt would say he'd just received a message from the gods: *Be wary of the obvious.*

Chapter Five

As soon as Yianni stepped inside, a man asked if he was there for the press conference.

"No, I'm here to meet with the mayor."

"About what?"

Yianni smiled. "I don't mean to sound rude, sir, but my business doesn't concern you. The mayor's expecting me, so why don't you just tell him Detective Kouros is here to see him?"

"Oh, so you *are* here for the press conference. The mayor left instructions for you to go directly inside." He pointed toward an atrium at the center of the building, where a lone olive tree grew beneath a pyramid-shaped skylight. A second-floor balcony, trimmed with scenes from classical Naxos, encircled the atrium floor.

At one end of the atrium, reporters milled about a podium, waiting for a press conference to begin. Yianni shouldn't have been surprised. It wasn't often that a mayor from a traditionally non-newsworthy island had the opportunity to draw national coverage. Announcing the now-famous reporter's disappearance would make headline news for sure.

Yianni recognized some of the reporters from Athens and stood back from them, not wishing to draw their attention.

"Detective Kouros, how nice of you to show up."

Yianni swung around to see a short, well-tanned man with a bouncing belly, badly dyed brown hair, and a well-rehearsed smile.

"I'm sorry, sir. I don't believe we've met."

"I'm the mayor." He extended his right hand. "The reception-ist told me you're here, and I came right down." He pointed to a staircase behind him. "After all, we don't want to keep the press waiting."

"Excuse me, sir, but I'm not here for a news conference. I'm here to ask you about your meeting with Nikoletta Elia."

"All in good time." He patted Yianni on the shoulder. "But first we must alert the press and my fellow Naxians to what has befallen her and assure them that we, their public servants, are doing all that we can to find her."

"We are. But having a news conference to announce her dis-appearance and my unit's involvement could endanger her life."

"I don't see how you can say that. It will mobilize the com-munity to look for her."

"If there's actually been a kidnapping, and the kidnapper learns he's the subject of a nationwide manhunt, the attention might spook him into doing away with her. Your local police are already doing all the right things. I'm only here to provide them with additional manpower."

The mayor's perpetual smile turned sharklike. "That's bull-shit and you know it. The local cops are inept and couldn't find a souvlaki at a soccer match. You're here because the reporter's newspaper and your minister insisted that your unit step in and take over the investigation. I will not be party to a cover-up of this poor woman's kidnapping."

Yianni leaned into the mayor. "I don't know who put those ideas in your head, but I suggest you reconsider whatever you plan on saying to the press."

Any semblance of a smile disappeared. "Is that a threat?"

"No, just some professional advice from one public servant to another."

"I was hoping you'd participate in the press conference, but it's far from necessary. You're here, and that's all the backup I need for what I have to say on the subject."

"Feel free to say whatever you think serves the interests of your island, but there's something I should tell you."

"What's that, another threat?"

"No, another fact. My chief arrives tomorrow, because he's also concerned with the safety of Nikoletta. You've now been warned about the risks to her life presented by proceeding with your press conference. If Chief Inspector Kaldis thinks that what you say to the media in any way jeopardizes her life, he'll tear you apart in the press, not to mention what he'll do to you in the eyes of all your perceived political friends back in Athens."

"I'm not afraid of him."

"Well, you should be. Perhaps you forget that our unit's mandate extends to investigating suspected official corruption wherever we find it. Why you're so hell-bent on undermining your local police chief, no matter the risk it presents to the reporter's life, will undoubtedly pique my chief's interest." Yianni put his hand on the mayor's shoulder. "Are you up for risking your political career for a few passing headlines and the chance to take a cheap shot at your police chief?"

He let his hand fall from the mayor's shoulder. "I'll be waiting here when you're done. We still have to talk about your conversation with Nikoletta."

The mayor turned and walked briskly toward the journalists, but with a noticeable slump to his shoulders. Reporters began shouting questions at him, but he paid them no attention until he was behind the podium and cameras were rolling.

He stared straight at Yianni as he spoke. "I'm here to answer any and all of your questions, but first let me say why I've called you here. I want you and the nation to know how proud I am of our island's professional hardworking police force, which has spared no effort to identify the poor tourist who tragically perished here."

"Is that why you called this press conference?" yelled a reporter. "Just to say thank you to the police?"

He stared at the reporter. "I wouldn't think any of you'd have a problem with that. On Naxos we value our police and everything they do to keep all of us, tourists and locals alike, safe and secure. Don't you agree it's about time they got the recognition they deserve?"

Yianni smiled. *Nicely played, Mister Mayor.*

———

Yianni had to give the mayor credit. He'd handled the sharp questioning with patience, offering little in terms of substance, yet tossing out a teaser to keep them coming back. "We expect very soon to identify the tourist who perished in that tragic fall onto the rocks below Grotta."

That prompted a shouted round of additional questions.

"It's part of an ongoing investigation," the mayor deflected, "and we'll provide you with more details as soon as we've confirmed them and notified the next of kin."

When the press conference ended, the mayor hurried out of the atrium, made his way up three flights of marble steps to the second floor, and headed straight for a doorway centered on a glass-enclosed office suite marked MAYOR—with Yianni right behind him.

Inside, the mayor stopped momentarily to speak with a woman

sitting at a desk in front of a set of French doors and across from the open door to a corner office. He glanced back at Yianni and grunted, "Follow me."

The office was furnished in what Yianni considered *politician traditional.* An imposing, highly polished wooden desk, a luxurious high-back leather swivel chair, a pair of far simpler guest chairs, an oval conference table with matching chairs, and a comfortable sofa set off to one side of the room. The sofa undoubtedly was meant for those occasions when, by sitting next to his visitor, the mayor could convey that his guest was among his most valued and trusted confidants.

The office also displayed the obligatory photographs of celebrities and powerful officials who'd passed through the mayor's life. Angled on his desk for all to see stood a photo of his wife, children, one dog, and one cat.

Without waiting to be invited, Yianni sat in a chair directly across from the mayor.

"Okay, Detective, I did what you wanted. What else do you need to know so that I can get you out of my hair?"

"I'd appreciate your telling me everything you recall about your meetings with Nikoletta Elia."

"It was *one* meeting, and I found her to be a charming and intelligent woman interested in fairly portraying Naxos to her readers."

"You're done with the press conference, and though I sincerely admire the way you handled the press, don't waste your charms on me. I've read her notebooks, and we both know that at one point she told you to stop bullshitting her with 'Chamber of Commerce' answers."

The mayor rolled his eyes. "Well, if you already know what we said to each other, why are you wasting my time asking me to repeat myself?"

"I have a couple of reasons. One, to see what she may have left out of her notes, and two, to decide whether I can trust you're telling me everything. So let's get back to what she asked and what you answered."

They sparred back and forth for the next twenty minutes, but the answers the mayor grudgingly gave were consistent with what Nikoletta had recorded in her notebook.

"So, my final question—at least for now—is who else did you suggest she interview for her article?"

"Let's be frank, Detective. As I see it, Nikoletta was into this story for the glory. It's why she wrote the piece about a computer criminal. Next, she wanted to write an article about what she thought was a war brewing between our tourism industry and agricultural interests. Contractors versus conservationists. Yes, she asked me for the names of the biggest, most important players on all sides of what she saw as a potential controversy. I wasn't about to give her the names of firebrands who'd stoke her into doing a hatchet job on the island, so I gave her the names of people who I knew would only say good things about the island. If she wanted revolutionaries and naysayers, she could find them on her own."

"Did she find them?"

"I don't know. My job is to protect the island, and that means its reputation. Encouraging bad press falls outside my job description."

"Okay, let's try a different approach. Who are the island's firebrands, revolutionaries, and naysayers?"

The mayor's face turned crimson. "All they'll try to do is wind you up with crazy conspiracies and theories. How's that going to help find the missing woman?"

"I won't know until I speak to them. But let me put your mind at ease. She never believed what you told her. Here's what she had to say."

Yianni read from his notes. "'The mayor must think I'm an idiot. He gave me a list of political cronies who'll give me only politically correct answers. He must be hiding something. I'll have to get leads elsewhere.'"

Yianni looked up. "Sounds like your recommendations didn't cut it with her. So…names, please. It'll speed up the investigation, and perhaps even save her life."

The mayor spit out a list of names, accompanied by various creative epithets.

As it turned out, every name mentioned by the mayor had found its way into Nikoletta's notebooks, which also contained a few that weren't on his list. She'd obviously been thorough in her research. Perhaps too thorough for islanders like the mayor, who don't like the threat of bad press.

Yianni thanked the mayor for his time and cooperation, but the mayor said nothing in reply, only pointed Yianni toward the door, not rising to shake his hand or show him out.

I guess that means I did my job.

———

After calling Andreas to brief him on how he'd indelibly ingratiated himself to the island's mayor and texting Dimitri the description of the man he'd been told was watching Nikoletta and the hacker the night they met, Yianni moved on to the next name on Nikoletta's list, Marco Sanudos, head of the Naxos Hoteliers' Association. They'd arranged to meet at Marco's hotel. A map showed it to be approximately five kilometers from Naxos town hall, close by a popular beach. Since it didn't seem that far, Yianni decided to use the motorbike rather than accept Dimitri's offer of a car and driver.

It was a sunny, warm morning, with very little wind, a perfect day for a bike ride along the miles of open beach that Naxos took such pride in offering to the world. Less than a kilometer into his planned route, Yianni realized the maps were not as precise in describing the state of the roads as he'd hoped, so much so that he should have taken Dimitri up on his offer of a driver.

The paved road running from the town hall south along the sea soon turned away from the beach and into a maze of back streets that had Yianni turning first one way and then another in an effort to keep moving parallel to the sea. When he came upon a broadly paved road running next to the beach, he thought he'd found his way, but it soon turned into a dirt road before joining up with a main road that took him away from the sea in the direction of the airport.

At a sign for Agios Prokopios Beach, he decided to put his faith in the saint whose namesake beach he was looking for and took a right, heading west. It took him past the salt pond he'd seen when his plane landed and along a narrow paved road winding between borders of bamboo windbreaks and ancient stone walls. He drove alongside fields and pastures of varying shades of greens and browns, some no doubt growing seed potatoes for Naxos's most famous crop. It was not the by-the-seashore sort of ride he was looking for, but still scenic. Missing, though, were road signs with even a hint at how to find Marco's hotel.

After a slew of wrong turns and dead ends, Yianni pulled over, took out his phone, and in an act some might see as a repudiation of divine guidance, switched his faith to GPS.

By the time he spotted the first sign for the hotel, he was already there. It sat atop a slight rise overlooking the beach. The resort complex, equipped with two huge swimming pools, a spa, shops, bar and dining facilities, tennis courts, and a private beach, had virtually everything required to keep the clientele happily on property, free to spend their time and money there and nowhere else.

He parked the bike by a freshly painted white building trimmed in cerulean blue and dominated by a soaring all-glass entrance-way framed in white marble. Yianni followed a sign marked RECEPTION pointing toward the building. A short, fit man a few years older than Yianni waited for him inside the door.

"Detective Kouros, I presume. I'm Marco Sanudos."

"How did you know it was me?"

They shook hands and the man smiled. "Very few of our guests arrive on motorbikes, and even fewer without luggage. Frankly, I was a bit concerned when you didn't show up at our appointed time, especially after the mayor called to tell me you'd been to see him and left."

"How nice of him to call."

"I think he was more interested in warning me to be careful of what I say to you."

"Does he have a habit of doing that, or is it a special honor reserved just for me?"

"He means well," Marco smiled, "as long as you're not inter-fering with his priorities."

"What's that mean?"

"May I suggest we continue this conversation in my office?"

He told a young woman sitting behind the concierge desk to send water, coffee, and pastries and led Yianni into a room behind reception. The room's only masonry wall was a long one shared with reception, the rest glass, arranged in a perfect semicircle looking on to the pool area.

"Wow, how do you get any work done in here? I'd either be mesmerized by the view or worried who might be watching me."

"The view you get used to, and the glass is one-way." He pointed to a stylish chrome and leather chair in front of a teak and chrome desk. "Please, make yourself comfortable."

Yianni sat down as a waiter arrived with a coffee tray. After the waiter left, Marco said, "What I didn't want to get into out there in front of my staff was that I'm much closer to your friend Dimitri than I am to the mayor. Dimitri told me you'd scuttled the mayor's plans for sticking it to him, and that really pissed him off."

"How do you know about my friendship with Dimitri?"

"He called me not long after the mayor did. He said you were a friend who could be trusted and that you'd likely get lost on the way here." Marco looked at his watch. "He asked that I let him know if you hadn't made it by now."

"I'm flattered everyone's so worried about me."

Marco smiled. "We've lost a tourist and may have lost a reporter. I guess no one wants us to lose a cop, too."

"So you know about Nikoletta?"

"The mayor told me. He also said not to share her potential disappearance with anyone."

Yianni nodded. "I can understand your concern about losing more folks. From my limited experience in getting from town to here, I'd say Ariadne and her Labyrinth crowd must have played a big role in laying out Naxos's street plan."

Marco laughed. "You're not the first to suggest that. But better roads come at a price, and I don't mean just their construction costs. They change the nature and character of a place. Easier accessibility means greater numbers of visitors to an area, and that brings other changes."

Yianni stared at Marco. "Whose side are you on? I'd expect you to be all in for tourism?"

"I am all in for tourism, just not to the point that I want to see our island trampled to death. I was born and raised here. My grandfather started this hotel, my father expanded it, and now it's my turn to shepherd it forward. I'm committed to sensible planning, sensible preservation, sensible progress."

"Nicely put. Does the mayor know you're after his job?"

"Not interested. This is my passion, not politics."

"Did you have this kind of conversation with the reporter?"

"Yes. I sensed she didn't believe I was sincere."

So far he's consistent with what's in Nikoletta's notebook. "What made her think that?"

"She asked whether I had plans to expand the hotel, and I said yes. Why not? This is a hotel area. We wouldn't expand onto the beach but onto property adjacent to the beach. There are plenty of other virtually undeveloped beaches that can and should be preserved as they are."

"My guess is your fellow islanders who own property on those undeveloped beaches wouldn't agree with you."

"They don't, but that's not unique to Naxos; it's a national problem. We only want *others* to bear the burdens of preserving our country's natural resources."

"Perhaps I was wrong in suggesting you're running for mayor. Sounds more like prime minister to me."

He shrugged. "Right now I'm confining myself to simpler issues, such as limiting the number of cruise boats allowed to dock on any given day."

"How big a problem is that?"

"It chokes the old town for the few hours they're in port, but otherwise they have a limited effect on the island. The bigger issue is expanding the airport."

"Is there a plan to do that?"

"There's a lot of wishful thinking in some quarters, and anxiety in others, because extending the runway to accommodate big jets would significantly impact the island."

"What do you think will happen?"

"Frankly, I don't think Naxos will have much say in it, one way or the other."

"Why's that?"

"Because the airlines, cruise lines, and airport authorities don't want Naxos to have an international airport."

"Why not?"

"The most expensive per-mile air route in Europe is between Athens and Mykonos. Mykonos has expanded its airport and operates twenty-four hours a day, seven days a week. It's a transportation hub for this part of the Cyclades. Big jets land there, and tourists head to its ports, where boats transport them to other Cycladic islands. It's a simpler and more profitable arrangement for big-time transportation interests than having another international airport so close to Mykonos. Santorini serves the same role in its part of the Aegean."

"Did you tell that to the reporter?"

"It didn't come up, but she might have heard it from someone else. It's not a secret."

"What *did* you tell her?"

Marco gave a thoughtful recitation of everything he could recall of their conversation, which matched what Nikoletta had entered in her notebooks. She'd also describe him as "cute," but Yianni decided not to share that bit with him.

"So, what do you think happened to her?" asked Yianni after Marco had finished describing his conversation with Nikoletta.

"I have no idea. Yes, there are strong passions on this island over its future direction, but enough to kidnap a reporter over a story about any of that?" He shook his head. "I don't see it."

"But what if she uncovered something someone didn't want exposed?"

"You mean corruption?"

"That's one possibility."

"I think it's safe to say that everyone on this island already knows who's corrupt, and a reporter threatening to expose what's already known wouldn't likely lead the bad guys to harm her. That would be a surefire way of generating far more serious trouble for them than anything she planned on exposing."

"So what's *not* known that could have endangered her?"

Marco again shook his head. "I don't know. There are crazies everywhere in this world, doing the unimaginable in the most unlikely locales. Who knows what could have happened here, who she met, what she said or did, even innocently, that triggered a response otherwise incomprehensible to rational, sane people?"

"That's not the answer I was hoping for."

"I truly wish I had a different one."

"Do you know anyone who might?"

"Sure, speak to the activist folks."

"Where would I find them?"

"Some of the island's most vigorous activists call Halki home, or at least consider it friendly territory. Besides, it's a cool village to visit."

"I can see why you represent so many disparate interests. You only have nice things to say about everyone."

He gestured no. "No, not everyone. But my disputes with them are unrelated to any of this, and even with my worst enemy, neither of us would go so far as to physically harm the other. It's just not our way." He smiled. "At least not when sober."

"On that note, thank you, I'll be on my way."

"Not yet, please. Dimitri sent a pickup truck to take you and your motorbike to your next appointment."

"Did he say why?"

Marco smiled again. "No, but my guess is that after your experience getting here, he doesn't think it's a good idea for you to be wandering about the island alone looking for whatever village it is you want to see."

"It's marked on a map. How difficult could it be to find?"

"What's the village's name?"

"Siphones."

Marco lost his smile. "Oh."

"What's that mean?"

"That village has been abandoned since the 1950s."

"It can't be the only abandoned village on the island."

"It's not."

"So, then what's with the *oh*?"

Marco hesitated. "Locals claim it's haunted."

"*Oh.*"

Chapter Six

Yianni stood alone outside the hotel entrance, speaking on his mobile with Andreas.

"So, how did your Naxos friendship tour work out with the head of the hotelier association? Better than with the mayor, I hope."

"A lot better." Yianni described his conversation with Marco in detail, leaving out only the parts about his trouble finding the hotel.

"What did you think of him?"

"Came across as a nice guy. He sounds like a politician, always trying to find middle ground."

"Always *seemingly* trying to find middle ground, but as you pointed out, his middle ground allows his hotel business to expand while cutting out potential competition from other beaches."

"But it does make sense, Chief. It might just be a matter of working out satisfactory compensation for those restricted from building on their property."

"I don't even want to contemplate what that process would be like, how long it would take, or the sorts of shenanigans it would bring into play. If Marco thinks getting an international airport on Naxos would be politically difficult to achieve in the face of opposition from other Cycladic islands, imagine what his *middle ground* proposal would involve. I assure you getting individual islanders to give up their property rights so that their neighbors can profit from land they're allowed to use will require nothing short of a political miracle."

"Okay, I get your point. But nothing Nikoletta could've written struck Marco as a reason for a local to kill her."

"So he says. He prefers the *random crazy attacker* scenario or, if not that, perhaps a cabal of vigorous village *activists.*"

"What do you think he's hiding?"

"I've no idea if he's hiding anything. But I do think he's trying to take the heat off like-minded Naxians by suggesting we concentrate on crazies and activists. To me the bottom line is simple. He may not like the mayor, and certainly the two men have very different styles, but they share a core principle: Above all else, protect the reputation of the island."

"In other words, I should continue doing what I'm doing. Question everyone, believe no one, and be ready for your arrival tomorrow."

"I'll let you know what flight. By the way, what are you driving?"

"Funny you should ask. I think I see my new ride headed this way."

"Come again?"

"I've been using a motorbike, but it's not good for the terrain I have to cover next, so Dimitri is sending me new wheels and a driver who knows the island."

"What kind of wheels?"

"Give me a minute; it's almost here." Yianni paused. "My oh my, you're not going to believe this."

"I'm all ears."

"Then I guess I should start humming the tune to that Eagles song about a girl in a flatbed Ford, because that's precisely what's headed my way."

Andreas groaned. "Call me later."

———

Officer Popi Sferes was twenty-three, two years out of the police academy and freshly married to a local. She wore her dark-brown hair in a tight bun, no makeup, a light-blue police blouse, dark police trousers, and black leather high heels. Yianni never understood why so many female cops wore heels, but in this case he did. Without them, Popi would've been barely tall enough to meet the police force's minimum height requirement.

She introduced herself as his driver and official guide to the island. "My chief thought that since my husband is local, my presence might help convince other locals to talk with you."

"Sounds reasonable."

"Reason doesn't necessarily work here."

"Meaning?"

"Let's get the bike into the bed of the pickup, and I'll explain later."

Yianni nodded and rolled the bike to the truck as Popi dropped the tailgate. Yianni braced himself to bear the brunt of the weight on the lift, and together they counted, "One, two, three, *lift*."

Yianni nearly lost his balance and dropped his side of the bike while Popi lifted her half with the strength of a man twice her size.

She smiled. "Surprised you, didn't I?" She reached for a set of tie-downs in the bed of the pickup, tossed one to Yianni, and together they lashed the bike in place.

"Sure did. Could you let me in on whatever brand of vitamins you use?"

"No vitamins, just the hard life of a farmer's daughter in the rock-infested Peloponnese, plus years of weightlifting competitions to make up for what has me wearing high heels whenever I'm asked to meet a visiting dignitary."

"I'm hardly a dignitary."

"Maybe not, but you didn't try mansplaining me into why I shouldn't be lifting the bike, so I'd say you qualify as a pretty good guy."

"My girlfriend gets the credit for training me well."

"Good for her." Popi walked toward the driver's door. "Are you ready?"

"Sure." Yianni opened the passenger's door and noticed a pair of women's flat shoes on his seat. He held them up. "What do I do with these?"

She slid onto the driver seat, kicking off her heels as she did. "I hate wearing heels." She took the flats from Yianni and put them on.

"So, what is it you promised to explain *later*?"

"It's a pitch I have for visitors to explain the nature of the people here. It saves them asking me a lot of questions." She turned on the engine and edged back out onto the road, headed in the general direction of the airport. "I can give you the Chamber of Commerce-approved version, or my cop-to-cop one."

"I think you know which one I want to hear."

"Just stop me if I bore you." Popi swallowed. "Naxos spent so many centuries occupied by foreign powers that some Naxians seem bred to be naturally suspicious of everyone and jealous of their neighbors. For example, the Venetian aristocracy that once lived within Chora's Kastro walls literally and figuratively looked down on whoever lived outside their privileged castle. That same sort of snobbery exists in many respects today among their descendants."

She reached for one of two bottles of water in a cup holder between the seats. "The other bottle's for you."

"Thanks."

"Then you have the farmers and herders who live outside of town. They're not only considered ignorant peasants by many who live in town, but they're also often consumed by rivalries with neighboring villages." She took a slug from the bottle. "On top of all that local bullshit, you've got the resentment Naxos as an island bears toward its neighbors, Paros and Syros, and vice versa."

"What gripes does Naxos have with them?"

"Basic islander jealousy pretty well covers it. But with Syros it runs a bit deeper. In antiquity, Naxos was rich and important far beyond any of its Cycladic neighbors, other than the holy island of Delos. But all that changed once Naxos was conquered. Centuries later, after Greek independence, Syros emerged for a time as the cultural and economic center of the Cyclades, and the airs adopted by Syriots riled Naxian pride to an extent they've never forgiven."

"You make them sound like rival football fans."

"Not a bad analogy," said Popi. "Which means I may not be of much help if whoever we're meeting with sees you as rooting for the other team."

"And the rival team for where we're headed would be...?"

"Greeks have a penchant for paranoid conspiracy theories. No telling how what you have in mind fits into their frame of reference."

Yianni shook his head. "So, what can you tell me about Siphones?"

"It's in a lovely location that's been abandoned for nearly seven decades for reasons no one seems clear about. Some suggest it was a lack of water, others say floods, a few claim villagers moved away after the emery mines closed and they lost their jobs or because it lacked a school for the children."

Yianni looked at her. "What do you think's the reason?"

"Hard to say, but other villages have persevered and continue to this day with far less in natural beauty and resources than Siphones. In fact, farmers still work the land there during the day but leave before dark rather than turning any of the abandoned homes into their own."

"Like I said, what do *you* think's the reason everyone moved on?"

"Honestly, I've no idea. There are rumors it was leprosy, but that seems somewhat dramatic...another quality we Greeks are known for." She paused. "Then again, there's the marble cross and plaque someone mysteriously erected at the village some twenty years ago. The plaque contains an engraved prayer dedicated to a saint revered for his magic and makes mention of healing the wounds from demons and their works of magic."

"And thus arises the haunted angle Marco mentioned."

"Some would even say cursed. At one point the plaque was smashed to pieces, and though it's been pieced back together on the ground, there's been no explanation for why someone went to the trouble of destroying something bearing a prayer asking for a saint to heal wounds."

Yianni shut his eyes and shook his head. "At the moment, I've got more than enough open mysteries on my plate. This new one I respectfully leave for you to solve."

"I just thought you might like to know the background of the people and place you're about to visit."

Yianni opened his eyes. "I know. I'm just complaining for the sake of complaining. Thank you for listening."

Popi smiled. "That's an admission I rarely hear from a man. Your girlfriend really did raise you right."

"It's been a challenge. For us both." He smiled at Popi. "But it's worth it."

She smiled back. "I know."

At a juncture with a main road just north of the airport, Popi turned left, then headed north.

"Are we heading back to town?" asked Yianni.

"Who's doing the driving?"

"Okay, I'll take that as a 'please shut up.'"

"No need to say please."

Yianni stared at her. "Why do I feel your husband and I have a lot in common?"

She turned right off the highway onto a narrow dirt road passing between broad swatches of farmland mixed in among fields of tall grass and newly baled hay. Tall bamboo, planted to protect the crops against strong Cycladic winds, lined both sides of the road, and of the handful of structures Yianni saw along the way, half looked to be businesses catering to tourists.

"Is this what most of Naxos is like?"

"Around here, yes. Away from here, no. We're on the edge of a fertile plain that spreads out south and east into major growing areas. Once we hit the highway, we'll be heading into the mountains and you'll get a bigger picture of where we are now."

"I think what you're trying to tell me is that down here, I can't see the forest for the trees."

"Yes, but more like you can't see the farmland for the bamboo. Naxos no longer has forests. Thanks to the practices of those who lived here before us."

Yianni stared out the window, wondering how this area might look a few years from now.

"Are you into goat herding?"

Yianni looked at Popi. "That's a strange question to come out of nowhere."

"You said you thought my husband and you had a lot in common."

Yianni paused for an instant. "Are you saying your husband's a shepherd?"

"That's for sheep. He's a goat herder and one of the best." Popi glanced at Yianni. "You seem surprised."

"I am. It's just so different from what we do."

"Not really. He spends much of his time like us, trying to keep critters in line who'd otherwise go astray at the first opportunity."

"Interesting perspective, but you must admit it's not the sort of career you hear much about these days."

"You do if you live in a rural community on Naxos. You may think being a cop is glamorous, but at least herding has profound biblical significance."

"We have more TV shows."

She smiled. "Good point."

Popi turned left onto a paved road, then right onto a two-lane highway lined with a hodgepodge of buildings and unkempt grounds typical of the sorts of businesses necessary for supporting a community.

She kept left each time the highway split. "Here's the road we want." She nodded toward a sign pointing left and marked KOUROS, KINIDAROS.

"Ah, at last, a chance to find myself," smiled Yianni.

"Huh?"

"That sign, it has my last name on it."

"Oh, I see, that was a joke. Next time warn me."

"I assume Kouros is where Naxos's famous six-meter long, unfinished marble statue of a young boy has lain on its back since the seventh century B.C.E."

"How'd you know that?"

"Trust me, if your last name also happens to be the term used to describe nude statues of young boys, you learn all about them, whether you want to or not."

Popi laughed. "Now *that's* funny."

"And I didn't even have to warn you." Yianni stretched. "So, how much longer until we get to Siphones?"

"We should make it in about a half hour, depending on traffic."

"What sort of traffic?"

"Slow buses, slow trucks, slow tourists, and of course, the ever-present possibility of goats on a road."

"You must know all the tricks for driving through a herd of goats."

"Yes, sit back, relax, and wait, because if you want to see a pastoral herder turn wildly insane, try driving through his herd and scattering his goats in every conceivable direction."

"Oh."

"Enjoy the ride."

They left the developed part of the island behind them, passed through rich bottomland plains, and began their climb up into the mountains. Each time the road narrowed down to run through a village, Yianni'd catch glimpses of the weathered faces of old men sitting on the front porch of their local *kafenio*. He wondered what thoughts passed through their minds as they sipped their coffees, watching so many vehicles stream by on their way to who knew where. Perhaps they thought of their children and grandchildren out working the farms and tending the flocks in the same age-old ways as they once had.

More likely how naive we city types are. Why would their kids, let alone their grandkids, be willing to put in the sort of fifteen-hour days of hard labor their lives once demanded?

As the pickup slowly passed close by a tiny, bougainvillea-draped stone house surrounded by daisies, poppies, and anemones, Yianni rolled down his window for a whiff of the scents. With that, he caught the rhythmic beat of cicadas nesting in a roadside patch of fig trees.

"Can it get any better than this?"

Popi smiled. "Just wait."

Once up in the mountains, the road turned to twists, switchbacks, and panoramic views of long, fertile valleys and stone-edged mountaintops. At times he'd see a slice of the distant deep-blue sea, or a mountain face shaved white for its marble. Down in the valleys, rows of olive trees swept up against fields of copper, emerald, and sage, while stone walls streaked with age held planted terraces snugly in place against sharply slanted hillsides.

In the bright early afternoon sunlight, every color showed true. Dots, dashes, spires, and blotches of green popped out against a richly earth-toned land deep into its seventh millennium of cultivation.

Roadsides boasted colorful flowers mixed with grasses, herbs, maquis, and gorse in among eucalyptus, fig, olive, oak, and other such hardy trees the ever-present rock and winds permitted.

Even the occasional concrete plant or marble quarry could not diminish the awe-inspiring majesty of the mountains' natural beauty or the timeless charm of old stone villages nestled against their slopes.

"This is truly beautiful," said Yianni, not taking his eyes off the view.

"I'm glad you like it," smiled Popi.

"It's hard not to. Do you live out this way?"

"I live south of here, by the Temple of Demeter."

"What's it like down there?"

"The temple sits on a hill with a view that every time I go by gives me more respect for the ancients' uncanny ability at picking the perfect sites for their holiest of places. Many consider it the most significant archaeological site on Naxos."

"Sounds like somewhere to take my girlfriend if she manages to get here this weekend."

"What's the lucky lady's name? My husband's is Mamas."

"Toni. She lives on Mykonos. Plays piano in a bar. Not exactly Mamas's biblical career, but it's a living."

"Speaking of intriguing, do you mind if I ask why we're going to Siphones?"

"I assume Dimitri told you about the missing reporter. She met some farmers in Siphones who were pretty outspoken about big money trying to ruin the island."

"They're not alone in that feeling. Especially among Naxians living outside of Chora."

"But aren't they used to that? After all, between the emery mines and marble quarries, this island's been getting sliced up for eons. And for much of the time, by foreigners."

"True, but what locals fear this time is a new type of foreign conquest. One fueled by big-money investors making changes in a few brief few years that outstrip the sum of all that the island has experienced in the past *six thousand* years."

"Sounds like the sort of fevered rhetoric that gets passions running high."

"You better believe it."

"Enough to kill someone?"

"I'm a cop; how could I ever rule that out?"

"What's your instinct, based upon living here?"

"There's a lot of tough, hard-thinking people on this island, and if they thought their way of life was under siege, I've no doubt they'd do what they felt they had to do to protect it."

"So much for the pastoral life."

She shook her head. "No, it's consistent. It is, after all, the responsibility of the herder to protect his flock from wolves."

Yianni stared at the side of Popi's face. "Are you suggesting it's reached the point where herders are going after the wolves?"

"No, I'm just answering your request for my instinctive opinion on what I believe could happen if those concerns aren't addressed."

Yianni looked straight ahead. *What the hell have I walked into?*

———

Just before the village of Moni, Popi turned left at a sign marked KERAMOTI-APOLLON. "We're ten minutes away from Siphones."

"I appreciated this brief chance at being a tourist. Thanks for driving."

"No problem. As often as I've been up here, I'm still blown away every time I see the mountains. I miss the ones back home in the Peloponnese."

She pulled off onto the side of the road just past a sign reading SIPHONES.

"Where's the village?"

"On the other side of the road. It steps down the hillside in terraces still farmed to grow crops like potatoes, cabbages, onions, tomatoes, and eggplants."

"How many old houses are here?"

"Hard to say, with so many in ruin, but I'd guess around thirty-five."

"That many?"

"This used to be a vibrant community, with lots of kids, lots of grapes, and lots of wine."

They walked across the road and stood at the edge of the hillside looking at the mountains to the south and west.

"They must get a hell of a sunset here."

"This view always makes me wonder why everyone left and, more significantly, why no one has returned."

Yianni nodded in the direction of a marble cross. "I assume that's where I'll find the plaque with the mysterious message."

"Yes."

He walked up the road to the cross and stared down at the remains of a broken plaque. Yianni knelt down to read the inscription. "It says precisely what you described." He took out his notebook and began to write.

"It's getting to you, isn't it?"

"That's the downside of being a detective. We can't resist a good mystery. But this time it's only curiosity, not professional interest." He stood up.

Popi pointed at a group of men gathered on one of the cultivated terraces. "Are those the ones you're here to see?"

"I won't know until I meet them. How do we get down there?"

"We walk under a bridge from the other side of the road. It's a bit overgrown, but that's the only way I know to get there." She started out across the road.

Yianni followed. "What's the snake situation on Naxos?"

"Ah, you're a city boy."

"As a matter of fact, my family is from your part of Greece, the Peloponnese."

"Then don't embarrass our roots by being afraid of snakes."

"I'm not afraid, just asking."

"Make a racket and watch where you step. They don't like you any more than you like them."

"I didn't say I didn't like them."

Popi managed to maneuver through a patch of tall thistle, and down nine stone steps to the edge of an overgrown four-meter stretch that ended at the mouth of a dark culvert running under the bridge. An algae sludge grew where a trickle of water seeped into the culvert from the hillside behind her.

Yianni stopped at the top and stared at the culvert. "You've got to be kidding."

"Don't worry; it's an old sluiceway for water running off the mountain. It's the water that still makes this place so attractive to farmers."

She picked up some stones and tossed a few into the weeds in front of her and the rest into the culvert. "That's to scare away whatever might be in there. But don't worry; I'll lead."

Yianni followed the path she'd made through the thistle and down the steps to where she'd stopped to throw her stones. "I take back what I said before about my having a lot in common with your husband."

"Why's that?" she asked from inside the culvert.

"Because the poor soul obviously has a lot more to contend with than I do."

As Popi continued though the culvert, Yianni heard, "Snakes, snakes, come meet the nice detective."

Chapter Seven

"Minister, I don't know who's pounding down your front door over this, but it's been only a little more than a day since we learned the reporter *might* be missing." Andreas switched the phone from his right hand to his left, picked up a pencil with his free hand, and began tapping the eraser end on his desktop.

"Detective Kouros is on Naxos conducting an investigation alongside the local police, and I'll be joining him tomorrow. If we do what you say you're being pushed to do and announce to the world that we believe she's been abducted, it will most certainly draw a lot of media attention, but as I've said before—and it deserves repeating—*that sort of attention could cause her abductor to panic and kill her.* Let's not forget there's been no ransom demand, so if there's been a kidnapping, her captor's motive is something other than ransom. If we can determine what that motive might be, it could be the lead we need to find her."

Andreas listened to the minister.

"Minister, I'm not questioning your motives or the sincerity of your concern for the reporter's safety. If I'm questioning anything, it's the agenda of whoever is pounding on you to do something that we both know is premature at best and fatal for the victim at worst."

He listened more.

"Of course there comes a time that alerting the media could be beneficial to a search, but we're not there yet."

And listened still more.

"By Sunday evening? That's virtually impossible."

Andreas and the minister argued back and forth on the date, but the most the minister would agree to was Monday at noon.

The minister hadn't revealed who was pressuring him to go public, but Andreas felt certain it was Nikoletta's publisher. What bothered Andreas was why her publisher was pushing so hard. Genuine concern for his reporter's fate? A sincere belief in the power of the media to help police generate leads? Or to sell newspapers and promote his paper's follow-up series on Nikoletta's reporting.

Whatever the reason, Andreas had until Monday to find Nikoletta. After that, the story of her disappearance would be all over the media, along with a slew of finger pointing at his unit for not finding her.

The sooner I get to Naxos the better. Andreas sighed—and snapped the pencil in half.

———

Yianni made it through the culvert, cursing all the way.

"That's certainly a novel way of clearing away critters," said Popi.

"It's the last time I'm doing something like that."

"Sorry to tell you, but that's the only way I know back to the truck."

"You can't be serious." He waved his hand in the direction of three men on a terrace below them. "Just get me over there."

They followed the sluiceway's flagstone bed beneath a canopy of fig trees and climbed up onto a path running by a group of tumbledown homes.

"What's that?" said Yianni, pointing at a dark pit.

"My guess is that's where they once stomped grapes to make wine. They still grow grapes here," she pointed at some vines, "but it doesn't look like there's much stomping going on anymore."

As they approached, the three men stopped their work, stood up tall, and watched the visitors approach. All three appeared lean and fit, dressed in similar jeans, work boots, and long-sleeved cotton shirts. Their difference lay in their choice of hats. One wore a broad-brimmed straw, another a Greek fisherman's hat, and the third an American-style ball cap bearing the symbol of an Asian tractor company.

Yianni waved as he stepped onto the terrace and approached the men. "*Yiasas.*"

The men did not return his wave or hello.

Yianni kept coming, smiling all the way. As he drew closer he noticed significant age differences in the men, accentuated by the varying years spent earning farmer tans on their faces, necks, and sinewy forearms.

He stopped in front of the man in the fisherman's hat, clearly the oldest of the three. "Good afternoon, sir. My name is Yianni Kouros. I'm a detective, and this is my colleague Officer—"

"We know Popi," said the man in the ball cap. "And don't waste your time talking to my father; he's not quite all there. Let him get back to his fieldwork before he gets upset and we have a hell of a time getting him home. He doesn't take well to changes in his routine."

Yianni looked at the one in the straw hat and nodded toward the old man. "Is he your grandfather?"

Straw hat looked at ball cap.

Ball cap nodded. "Answer the man, son."

"Yeah, we're all family."

The old man wandered away, and no one tried to stop him.

"He'll be okay," said ball cap. "He's like an old burro. Knows every inch of his land blindfolded."

"I don't mean to interrupt your work," said Yianni, "but if you could spare us a few minutes of your time, I'd appreciate it."

"The police chief said you wanted to know about that reporter who was nosing about here a few days ago."

"That's right."

"Why do you want to know about her?"

"She wrote a newspaper article about a man she met in Chora, and we're following up on that."

"You mean the computer guy?" said the son.

Yianni nodded. "We're looking for leads on who he might be."

That was the best cover story he could think of to hold off speculation over why cops were running all around the island asking questions about the reporter.

"Why don't you ask her?" said the son.

Yianni liked it better when the son was quiet. "Reporters like to protect their sources, so we have to go at it differently. I'm sure you aren't interested in protecting a criminal."

"What do you want to know?" said the father.

"What you talked about with her."

"How's that going help you find your man?" the son asked.

The kid was getting on Yianni's nerves.

Popi put her arm around the son. "Come, let's go find your grandfather and let your father and the detective talk."

He seemed reluctant to leave, but his father nodded, and he went with Popi.

"The reporter came here looking for dirt on how we felt about the growth of tourism on the island."

"What sort of dirt?"

"Who's corrupt, who are the big players behind development efforts, and what sorts of things they're doing to get their way. She also wanted to know about anyone I knew who was against development and what they were willing to do to stop it."

"What did you tell her?"

"The truth. There's corruption all across Greece. This place is better than most. Same thing with development. Places change; people move on. Just look around you." He waved his hand. "Grandfather was born here, but everyone's moved away. This place died, a new place somewhere else was born. It's part of the cycle of life."

Yianni stared at the man. "What's your name?"

"People call me Junior."

"Mine's Yianni. The thing is, Junior, I've heard you're not too happy with what's happening on your island. That foreign investors are coming to ruin Naxos, and you're all in for doing whatever it takes to see that doesn't happen."

Junior shrugged. "I don't know who'd have told you that, but I'm just a simple farmer. What do I know about foreign investors?"

"You live on an island where for millennia its people have lived under the domination and control of foreigners. Everywhere you look are reminders of that history. So, please don't bullshit me by saying you have no opinion on foreign investors threatening to occupy your island."

Junior glared and clenched his fists. "Are you calling me a liar?"

Yianni looked him straight in the eyes. "No, I'm calling you a bullshitter."

For an instant neither man moved or blinked.

Junior smiled. "Okay, that name I can accept."

Yianni returned the smile. "So, what did you tell her?"

"What I thought would impress her."

"I don't follow."

"Look, let's be realistic. I'm a bit old to be running around with those revolutionary types on the mainland tossing Molotov cocktails at what they see as symbols of their enemies. But I could tell she was looking for just that sort of angle for some story she was writing about farmers versus developers. So I made myself seem like a revolutionary."

"But why would you do that?"

"I may be too old to run around with revolutionaries but not too old to want to get into their pants."

Yianni felt certain his jaw had dropped. "Are you saying you slept with the reporter?"

Junior gestured no. "I tried my best routine—even tossed in a line about how the European Union with its memoranda has been occupying our country for a decade. But none of that worked. She took my story and took off. Didn't even accept my offer of sharing a bottle of homemade wine."

Nikoletta had left that bit about her afternoon out of her notebook. Perhaps because as a Greek woman she was used to that sort of approach from the men she met.

"But I heard that a group of you told her you'd burn down the foreigners' projects if necessary."

Junior smiled. "You heard right. More Molotov cocktail talk. The group you heard about was me, my son, and my father. I'll let you decide whether Grandpa could have agreed on anything. As for my son, he's bright for sure, but as you've seen, he goes along with what his father says."

Yianni burst out laughing. "What is it about Greek men that leads them to think they have a chance with every woman?"

"I don't know, but why do you think my son wandered off with Popi when he was having such a good time tormenting you?"

Yianni turned to look for Popi. She was nowhere to be seen.

"Don't worry. She's in no danger. Aside from her having a gun and a husband who could lift a bull, my son's a gentleman. It's just the thought of the possibility that makes men vulnerable to a woman's charms."

Yianni yelled out her name.

"Besides, Popi was raised on a farm among four brothers and learned how to handle men by watching them grow up making fools of themselves. Something we all seem to do from time to time."

Yianni saw Popi walking toward them with son and Grandpa in tow.

"See, I told you there was nothing to worry about."

Yianni hesitated. "Perhaps you could answer another question for me?"

"I'll try."

"Is there a way to get back up onto the road other than going through the culvert?"

"Yeah, head up the hillside below the monument and over the wire fencing. That will get you back on the road."

"Thanks."

"No problem. Just one thing."

"What's that?"

"Be careful of the snakes in the brush if you go that way."

———

Yianni grudgingly admitted to Popi that a few seconds' scoot through the culvert beat three minutes of not knowing what lay ahead of you in the underbrush.

Safely back in the pickup, he checked his phone for messages and saw one from Andreas telling him they only had until Monday noon before the whole world knew Nikoletta was missing. He called back, and when put into voicemail, left a brief message describing his interview with the Siphones boys.

"Everything okay?" Popi asked.

"Just routine stuff." He put his phone back in his pocket. "Before I forget, thanks for steering the son away from his father so I could speak to him alone. You did well, Officer."

"Thank you. I know the son. In fact, I know the whole family. The father sometimes hunts with my husband."

"That explains how he knew so much about your background."

"Hunting gives hunters a lot of time to talk among themselves. Sometimes too much time."

"He only told me good things, such as how your growing up among four brothers taught you to deal with Greek men."

"I wouldn't say that I'm fully up to speed on the intricacies of what makes them tick, but being the only sister had its advantages, even if I didn't appreciate them at the time."

"Meaning?"

"I was the baby of the family, so my brothers called me *Runt*, as in runt of the litter."

"Ouch. That must have hurt."

"But woe be unto anyone else who dared call me that or messed with me. My brothers were very protective. Too protective at times. They still tease me. Now, though, their favorite line is that I married Mamas because he's the only guy I ever dated big and strong enough to handle them."

"The father mentioned something about your husband being able to lift a bull."

"More like a calf, a big calf." Popi paused. "Do you mind if I ask the context in which that subject came up?"

Yianni wondered how much he should tell her, but if she hadn't drawn the son away he'd likely never have learned a thing from the father. "No, I don't mind. Just keep it among ourselves. This isn't gossip to share with anyone, including our cop colleagues over coffee."

"Understood."

"He claimed that everything he told the reporter was made up to impress her. That none of it was true."

"Did he say why he made it all up?"

"To use his words, he wanted to get into Nikoletta's pants by convincing her he was a Molotov cocktail–tossing activist."

She nodded. "That makes sense. It's priority number one for men in their dealings with women. At least most men, and not just Greek men."

"I'm not sure I'd go that far, but then again, I'm not in your shoes." He smiled. "Either heels or flats."

Popi laughed. "A deft change of subject."

"In this case, though, I believe the father," said Yianni.

Popi nodded. "From what I know of him and his family, I'd agree they're not the Molotov cocktail–tossing sort." She started the engine. "So, where do you want to go now?"

"I'm famished. Haven't eaten since breakfast, aside from a couple of cookies at Marco's hotel."

"There's a terrific taverna up the road in Koronos, and the drive there offers some of the most spectacular views on the island. Every time I'm up this way I eat there. It's a winding mountain road with plunging views into emerald valleys running out to the sea. Are you up for that?"

"How could I not be?"

She edged back onto the road around an old pickup that had parked off to the side of the road just beyond them.

"I've got a whole list of people to chase down, but not an address or telephone number for one of them. All I have are their names and their villages. Nikoletta apparently found them by going to the villages, striking up conversations with locals, and getting them to tell her where she could find their village's main *activist.*" Yianni turned to look out the side window. "She must have a real gift for getting people to talk. I find most villagers to be closemouthed when it comes to speaking to strangers."

"That's because you're a cop, and activists are wary of cops. In my experience, once you get them talking, the hard part is getting them to stop."

"But how do I find them?"

"I should be able to help you with that. This is a fiercely independent island, with tough people, but it's still a small community and if you're known and trusted, you can get that sort of information."

"Here are the names." Yianni pulled out his notepad and read off a half dozen names and villages.

"Oh, boy."

"Dare I ask what that means?"

"Remember what I said before about getting activists to stop talking? Well, you've got the equivalent there of a Eurovision competition among the biggest talkers on the island. I suggest you plan on spending the better part of a day with each one on your list. That is if you want a shot at getting any of your questions answered. They'll spend most of the time preaching to you about why they're right, the rest of the world is wrong, and you should join them in their cause."

Yianni thought of the new deadline Andreas had delivered. "I don't have that kind of time."

"I wish I could tell you something different, but they'll bend your ear for sure."

Yianni leaned his head back, shut his eyes, breathed in deeply, exhaled, and opened his eyes. "What's the chance of our getting all of them together in one place to meet with me as a group?"

"You mean turn it into an activist convention? They'll be

competing like cats for attention to show who's the most important."

Yianni smiled. "That's the point. They'll each have heard the other's pitch so many times they'll be shouting one another down to stop with the canned speeches. We might actually be lucky enough to get them competing with each other over who's giving better answers to my questions."

"Optimism is an admirable trait, Detective." Popi bit her lower lip. "I must admit, it's an interesting idea, and if we promise them food, wine, and liquor, it just might work. We can bill it as Athens reaching out to Naxos's leading thinkers in an effort to learn what's truly on the people's minds."

"That's laying it on a bit thick, wouldn't you say?"

"We're talking about self-styled politicians, and regardless of where they fit on the political spectrum, they all share one common trait: they love an audience."

Yianni smiled. "Are we back to your view on men?"

"In this case it's a gender-neutral phenomenon."

Yianni sat quietly for a moment. "Do you really think you can pull it off?"

"I can try. Once they learn who else is being invited, they'll all likely want to be in on it, if only not to lose out to a rival if something good comes out of the meeting. I suggest we hold our little get-together in a place activists consider friendly territory."

"Okay, go for it. Try to set it up for tomorrow afternoon. He'll be here by then, and I'm sure he wouldn't want to miss it."

"Is he a masochist?"

"No, more of a cat wrangler."

Andreas was doing his best to clear his desk of a mess of burning bureaucratic emergencies, but his usual approach—handing them off to Maggie—wasn't available. She had her own fires to put out, so he decided to take a different tack: Ignore everything, leave the office early, and spend the rest of the day with his children.

Andreas made it as far as his car before his mobile rang. It was a Naxos caller, but he didn't recognize the number.

"Hello, Kaldis here."

"Chief Inspector?"

"Yes, who's calling."

"It's Dimitri from Naxos."

"Oh, sorry, Chief. I didn't recognize your voice. You sound so serious."

"There's been an accident."

Andreas's heart skipped two beats. "Involving Yianni?"

"Yes."

Andreas swallowed. "How is he?"

"Banged up but hanging tough."

"How banged up?"

"As far as his doctors can determine, it's two broken ribs, but otherwise only sprains, bruises, and cuts. He was knocked around quite badly but doesn't appear to have sustained a concussion or internal organ damage. Still, they're keeping him heavily medicated and want him to rest undisturbed for now. Which means no questions from us."

"Thank God he's okay. Where is he?"

"In our Naxos General Hospital. That's where the ambulance brought them."

"Them?"

"My officer was driving. She wasn't as lucky as Yianni."

Andreas's heart dropped. "How is she?"

"Don't know yet. She was in a coma when they airlifted her to Athens. I'm waiting for word."

"What happened?"

"Their pickup went off the road just outside of Koronos, a mountain village up north. No idea yet if it was mechanical failure, or she swerved to avoid hitting an animal on the road, or something else."

"Something else like what?"

"At this point we're ruling out nothing."

Andreas drew in and let out a deep breath. "I'll be there tomorrow morning. When do you think you'll have a better fix on what happened?"

"We sent a mechanic and accident investigation team to the site. As soon as I hear anything from them, I'll let you know."

"What do you know so far?"

"The pickup went off a narrow two-lane mountain road at a sharp curve to the driver's left, over a cliff edge to the right, rolling before getting hung up on a massive boulder. It was a miracle they hit the boulder, because if they hadn't, the pickup would have rolled all the way down into the valley and they'd have had no chance of surviving."

Andreas crossed himself.

"Who found them?"

"A tour guide driving tourists back from Koronos saw the pickup on its back up against the boulder and called it in."

"Did the guide see what happened?"

"No."

"Bad luck."

"As a matter of fact, very good luck. It turned out that one of the tour guide's clients was a doctor, and she was able to stabilize them until the ambulance arrived."

Andreas crossed himself again.

"What are your instincts on the cause?"

"Let's just say Popi was familiar with the road and used to goats darting out from nowhere. She knew you don't swerve if you can't brake in time, especially in the mountains. Better a dead animal than you."

"So, we're left with something mechanical or your *something else*."

"That's how I see it."

Andreas fluttered his lips. "Please keep me in the loop on how they're doing, and let me know when I can speak with Yianni."

"Will do."

"Thanks."

They said goodbye, and Andreas put down the phone. He shut his eyes and said a brief prayer. He opened his eyes and wondered whether this was just a tragic coincidence or *something else*.

He knew what he had to do next. He just wasn't sure how best to go about it. He hoped the words would come. He looked at his phone, found the number he wanted, and called Toni.

Chapter Eight

Toni had heard so many good things about Naxos that she couldn't wait for tomorrow to come to join Yianni there. But that was before she spoke to Andreas. By the time they'd hung up, everything he'd told her was a blur, and she could only recall him saying there'd been an accident, Yianni was fine, but the doctors wouldn't allow him any visitors or callers.

To Toni, that did not sound like *fine*.

Her immediate reaction was to call the hospital and ask to speak to Yianni, but all that would do is kick her anxiety level into even higher gear once the hospital inevitably told her what Andreas had said. *No callers.*

She knew what she had to do next. She called her boss and told him she couldn't work tonight because her boyfriend had been in a serious accident on Naxos, and she had to get over there right away. Her boss said that if she didn't come to work tonight, she was fired.

She said that since the bar would be closed for the weekend anyway, what was the big deal?

He said it was nonnegotiable.

She said, fine, if he wanted to play a hard-ass, she'd tell his wife about his girlfriend. He said he didn't care.

Then she told him she'd tell his *girlfriend* about his *boyfriend*.

He paused for a moment before wishing her safe travels and asking that she please make it back to the bar as soon as Yianni was better.

Now she sat in the new port of Mykonos, waiting for the next boat to Naxos. The trip would take less than an hour, but she had absolutely no idea what she'd do once she got there. All she knew for certain was that she had to get to Naxos. Somehow she'd figure out what to do next.

After all, improvisation is how I make my living.

———

Lila hadn't been off the phone since Andreas called to tell her of the accident. She insisted on coming with him to Naxos, if only to comfort her friend Toni.

Her first call was to her mother, who agreed to watch the children and suggested Lila immediately call a close family friend to see if she could stay at her summerhouse on Naxos. The friend told her she was away, but Lila should use the home as if it were her own for as long as she needed.

That led Lila to call Maggie. Lila knew Maggie and her boyfriend, Tassos, would be headed to Naxos to be at Yianni's bedside. Tassos was Andreas's and Yianni's longtime police mentor and chief homicide investigator for the Cyclades. Lila invited Maggie and Tassos to stay with her and Andreas at her friend's house and said she'd pick Maggie up tomorrow in time to catch the first plane to Naxos. Maggie confirmed that Tassos would join them there by boat from Syros, and Lila said to tell him they'd meet him at the port.

With arrangements made, her next call was to Toni.

No answer.

She kept trying.

———

By the time the ferry docked in Naxos, Toni had a plan. The worst it could do was get her arrested, but since her boyfriend was a cop, she figured he'd be able to make things right…once *he* was right.

Stop thinking like that, she thought, and whispered to herself, "He's fine, just like the doctors said."

She knew she had to calm down if she wanted to pull this off, so she decided to walk to the hospital rather than take a taxi. The hike would bring her around. She pulled on her small backpack, disembarked, and headed for town. Her immediate problem was that she had no idea where to find the hospital. She stopped at a car rental agency by the entrance to the pier and picked up a map.

The hospital was about a kilometer away, depending on the route she took. She picked one crossing the harbor front that turned left at the main road into the port. The road ran by storefronts filled with goods aimed at enticing passersby, but Toni noticed none of it in her haste to reach the hospital.

The neat, one-story, white stucco and blue-trimmed medical center sat on the left, just beyond a rotary. She headed straight for the door marked ACCIDENTS AND EMERGENCY and joined three others sitting along a wall in the reception area, while a half dozen more waited in line for the receptionist.

The receptionist paid her no mind, and Toni sat as if patiently waiting for someone to arrive. The opportunity Toni'd been hoping for came in the form of an animated and rapidly accelerating conversation between the receptionist and an elderly local woman complaining loudly over how long she'd been waiting to see a doctor.

Toni stood and matter-of-factly strolled past the two combatants as if looking for a toilet. In the midst of her battle with the woman, the receptionist barely glanced at Toni. With a quick peek back to be certain the receptionist's eyes were not on her, Toni went left and darted through a door reading PATIENTS AND HOSPITAL PERSONNEL ONLY. It led into the emergency treatment room, which, as with most public hospitals these days, was staffed by overworked, underpaid professionals possessing neither the time nor inclination to care about who passed through their unit.

She aimed for a door at the far end, walking as if she knew precisely where she was headed. Once through the door, she circled back toward the reception area but entered the corridor beyond where she could be seen by the receptionist. Toni had no idea where Yianni could be in the building, and though Greek hospitals might not be finicky about who walked through their halls, if she started opening doors to patient rooms, she'd likely be escorted out in short order.

She heard a door open around a corner ahead of her. A serious-looking man in a white coat turned the corner headed straight for her. She gave him her most innocent smile. He said nothing until he'd passed her.

"If you're looking for a patient, Miss, their rooms are down this corridor in the halls to the left and right."

She turned to thank him but he'd already disappeared into the treatment room.

Thanking Lady Luck instead, Toni hurried down the corridor toward the rooms. At the intersection of the corridor with the hallways, she paused to listen for voices.

She peeked around the corner to her left. A nurse sat on a chair with her back to Toni, facing a monitor and chatting on her mobile. The nurses' hallway and the hallway to Toni's right each had four doors, a pair on each wall.

Toni's only chance at getting to Yianni without being seen by the nurse was if he was in one of the rooms to Toni's right.

Lady Luck, I need you again.

She crept along the wall leading to those rooms, paused at the first door, and listened. She heard a young woman singing a Greek lullaby.

She moved on to the next door but heard nothing. She'd reached for the door handle for a quick peek when she heard people in the room directly across saying goodbye. She yanked at the handle and jumped inside, just as a couple walked out of the other room loudly repeating their goodbyes. No way Yianni would be in there.

If Yianni wasn't in this room, or in the fourth room in this hallway, Lady Luck had let her down. Toni turned and looked at an empty bed. She shut her eyes and willed herself to believe Yianni was behind that fourth door.

She drew in a deep breath and reached for the door handle. That's when she heard an alarm.

How could they have found me?

She heard voices shouting and people running down the hall in her direction.

Oh well, I almost made it.

She opened the door, prepared to tell the truth, in time to see the nurse from the monitor race into the fourth room followed by the helpful man in white.

Yianni must be in there.

She ran to the fourth room's doorway and saw the two frantically working on a man hooked up to wires and tubes. An old man.

This was her chance. She raced across the corridor to the other four rooms and opened the first door. No Yianni. She opened the second. No Yianni. She opened the third. Her heart jumped at the sight. IVs, tubes, and monitors all connected to a sleeping, bandaged Yianni. She closed the door behind her, crept around the bed to a chair up by his head, sat, and smiled. "I'm here," she whispered.

She mouthed a thank you to Lady Luck, then thought of the old man whose crisis had generated the distraction. She hadn't seriously prayed in years, and long ago had lost all interest in organized religion, but if ever there were a time for appealing to an everlasting being on behalf of Yianni and the old man, this was it.

Toni sat quietly, drifting between joyful memories and abject fears for the future. She was deep in thought when a nurse bolted into the room, each startling the other.

"What are you doing in here?" the nurse demanded.

"He's my boyfriend. I'm just sitting here, not touching him, not saying anything. Just being here for him."

The nurse raised her voice. "I don't care who you are. You're not allowed in here. I don't know how you got in here, but if you don't leave at once, I'll call the police."

Toni gestured with her hand for the nurse to lower her voice.

"Don't tell me what to do; just get out of here." She pointed toward the door. "And I mean *now*."

Toni smiled and spoke softly. "Let's look at the situation. I've been in here for a good hour. Perhaps you can explain to the police how you allowed a complete stranger to gain access to a critically injured one of their own and remain undetected long enough to have done only God knows what sort of harm to him." Toni shook her head. "Come to think of it, I guess the police aren't your main concern. After all, how are you going to explain to your superiors what happened? This just might rise to the sort of thing that justifies terminating your job. Is that the kind of risk you want to take in this horrible economy? And for what?"

"You don't—"

Toni held up her hand. "Let me finish, please. I'm trying to help you out here. Why get into a fight that you can only lose? After all, the worst that happens to me is my boyfriend's buddies escort me outside, thank me for caring so much for him, and tell me to come back to see him tomorrow."

Toni raised and dropped her shoulders. "So, what's it going to be? A confrontation you can only lose or an act of compassion allowing all of us to win?" She pointed to Yianni. "Especially him."

The nurse closed her eyes and stood perfectly still—as if counting to ten—then abruptly turned and walked out of the room.

"I don't think I won a friend in that exchange," she whispered in Yianni's direction. "But I don't care, as long as I won the battle."

Toni went back to sitting quietly by Yianni's bedside, watching him sleep, and taking care to do nothing to disturb him. She noticed that his hand closest to her had begun to twitch ever so slightly. She reached over so that his twitching hand touched the top of hers. She felt him weakly grip her hand and lightly squeeze.

She struggled to fight back tears.

This battle she lost.

———

Andreas heard his cellphone ring. "Honey, would you grab my phone please? It's on the kitchen counter. I'm in the middle of changing the baby's diaper."

He tickled Sofia's belly. "Promise you'll never tell any of your tough guy daddy's buddies what you just heard him say." He tickled her again. She giggled. "I'll take that as a yes." Andreas finished securing her diaper, kissed her belly, and snapped up the bottoms to her onesies jumpsuit. "They wouldn't believe you anyway."

I can hardly believe it myself. He smiled. *And I owe all of this to the nanny's night off.*

"It's someone from Naxos named Dimitri," said Lila.

"Coming." Andreas carried Sofia from the nursery across the

apartment to the kitchen. He handed Sofia off to Lila in exchange for his mobile.

"Hi, Dimitri. How are our cops?"

"No change, which I'm told is a good thing."

Andreas clenched his jaw. "Let's hope so."

"I have news from my guys at the accident scene. That boulder was a lucky break for them for more than one reason. If the pickup hadn't hung up on it, they wouldn't have had such an easy time determining the cause."

"Easy time?"

"Like a neon sign announcing, 'Look here,' is how they described it. The driver side of the truck was caved in from the front wheel to beyond the door. Something hit it and sent it on its way off the road."

"What kind of something?"

"Likely another truck, or at least something big enough to inflict that much damage without its driver also losing control on impact. The place where it happened and timing were ideal for knocking them off the road. It was in the middle of a sharp left-hand curve, meaning momentum already had the pickup moving toward the edge when the collision occurred."

Andreas rubbed at his eyes with the thumb and forefinger of his free hand. "How can they be sure the damage wasn't caused by the pickup rolling over before hitting the boulder?"

"Indentations along the side of the pickup indicated impact with a bumper, and though the paint color on the impacting vehicle was close to the color of the pickup, it wasn't quite the same."

Andreas dropped his free hand down to his side. "How could Popi have missed a truck swerving into her lane?"

"That's one of many questions I hope each of them will soon be able to answer."

Andreas paused. "So, what's your gut telling you on this one? Another coincidental accident?"

"I'd sure like to think so. Otherwise, someone's out there targeting cops just for asking questions about the reporter."

"Can you think of any other reason why Popi might be a target?"

"Nope."

Andreas nodded. "Same with Yianni. At least not a target for anyone who'd bother to go to the trouble of making it look like an accident."

"That sort of thinking is what has me worried."

"Me too, and why I'm on tomorrow's morning flight to Naxos."

"By then we hope to have an ID on the dead tourist whose description matches the one Yianni obtained of the guy in the bar watching the reporter and her interview. It's not easy identifying foreigners like him unless they're in an accessible database or have been reported missing."

"Let me know as soon as you hear anything."

They exchanged goodbyes.

"How's Yianni?" asked Lila, still holding Sofia.

"No change."

"What about Toni?"

Andreas shook his head. "I don't know. I sensed she was in shock after I told her what happened, and I haven't heard from her since. Have you spoken to her?"

"No. I keep trying her on her mobile, but there's no answer."

Andreas bit at his lip. "I sure hope she's okay."

"She's a tough cookie. Lord knows what she's up to."

"I'm sure we'll find out soon enough." He walked to the refrigerator, opened it, and took out a beer. "Want one?"

"Since when have you switched to beer?"

"I read it's healthier than wine."

"And more fattening."

"Are you suggesting I'm fat?"

"No, but ask me again after you're on this beer kick for a month or so."

"Mommy, Daddy, come see what I did," shouted Tassaki from the living room.

"Dare we imagine?" said Lila, leading the way.

Tassaki sat on an Oriental rug covering part of the room's white marble floor. Spread out on the marble in front of him was a completed jigsaw puzzle depicting the Acropolis.

"Wow," said Andreas. "You did all that by yourself?"

"Yes, and it looks just like the real one." Tassaki smiled as he pointed out the window at the apartment's unobstructed view of the Acropolis.

"We're so proud of you," said Lila.

Sofia gurgled.

"Sofia is too," smiled Andreas.

"Now run off and get ready for bed. Then daddy will come read you a story."

"Yay!" Tassaki jumped up and ran off to his room.

"How many pieces are in that puzzle?" asked Andreas.

"Two hundred fifty."

"I couldn't do it."

"I wouldn't have the patience."

"Maybe you should bring one of his puzzles to Naxos," smiled Andreas.

"What are you trying to tell me?"

"Just that I'm going to be very busy there."

"We've been married long enough for me to have already figured that out."

"Just saying."

She stared at him. "I certainly hope you don't think I plan on getting in your way. I'm going to see Yianni and be there for Toni. Maggie and I—and if she's up to it, Toni—are more than capable of hanging out together and taking care of ourselves."

Andreas cleared his throat. "To pick up on your point, we've been married long enough for me to know your capabilities. I just don't want you doing something that attracts the wrong kind of attention."

"And just what's that supposed to mean?" Lila's hands now rested in fists upon her hips.

"Like drifting over into my line of work."

"That's just your cop brain talking." She waved him toward Tassaki's bedroom. "Go read your son a story. You won't be seeing him for a few days."

"I wish it were only my cop brain."

"What makes you think it isn't?"

"A journalist is missing and two cops are in a hospital, the apparent common connection being questions asked that someone didn't want asked. I don't want your healthy curiosity turning unhealthy."

Lila sighed. "Go read your son a bedtime story." She paused. "You both could use one."

Chapter Nine

The morning flight out of Athens had Andreas, Lila, and Maggie in Naxos by eight. After picking up their rental car, they made it to the hospital by nine. Dimitri was waiting for them outside Yianni's room, unsmiling.

"What's wrong?" asked Andreas.

"Is Yianni all right?" said Lila.

He faced Lila, but his expression did not change. "I'm Dimitri."

"Excuse me, Chief, I should have introduced my wife," Andreas nodded at Lila, "and our police colleague, Maggie Sikestis."

"Better known as his administrative assistant," said Maggie, extending her hand.

Dimitri shook their hands. "It's a pleasure to meet you both. I just wish it were under better circumstances. Yianni is fine. It is my officer who's not. She's still in a coma, but an infection has set in, and they may have to remove her spleen."

"Oh, my God," said Lila.

Andreas's head sagged and he exhaled deeply. "I can't wait to catch the bastard who did this." He looked up at Dimitri. "Have you spoken to Yianni?"

"No, I was waiting for you to get here. But he's awake and talking."

"Talking to whom?"

"His girlfriend."

"Toni?" said Lila. "What's she doing here?"

"That's a story no one seems willing to tell, but she's here. Been with him since late yesterday afternoon and hasn't moved from his bedside."

Lila smiled. "That sounds like our Toni. Can we see him?"

Dimitri shrugged. "You'll have to ask Toni. It seems the hospital has ceded all decisions to her."

Andreas opened the door to Yianni's room and motioned for Lila, Maggie, and Dimitri to step in ahead of him.

Toni jumped up from her chair and hurried around the bed to embrace Lila, tears welling up in her eyes. "I'm so glad to see you."

Lila hugged her tightly. "I've been trying to reach you since I heard what happened."

"I know." Toni released her grip and stepped back from Lila. She took Andreas's hands and kissed him on both cheeks. "I turned off my phone. I didn't want to speak to anyone. I just wanted to focus on Yianni." She hugged Maggie.

"Any chance of me getting included in this party?"

Andreas looked down at Yianni. "Would you please not disturb us while we're commiserating over how worried you had us?"

"Yeah, at least let us get to the really tearful parts we rehearsed on the plane," said Maggie.

Lila walked to his bedside and touched Yianni's hand. "Your buddies over there are all macho now, but you should have seen them on the plane. Never saw them so worried."

"It was a tiny plane and a lot of wind," said Maggie.

Andreas moved in next to Lila. "Good to see you back to your lousy sense of humor self."

"Glad to be seen. When we went off that road, I never thought we'd be seen again, except at the funeral."

"You don't have to talk about any of that now," said Andreas.

"How's Popi?"

Andreas glanced at Dimitri.

"She's fine," said Dimitri.

"Where is she?"

Dimitri paused. "Athens."

Yianni's face tightened. "Then she's not fine. Stop bullshitting me."

Andreas stared at him. "She's still in a coma, but stable."

Yianni shut his eyes. "That poor kid. I can't wait to get my hands on the bastard who did this."

Toni went back to her seat by Yianni's bedside and took his hand.

"There seems to be a consensus on that point," said Maggie.

Yianni's eyes remained closed. "We left Siphones and were driving to Koronos for lunch. Everything was going smoothly, until we went into that curve." He drew in and let out a deep breath, and opened his eyes. "This red Fiat came whipping round the curve on its side of the road—"

Dimitri cut in. "A red Fiat knocked you off the road?"

"No. Right behind it, almost up against the Fiat's bumper, was a white straight-job. I thought it was preparing to pass the Fiat once it got around the curve. Instead, as we were opposite the Fiat the truck swerved into our lane, and..." Yianni shut his eyes again and shook his head.

"What's a straight-job?" asked Lila.

"A truck about the size of a small bus," said Dimitri.

Yianni opened his eyes. "How bad off is Popi, really?"

Andreas answered. "They may have to remove her spleen."

Yianni winced. "How's her husband holding up?"

"He went with her on the airlift to Athens," said Dimitri. "That's all I know."

Yianni squeezed Toni's hand. "Good. I'm glad he's there."

Andreas bit at his lip. "Do you think it was an accident?"

Yianni stared at him. "Not a chance. The bastard was looking straight at us when he swerved into us."

"Can you describe the driver?"

"Dark eyes are all I remember."

"How do you think the attacker knew you'd be on that road to Koronos?"

Dimitri interrupted, "From Siphones, there are only two ways to go. Perhaps he just guessed right."

"Or he was virtually certain where we'd be headed," said Yianni.

"How would he know that?" asked Andreas.

"Popi told me that every time she's in the area she eats at a particular taverna in Koronos."

"That means your attacker knew Popi's routine," said Maggie. "I know."

"Or, assuming a hit team, they were prepared to catch up with you from behind if you'd turned the other way," said Andreas.

"Why do you say team?" asked Dimitri.

"We've heard nothing from the Fiat driver, for one thing. Also, a big truck roaring along a curvy two-lane mountain road likely raises a caution flag in most drivers' minds, but seeing one hugging the bumper of another vehicle makes you more concerned for the other driver than yourself. It slows you down just enough to make you an easier target."

"In other words, we're dealing with an orchestrated hit," said Dimitri.

"Seems like it to me," said Andreas.

"Then we were damn lucky to have survived. According to what I read in Nikoletta's notebooks, that hacker doesn't miss a target."

"Which kind of makes you wonder," said Andreas.

"About what?" asked Toni.

"Our man's trademark has him making deaths look like accidents. What happened here checks that box, but he always works alone and doesn't take risks that might come back to haunt him. In this case, at least two people were likely involved, a truck driver and a car driver, and the paint on Popi's pickup and the straight-job don't quite match. Yes, it might have been overlooked by investigators if the pickup had rolled all the way down the mountain, but the clear paint differences would be just the sort of mistake our man takes pride in avoiding."

"So who else could it be?" said Maggie.

"Anyone." Andreas looked at Dimitri. "Any luck yet on identifying that dead tourist?"

Dimitri gestured no. "Like I said before, identifying tourists is difficult."

"Have you tried our Greek databases?"

"For a foreigner?"

"Maybe he wasn't a foreign tourist?"

Dimitri exhaled. "Will do."

Andreas turned to Yianni. "What were you planning on doing next?"

"Having a big meeting with all the activist leaders Nikoletta interviewed. Popi was going to set it up using her local connections."

"So much for that, I guess," said Dimitri, quickly adding, "at least for now."

"Not necessarily," said Andreas. "Tassos Stamatos's boat arrives in less than an hour. He has local connections everywhere and might just be able to set up that meeting."

"If anyone can, it's Tassos," said Maggie. "Everyone in the Cyclades seems to owe him favors."

"Or worries about what he has on them," said Yianni.

Andreas looked at Dimitri and nodded toward Yianni. "He's Yianni's hero."

"Can't help it; he's my Greek version of John Wayne."

"A shorter, stockier Rooster Cogburn version, no doubt," said Andreas with a smile.

"Easy there, that's my guy you're talking about," growled Maggie.

"Enough already," said Yianni. "Just set up the meeting for tomorrow so that I can make it."

"But you're all bandaged up," said Lila.

"It'll generate sympathy. And make me look like a tough guy."

"Not as tough as the guy who put you here," joked Andreas.

"You're staying right here until the doctors say you can leave," said Toni.

"Then I want to talk to the doctors."

"Fine," she said.

"Alone."

"Why?"

"You intimidate them."

"That's not a good reason."

"Okay then, because you intimidate me."

Toni patted Yianni's hand. "Get used to it."

———

Andreas and Maggie were waiting for Tassos when the massive Blue Star ferry docked at the port. Andreas had used his badge to park next to the Harbor Police post by the end of the pier, saving Tassos a three-hundred-meter walk lugging baggage.

Tassos hugged and kissed Maggie. "Great to see you, my love."

He looked at Andreas. "Good to see you, too, fella." They embraced and slapped each other on the back.

"You look terrific. Slimmer than I can ever remember."

"I owe it all to my prison warden here. Maggie keeps everything I'd like to eat under lock and key, leaving me to battle rabbits for food."

"That visual works for me. You out in your garden on all fours, hopping around after lettuce and carrots."

"Don't knock it 'til you've tried it." Tassos looked inside the three-row SUV. "Hey, where's Lila?"

Andreas picked up Tassos's bag and put it in the far back seat. "She's at the hospital keeping Yianni company while Toni takes a break to shower and catch a bit of a nap in Yianni's hotel room."

"How's the kid doing?"

"He's almost as tough as you." Andreas smiled. "I'm not worried about him. Come on, jump in the car, and we'll go see him."

Maggie opened the passenger side rear door and stepped inside. "Sit up front," she said to Tassos. "I'm sure you two have a lot to talk about."

"Don't we always," said Andreas.

He carefully maneuvered the SUV through the crowd of pedestrians headed toward the taxis, hotel buses, and car rental offices far ahead. "This place is packed."

"Always is when a boat lands. A real bottleneck for the whole town," said Tassos.

"I can't imagine what it must be like when one of those behemoth cruise ships lands," said Maggie.

"Naxians can. It's what motivated some of them to wage a humongous battle against the town's plan to expand the port by seventeen acres."

"When was that?" asked Andreas.

"Back in 2007. Town hall wanted to expand the port to accommodate five cruise ships. Thirty-three citizens filed a lawsuit against their plan and won it in 2008 when the Greek Supreme

Court found the study on which the expansion was based to be insufficient."

Andreas shook his head. "That sort of activism must have really pissed off town hall."

"That's an understatement. Participants in the Case of the 33, as it came to be called, and their supporters were vilified for opposing the plan. Threats of physical harm were reportedly made, CURSE THE 33 appeared emblazoned on signs at rallies and in graffiti, and boycotts were called against businesses tied to the thirty-three. The more overtly threatening tactics largely subsided once the media in Athens got word of what was happening and turned the situation into an embarrassment for the island. But even today, pockets of resentment remain and some still boycott the original thirty-three."

"What happened to the thirty-three?"

"Actually, there were more than thirty-three actively in opposition, but since the law required those acting as plaintiffs to be directly affected by the plan, some of its strongest opponents weren't officially named as part of the thirty-three. After their court victory, the group disbanded, though some members later ran for office, and their party is now the third-largest vote-getter on the island."

"So they gave up good works to became politicians," said Maggie.

"Not all of them, my love. Some of the thirty-three organized an environmental group that's very active on a lot of fronts."

"Such as?" said Andreas.

Tassos looked at Andreas. "Why do I get the impression you're interested in what I'm saying for more than its historical significance?"

"Just keep talking, Professor, and I'll tell you after you're done."

"He's never *done* talking. Here take this." Maggie held out a bottle of water.

"Ignoring those slights, I shall continue." Tassos paused to take the bottle and twist off the cap. "So, back to today's hot environmental issues on Naxos..." Tassos took a long sip of water and stuck out the thumb of his free hand. "Number one is windmills."

"Windmills?" said Andreas, "I'd think environmentalists would be all for them."

"They claim they're not as efficient as other methods and that those behind them are actually seeking to create an industrial park for purposes of selling energy off-island, not to conserve and protect the island."

"Interesting."

"The other hot button issues are much the same as those confronting most islands." He popped out a finger. "Private businesses using public spaces like beaches for their umbrella, kitesurfing, and taverna businesses. Three," another finger shot up, "protection of wildlife, like sea turtles. Fourth," another finger, "where do you place stops on tourist development? And that issue raises more additional and complicated issues than I have fingers to count on."

"And please do spare us your toes."

Tassos waved Andreas off. "Bottom line, there's a lot of activism here, and it's not just a right versus left political thing. Naxians are proud of their independent lifestyle, and many have genuine concerns over what constitutes sustainable development and what threatens to destroy the way of life they treasure. These are not new concerns. Back in the 1990s, there was talk of expanding the airport to accommodate bigger planes, and twenty-three communities came out publicly against it."

"God sent you to me today for a purpose," said Andreas.

"Glad you finally figured that out."

"Stop this blasphemy," said Maggie, crossing herself.

"I need you to reach out to your contacts here to arrange a meeting."

"What sort of meeting?"

"With the activists interviewed by Nikoletta Elia." Andreas brought Tassos up to speed on the case.

"Don't we need Yianni at the meeting?" said Tassos. "He's the only one who's read the reporter's notebooks."

Andreas nodded. "I know. But there's no choice. We only have until Monday before the minister goes public about the reporter's disappearance."

"That could get her killed," said Tassos.

"Tell me about it."

"I guess that means the three of us have some serious reading to do before tomorrow," said Maggie.

"We can divide it up among us," said Tassos.

"If you set up the meeting, we'll do whatever has to be done to make it work."

Tassos pulled out his mobile, found a name, and pressed it. "Now, please be quiet while I try to be charming."

Andreas glanced back at Maggie. "My, Maggie, it sounds as if you and I are in for a novel experience."

She rolled her eyes. "To quote you, oh wise one, 'Tell me about it.'"

———

By the time they reached the hospital, Toni was back in her chair next to Yianni.

"I thought you were taking a nap," said Andreas.

"Couldn't sleep. Too wired," said Toni.

"You should take one of the pills they're giving me. It will put you right out," said Yianni.

"Or take a ride with this guy, listening to him attempting to be charming." Andreas nodded at Tassos walking into the room behind Maggie.

"Tassos, you old devil, so good to see you," said Yianni, struggling to sit up in bed.

"Don't move," said Tassos.

"It's not me that's weak; the meds only make me feel that way. The nurse had me walking while you were out. With any luck, they'll release me tomorrow morning."

"Don't push it," said Andreas.

Yianni frowned. "But we've got to set up that meeting if we hope to have any chance of finding the reporter before Monday."

"It's all taken care of," said Tassos. "I spoke to an old friend from Junta days, and he said he'd do what he could to set up the meeting."

"'Do what he could' doesn't sound very promising."

"The guy I spoke to was one of the Junta's fiercest opponents. They threw him in prison, and I was the only guard who made sure he was properly taken care of, which included protecting him from some of my colleagues who thought they could use him as a punching bag. Since then he's always thought of me as a brother. But more importantly, he's from Naxos and a legend on the island among the sort of people the reporter met with. To them, getting a request from my friend is a royal command."

"I think 'royal command' might be the wrong analogy, considering their politics," said Lila.

"Trust me, he'll make it happen. In fact, he's reaching out as we speak. He'll set it up for someplace where they'll all be comfortable, around siesta time so as not to interfere with their distinctly varied lines of work."

"What sorts of work?" asked Andreas.

"He said we've got a shepherd, a chef-restaurateur, an artist, a bookseller, and a farmer."

Yianni nodded. "And, according to Nikoletta's notebooks, each is firmly committed to different strongly held opinions. It should be quite a get-together. I can't wait."

"Like hell you'll be involved. Your pulse rate is moving up on the monitor just talking about it." Toni pointed at blinking lights above the bed.

"That's because my medication is wearing off, and having you so close to me is giving me intriguing thoughts."

"Flattery will get you nowhere."

"How about laid?"

Toni shook her head. "Please excuse his language. It must be his medication talking."

"I think it's our cue to leave," said Lila.

"No, we've got work to do," said Yianni.

"Your only job is to rest and get better. We'll take care of the meeting," said Andreas.

"But, like I said, I'm the only one who's read Nikoletta's notebooks."

"We'll read them tonight. Toni brought them here from your hotel room."

"I still think I should be at the meeting."

"Only if the doctors say so. And that's an order. I also think it's time we leave you two lovebirds alone."

"Toni, go with them. I'll be fine."

"Not a chance. When you leave, I leave, not before."

Yianni squeezed Toni's hand and winked. "More motivation for me to get out of here ASAP." He looked at Andreas. "Where are you staying?"

"At the home of a friend of Lila's family, about fifteen minutes south of Chora toward a beach area known as Plaka."

"That commute time assumes you know where you're going. From my experience with Naxos roads, you're in for a longer adventure."

"Use GPS," Toni told Andreas.

"You're wasting your breath," said Lila. "He's a man."

Andreas spread his arms. "What did I do to deserve this unprovoked attack?"

"You're right," nodded Lila. "It's not your fault you were born a man."

"Make that a Greek man," added Maggie.

Tassos patted Yianni on the leg and waved for everyone to leave. "I think I'd better retreat before this skirmish accelerates into an all-out separate bedrooms battlefield."

"Like I said, a Greek man. If you want to get his attention, feed him or threaten not to fuck him."

"Maggie, such language," said Lila, feigning horror.

"It comes from too many years hanging out with cops."

Toni looked at Lila. "I'll call you later and let you know what the doctor says."

"There's really no need for all of you to leave," said Yianni.

"Of course there is. You've just been fed." Toni smiled. "Now it's time for that other thing."

"What other—" Yianni's face lit up. "Bye, everybody."

———

A few minutes after his visitors had left his room, Yianni turned to Toni. "Well?"

"Well what?"

"What you promised."

"You've got to be kidding. I was joking. Here you are, wired up to a monitor and IV twenty-four hours after going through a car wreck, and you want to have sex? In your hospital bed, no less, when a nurse could walk through the door at any moment." She shook her head. "You *are* nuts."

"No, just excited. After all, I survived a near-death experience, with no seriously broken bones or internal injuries."

"But you have two broken ribs."

"I've had those before. Besides, if I'm discharged tomorrow, I'll want to have sex as soon as we're alone at the house, but you still might be afraid for me."

"Damn right."

"That's the brilliance of doing it here, while I'm hooked up to these machines. We can tell if I'm overdoing it and should stop."

Toni stared at him. "You do realize what you just said is among the most creative lines I've ever heard from someone desperately trying to get into someone else's pants? And in all my years of working in bars, I've heard a lot of them."

He smiled. "So, did it work?"

She leaned in and kissed him on the cheek, then on the lips. "Not totally."

"What does that mean?"

She kissed him again and looked up at the monitor. "Your pulse is beating faster."

"I'd certainly hope so."

She pressed her lips against his, opened her mouth and felt him press his tongue hard against hers. She glanced up at the monitor and mumbled, "Faster."

He kissed her more deeply and felt her hand slide under his blanket, beneath his gown, and down to where he was growing hard. She squeezed and slowly slid her hand up and down as she squeezed.

Again, she looked up at the monitor. "Faster."

"Yes," he whispered, "faster."

She pulled back from kissing him. "Uh-uh."

"What—"

Toni dropped her head beneath the blanket and brought her mouth to where her hand had been.

Neither noticed or seemed to care when the alarm went off on the monitor, and by the time the nurse responded, it was as if nothing had happened.

"Everything okay in here?" she asked.

"Yes, fine," said Toni.

"Are you sure?" she said, looking at Yianni.

Yianni nodded, closing his eyes. "I'm sure."

The nurse nodded back. "Funny thing about these monitors. In all the years I've been watching them, there's a certain pattern they follow when I leave young couples alone in the room. Congratulations, you two rang the bell." She smiled, stared for a few seconds at a red-faced Toni, and walked out.

"Busted," said a still-blushing Toni.

"Me too," said Yianni, sighing contentedly. "Thoroughly and totally busted."

Chapter Ten

Directions to the home of Lila's friend had Andreas turning left out of the hospital parking lot and following signs to the village of Vivlos. From there he made a right at a "big church" onto a paved road running toward Plaka Beach and a house identified by a white gate that opened by punching 1821# into an adjacent keypad.

With only a few brief wrong turns, they'd made it to the gate in less than twenty-five minutes.

Beyond the gate and a wide stone parking area lay an all-white stucco house set high above patches of pasture and farmland running out to the beach. The home paid clear homage to the traditional Cycladic cubist style, but with a modern flair most noticeably reflected in its oversized windows and broad terrace facing west toward the sea.

A housekeeper stood waiting for them at the front door. She explained the layout of the house, pointed out their respective bedrooms, and emphasized that at her employer's instructions the refrigerator had been fully stocked in anticipation of their arrival.

After offering many "thank yous" and "not necessaries" to the housekeeper, they went to their rooms to unpack. Lila took the opportunity to call her mother and check in on the children. That led to Tassaki taking the phone from his grandmother and describing in great detail, first to his mother and then to his father, all of the wonderful things he'd been doing with his *yiayia* and *pappou*.

By the time Andreas and Lila came out of their room, Maggie and Tassos were sitting on the main terrace reading the reporter's notebooks.

"How's the reading going?" said Andreas.

"This is interesting stuff," said Maggie. "The reporter's good at what she does."

"Which notebook are you reading?"

"The one covering her interview with the hacker."

"Anything jump out at you?"

"So far, based on the level of detail, only that he's likely telling the truth. Hard to imagine how he'd know all this if he hadn't planned the hits."

"So, if *you'd* paid him to do a hit, I assume you wouldn't be happy with all the publicity he's drawn?"

"For sure."

Andreas looked at Tassos. "Which one did you pick?"

"I passed on reading her interviews with politicians and hotel guys. I'm sure it's all politically correct bullshit. I took notebook number three, which includes her interview with the farmers Yianni and Popi met with before getting run off the road. Nothing exciting yet, but I just started reading."

Andreas looked at the remaining three notebooks. "Eenie, meenie, miney—"

"Here you are, folks," said Lila, carrying a tray of snacks out to the terrace.

The housekeeper followed with glasses and two large bottles of water.

"What do we have here?" asked Tassos.

"Only good things. Crudité, fruit, low-fat Naxos *anthotiro* cheese, and pita bread."

"Same food, different island," said Tassos, grabbing a carrot stick.

"Shut up and read," said Andreas, picking a notebook. "I'll take number five, her final day before disappearing."

Andreas handed another notebook to Lila. "Since you're here, come join in on the group read. Here's notebook number four, covering her time with the activists."

Lila took the notebook and a glass of water, found a comfortable chair, and sat down. "The housekeeper is preparing lunch, so happy reading."

Once settled in, each read silently, moving about only to get something to eat or drink from the table between them.

A half hour into their reading Tassos blurted, "Oh, my God."

"What is it?" said Andreas.

"I can't believe this guy is still alive."

"What guy?"

"The grandfather of the trio in Siphones."

"How do you know him?"

"It's a very long story."

Andreas rolled his eyes. "Is there any other kind of story you tell?"

"Do you want me to tell it or not?"

Andreas waved his hand at Tassos. "You've primed your audience, so just get on with it."

"I met him here during the Junta Years. He'd been shaped by an unimaginably hard life trying to survive World War II as a young boy in one of Naxos's poorest mountain villages. Starvation plagued those places, and you survived by doing whatever you had to do to feed your family. In his case, he became legend for his talent at finding ways to steal food and livestock from farmers and herders on the plains below." Tassos took a sip of water. "After the war he honed his foraging skills in a different direction, the artifacts market. Naxos was filled with unexcavated ancient sites, and he had a gift for finding them and their treasures."

"He must have made a fortune," said Lila.

Tassos gestured no. "He wasn't a businessman, just a thief. He'd find the treasures but sell them off to middlemen for virtually nothing compared to their true value to collectors."

"Dare I ask how you got to know him?"

"Not in the way you're thinking, wiseass. When I worked as a prison guard for the Junta on Giaros, I'd sometimes be detailed to another island, and when the Junta decided to build a major highway on Naxos running from Chora to Alyko, I spent a lot of time down in Alyko assigned to keep an eye on things."

"Where's Alyko?" said Lila.

"About a half hour south of Chora."

"What sort of 'things'?" said Andreas.

"They built the road to connect Chora and a big hotel project in Alyko overlooking the sea."

"The Junta was building a hotel?" said Lila.

"They encouraged a lot of hotel construction, but this was a foreign corporation's project. Anyway, I was there to make sure it wasn't disturbed."

"Disturbed how?"

"By trespassers intruding on the property while construction was underway. Mostly, we chased away herders with their animals and locals walking dogs."

"Why do I have the feeling this story has a lot more to go?"

"The farmer was working there, and he seemed at first like any other manual laborer, digging holes. He'd dig in one place, leave it open for a couple of days, and then cover it up and dig another hole somewhere else."

"Why?"

"Whenever I asked him that question, he always gave me the same answer. 'Keep your nose out of other people's business.'"

"Something we all know you can't do."

"Back then I wasn't as aggressive. Besides, I was a young man with a sweet Junta job and didn't need to risk pissing off someone who was doing something my superiors must have known about. No way he could be digging all those holes and not be noticed."

"Did you ever find out why he dug the holes?"

"I have a pretty good idea. Every night the same old man would walk his dog onto the edge of the property and I'd have to shoo him away. It became a ritual, and we'd talk for a bit before he'd head back home. One night he asked me why the caïques came in so late at night to the concrete pier just below the hotel construction. I said I didn't know anything about those boats, but they were probably there to unload supplies. He said, no, they were *loading*, not unloading, and always gone before dawn."

Tassos reached for another carrot stick. "Years later, after the project had gone bankrupt and the Junta'd been overthrown, I heard from someone in the artifacts business that Naxos was filled with ancient burial sites—"

"Antiquities smuggling," said Lila.

"You win the prize," said Tassos. "The ancients buried their dead with whatever they'd need in their next life. Many of the treasures in the island's Archaeological Museum came from gravesites. Though it hadn't registered with me at the time, locals used to call the construction 'the gravesite project.'"

"So the holes the grandfather dug were on ancient gravesites?" said Andreas.

"Based on his history, I've no doubt that's true. But there's a lot more to the story. In later years he went back to farming. He'd done what he'd had to do to keep his family alive, but he didn't want his children and grandchildren following his ways. He became active in the conservation resistance to preserve the beauty and history of Naxos. He galvanized village opposition to expanding the airport, rallied locals to successfully challenge efforts to resurrect the failed Alyko hotel project, and openly supported the Case of the 33."

"Then the reporter was right about the old man, his son, and grandson being activists, and what Yianni was told about the grandfather was bullshit," said Andreas.

"I don't know about the other two, but it's sure BS about the grandfather."

"Why would they lie?" asked Maggie.

"That's something to ask them."

The housekeeper stepped out onto the terrace. "Lunch is ready. Shall I serve it out here?"

Lila and Maggie jumped up. "We'll help you," said Lila.

"Not necessary," said the housekeeper.

"We need a break," said Maggie, following Lila and the housekeeper inside.

"From what?" said Tassos.

"Don't worry about them. I'm still listening. Is there anything more you have to tell me?" said Andreas.

"Nope." Tassos jerked in his seat and reached into his pants pocket. "My mobile's on vibrate." He looked at the phone screen. "Perhaps I do. The call's from my friend who's trying to set up the meeting for tomorrow."

Tassos held the phone against his cheek with his shoulder, crossed his fingers on one hand, and reached for a pita with the other.

"A true multitasker," smiled Andreas.

Tassos nodded yes as he said into his phone, "Make me smile, my friend."

———

Tassos listened patiently as his friend described what he'd gone through to arrange the meeting. Apparently, word was out to many that the reporter had disappeared, and some of those that Tassos's friend had contacted now worried for their safety and that of their families.

"Who has them worried?"

"They're too worried to tell me," said Tassos's friend.

"Jesus."

"No need for you to worry, though. I convinced them they'd be much worse off if they didn't speak to you."

"How'd you do that?"

"By playing on their natural fears that the government is a police state capable of all kinds of merciless deeds."

"And they believed you?"

"Why not? I believe it. After all, do you forget where we met? I was a political prisoner under a fascist regime."

"But times are different now?"

"Are they?"

Tassos had been down this road before with his friend. "Okay, I get your point. Let's move on. What—not who—has them worried?"

"It's conjecture based upon gossip, but when you toss in an element of truth, even lies gain credibility. Here we have an Athenian journalist writing about big money angling to slice up the island for *private gain,* and Naxians remember how Athens media helped the thirty-three defeat a *public benefit* project backed by the local government to expand the port. The last thing modern-day privateers want is the national press focusing on what they have in mind for Naxos and its treasures."

"What are you saying?"

"Even among opponents and supporters of the port project, there were violent skirmishes. Passions run high in disputes over development."

"But we're talking about kidnappers and potential murderers?"

"I'm not suggesting there was anyone like that involved in the port dispute, but now we're talking about private projects capable of generating at least as much passionate resistance. You're a cop, do you have any doubt that among all the private projects percolating around here there aren't bad actors from dangerous places around the world looking to launder money made in the most mercenary of ways? For them to do physical harm in pursuit of monetary gain is not a reach at all."

"Do you have any particular projects or bad guys in mind?"

"Nope. For that you'll have to speak to the people I've pulled together for your meeting."

"Tell me about them."

"They're from different parts of the island. Some are native to Naxos, others expats, but all vigorously oppose unrestrained development."

"Who ever admits to being *in favor* of unrestrained development?"

"Good point. Come to think of it, I've never heard a politician say anything remotely like that, even those who love pouring concrete over any open space they can find. But the ones coming to your meeting actually live their lives keeping that commitment."

"I assume you know them all."

"Yes, and if they're locals, most of their parents and grandparents as well. The bookseller's late grandfather and I were together in resisting the Junta, though he never got arrested."

"Poor guy, he never got to meet me."

"I'm sure he regretted that. He was a lawyer, and his son

followed in his footsteps, but the grandson opted for bookselling as a better life choice."

"Hard way to make a euro."

"He has the benefit of a grandfather who left him several rent-producing properties to subsidize his lifestyle."

"Where's he live?"

"In Chora, above his bookshop. The others all live in villages out of town. The farmer raises olives in Eggares and runs an olive-press museum in the center of the village."

"What's his family tree?"

"Hers. She's a sixth-generation Naxian farmer. There's another woman in the group. She's an artist who lives in Halki and runs a very successful art gallery called Alex's Fishbowl. She's an expat. Been here for thirty years. One of the most articulate of those seeking to market the preservation of Naxos as a selling point for tourism."

"Interesting crew."

"It gets better. The chef-restaurateur has one of the best places on the island. It's less than a half hour out of Chora, down toward Alyko. We've set up the meeting in his taverna. He was a driving force behind the Case of the 33 and is still a strong voice among conservationists opposing the windmills and private exploitation of public lands."

"And the shepherd?"

"He's perhaps the most interesting. He's of one hundred percent Cretan blood, born and raised in the mountain village of Apeiranthos but married an American girl and now lives in Sangri by the Temple of Demeter."

"Why do you say he's the most interesting?"

"The list of names you gave me included his wife, not him, but when I called her she said she'd have to speak to her husband. He called me back to say he wanted to come instead of her. I was surprised because his roots and village aren't known for friendly cooperation with authorities."

"Do you think he's coming to cause trouble?"

"That's what I thought at first, too, so I asked him that straight out. He said he's coming because he's a close friend of the husband of the cop who was hurt in that pickup rollover outside of Koronos. He said he wants to do what he can to help find whoever's responsible."

"Sounds like he's suggesting what happened to the reporter and his friend's wife are related. Did he say why he thought that?"

"We're in Greece, friend. People see conspiracies in the number of raisins in a cereal box. Who knows what he thinks or the basis for his thoughts. That's why I set up your meeting, so you can be the super detective who ferrets out the answers."

"Just for the record," said Tassos, "I want you to know that you're just as ornery as ever."

"I think you mean *we're* just as ornery."

"I know."

"But I still love you."

"Me too," said Tassos. "Thanks for all your help, and stay well, old friend."

Tassos hung up but didn't move. He sat staring out to sea. *Where had all the years gone?* Each time he said goodbye to an old friend, his thoughts ran to whether that might be the last time they spoke. *Snap out of it, Stamatos. You've got a great woman, great friends, and a great life left to lead.*

"Would you please come back to planet earth and tell me what he had to say?" said Andreas.

Tassos rose from his chair. "Let's have lunch while I tell you."

Over a lunch of chicken *kalamakia,* beef *keftedes,* fried zucchini, *graviera* cheese, fresh bread, and a large Greek salad, Tassos shared what he'd heard from his friend.

"Sounds like an interesting group of people," said Lila.

"With strong opinions," said Maggie.

"And some real leads," added Andreas. "We're meeting at three, so we should plan to leave here by no later than two thirty."

Tassos motioned to the housekeeper. "May I have another *kalamaki,* please?"

The housekeeper paused as if confused, nodded, and went into the kitchen.

"Why don't we visit Yianni and leave for the meeting straight from the hospital?" said Lila.

"Good idea."

The housekeeper returned with a plate bearing a single straw and placed the plate in front of Tassos.

"What's this?"

"Your *kalamaki,* sir."

Andreas burst out laughing and said to the housekeeper, "I bet you're from Thessaloniki."

She nodded yes.

Andreas laughed again. "In Thessaloniki, if you ask for a *kalamaki* you get a *straw.* Down here you'll get chicken or pork on a skewer."

"Then what do they call meat on a skewer?"

"Souvlaki, which means the same thing to everyone."

"Just ask for souvlaki and avoid the problem," said Maggie.

Tassos shook his head. "I guess I'm still not too old to learn something new."

"What do they call *keftedes*?" asked Lila.

"Meatballs are meatballs everywhere," smiled Andreas.

Ring, ring.

"Not my phone this time," said Tassos.

"It's mine," said Andreas, pulling his phone from his pants pocket.

"Kaldis here."

Pause.

"Hold on, Adoni. I want to put you on speakerphone."

Andreas set his mobile on the dining table. "It's our head tech wiz back in GADA with news. I'm here with Maggie and Tassos. What do you have for us?"

"I heard about Yianni. How's he doing?"

"His hard head finally came in handy," said Andreas. "He's doing great. I'll tell him you asked."

"Thanks, Chief. Nikoletta Elia's editor just left. We examined his phone and analyzed the voicemail left by her possible kidnapper. The caller used a state-of-the-art scrambler. No way we could unscramble it, not even to say whether the caller was a man or a woman."

"Damn."

"But there's more."

"More bad news?"

"Depends on what you're expecting. We'd also examined the reporter's mobile and came up with the number of the last call she'd received and answered on that phone. It came through at about the same time as she disappeared from her hotel."

"Why didn't you tell us that before?"

"I did, in a voicemail I left yesterday for Yianni, before I heard what happened to him."

"Okay, go on."

"As a result of our examination of the journalist's phone, I have potentially significant news for you."

"Why is every cop so dramatic?" said Maggie.

"Because we strive for recognition of our small victories amid an ever-losing battle with the dark side," said Tassos.

"I like that," said Adoni.

"Just make your point, please," said Andreas.

"We came up with the same number as the caller who left the message on the editor's phone."

Silence.

"Dare I ask if you know whose number it is?" said Andreas.

"I have a name but no other information."

"What's the name?"

"Petros Zagorianos."

"Never heard of him." Andreas looked around the table and received a group shrug.

"It could be an alias. The phone was purchased at a shop on Naxos the day before Nikoletta disappeared."

"Do you know anything else about this Petros character?"

"Not a thing."

"Is that all you have on the phones?"

"Yeah. I hope it helps."

"It's a good start. Thanks."

Andreas clicked off. "Any thoughts?"

"Yeah," said Tassos. "Call Dimitri and see if he's ever heard of this guy."

Andreas dialed.

"Dimitri, it's Andreas. You're on speaker with my crew."

"Small world, I was just about to call you."

"I wanted to know if you ever heard of a Naxian named Petros Zagorianos?"

Pause.

"Dimitri, are you still there?"

"Did you say Petros Zagorianos?"

"Yes."

"I was calling to tell you we have an ID on the tourist who took a header on the rocks the night the reporter disappeared.

He was born on Naxos as Petros Zagorianos but emigrated to the U.S. as a child, and the name on his U.S. passport is Peter Zagori."

Andreas leaned in toward the phone. "When did he last enter Greece?"

"According to Immigration, the day before the reporter disappeared. He arrived on Wednesday. She disappeared early Thursday morning."

Andreas looked at Tassos. "The same day he bought the phone."

"What phone?" asked Dimitri.

"The one used to call Nikoletta the night she disappeared and to call her editor yesterday to say she was okay."

"But Zagori couldn't have called her editor. He was dead for nearly two days by then."

"I know," said Andreas. "Which means if we find Peter Zagori's phone, we likely find his killer."

"And whoever has Nikoletta," added Tassos.

"Any other info on Zagori?"

"Not yet, but based on your suggestion we ran him through Greek databases and he popped up with a Greek military record. He came back from the United States to serve his time in the army. That's all we have on him over here, but we've put in a request with the United States for anything they might have. I'll let you know as soon as we hear back."

"Thanks. How's Popi doing?"

"Stable is all we're hearing. The infection seems to be under control. They may not have to remove her spleen."

Andreas pumped his fist into the air. "Thank God. If you speak to her husband, please pass along our thoughts and prayers."

"Will do. Bye,"

Andreas shut off his phone and looked at Tassos. "What do you think?"

"That we've got one hell of a mystery to solve."

"And less than forty-eight hours in which to do it."

"Back to the books, boys and girls," said Maggie.

"Once we finish, let's go to the beach," said Lila.

"I can't go. We really have a lot to do," said Andreas.

"Sure you can. From what I've heard, until you meet with those folks tomorrow, all you have to do is think and toss around ideas. That can be done on a beach as well as in one of these chairs. Besides, a swim will clear your head and make all of us think better."

Andreas raised his hands in a sign of surrender. "Fine. Off to the beach it is. But I get to pick which one."

"Deal."

Chapter Eleven

Though their deal had Andreas picking the beach, when he passed on nearby Plaka Beach for a beach at least twenty minutes south, there were grumblings among his crew. Lila argued that Plaka was a perfectly exquisite sandy beach offering organized services for those who wanted them, and since neither she nor Andreas had ever been to that other beach, why risk messing up what remained of their day by heading toward the unknown?

Andreas did not relent. He drove back to Vivlos, turned right onto the main road, and followed it to its end before turning right onto a narrower paved road running between cedar-dotted sand dunes. Parked cars sat off on both the sides of the road. He turned left at what seemed more of a sandy path than a road, and followed it to where it opened up into an impromptu parking area separated from the beach by a line of cedars.

"Here we are, folks. Welcome to Alyko Beach."

Lila and Maggie hurried down to the beach, carrying bags filled with what they deemed essential for a day by the sea. Andreas and Tassos followed, carrying snacks, water, bamboo beach mats, and two beach umbrellas to shield them from the sun.

"Wherever you ladies pick is fine with us," said Andreas, glancing at a nodding Tassos.

"This place is gorgeous," said Lila looking south. "The beach must go on for half a kilometer with not a structure in sight."

"If you look south," said Maggie. "But up on that rise beyond the cedars to the north there's a church and what looks to be the skeleton of some sort of abandoned concrete and stone construction."

"But it's a small church," said Lila, "and the other structure looks to be only a story tall and is hardly noticeable up there off among all those cedars."

"I wonder what it is?" said Maggie.

Tassos looked at Andreas but said nothing.

"Frankly, I don't care. I'm just happy to be on a lovely white beach with crystal clear water that's utterly devoid of music, chairs, tavernas, and anything else man-made." Lila put her beach bag down ten meters from the edge of the water and, with a flourish suggestive of a conqueror claiming territory, said, "How's this?"

"Perfect," said Maggie.

Andreas gathered up rocks as Tassos scooped out a hole in the sand. They planted one umbrella in the hole, secured it in place from the wind with the rocks, and repeated the process for the second umbrella.

After they'd set up and spread out their things, Lila turned to Andreas. "How did you know about this place?"

"Tassos told me."

Tassos grinned.

"When were you here?" asked Maggie.

"Long before I met you, my love. I was but a young man of twenty serving my country." He nodded toward the structure on the hill north of them. "I was here when that was being built.

As you guessed, it's a long-abandoned project. A hotel project, to be precise."

Maggie nodded. "So, that's where you met that grandfather from Siphones."

"Yes. He was around forty then."

"And the beaches surrounding it sounded so idyllic I thought you'd like to see them," said Andreas.

Lila rolled her eyes. "I wondered why you agreed so quickly to come to the beach in the middle of a case that has you stressed out. It's not like you to risk relaxing, especially with Yianni in the hospital."

"I'm not stressed out," he barked.

"Yeah, sure. But at least admit that you brought us here so that you could check out that place." She pointed north.

Andreas shrugged. "Sure, we're here, so why not? Besides, it could be interesting for other reasons. I hear artists have done some extraordinary things with it."

Lila stood. "I'm going swimming. If you can bear to wait until I return before gallivanting off on your little expedition, I might join you."

Andreas lay back on his towel, staring straight up at the sky through a space between the umbrellas. "Lord spare me from doing good deeds unappreciated by mere mortals."

Lila kicked sand on his legs. "Like I said, wise guy, wait for me." She turned and ran toward the sea without waiting for a reply.

"I think the tag line to that exit was, 'or else,'" said Tassos.

"Don't I know it."

"Good," said Maggie smiling. "We've obviously trained each of you well."

———

Lila swam for twenty minutes, dried in the sun for ten more, changed into a one-piece bathing suit, and said to her husband, "So, are you ready for our hike?"

Andreas got up from his towel, grabbed a T-shirt, and slipped into a pair of sandals. "I thought you'd never ask."

"Are you guys coming?" Lila asked Maggie and Tassos.

"Nope, you two are old enough to go off exploring on your own," said Tassos, stretched out on a towel under an umbrella.

Andreas took Lila's hand and led her up toward the SUV.

"Why don't we just walk along the shore over toward the church?"

"While you were swimming, I noticed a pickup parked over by the church drive out to where we parked. It'll be a lot easier following that road than struggling past rocks and brush in bathing suits."

Their walk along the road to the church took five minutes, the last minute alongside a half dozen or so decrepit concrete shacks across the road from the church.

"What are those buildings?" Lila asked.

"My guess is they're part of the old hotel project, but from the shutters and doors, I'd say that at least some of them were used after the project was abandoned. For what purpose or by whom, I've not a clue."

They continued their walk, passing more faded structures and rows of unfinished stone and concrete walls. Andreas stopped at a still-serviceable concrete pier jutting out into the sea. "It's right where Tassos said it would be."

"Why didn't he come with us if he knows so much about the place?"

"He said it's been too many years for him to remember where that Siphones grandfather dug his suspicious holes."

"That doesn't sound like Tassos."

"I know," said Andreas. He shrugged.

"Maybe he doesn't want to be in a place that reminds him of his time in service to the Junta?"

"No, he came to grips with that long ago. My guess would be it's something far simpler. Like he's afraid to take the walk. Maggie said he's watching his weight but is reluctant to do more than minimal exercise."

"If I'd known that, I'd have insisted he come with us."

"I know; that's why I didn't tell you."

Lila went to smack him, but before she could, Andreas bolted toward a dirt path leading up to a wide promontory overlooking the sea.

"Ha ha, too fast for you."

"We'll see about that," said Lila charging after him. "You're in sandals and I'm in sneakers."

"Yeah, but I'm more afraid of you than you are of me," Andreas yelled, not turning or slowing down.

As they neared the top, the scope of the project they'd seen only part of from the beach came into view. One- and two-story stone skeletons tracked along the rim of the cape in an architectural theme reminiscent of the Roman Coliseum's penchant for archways.

They stopped.

"This is amazing," said Lila.

"I've never seen anything like it." Andreas turned to face the sea and swept his hand across the horizon. "I'd bet this view is what attracted the hotel project here in the first place."

"Why do we Greeks insist on selling our very souls?" Lila sighed. "But having said that, I must admit that compared to many of the modern-day hotel projects plaguing us, this one actually looks to have tried fitting in with its setting."

"Don't be so sure about that. It wasn't finished. Who knows what it would have looked like then."

"Sadly, you're right. But with any luck we'll never know." She took his hand. "Come, let's look around."

They left the shrubbery-lined path to walk between the perimeter buildings into a broad, open space covered in concrete. Unkempt gorse and other hardy greenery competed for random patches of available dirt.

"This must have been the intended main entrance and parking area," said Andreas. "Be careful where you step; parts of the concrete have collapsed. This entire area must be hollow below." He pointed to a hole just in front of them.

Lila poked Andreas on the arm. "Do you see what I see?" She swung around in a circle. "They're beautiful, they're stunning, and they're all around us."

Huge, colorful murals of mythical creatures—faces, birds, and omens—leaped out at them from almost every vertical surface. Long-abandoned concrete walls had been turned into gigantic canvases, one more challenging to the senses than the next.

"I've heard of this place, even seen photographs of some of the art, but I never imagined how overwhelming it is to see them here, in the surroundings that inspired their creation." She swung around again. "They were painted a few years back by a Balian street artist who lives in Athens." She pointed to a doorway leading into a skeletal maze of unfinished rooms and hallways. "There are more inside." She headed toward the doorway.

Andreas yelled, "Remember, be careful where you step." He watched her disappear inside. "I feel like I'm talking to Tassaki," he muttered. *But at least with him I have a shot at being listened to.*

He stood alone on the concrete, staring first one way and then another. He had no idea what he was looking for here that might tie into Nikoletta's disappearance, nor even a hint of where he should start to look for inspiration. He decided to take his mind off the investigation and just tag along with Lila. He followed the path she'd taken inside through an archway now doubling as the gaping, wide-open mouth of a sea monster. *Perhaps that's what happened to Nikoletta—she was swallowed up by some mysterious creature.*

So much for putting the investigation out of his mind.

He wandered from room to room, taking care not to step too close to the many holes, some of which promised to the inattentive a fall of a story or two. With all the tourists this artwork must draw, he was surprised no efforts had been made to repair or at least cover over the holes. But, then again, with the entire country still in the midst of financial crisis, there wasn't enough money available for far more pressing crumbling infrastructure projects directly affecting the daily lives of everyday Greek voters.

He stopped to look at a small mural obviously painted by a different artist trying to pass himself off as the original. An awkward impersonation, to say the least.

Impersonation...? Andreas stared straight ahead. *What if whoever attacked Yianni and Popi was trying to impersonate Nikoletta's mystery man?*

That could mean the telephone calls to Nikoletta and her editor were made by the man Nikoletta interviewed, and everything he told the editor was legitimate. *The hacker is keeping her safe from impersonators trying to harm her.*

Andreas felt he was onto something but needed more than instinct before pushing his theory. If his hunch was correct, then Nikoletta faced no danger from her "captor," but if wrong, she could die. Or already be dead.

Maybe the answer will come from what the Americans have to say about Peter Zagori. Given the calls from Zagori's phone, Andreas had no doubt he'd been killed by the hacker. But why? Certainly not for his mobile.

He nodded to the mural that had sparked his possible epiphany.

"Thanks for the inspiration whoever you are. Keep up the good work."

———

After another half hour of wandering through the ruins, Lila agreed it was time to rejoin Maggie and Tassos on the beach. They walked along the path past the church, every so often catching a glimpse of the beach below through a break in the cedars.

"I could use another swim," she said.

"I'm in need of one too. It's a warmer day than I thought." Andreas turned his head to glance at the beach and came to an abrupt stop.

"What is it?"

"Three men are surrounding our umbrellas, and Maggie's standing between them and Tassos."

"Is something wrong?"

"I don't know, but I'll meet you there." Andreas jumped into the brush, slipping and sliding along the rocks until he'd made it down to the beach. He kicked off his sandals and broke into a trot, aimed straight for his friends and some very loud music. The closer he came, the louder the music. He watched one of the men grab Tassos's umbrella and throw it toward the sea.

"*Whoa, there*," yelled Andreas. "Let's calm things down, fellas."

The man who tossed the umbrella responded in English. "Fuck off, mate, unless you want some of what this old asshole's gonna get." The man stood about as tall as Andreas and had the bull-like build of Yianni.

Andreas changed course to pick up the umbrella, saying in English as he did, "You're obviously not from around these parts, but that's not the way we talk to strangers in Greece." He collapsed the umbrella and wrapped it tightly shut as he walked toward the men.

"I said fuck off." The man pointed to his two friends, each the size of a professional rugby player. "Take care of him. I'll take care of the old fart and his pig of a woman."

Maggie swung around to face Tassos, saying in Greek, "Don't you dare let him goad you into a fight."

"Yeah," said Andreas, in English, "give me a chance to reason with these fellas." He stopped five meters from the men. "Why don't you go back to your blanket and sleep off whatever has you all fired up? Honest, that's a much better choice than what you'll face if you insist on taking this route."

"I said, take care of him," growled the man. "Do it *now*."

"Oh, so you're in charge. Just for the record, permit me to explain whom you and your friends are about to assault. We're both Greek policemen, so no matter how what you have in mind turns out, you and your buddies are in for a mass of hurt."

"Cops? I love beating up cops."

"Nah, be honest, you like your buddies to beat up cops. You only have the balls to go after old men and women, and only then when you're drunk enough to think you have the courage. Like now. You're a...uh what's the word?" He looked at Maggie.

"Pussy."

The leader swung around toward Maggie.

"Hey!" Andreas put a little heat into his voice to catch the guy's attention. "Like I said, no balls, only guts when you're high enough to go after easy targets. Why don't you try me, asshole?"

The leader paused for an instant to look at his friends, then charged at Andreas as if headed into a scrum, arms spread wide and eyes glaring. A pace before the raging man reached him, Andreas slipped to the man's right, causing the man to stumble and giving Andreas the opportunity to drive the pointed end of the umbrella into the side of the man's right knee, sending him crumpling to the sand. The man clutched his leg and howled, just as Andreas delivered another pointed shot to the man's left shin, followed by a haymaker from the umbrella's blunt end to the man's jaw.

Andreas stepped back. "Are we done yet?"

The man growled and lurched along the sand toward Andreas.

"Not yet, huh? Well, have it your way." Andreas stepped back as the man tried to get up. Andreas stepped forward with his left foot, as he brought his right foot forward and up in a fierce pendulum shot of a kick to the man's balls.

As the man lay writhing on the ground, Andreas turned to his mates. "Here in Greece we prefer football, though you might call it soccer. Now, would you two mind removing your buddy from our area of the beach?" The two men looked at each other and charged at Andreas. He stepped back and braced for their attack.

CRACK!

The sound echoed across the beach, stopping the two men in their tracks.

"Okay, assholes, I've had all that I can take from your loud-ass music and bullshit machismo." Tassos stood with his gun aimed at the chest of the bigger of the two men. "If you aren't off this beach with your hurt buddy in two minutes, I'm going to start taking target practice at your kneecaps."

The men stood frozen in place.

"I said *move.*" Tassos fired another round at their feet.

One tossed everything of theirs into a blanket and ran with it Santa Claus-style toward the parking area while the other helped their staggering leader struggle along after.

Andreas watched to make sure they'd left before turning to Tassos.

"That was a highly inappropriate use of a firearm."

"Yeah, tell me about it."

Maggie said, "I wondered why you seemed so calm when they threatened you for asking them to turn down their music. For a moment, I thought you'd forgotten your English."

"Yeah, I should have shot their music box instead. That would have ended the confrontation right there."

"I remember the days when you wouldn't have needed the gun to take care of those three," said Andreas.

"So do I, but times change."

Andreas nodded. "They sure do. And by the way, why didn't you pull your pistol and put an end to it all before I had to fight the guy?"

"I figured he needed his ass kicked and you needed some practice."

Andreas shook his head. "Those three weren't the only assholes on this beach today."

"Yeah, it was their bad luck we all happened to end up in the same place on the same day."

Same place, same day. Andreas froze. "That *can't* be."

"What can't be?" said Tassos.

"That dead Greek-American, Zagori. He couldn't have been in the bar the night Nikoletta met the hacker. He wasn't even in Greece until days later!"

"Maybe it's just a coincidence the two men resembled each other?" said Maggie.

"We hate coincidences," said Andreas.

"But this time, maybe it is?" said Tassos.

"Meaning that lead's a dead end. Damn it."

"*Is everything all right?*" shouted Lila running toward them. "I heard shots and saw three men hurrying off like fleeing thieves."

"It was just another drunken tourist episode," said Tassos.

"Yep," said Andreas. "The kind that comes to our country on

holiday thinking they can do anything they want, and too many of us let them do just that." He nodded toward Tassos. "Unluckily for those three, Tassos isn't one of them."

"All this excitement has me hungry," said Maggie. "What do you say we get something to eat?"

"Good idea," said Lila.

"Just one question," said Maggie, looking at Andreas. "What was that bit about *old men and women?*"

He smiled. "I just used that for dramatic effect."

"I would certainly hope, because I was a pretty good footballer myself."

"That's good to know. I'll keep it in mind."

Tassos nodded. "I also learned something today,"

"What's that?"

"Always bring an umbrella to the beach."

Chapter Twelve

After leaving the beach, they followed the highway north toward Chora. A few minutes later they entered the area of Kastraki, passing between fields of hay, olives, and pasture, all bordered in the distance by clusters of modern white villas. Beyond a row of beach pines, Andreas turned right into a dusty parking lot and stopped beside a pale ochre roadhouse cloistered by olive, fig, apricot, and pomegranate, well-tended gardens, and a veranda draped in bougainvillea, hibiscus, and grape.

"What's this place?" asked Lila.

"Tassos's friend said it might be the best taverna in the Cyclades."

"It's where our meeting is set for tomorrow," said Tassos. "I figured since we're in the area, why not take a peek at it?"

"As long as the food is good, I don't care about your ulterior motives," said Lila, opening her rear door and sliding out.

"Ditto on that," said Maggie, getting out the other side.

Andreas looked at Tassos. "Hardly a serious wisecrack from the crew in the back. I guess they really are hungry."

"They're not alone in that. And that's not a coincidence; it's a fact."

Andreas shook his head. "I still can't believe a Zagori look-alike was in that bar nights before the real Zagori arrived on Naxos."

"I admit it's freaky. But what other explanation is there other than coincidence?"

"That's what I'm asking you."

"Perhaps lunch will inspire me."

They caught up with Lila and Maggie waiting just inside the entrance to a large empty room next to an open kitchen. A bearded young man said hello and led them out onto an even larger L-shaped veranda where diners happily chatted away at traditional taverna chairs and tables painted terracotta and olive.

"I think I'm going to like this place." Lila pointed to a small ceramic tile depicting a fish and olives mounted onto a concrete pillar supporting the veranda's beam and double-slatted roof. "I love the little touches."

"Yeah, I was thinking the same thing," said Tassos.

Maggie poked him. "Nobody likes a smart-ass."

"That's okay," said Lila. "We know he's only trying to hide his sensitive side."

The young man showed them to a corner table on the side of the veranda farthest from the road.

"I suspect that big room next to the kitchen is for use in the winter," said Lila.

Tassos nodded. "A lot of tavernas are like that. Summers, everyone wants to sit outside, winters it's back inside."

They ordered off the menu and from a wall-mounted chalkboard listing specials, each picking a dish for the table to share. As courses like mussels in wine, grilled figs with local cheese, deep-fried little fishes, and sardines stuffed with capers and cherry tomatoes drew praises of "best ever," "fantastic," and "amazing," they expanded their order to mackerel and fava, shrimps in lemon, rabbit in tomato, oven-cooked chicken with potatoes, and a few repeats. All accompanied by the house's homemade wine.

At the end of the meal, after the plates had been cleared and desserts refused amid myriad I-must-watch-my-waistline excuses, a man in his late thirties came to their table carrying a tray filled with fruits.

"These are from our garden. Compliments of the house."

"Thank you," said Andreas. "This had to be one of our best meals ever. Our compliments to the chef."

The man nodded. "I thank you. Praise like that is what keeps me cooking."

"You're the chef?" said Lila.

"Yes and an owner."

Lila smiled. "I agree; it was a wonderful meal."

Chef nodded. "Thank you, *keria.*"

"May I ask you to sit with us for a moment?" said Andreas.

Chef looked around the room. "For a minute, I can." He pulled up a chair and sat next to Andreas.

"Since we're talking, I thought I should introduce myself so that tomorrow you don't wonder why I hadn't."

"Tomorrow?"

Andreas extended his hand. "My name is Andreas Kaldis. I'm chief of GADA's Special Crimes Unit. We're part of that meeting taking place here tomorrow at three, but I want to assure you our reason for being here today has absolutely nothing to do with any of that. We're here solely because of the food. We kept hearing this is the best taverna on the island, so after swimming at Alyko Beach, we decided to come here."

Chef nodded thanks to everyone at the table. "Now, it's my turn to compliment you on your choice of Alyko. It's my favorite beach. Let's hope it doesn't change."

"We all agree with that," said Lila.

"I assume you saw what remains of the Junta's abandoned hotel project?"

"Yes," said Andreas.

"It's a tragedy what we Greeks do with God's gifts of natural beauty."

"My thoughts exactly," said Lila.

"Thankfully, the courts stopped it from going forward," said Andreas.

Chef winced. "For now."

"What do you mean?" said Andreas. "Didn't the Supreme Court decide it was government land and couldn't be built upon?"

"I'm sure you know better than I that nothing is certain these days. With our government desperate for money, there's no telling what might happen if the right deep-pockets foreign investor decides to offer an extravagant sum in exchange for permission to build there."

Maggie crossed herself. "I pray not."

Andreas leaned forward. "Is there any talk of such a deal in the works?"

"Not that I know of, but those who'd like to make it happen aren't likely to let me in on their plans."

"The whole project would have to be demolished, from the ground up," said Andreas. "Correction, make that from *below* ground up. Its concrete base is collapsing."

Chef nodded. "Every once in a while a herder complains to me of a goat falling into one of those holes. They're deep. Much deeper than you'd think necessary for a hotel project."

"I wouldn't know," said Andreas, "but hotels put a lot of their support services underground."

"Not sure how much of that they did back in the early 1970s," said Chef, "but if you ask the locals, they're convinced all that concrete covered open space was just that, a cover for smugglers digging for antiquities deep below the surface."

Andreas glanced at Tassos. "Yes, I've heard those rumors. Do you think they're true?"

He smiled. "You're a police officer. If I started talking to you about the number of locals and others who have personal collections of artifacts found around that hotel site, you'd be duty-bound to send the minister of culture a memo, which, if I were lucky, would *only* get me disowned by my family and run off the island."

Andreas patted Chef on the shoulder. "I understand, but don't worry, there will be no such memo."

A bearded younger man came to the table. "Excuse me, but they need you in the kitchen."

Chef stood and Andreas quickly did the same.

"Thank you for a wonderful meal."

"You're welcome. See you tomorrow."

"For sure."

Andreas sat down and watched the man walk back to the kitchen. "What do you think, Tassos?"

"I think he's telling the truth."

"I meant about someone resurrecting the hotel project."

"I agree with him. There's no telling what might happen in this economy. But it would be interesting to know if anyone's expressed an interest in reviving the project."

"I'll ask my father," said Lila. "Perhaps he knows or knows someone who would."

"Any excuse to call home to speak to the kids," said a slightly tipsy Maggie.

Lila laughed. "No guilt feelings here. I'm sure they don't even realize we're gone."

"Besides," said Andreas, "it leaves my lovely wife more time to have me all to herself."

Lila pulled her phone out of her bag and hit a speed dial button. "Be still my heart."

"I see the wisecracks are back," said Andreas.

"Just in time for the trip back home," said Tassos.

"Lucky us."

———

By the time Lila and Andreas finished checking in on the children and explained to Lila's father what Andreas wanted to know about the hotel project, they were back on the road heading home, and the sky had taken on the distinct burnt-orange tones of another magnificent sunset.

"We should bring the kids here," said Andreas.

"After spending this weekend with my parents, who no doubt will spoil them rotten, I think it's safe to say we'll have been knocked out of first place on their preferred holiday escorts list."

"Grandparents have a knack for doing that," said Andreas.

"Especially with your mother joining in on triple-teaming us," said Lila.

"God bless them all," said Maggie, crossing herself.

"I wonder how Yianni's doing," said Tassos.

"Toni texted me that everything's looking good," said Lila. "They might release him as early as tomorrow morning."

Maggie crossed herself again.

"What about Popi?" said Andreas.

"No word yet, other than hopeful."

Andreas exhaled. "Bastards."

Ring.

"That's mine," said Lila. "It's my father."

"Hi, Dad."

Pause.

"I'd put you on speaker but the reception's a bit sketchy here, and Andreas is driving, so tell me what you have for him and I'll pass it on."

She listened intently for several minutes.

"Thanks, Dad. Love you too."

Lila put her phone back in her bag. "He said you can call him later if you like, but here's what he's learned. Years after the Belgian entity that owned the project declared bankruptcy, a Lichtenstein company claimed ownership of the Belgian's shares and the right to continue the project. The person behind that claim was a Greek shipowner known to my father. He got tied up in court for years on any number of grounds and ultimately got nowhere with it. My father has no doubt that if someone offered him the right deal in cash, a partnership, or some combination thereof, he'd take it in a heartbeat. My father also said that whoever tries to develop that site faces serious public opposition from both local and national community activists on the order of what's stymied the redevelopment project at Athens's old international airport."

"Do you mean there actually are people out there who dare distrust the intentions of our elected leaders?" smirked Tassos. "Next thing you know, they'll be losing faith in God to deliver us from evil."

"*Tassos,*" said Maggie, "how *dare* you equate God's love to those minions of the devil who deceive and mislead us with false promises?" She crossed herself three times. "Especially after being spared who-knows-what horrible fate back on that beach."

Silence.

"Is everything okay?" said Lila softly. "I've never seen you act so seriously."

"I'm not *acting.*"

Lila leaned in toward Maggie. "You're calling out to God and crossing yourself far more than I've ever seen you do before."

"How dare you criticize my right to practice my religion as I see fit?"

Tassos and Andreas glanced at each other.

"Maggie. I repeat: Is everything okay?"

Maggie shut her eyes, drew in a breath, and exhaled. "I don't want to talk about it."

Lila nodded. "Okay."

Maggie looked out her side window.

Not a word was spoken for more than a minute.

"Beautiful sunset," said Tassos.

"A beautiful, blinding sunset," said Andreas, pulling down the sun visor as he turned west at Vivlos, aimed straight into the setting sun.

Maggie coughed. "Sorry I raised my voice."

"No need to apologize," said Lila. "You're among friends."

"I know." Maggie dabbed at her eyes. "And I love you all dearly." She turned back to the window. "I think I had too much to drink."

She said nothing more.

———

When they reached the house, Maggie hurried inside ahead of the others, closely followed by Tassos.

Lila and Andreas hung back, as if admiring the fading sunset.

"What do you think?" said Lila.

"She's definitely edgier than I've ever seen her."

"Do you think it's her health?"

Andreas shook his head. "I don't know, but I pray not."

"Maybe she's worried about Yianni?"

"I wouldn't think so. He's out of danger. But, again, I don't know."

"She needs someone to talk to about whatever it is."

"Greeks aren't big on that sort of thing."

"I know that. I meant a friend, not a psychiatrist."

Andreas took Lila's hand and headed toward the door. "She has you, she has me, and most of all she has Tassos. When she wants an understanding ear, she'll have it."

———

Tassos closed their bedroom door and spoke softly. "What's bothering you, Maggie?"

She sat on the bed, looking at the floor. "Nothing."

"That's reassuring. I thought it might be something serious, like you've given up on your plan for achieving world peace."

"It's not funny."

He sat down next to her. "I know." He put his arm around her shoulders, drew her to him, and kissed her on the forehead.

Maggie leaned in against his chest and cried uncontrollably, finally sniffling to a stop after a succession of deep breaths. All the while, Tassos never uttered a word or softened his embrace.

"Thank you," she sniffled.

"No reason to thank me. I'm here for you the same as you've always been for me. All that matters is that something serious is bothering you. Do you want to tell me what it is?"

Maggie shut her eyes. "Perhaps I've been on the job too long. Seen and heard too much."

"Is this about Yianni or the other cop?"

"No." She opened her eyes and sat up straight. "It's about you."

"Me?"

Maggie paused. "You've been a bit down since your heart incident. The doctors say you're fine, and you've been following their instructions better than I ever hoped, but your mood worries me. You're not back to your old self. It's as if you're counting

down how many years you have left, rather than living them."
She sighed, followed by a deep swallow. "On the beach today
when those three animals were ready to hurt you, I felt helpless
to protect you."

"There was no need for you to protect me."

"I didn't know that. All that I knew was that the one person on
earth who means more to me than my own life could have been
killed today over loud music on a beach."

"This does not sound like you at all."

"I know. As I said, perhaps I've seen too much and realize
how, in an instant, a fit of temper can wreck more lives than just
the victim's."

"What do you want me to do? Resign from the force?"

"No, that wouldn't change you. You'd still be the same aggressive grump you've always been, just without a gun and a badge."

"Well then, what is it you want me to do?"

Maggie grabbed his free hand. "Promise me you'll learn to let
these lesser offenses to your sensibilities slide by. You can find a
reason to get into a fight these days almost anywhere you look,
and that's before anyone even begins talking politics."

"You're saying you want me to be more laid-back?"

She sighed. "Yes, I guess that's right. I miss your old self."

"Fine. But you'll have to promise to do something for me in
return."

Maggie cocked her head. "Why do I sense what's coming?"

Tassos leaned in and began kissing her on the neck.

"Because you never miss a thing."

———

"Hello."

"Yes?"

"Is this Detective Kouros?" The voice was deep but tentative.

"Yes, who's this?"

"Popi's husband."

Yianni's heart jumped. "Is she okay?"

"She's out of her coma."

"Thank God. My thoughts and prayers have been with you both."

"Thank you."

The line remained quiet for so long Yianni thought they might have been disconnected.

"I got your number from Dimitri and meant to call you before, but things just...well...I guess all I can say is I didn't."

"No problem. I'm glad that you called now with good news."

More silence.

"How are *you* doing?" Mamas's voice still sounded tentative.

"With any luck I'll be out tomorrow and back to catching the bastards who put us in the hospital."

"It's why I called you."

Yianni paused. "I don't understand."

"I think I can help you find them."

Yianni swallowed. "I, uh, understand how upset you are. Believe me, I do, but this is a police matter, and I don't think it's a good idea for you to be involved in hunting them down. As much as I agree with your motives, and I don't doubt you'd be a great help, tempers could flare and you might get yourself in some serious trouble."

"I know." He seemed struggling to restrain his voice. "When I thought Popi might not survive, I promised myself that if she passed away I'd hunt down and slaughter everyone responsible, one by one."

Yianni had no doubt the man meant it.

"But when she woke up, I felt reborn. Like I had a new reason for living. I realized then that going after the ones who'd tried to kill her would only put her and our future in danger again. That's when I decided to leave retribution to you."

"A wise decision." Yianni exhaled. "The police found the truck and car involved in attacking us."

"The drivers were hired that morning to run a motorbike off a mountain road, but when you ended up in Popi's pickup, their instructions must have changed."

Yianni stared at the phone for a moment. "Wait. How do you know all this?"

"Yesterday, someone I know from Naxos visited me in the hospital. He said he had something he had to tell me in person." Mamas paused. "I'm sure I don't have to tell you, Detective, that there are some very nasty people out there, and the one who came to see me is among the worst. But we grew up together. Our families have known each other for generations."

Yianni heard Mamas swallow.

"He'd been offered a huge fee to kill a cop on a motorbike. But it had to look like an accident and happen that day. He was told he'd find the cop at a hotel west of the airport and should follow him until he found the right place to run him off the road. He said he turned down the job. Even at that price, it wasn't worth the risk of killing a cop."

"I wonder what's the going rate for two cops in a pickup?"

"He said he didn't know for sure what happened after he turned down the offer, but he guessed someone involved in the plan saw you in a pickup and the plan changed."

"Why would such a bad guy tell you all this?"

"Self-preservation. He knew if I somehow thought he'd had anything to do with what happened to Popi, he was a dead man. As soon as he heard about the crash, he knew he had to tell me. He did it in person because he knew I'd need to look him in the eye to believe him."

"Do you believe him?"

"I believe he wouldn't do anything to harm Popi."

"What's his name?"

"I promised I wouldn't say."

Yianni decided not to push the point. "Does he know who was involved?"

"He knows who *tried* to hire him."

Yianni clenched a fist. "Who?"

"He's a local, another of the nasty ones. His name is Spyros, but everyone knows him as Honeyman."

"What's a Honeyman?"

"It's his nickname. He works a honey-selling routine on tourists out of the back of his old pickup truck. He's quite a fast-talker, convincing tourists that the supermarket honey he's selling them at three times the price comes from his own bees."

"Happens everywhere," said Yianni.

"But for him it's just a cover for how he makes his real money. He drives all over the island selling his honey, picking up bits of information here and there, and selling it to whoever might be interested."

"Sounds like a spotter for burglars."

"More likely he's one himself. Among other things…" Mamas's voice sharpened, "But being involved in a murder plot is way beyond anything I've ever heard said about him before. Considering the risk, there must be some real money or pressure involved."

"I take it you don't see him as the top dog in this?"

"No way. He likes to hear himself talk, and he thinks he's clever, but he's a small-time grifter. He did it for somebody else."

"Where can I find Honeyman?"

"Hard to say. He's always on the move, likely up and out of his house before dawn and not back until after dusk. Dimitri should be able to find him. Come to think of it, your best chance at catching him might be at night when he's home."

"Where's his house?"

"I couldn't give you understandable directions, certainly not for finding it at night, but Dimitri will know how to get there."

Yianni hesitated. "One question. What do you think the chances are that Honeyman knew the taverna we were headed to was Popi's favorite?"

"He could have found that out from any number of people. Popi always talked it up as her favorite place on the island. How's that important?"

"I'm trying to figure out how Honeyman knew when, and which way, we'd turn coming out of Siphones. Hard to imagine he'd leave something that important to chance."

"I don't think he did. One of his usual places for parking his pickup and setting up his honey operation is along the road running past Siphones. Your only choice out of Siphones is to head south toward roads connecting back to Chora or north toward Koronos. All he had to do was wait until he saw which way Popi was headed and call the drivers. My guess is they expected you to head toward Koronos and were waiting up that way, but if you'd gone south, they'd have tried to chase you down from behind."

Yianni shut his eyes, drew in a deep breath, and thought back to when they left Siphones…and of that old pickup parked off to the side of the road.

He exhaled and opened his eyes. "I think it's time to arrange for Naxos's finest to pay an official visit on Mr. Honeyman."

Mamas's voice lightened up, "I was hoping you'd say that." He paused. "I'm sure Popi is too."

Chapter Thirteen

In the moonlight, to the tempo of what seemed a million cicadas, the SUV and a marked police car crept lights-out down a rutted donkey path toward a ramshackle stone farmhouse at the bottom of a hollow. Not a glint of light came from the farmhouse. Beyond the house, parallel rows of beehives ran off in the direction of a long-neglected shepherd's hut.

The vehicles stopped thirty meters from the house, and two men got out of each vehicle. Two approached the front door, and two went to the rear. The men at the front stood to each side of the door as the taller of the two knocked twice on the door.

"Spyros, it's Chief of Police Dimitri. Open up."

No answer.

He banged on the door three times. "Police, open up."

No answer.

He banged away, shouting all the while. "Spyros, it's the police. Open up. We know you're in there."

The front door opened. "Easy guys, it's me," said Tassos. Behind him stood a uniformed Naxos cop holding a teenaged boy by the arm. "This one tried scooting out the back door."

"Who are you?" asked Andreas.

The boy said nothing.

"I said, who are you?"

Dimitri interrupted, "It's Spyros's son." He looked at the boy "Why did you run?"

No answer.

"Do you want to go back to bed or be arrested? A simple choice. Now tell me why you ran?"

The boy shuffled his feet. "I was afraid."

"Of what?"

"Of you."

"A guilty conscience over some crime you committed that you thought we knew about, perhaps?" said Tassos.

The boy looked down at the floor.

"Where's your father?" said Dimitri.

"I don't know."

"And your mother?"

"She's in Athens with my sister."

"Doing what?"

"I don't know."

"What's your father doing?"

"I don't know."

Tassos whispered to Andreas, "My guess would be off doing a little while-the-cat's-away-the-mice-will-play action."

"When will your father be back?" said Andreas.

"I don't know."

"You've got that 'I don't know' bit down pretty well," said Tassos. "Why don't you tell us what you do know about where your father *might* be."

"I don't know."

"When's the last time you saw him?"

The boy hesitated.

"Remember the choice I offered you," said Dimitri. "Back to bed or back with us."

"Two days ago."

"Do you mean the day before yesterday?" said Andreas.

He nodded. "In the morning."

"When did your mother and sister leave for Athens?"

"Three days ago."

"Are you alone?"

He nodded.

Dimitri said to his cop, "Check out the house to see if anyone else is in here."

Tassos walked to the back door and stared out at the beehives. "Didn't Popi's husband tell Yianni that Honeyman's game was to buy honey at the supermarket and resell it to tourists as his own?"

"Yeah," said Andreas.

"Then why all the hives?"

Tassos looked at the boy. "Does your father raise bees?"

The boy gestured no. "My sister is allergic to bee stings. She almost died from a bee sting, so mother made him give up the bees."

"Is that when he started passing off store-bought honey as his own?"

The boy nodded.

"I have to admit, his improvised method for supporting his family earns my grudging respect," said Tassos.

"Don't get too carried away with the admiration," said Dimitri. "Honeyman has been passing off store-bought honey as his own since before he was his son's age. He found that a lot easier way to make money than raising bees." He looked at the boy. "That's the same sympathy pitch his father gives to any tourists who happen to discover they've been hustled and come back looking to complain."

Tassos looked at the boy. "Ah, so the little rotten apple doesn't fall far from the tree." He motioned for Andreas to follow him as he walked to the back door, headed toward the hives. "Come. Let's see what we have here."

"Bees," said Andreas. "And they sting when their rest is disturbed."

"What troubles me," said Tassos, as he approached the first row of beehives, "is that even with the bee shortage in Greece, these hives are worth money, and I can't imagine why he wouldn't sell them, rather than leaving them to rot."

Tassos held his flashlight up to the first hive in the row. He stepped forward and tapped on the hive. Nothing happened. Next, he shook the hive. Nothing happened.

"So far so good," he said.

"They're just waiting to ambush you for taking off the top," said Andreas.

"We shall see. Here, hold the light so I can lift the lid."

Andreas took the light and Tassos lifted off the top.

"No bees."

Andreas stepped forward and shone the light down into the hive. "What's down there? I can't see in."

"I have a buddy who raises bees on Syros. I'll have to remove the feeder section to see into the body of the hive." Tassos pulled and tugged at the top section. "My buddy uses a pry bar to do this." He kept tugging until the feeder came off.

They looked inside.

"What the hell is this?" said Andreas, holding the light.

"It should be filled with frames that hold the honeycombs. Instead we've got a different kind of honey." Tassos reached in and pulled out a piece of ceramic.

"A potsherd." He reached in again and pulled out another piece. He held them both up to the light. "They look to be from the same urn." He took the light from Andreas and stared into the hive. "From my onetime experience in this business, I'd say that this hive contains all the pieces of at least one very old urn." He carefully put the pieces back in the hive and replaced the sections.

Tassos aimed the light at the rows of hives. "If all those hives are stocked like this one, I'd say we've hit upon a serious antiquities-smuggling operation."

"How would that tie into Honeyman arranging for a hit on Yianni and Popi?"

"It may not."

"Another coincidence?" said Andreas.

"I'm just as suspicious as you are of coincidences, but it's a possibility. After all, I haven't seen or heard anything that ties the reporter, Yianni, or Popi to antiquities smuggling. Have you?"

"No." Andreas waved his hand at the hives. "But here we've got this honey seller sitting atop a fortune in illegal antiquities, organizing a frantically ill-conceived hit on two cops looking to find a missing newspaper reporter writing a story about tourism versus preservation. It makes no sense."

"Maybe Honeyman is more than just a honey seller. Perhaps he's a *really* bad guy." Tassos paused. "Possibly even Nikoletta's mysterious guy?"

"Wouldn't that be a fateful twist?"

"Is a fateful twist any different than a coincidence?"

"Let's go back inside and talk to the kid some more. Then I'll answer your question."

"I'll meet you later. I want to check out that shepherd's hut."

"For what?"

"Who knows what other wild coincidence or fateful twist might be lurking in the shadows?"

"Good point," said Andreas, turning back toward the house. *Who knows, indeed?*

———

Their efforts at getting the boy to talk began with wading through the boy's defensive barrage of "I don't knows" and "I haven't spoken to my father in two days." Once the boy admitted that his father had never left him alone this long before, it didn't take much to convince him his father might be in serious trouble, and by keeping quiet he wasn't helping him.

The boy knew all about the beehives but swore nothing in them was his family's. His father had told him he ran the beehives as a hotel for other people's property—he called the items *guests*—and also provided transfer services for guests requiring a pickup from or delivery to a plane, boat, or other place on the island. He'd transport the *guests* hidden beneath a tarp in the back of his truck. Sometimes the boy helped his father transfer guests from the truck into the hives. At other times he'd help move guests out of the hives, either back to his father's truck or into a stranger's vehicle, but no matter what, his father would smile and say, "Sure beats beekeeping."

The more the boy talked, the more noticeably anxious he became for his father.

"When's your mother coming back from Athens?" asked Andreas.

"I don't know. When she left she said next week."

"Does she know you're alone here?"

"No, I didn't want her to worry."

Andreas nodded. "Is there anyone you can stay with until she's back?"

"My aunt."

Andreas looked at his watch. "It's about a half hour before dawn. We'll call her after sunrise."

"You've been most helpful," said Tassos. "I have just one more question."

The boy tensed.

"How did you know which *guests* went in which hive? And which guests belonged to the strangers who came to collect them?"

The boy pointed at a loose-leaf notebook on a shelf behind the kitchen table. "It's all in there."

Tassos pulled it off the shelf, opened it, and spent a minute quickly looking through it. He smiled. "It sure is. Thanks, son, you can go back to bed now."

The boy hurried out of the room.

"What's in the notebook?" asked Dimitri.

"Separate ledger pages for each hive, recording guests, dates of check-in and checkout, and initials, which I suspect represent who was paying rent on the particular hive."

"Any way to put a name to the initials?" said Andreas.

"Not as far as I can tell."

"Maybe we'll find a key somewhere else in this mess?" said Dimitri.

"I'd like to think so," said Tassos, "but the truth is there's only a half dozen or so sets of initials, so he probably doesn't need to keep a list in order to know the names that go with them."

"I guess we'll just have to find Honeyman and sweat him." Andreas looked at Dimitri. "But until then, and until the Ministry of Culture gets its people here to catalog and take custody of all this, you better keep some cops here. It would be a real embarrassment if any of what we found disappeared while in the hands of the police." He spread out his arms, stretched, and yawned. "Make that a *career-ending embarrassment* for everyone involved."

"It's going to be a busy day," said Dimitri. "And you've got that meeting at 15:00."

Andreas nodded. "Plus Yianni's checking out of the hospital this morning."

"Don't worry about picking him up. I've arranged for an ambulance to take him to your house."

"That's very kind of you."

"It's the least I could do for you after all you've done for me."

"What have we done for you?" asked Andreas.

"I agree that losing any of these artifacts would be a surefire career-ender. But on the other hand, finding them should put us all in line for serious promotions."

"I don't want one," said Andreas.

"Me either," said Tassos. "But I'll tell you what. If you take responsibility for protecting all this stuff and coordinating things with the Culture Ministry so that I can get out of here and back to bed, you can have my promotion."

"Mine, too."

Dimitri smiled. "Deal."

———

Yianni refused to leave the hospital in an ambulance. He said he was fine. Toni told him to get over his macho stubbornness and think of it as a limo or else she was going straight back to Mykonos. They compromised on Yianni sitting up front with the driver.

When they arrived at the house, Lila and Maggie were waiting for them outside the front door. "We had to put the brass band on hold," Lila said, exchanging cheek kisses with Yianni and Toni, "because the men of the house are sleeping."

"They were up until after dawn," said Maggie.

"I know," said Yianni. "I spoke to them on their way back to the house."

Toni poked Yianni in the arm. "This one kept waking up all night to check his messages."

"They promised to message me once the raid was over. How could I sleep?"

"There's a bedroom waiting for you two whenever you'd like it," said Lila.

"I'll take you up on that offer," said Toni. "After two days of dozing on a hospital chair, I could use a bed."

"What time do they plan on leaving for the meeting?" asked Yianni.

"We're leaving at two thirty," said Maggie.

Yianni perked up. "You're going with them?"

"So am I," added Lila. "Each of us read a different notebook, so we all have to be there."

"I read two," said Maggie. "Besides, the restaurant we're meeting at is terrific."

"It'll be like a family outing," said Maggie.

"Well, I guess that settles it," said Yianni.

"Settles what?" asked Toni.

"We're all going."

"No you're—"

Yianni cut Toni off. "Nonnegotiable. As Maggie said, it's a family outing, not a police action. Besides, I'm the only one who's read all of the notebooks and spoken to people named in two of them. I have to be there."

"Your health is more important. And need I remind you again: *You just got out of the hospital.*"

"And now I'm going to take a nap. I'll be fine."

Toni shot him the middle finger and glared. "Fine, but if that meeting puts you back in the hospital, get yourself another nursemaid."

Yianni leaned over and kissed her on the cheek. "Never."

———

Yianni sat in the front passenger seat next to Andreas, while Lila and Toni occupied the far rear seats and Maggie and Tassos had the middle row.

Andreas glanced at Yianni. "Are you comfortable?"

"Yes."

"Are you sure?" asked Maggie.

"Yes," said Yianni. "Please stop worrying about me. I'd be more concerned about how we're going to play this. If we're not careful, it could turn into the opening line to a bad joke. 'Three couples walk into a restaurant…'"

"Or a caper movie starring Charlie's Angels and the Three Stooges," quipped Maggie.

"Okay, children, behave," said Andreas. "This is how we're going to play it. I'll introduce each of you and explain why you're there. Yianni, Tassos, and I will do most of the questioning. If any of you have a question or think there's something we missed, don't just blurt it out. Let me know what's on your mind. There may be a method to what you see as our utter stupidity."

"Or there may not be," added Yianni.

"As I can attest," said Tassos.

"Thank you, gentlemen, for demonstrating another point I want us all to keep in mind. The key to this afternoon is *to remain serious*. That means, staying on message. The message being: *We need your help to save a young woman's life*."

"I guess we're done with denying she's disappeared," said Yianni.

Andreas nodded. "That's a secret I think it's safe to assume is long out of the bag among many Naxians and certainly is with those we'll be meeting. Besides, it's Sunday afternoon, and we only have until noon tomorrow before the whole world knows."

Yianni adjusted himself in his seat. "I know you've been talking among yourselves about the notebooks, so it would be helpful to me if you'd each give a quick rundown on what you found significant in whatever notebook you read. That way, I'll know if I missed something or have something to add to your take."

"Sure," said Andreas. "Maggie, since you read the notebooks covering Nikoletta's interview with the hacker, and with the mayor and hotel association guy, why don't you start?"

One by one they described their respective notebook's high points and what they thought significant. When they'd finished it was close to two thirty, and they were less than a kilometer from the taverna.

"Well done, class, and we're right on time. Now remember what I said: Stay serious, and stay on message."

Chapter Fourteen

Andreas parked behind the taverna at the edge of an olive grove. His party entered single file through an open back door and found their way onto the veranda, where three men and two women sat on the far side of a long table spanning the rear of the space.

Timeliness was not a traditional Greek trait, yet the five they'd come to meet were all there, and from the number of bottles, plates, and cigarette butts in front of them, had been there for quite a while. Andreas took that to mean they'd been meeting among themselves in preparation for their meeting with him. A prudent thing to do.

"Welcome," said Chef from his seat between two men and two women. "Please excuse us for not standing, but we're sort of wedged in here."

"No problem," said Andreas, walking up to a chair directly across from Chef's extended hand. "Sorry we're late."

"You're right on time." They shook hands and Chef turned first to the women seated next to him to Andreas's left and then to the men seated to Andreas's right. "This is Chief Inspector Andreas Kaldis, head of GADA's Special Crimes Unit. He requested this meeting." Chef turned back to Andreas. "Perhaps you'd like to introduce your colleagues to us, some of whom I've already met."

"As very satisfied customers," added Andreas. "My pleasure, but before I do, please allow me to express my gratitude to each of you for taking the time to come here today. We truly need your help, or rather the reporter to whom each of you spoke, Nikoletta Elia, needs your help."

He paused. When no one asked *why* their help was needed, he knew they were indeed already aware that Nikoletta had disappeared.

"I've brought five colleagues with me, because the situation we're facing is serious and urgent. I trust you'll keep what we talk about this afternoon in strict confidence, as the safety of the reporter may depend upon our discretion."

He pointed at Tassos. "This is Tassos Stamatos, chief homicide investigator for the Cyclades. And this is Detective Yianni Kouros, who works with me at GADA." Both men nodded to the group and sat to Andreas's right.

"Maggie," he said, "is my personal assistant at GADA. And Toni is an expert at recovering missing items and persons. Finally," he nodded at his wife, "Lila Vardi specializes in the study of erratic behavior." As they sat to Andreas's left, he made a mental note to compliment Lila and the others for keeping a straight face at her introduction.

Chef introduced those seated on his side of the table: Farmer, Artist, Bookseller, and Shepherd.

Except for Andreas and Chef, no one had said a word since Andreas and his group walked onto the veranda. Nor had anyone asked about Yianni's bandages, which Andreas took to mean they already knew how he'd earned them.

Andreas looked at Farmer. "May I start with you, Miss?"

"It's Ms."

"My apologies. I believe you were the first of this group to speak to the reporter."

"We're not a group. We're each independent of the other, with independent views, principles, and goals."

"I did not mean to suggest otherwise. Did you have the occasion to discuss any of that with the reporter?"

"The reporter is a woman with a name. You should use it."

Andreas forced what he hoped looked like a sincere smile. "I'm actually working quite hard at trying to save Nikoletta's life, so if you'd meet me halfway on this back-and-forth over what you two talked about, it might be of great help in that endeavor."

"Are you suggesting I'm not cooperating?"

"Oh, shut the fuck up, already, and answer the man's question," growled Artist. "This isn't an equal rights confrontation; it's an attempt to save a sister's life. So stuff the bullshit and get to what you talked about with her."

"Go to hell," said Farmer.

This was not working out as Andreas had hoped. "Uh, folks, could we try kickstarting this again? Please remember why we're here." He stared straight at Farmer.

She stared back. "Nikoletta wanted to know how I felt about the island's expanding tourism. I said I wasn't against it as long as it was measured and in keeping with the environment. She told me that was a wonderful phrase to crochet on a pillow, but what did I *really* think?"

Andreas nodded and said nothing.

"That's when I told Nikoletta that strangers were buying up some of our finest virgin beachfront property in areas where development was forbidden."

"What sorts of strangers?" said Andreas.

"I don't know. They're using foreign companies."

"How do you know this?"

"I come from an old Naxian family with relatives everywhere, and many with beachfront property were approached."

"Why do you think strangers are trying to buy up that kind of property?"

"Because they see the writing on the wall. Naxos is gaining in popularity, and they're betting that sometime soon mounting pressure for development will make the government ease up on restrictions."

"Let's hope that day never comes," said Lila.

Andreas glanced at Lila, and she looked back at him.

Farmer smiled at Lila. "Exactly. Stand your ground."

Andreas swallowed. "What else did you and Nikoletta talk about?"

"That's about it."

"Did you give her the names of those buying or attempting to buy the properties?"

"She asked, but I said I didn't remember."

Andreas paused to compose his next question. "Does that mean you remember now?"

She spread her hands out in front of her. "Is it important?"

"It might help save her life."

"How?" asked Bookseller.

"If I knew that," said Andreas, "I wouldn't be asking for the names."

"But naming names is frowned upon on this island."

"Snitching is frowned upon just about everywhere," added Chef.

"In some of our villages it can lead to a vendetta," said Shepherd.

Andreas held up his hands. "From the way everyone's reacting, am I correct that all of you know of this effort to buy up properties?"

At first no one responded. Then, one by one, each nodded yes.

"So, how many different buyers are we talking about?"

Silence.

"Come on, at least tell me that."

Bookseller raised his hand. "I can't say for sure, but my father's a lawyer and his clients have received offers for their property from a lot of different foreign companies."

Andreas suppressed a sigh at the continued vagueness.

"But they all had one thing in common."

"What's that?"

"The same local approached each of them on behalf of a different foreign company."

Andreas leaned in toward Bookseller. "Could you please give me that person's name?"

Bookseller looked at his colleagues, but none reacted.

"I assume from their silence that no one disagrees with your telling me."

"I don't know his full name, but everyone calls him Honeyman."

Andreas hoped his poker face had held up as he turned to Farmer. "Is that the name you couldn't remember for the one who approached your relatives?"

"Yes, Spyros the Honeyman. That's the one." She smiled.

"Why are you smiling?"

"All the locals know he's a fast-talking con man, and they'll have nothing to do with him. Which means whoever's buying isn't local. No Naxian would ever use him as their intermediary."

Andreas paused. "Did Nikoletta ask all of you what you knew about people trying to buy and develop beachfront property?"

All nodded yes.

Why then, Andreas wondered, *had not a word about any of this appeared in Nikoletta's notebooks?*

Where to go next with the questioning? And, more to the point, what else could Nikoletta have not recorded from her interviews?

"Chief?" said Shepherd.

"Yes, sir."

"I'm a close friend of Popi's husband."

"Yes, I know."

"He told me what happened, and that got me to thinking about the really bad guys on this island. There's the one the reporter wrote about and the ones who tried to kill Popi and you." He nodded at Yianni.

Yianni nodded back.

"It's said bad things come in threes. Well, I have a third for you, Petros Zagorianos."

Yianni raised an eyebrow. "Do you mean Peter Zagori? The tourist who died in a fall from Grotta?"

"Yes, but he's no tourist. He's from a village close to mine. He was a bad kid and a worse adult. He went to America, changed his name, and became a hired killer. His family actually bragged about it. It's that kind of family."

"Are you saying everybody knows he's a hired killer?" said Andreas.

"No, just those from his village and some in a neighboring village that shares its Cretan roots."

"May I ask the name of Zagori's village?"

"Filoti."

Andreas stared at him. "I think I know the place. We spent most of last night there." *With Honeyman's beehives.*

———

The rest of the afternoon was interesting and, when food started coming out of the kitchen, tasty as well, but Andreas's thoughts focused on Honeyman. In less than twenty-four hours of poking into the background of this seemingly simple local grifter, Spyros had been exposed as central to a high-end antiquities-smuggling operation, the island's front man for a host of clandestine real estate ventures and a broker for contract killings. *How could an experienced investigative reporter like Nikoletta not have discovered at least some of those same things?* Perhaps she had, possibly much more. All of which kept leading Andreas back to the same question. *Why didn't she put any of this into her notebooks?*

Andreas excused himself from the table and went back to the SUV. From there he called Dimitri and asked him for the Athens address of Honeyman's wife and daughter. If Honeyman was there, they'd arrest him on the spot. If not, they'd keep an eye on his family until they found him. Attempted cop killers earned that kind of attention. Besides, characters this dirty could be involved in anything, and with Honeyman's fellow villager and contract killer Peter Zagori's body turning up at the scene of Nikoletta's disappearance, Andreas had no doubt Honeyman was somehow tied into whatever happened to the reporter.

By the time he returned to the taverna, Andreas had heard back from Dimitri with the address and passed it along, together with instructions, to the GADA officers he wanted to make the arrest. All they needed now was luck. Inside, the meeting was breaking up. Andreas joined in thanking everyone for coming and offered his help should the day ever come that one of them might need it.

Artist hugged Lila. "Please do stop by my studio in Halki. I'd love to introduce you to some of the other board members of our environmental organization. I sense we share the same sensibilities."

"That's very flattering," smiled Lila.

"And she's speaking for both of us," said Farmer.

"You're on the same board?" said Andreas.

"Of course, why else would I let her speak to me the way she does? It livens up our meetings."

"Don't believe it. She's a royal pain in the ass," said Artist, taking Farmer by the arm and tugging her toward the door.

Lila smiled. "It still will be my pleasure."

"I hope we helped," said Bookseller.

"You certainly did. Thank you," said Andreas.

"I want you to catch the bastards who did this," Shepherd told Yianni.

"You can count on it, if only for Popi's sake."

Shepherd shook Yianni's hand, nodded to Andreas, bowed to the women, and followed Bookseller out the door.

Andreas turned to Chef and smiled. "I really owe you a big-time favor. We couldn't have accomplished this without you."

"It was the right thing to do. You were vouched for by a man we all respect, and we agreed before you got here that since we'd shown up, we had to follow through and do what we could to help, even if some of us were less than thrilled at the notion of helping the police."

"Understood," said Andreas. "But I meant what I said: If there ever comes a day when you need me for anything, don't hesitate to ask."

"Well, now that you mention it, there is one thing."

So soon? Andreas wondered what was coming.

Chef handed a paper to Andreas. "You can pay the lunch bill."

——

Once in the SUV and headed back to the house, Andreas brought Tassos and Yianni up to speed on his efforts to track down Honeyman.

"I'm sort of getting used to driving this road," said Andreas, glancing off to his left.

"Too bad you don't get to see the scenery," said Lila. "It's amazing just watching the shadows play off against the hills and valleys. So many shades of color."

"My favorite part," said Toni, "is that elevated stretch of road bound by a long line of eucalyptus trees framing everything between us and the sea."

"My favorite part is the food," said Tassos.

"That explains why you were so quiet during our meeting," said Andreas.

"I thought you handled it quite well and saw no reason to speak."

"That generally means we both missed something."

"Speaking of missing something..." said Yianni.

"What's that?" asked Andreas.

"With all these folks talking to Nikoletta about foreign efforts to buy up beachfront property, why's there no mention of any of that in her notebooks?"

"That bothers me too," said Andreas.

"What do you mean?" asked Toni.

"Just that," said Yianni. "There's not a word about any of that in her notebooks."

"That can't be true," said Toni, leaning forward.

"I've read them all and, believe me, there's no mention."

Toni shook her head. "While Andreas was outside and the rest of you were chatting among yourselves, I was talking to Artist and Farmer. Artist said she noticed that none of us was taking notes. I said I hadn't noticed. She asked me if we were recording the meeting, and I said not that I knew of. She said that was good, because she wouldn't want what she'd said to Farmer recorded on audio for posterity. All of us laughed. That's when Farmer said how impressed she was at the reporter's thoroughness as a note-taker, taking down almost every word."

"We already knew that," said Yianni.

Toni bristled. "Well, then you probably already know this too, *Detective*. The artist said Nikoletta was not only thorough but organized. She brought two notebooks with her, and when she started asking questions about the efforts to buy up property, she switched to the second notebook. When she'd finished asking those questions, she went back to her first notebook. And while Artist was telling me all of that, *Detective*, Farmer was nodding in agreement."

"*Another notebook?*" said Andreas.

"I never saw a sixth notebook," said Yianni. "Where the hell could it be?"

"I don't know," said Andreas, "but I'm going to have Dimitri leave us a car at the house. Tassos and I will use that one and leave the SUV for the rest of you."

"Hey, what about me?" said an irritated Yianni.

"You've done enough for your first day out of the hospital. Rest up, because tomorrow could be D-day for us all."

"Where are you two planning on going?" said Maggie. "Tassos isn't exactly up to storming beachheads."

"Don't know yet, but the logical place to start looking for the missing notebook is back at Nikoletta's hotel."

"A *sixth* notebook," said Yianni. "I can't believe it."

"Believe it, Detective." Toni leaned across the middle seat and patted him on the head. "Whether or not you apologize."

———

The battered blue-and-white police cruiser had seen better days, but Andreas was happy to have it. The dents and scrapes gave it the sort of character that made other drivers hang back out of fear that they might be its next victim.

"So, what do you think happened to the sixth notebook?"

Tassos looked out the passenger side window. "The obvious answer is someone took it from her hotel room."

"Before or after she disappeared?"

"Could be either, though if after, the night security guy is the chief suspect."

"Dimitri's asking the hotel owner to bring him in early so we can question him."

"What if no one took it?"

Andreas slowed down to allow a half dozen hobbled goats to cross the road. "Then Nikoletta must have done something with it."

"Like what?"

"Hidden it, lost it, given it away, taken it with her, or destroyed it. If we find it, or find her, we might find out."

"I wonder what's in it?"

"Don't we all."

Ten minutes later, Andreas pulled up in front of Nikoletta's hotel. "Time to see where this new twist takes us."

"Speaking of twists, I already feel like a pretzel. This damned seat doesn't go back."

Andreas looked back and laughed. "It will if you move the case of water from behind it."

"Son of a bitch," said Tassos, wedging his way out of the seat.

"I'm sure Dimitri put it there because he thought we might need the water."

Tassos opened the rear door and lifted the case onto the back seat. "Well, it's enough to last us for a week. I hope he doesn't think we'll be driving this piece of crap for that long."

"Chief Inspector Kaldis?"

Andreas turned to see a tall, slim man standing outside the hotel entrance. "Yes?"

"I'm the owner of the hotel. Welcome."

The three men shook hands.

"We'd like to speak to your night man, Anargyros."

"I tried to get him to come in earlier, but he can't make it before eleven."

"Damn," said Andreas.

"Perhaps there's something I can help you with? Come, let's go into my office."

As they walked by reception, a dark-haired, perky young Greek woman smiled. "Hi."

Tassos and Andreas smiled back.

Once inside his office and seated around his desk, the owner said, "So, what can I do to help you?"

"How long have you known Anargyros?"

"Many years."

"Do you trust him?"

"If I didn't, he wouldn't be working here."

"I understand he has a drug problem."

"*Had*. He's worked hard at beating it."

"Does he have access to your guest rooms?" said Tassos.

"He knows where the keys are, so I guess the answer is yes."

"Who else has access to those keys?" said Andreas.

"Theoretically anyone."

"How's that?" said Tassos.

"When guests go out of the hotel they're required to leave their keys with us, and we place them on top of the reception desk for them to pick up on their return."

Andreas leaned forward. "So, after she left the hotel at four that morning, anyone could have picked up her key and gotten into her room, assuming they got past Anargyros?"

"As a matter of fact, not that night. When Nikoletta ran out, she took her key with her. We had to have a new one made."

Andreas slouched back in his chair. "Damn."

"What are you looking for? If you told me, perhaps I could be of better assistance."

"We think someone took something from her room."

"What sort of thing?"

"A notebook," said Tassos.

"Let's speak to my receptionist. If anyone on the hotel staff knew what happened to it, she would." He picked up his phone. "Marine, could you please come in for a moment."

Five seconds later the perky woman stepped into the room. "Yes, sir?"

"These gentlemen are with the police, and they are looking for a notebook that belonged to Nikoletta Elia."

"What sort of notebook?"

"The size we used in school," said Tassos.

"Way back in the days before computers," smiled Andreas.

"About this size?" said Marine, making a shape with her hands.

"Yes."

"No, I never saw a notebook."

Andreas exhaled. "Well, thanks anyway."

"But she did ask me to send off a package for her of about that size."

Andreas and Tassos sat up in their chairs.

"When?" asked Andreas.

"A day or two before she disappeared."

"She disappeared early Thursday morning," said Andreas.

Marine thought for a moment. "She gave me the package on Tuesday afternoon. Said it had to get to Athens right away."

"And you mailed it?" said Tassos.

"No, she wanted it sent by air courier that evening, no matter what the cost."

"Where did she send it?"

"I'll have to check my calendar. That's where I keep a record of such things."

The owner motioned for her to get it.

"You run a tight ship," said Andreas.

"We try."

Marine returned with a large calendar. "Let's see. Last Tuesday. Oh, here it is."

She put the calendar down on the desk between the two policemen and pointed with her finger to an entry. "That's the name and address."

Tassos read the name out loud. "Giorgos Pappas."

Andreas's jaw tightened. "Nikoletta's editor."

Chapter Fifteen

"Pappas? It's Kaldis here."

"Have you found Nikoletta?"

"Not yet."

"Then why are you calling me? I don't need stroking."

"What you need is a hard kick in the ass, but I'd rather deliver that to you in person."

"What—

"Just shut up and listen. In your moments of deep concern over the fate of your reporter, did you happen to forget to tell me a few things?"

"What *things*?"

"Let me be clear about this, Giorgos. From the way you're reacting, you might want to consider hiring a lawyer before getting yourself into deeper trouble than you're already in."

"Is that a threat?"

"If you're guilty of what I have in mind, you'd better believe it is."

"Would you mind telling me what you're talking about?"

"Let's start with that notebook you neglected to tell me about."

"What notebook?"

Andreas said nothing.

"I said what note—Wait, are you talking about the one Nikoletta sent me a couple of days before she disappeared?"

"Brilliant. Amazing how you figured that out all on your own."

"Just hold on a minute. It never entered my mind that it might be relevant to her disappearance."

"Bullshit."

"Like hell it is."

"Then convince me why you didn't think it relevant."

"Fine!" he yelled. "When Nikoletta's interview story broke, I wanted her back in Athens to work on our planned follow-up series, but she insisted she needed more time to finish her tourism piece. I told her to forget about it and get her ass back to Athens. Frankly, I thought she was looking for a way to extend her stay on Naxos at the paper's expense. Underpaid reporters have been known to do that sort of thing."

"You're not convincing me."

"I agreed to give her more time, but then my publisher started busting my balls to get her back in the office at work on the series. He'd never liked the tourism piece, said death and disaster sold newspapers. I told her the only way she could stay on Naxos was if she gave me something to convince our publisher that her time spent there was worthwhile. She said she couldn't divulge her sources on the tourism piece but that she'd come across something that might just do the trick. She learned about a local character who has a hand in just about every hustle on the island. He's a small-time grifter, and his story wasn't part of her tourism piece, but it's the sort of roguish tale people like to read. I thought it might appeal to our publisher. I told her to get me what she had right away, and she promised to send her notes to me by courier."

Andreas had a pretty good idea of the answer to his next question. "And the rogue's name is?"

"Unknown. She just called him Honeyman."

"How could you possibly have thought none of this might be relevant to her disappearance?"

"If I had, I'd have told you."

"Did she send you her notebook, then?"

"I received a package from her late that afternoon, just as I was heading off to a dinner party with my wife."

"Did you read her notes?"

"No, I forwarded them on to my publisher. I wasn't about to get in the middle of a brouhaha between him and Nikoletta. I'd let him make the call."

"What did he say after he read them?"

"I don't know if he ever did read them. She disappeared and all we've focused upon since then is finding her, not her stories."

"Do you have a copy of the notebook?"

"No, like I said, it was late and I was running out of the office so I just routed it on to my publisher."

"Do you have his number?"

"Of course, but why do you want to contact him?"

"To find out what he did with the notebook—and to read it."

"Good luck with that."

"What do you mean?"

"He's big on protecting journalists' sources, and if Nikoletta's notebook could possibly expose her sources, he's not going to agree to turn it over without her consent."

"A rather interesting dilemma, isn't it? She may die because he wants her consent to turn over what could possibly save her. And you guys complain about how fucked-up the government is." Andreas struggled to control the outrage in his voice.

Andreas heard Pappas breathe in and exhale. "You can try, and I hope you convince him." He gave Andreas the number. "Good luck."

Andreas hung up without saying goodbye. He looked at Tassos sitting next to him in the police car. "Did you hear that bullshit?"

"Somebody is either very stupid or thinks we're very stupid." Tassos shook his head. "Pappas harangues you to find his allegedly kidnapped reporter, yet never bothers to tell you that two days before she disappeared he received a notebook from her containing her notes on a story involving a *rogue* from the same island on which she's gone missing."

"Hard to believe what he said is true. So hard, in fact, that it could get one to thinking it must be true."

"I consider the part about his publisher busting his balls to be a particularly novel way of attempting to justify withholding evidence."

"Let's see what his publisher has to say." Andreas dialed the number Pappas had given him. The call went into voicemail. Andreas identified himself and asked that he please call him back immediately, as it concerned his missing reporter.

"When do you think you'll hear back from him?"

"That depends on whether Pappas gets to him first. Curiosity should have him calling me right back, but in this instance, maybe not."

"What do you think the chances are that this whole thing's been staged to sell newspapers?"

"But for the attempted hit on Yianni and Popi, I'd have seriously considered that possibility. I don't see that now."

"So, what's next?"

"We wait"

"For what?"

"I don't know."

———

Andreas drove down to Chora's harbor and, after searching unsuccessfully for a legal parking space, parked in a spot marked NO PARKING ANYTIME.

"Ah, the advantage of driving a blue-and-white," said Tassos.

"Why not? We're on official business waiting for the telephone call that could break our case wide open."

"This place looks good," said Tassos, steering him into a taverna close by the harborside piazza.

They sat where they could watch the children at play in the square, darting every which way on their bikes, scooters, and skateboards.

"Watching kids play always makes me miss my own."

"You'll be back with them soon enough," said Tassos.

"Doesn't it amaze you how when children get to play on their own, away from grownups, it looks like sheer chaos, yet they somehow manage to adhere to an overriding pattern of order that keeps their play from ending in disaster? What do you think it is? Some instinctive thing, like birds knowing how to fly in formation?"

"Whatever it is, it's not a lasting influence, because by the time they're fully grown they've learned it's every man for himself."

"You're one hell of a cynic."

"As if you're not."

Andreas shook his head from side to side. "Just enjoy the moment."

Ring, ring.

"So much for the moment."

"This could be the call we're waiting for." Andreas pulled his phone out of his pocket. "It's Dimitri." He held the phone so Tassos could hear.

"Hi, what's up?"

"We found Honeyman."

"Terrific, where is he?"

"Not sure right now, but when my cops found him he was facedown at the bottom of an abandoned quarry, with one end of a rope tied around his neck and the other end tied to a slab of marble."

"Oh, shit." *So he never made it off Naxos.*

"It's not clear yet when he died, but hikers saw him late this afternoon. As far as we can tell, he and his slab were tossed off the top of the quarry a hundred meters or so above where they found him."

"What are the chances it's a suicide?" said Andreas.

"I can think of a lot less terrifying ways than a header off the top of a cliff with your neck lashed to a slab of marble. Besides, his hands were tied behind his back."

"Well, at least this one wasn't staged to look like an accident."

"Is that good or bad?" said Tassos. "It could mean that whoever's behind this is now desperate enough to use amateurs to eliminate loose ends."

"The question is, was our mastermind desperate enough to step out of the shadows in order to take out Honeyman?" Andreas paused. "Hmm…if someone from Naxos killed Honeyman, what do you think the chances are that Honeyman knew who killed him?"

"Pretty good," said Dimitri. "It could have been the same guys he'd sent after Yianni and Popi. Wouldn't that be poetic justice?"

"If they're locals known to Honeyman, would they be known to you too?" asked Andreas.

"If they're the blunt, slash-and-burn sort of bad guys who bounce in and out of prison and not some sophisticated pro like Nikoletta's, I'd say the chances are pretty good."

"Well, then, to quote one of my favorite movies, I think it's time we rounded up *the usual suspects.*"

With an assist from GPS and a call to Dimitri, Andreas and Tassos found their way back to Honeyman's house. It was close to midnight, but lights were on inside the house, and as the car rocked its way along the old donkey path, a uniformed cop stepped out of the house, trained a light on their car, and waved for them to park next to another marked cruiser.

Once inside, the cop told them it was his partner's turn to keep an eye on the beehives while he watched the empty house. He complained about how this extended guard duty detail was already straining the Filoti Police station's ability to provide normal coverage to large areas of the island. Andreas assured him that the Ministry of Culture had promised to take possession of the items in the beehives on Monday.

The cop looked at his watch and pointed out that, as of two minutes ago, it was Monday.

Andreas smiled and told him to go hang out with his partner if he wanted to, because he and Tassos had some reading to do.

Andreas took Honeyman's ledger from its shelf in the kitchen and set it on the table. He carefully read through the ledger sheets, jotting down each set of initials, hoping to find a clue to someone's identity. He found six sets of initials—JSS, GTS, AKS, KSM, RIM, and BZ—but no clues or key to the abbreviations. A handful of beehives had apparently been hiding treasures for almost two and a half decades. Over ensuing years, other beehives came online, until every beehive had replaced its bees with antiquities. It looked like Honeyman had started off small and expanded his business significantly. A regular entrepreneur.

Andreas shook his head. "The same initials listed twenty-five years ago are listed in the new entries."

"I've heard that honey prolongs life."

Andreas waved off Tassos's attempt at humor. "Honeyman's clients didn't just show up one day and say, 'Hi, I have pilfered antiquities I'd like for you to hide in your beehives.' I'd bet my pension they've been involved in antiquities trafficking for a lot longer than Honeyman's run his business."

"Your pension? That's not much of a bet, but I still wouldn't take it."

"If I'm right, then there must be others who worked with Honeyman's clients before they came to him, which means there could be people out there who know the names tied to those initials. We just have to figure out how to find them."

"Assuming they're still alive." Tassos yawned.

"Getting a bit tired, are we?"

"It's been a long day."

"I'm feeling it myself. I must be getting older."

"With every passing day. My gardening keeps me young. That and chasing bad guys."

"Perhaps I should become a farmer," said Andreas.

"You could do worse, and no better place to learn than Naxos."

Andreas sat up in the chair. "That old farmer in Siphones. The one you know. He was with his son and grandson the afternoon Yianni and Popi were attacked."

"He's still perky enough to teach you a few things, I guess." Tassos yawned again.

Andreas smacked his hand on the table. "Stop that before you get *me* to yawning. If anyone knows who belongs to these initials, it's the grandfather. You told me he's been involved in antiquities smuggling on Naxos since before the Junta."

"But didn't his son say he's senile?"

"That's a convenient way to keep people from bothering him, but it doesn't mean he *is*. I think Yianni, you, and I better pay him a visit first thing in the morning."

"For a farmer, that's dawn."

"Okay, let's say nine."

"But that doesn't give us much time if the newspaper's going public with the story at noon. If that happens, we'll go from the few on Naxos who are aware and the many here who suspect she's disappeared, to all of Greece knowing she's vanished and spook the kidnapper for sure."

"Maybe not. I plan on having a talk with Pappas first thing in the morning." Andreas smiled. "Which to this cop means dawn."

———

"Hello." The sleepy voice came through the phone with a mix of confusion, anxiety, and budding rage.

"Good morning, Giorgos. Wakey, wakey, today's a big day."

"*Kaldis?* Have you gone mad? Do you know what time it is?"

"Of course I do. It's time for you to get your ass out of bed and convince your publisher to extend his noon deadline until midnight."

"You *are* mad. How the hell do you expect me to do that?"

"I know what I'd have told him if he'd bothered to return any of the many messages I left for him."

"And what would that be?"

"Simple. If he sticks to his noon deadline and tells the world Nikoletta has disappeared, I'll call a press conference to announce that your distinguished publisher is in possession of documents that could help the police locate his missing reporter but refuses to turn them over."

"With his power and connections, you wouldn't dare."

"Try me."

"Do you have any idea who you're dealing with?"

"The question is, does he?"

"You'll be making an enemy for life."

"Tell him to get in line." Andreas paused. "Are you done yet with this who-has-a-bigger-one ping-pong match?"

Pappas cleared his throat. "What is it you really want?"

"Like I said, I want him to hold off until midnight. Of course, if he's dead set on going ahead at noon, he could outmaneuver me by simply turning over the sixth notebook, but I don't think either of us believes he'll do that. Do we?"

"I've no idea what he'll do." Pappas paused. "Just so you know, I told him about our last conversation and urged him to cooperate, but he said his commitment to preserving his reporter's sources is sacrosanct."

"As is my commitment to preserving his reporter's *life*. Have a nice day."

Andreas hung up and looked at Tassos. "How did I do?"

"Like someone who went out of his way to turn his and his family's past, present, and future into the most-favored targets of the most powerful publishing family in Greece."

Andreas smiled. "Good, then he got the message."

"When are we leaving for Siphones?"

"Let's give Yianni another hour of sleep. He needs the rest, and we need him with us to make the introductions."

"Great, then there's time for breakfast."

"Is that all you care about?"

"No. Since Maggie put me on this strict diet, I think of other things."

"Like what?"

"Lunch."

Andreas smacked his forehead and sighed. "Why do I keep feeding you these straight lines?"

"Hey, it's a skill."

Ring, ring.

"Who the hell would be calling me at this hour?"

"Now you sound like Pappas. Maybe it *is* Pappas?"

Andreas looked at the screen, gestured no, and put the call on speakerphone. "Hi, Dimitri, what's up?"

"Obviously, you are. I was prepared to leave you a message."

"The early bird gets the worm and all that."

"Well, it seems likely there's something much larger than a worm we're looking for."

"That sounds ominous."

"Because it is. The preliminary autopsy's in on Honeyman. He died before hitting the bottom."

"Mercifully, I hope."

"A bullet to the head."

"It beats flying wide-awake off the top of a cliff wearing a rope necktie anchored to a slab of marble," said Tassos.

"Why do I sense you're just getting to the *ominous* part?" said Andreas.

"Last night we began rounding up the usual suspects, as you called them. A couple of hours ago, we found two ripe ones in a stolen car down behind the airport. Each with a bullet through his head."

"Don't tell me. The bullets match the one pulled out of Honeyman," said Andreas.

"Too soon to tell, but since it looks as if they've been dead for about as long as Honeyman, I wouldn't be surprised if they match."

"I'd be surprised if they don't," said Tassos. "Sounds like whoever got rid of Honeyman also took out the other two."

"One of the victims was at the top of our list of likely drivers in the attack on Popi and Yianni."

Andreas bit at his lower lip. "So, what do we have here? A sophisticated killer who kills Honeyman and then hunts down the other two? Or an amateur who somehow knew the two well enough to lure them to a convenient place for eliminating them as potential witnesses?"

"Or some combination thereof," said Tassos. "My guess is it's closer to your amateur scenario, because with the police hunting for them, it's hard to imagine how their killer would have been able to find them if they didn't want him to."

"But couldn't Nikoletta's computer guy have found them?" said Dimitri.

"Unless he's wired into the local bad-guy network, somehow used his skills to get a GPS reading on them, or has superhuman powers, I don't see how he could," said Andreas. "Besides, none of this bears the mark of a master at work."

"Perhaps he's just trying to confuse us by appearing sloppy," said Dimitri.

"I don't see it that way," said Andreas. "I'm into believing there's a new player involved. But I'm not sure what team he's playing for."

"What's that supposed to mean?" asked Tassos.

"Are these killings because of what *else* Nikoletta might write about her hacker? Or did her activist research trip a different alarm among some very bad people?"

"Or are they dead because of something completely unrelated to anything we know or imagine?" said Tassos.

"That too," said Andreas, drawing in and letting out a deep breath. "But since we'll never know if it's something unknown until we've eliminated the known, I say we go with what's tied to the highest body count. Namely, Honeyman. More specifically, his involvement in antiquities smuggling and development-project buyouts."

"In other words, it's off to Siphones," said Tassos.

"Yes."

"Right after breakfast?"

Andreas nodded. "But be sure to make it a big one. It's shaping up to be a long day."

Chapter Sixteen

By the time Toni, Lila, and Maggie sat down to breakfast, the men had left.

Lila picked up her coffee cup. "Well, we've got a car and the day all to ourselves. What would you like to do?"

"I'd like to see more of the island," said Toni.

"Me too," said Maggie.

"Sounds good to me." Lila took a sip. "We could stop by and say hello to the women we met yesterday."

"They're an interesting pair," said Toni. "The farmer not only grows olives but runs a museum dedicated to the history of olive-growing in Eggares. And then there's the artist's gallery in Halki."

"Both are lovely villages," said Lila, "and I'm sure they'll have suggestions on what else we should see."

Maggie reached for a croissant. "What time do you want to leave?"

"In about an hour," said Lila.

"Finally," said Maggie with a smile. "A day away from intrigues and mystery."

Toni raised her cup. "And hospital rooms."

———

Andreas, Tassos, and Yianni made it to Siphones by eight thirty a.m. They stood on the side of the road above the abandoned village and saw no one.

"The broken plaque with the mysterious inscription is up there." Yianni pointed to the right.

"No one's here yet, so we might as well take a look at it," said Andreas, walking toward the marble cross. "Who knows? Maybe we'll be struck with some brilliant insight that solves Popi's mystery and makes her day."

Looking at the cross, Andreas said, "So, where's the plaque?"

Yianni pointed to broken pieces of marble in the grass by the base of the cross. "I've written it all down in my notebook."

Andreas crouched and read the inscription aloud:

"TRIBUTE DEDICATION TO SAINT CYPRIAN.
OH SAINT MIRACLE WORKER
I WILL NEVER CEASE TO THINK
OF THE MANY MIRACLES YOU'VE DONE FOR US
FAITH IS TAKING ROOT IN MY HEART
EXHILARATION OVERFLOWS
AS DOES MY GRATITUDE TO YOU
TO THE WALKER PASSING BY
HE MAY BRING FAITH THAT SAVES US
FROM EVERY CALAMITY
FROM CHRIST YOU TOOK YOUR JOY
TO HEAL THE WOUNDS FROM THE DEMONS
AND FROM THEIR WORKS OF MAGIC
PUT ON THE FAITHFUL WHO CALL ON YOU
TO UNBIND ALL THOSE WITH LOVE
WITH A FAITH THAT IS VAST."

"Sure sounds mysterious to me," said Tassos. "I know some pray to Saint Cyprian to break curses and spells, if you go in for that sort of thing, but you have to read an extremely long prayer to invoke his assistance."

"I don't have a clue to what it means," said Andreas.

"Maybe the grandfather knows something about it," said Yianni.

"I've more important questions to ask him," said Andreas.

"Speak of the devil," said Yianni. "Look who's pulling up."

"Let's hope not," said Tassos, crossing himself.

A sun-bleached maroon Toyota pickup stopped by the side of the road across from their police car. The father got out the driver side, the grandfather the passenger side. One grabbed a hoe from the bed of the pickup, the other a shovel, and together they walked away from the cops alongside a stretch of goat-wire fencing strung parallel to the road.

"I wonder where the boy is," said Andreas.

"I wonder where they're going," said Yianni. "The way into the village is through a culvert, on the other side of the road."

The two men stopped, pulled open a narrow gate made of the same fencing, and stepped onto a set of stone steps mounted nearly invisibly up against a retaining wall made of the same stone.

"Son of a bitch," said Yianni. "When I asked the father if there was another way back onto the road he didn't tell me about the steps."

"You're such a trusting soul," said Tassos, making for the steps.

Yianni called out for the two farmers to wait for them. By the time they'd caught up, the grandfather had started working his hoe on a patch of unplanted soil.

"Didn't expect to see you again, Detective," said the father.

"I missed exploring culverts, Junior."

Junior grinned.

"This is my boss, Chief Inspector Andreas Kaldis, head of GADA's Special Crimes Unit and Chief Homicide Investigator for the Cyclades Tassos Stamatos."

Junior's grin abruptly faded.

"We're here because we don't think you told me the whole truth."

Junior clenched the shovel tightly in his hands. "Are you calling me a liar?"

"Don't bother to run that routine past me again. And in case you're wondering about these bandages I'm wearing, right after the last time we spoke, somebody tried to kill me and your hunting buddy's wife, Popi." Yianni pointed to the shovel. "Nothing would give me greater joy than for you to try using that on me. It would answer a lot of questions, plus give me the opportunity to vent a whole lot of pent-up rage."

"I had nothing to do with what happened to you or Popi."

"Just drop the fucking shovel."

Junior froze for an instant, then dropped the shovel.

"A wise decision," said Andreas. "No one is accusing you or anyone in your family of having anything to do with what happened the other day, but we do have some questions for your father."

"My father knows nothing about any of this. As I told him," pointing at Yianni, "he's not all there."

"Well, we still have questions for him," said Andreas.

"Klefteraki, how are you, my friend?" Tassos yelled out to the grandfather.

The father whirled to face Tassos. "Why did you call him that?"

"We all did back in the day. It was his nickname."

"I haven't heard him called that in forty years."

"Little Thief may not sound like a compliment, but that was his nickname when we first met. If we're trying to jog his memory, why not try a blast from the past?"

Junior shut his eyes, shook his head, and waved toward his father. "Okay, go ahead and try, but don't upset him."

Tassos walked over to the grandfather. "Klefteraki, it's Tassos. We worked together down by Alyko on that Junta hotel project. You did digging; I did guarding."

The grandfather looked up and studied Tassos's face. "I don't remember you."

"I was the one you always told, 'Keep your nose out of other people's business.'"

The grandfather kept staring at Tassos's face, then suddenly smiled. "I remember you. But you were so thin and good-looking then."

Andreas suppressed a laugh. Yianni wasn't as successful, and the grandfather shot him a stern look. "You need to show more respect to your elders, young man."

"Don't mind him," said Tassos.

"I apologize, sir."

"That's better." The grandfather turned back to Tassos. "So what can I do for you…uh…"

"Tassos."

"Sorry, I have such trouble with names these days."

"I do too. But that's sort of what I'm hoping you can help me with."

"Names?"

"Yes."

"From back then?"

"Yes."

"That's a long time ago."

"I know, but I think these names were important to you then."

He leaned against his hoe. "What are the names?"

"That's what I need from *you*. All *I* have are initials."

"Oh, my, I don't know how I'll possibly remember names from initials."

"Well, let's try. They're JSS, GTS, AKS, KSM, RIM, and BZ."

The grandfather's eyes appeared to glaze over. He closed and opened them three times. "Please, say them to me again."

He squinted and began nodding in concentration as Tassos repeated the initials.

He shook his head. "I'm sorry. I recognize nothing."

"Excuse me," interrupted Yianni. "Perhaps I can help, sir." He pulled his notebook out from his pocket and showed a page to the grandfather. "Can you tell me who wrote this?"

The grandfather leaned in close to the paper and carefully mouthed the words. His face lit up. "Yes, it was Giannis Nikiforou Konstantakis, a grocer up in Koronos."

He paused to swallow. "His mother, Sofia, was from here, and she twice saved him from the devil. He erected the plaque to honor her deep faith in God…"

He paused, shut his eyes, and gently rocked from side to side. "And her answered prayers to Saint Cyprian that he use his magic powers to save her son from the devil and bring joy back to his life."

"I thought the plaque had to do with the reason everyone left the village," said Junior.

"Yeah, like ghosts or disease," said Yianni.

"Ridiculous," said the grandfather. "People abandoned our village for the same reason as people abandoned other villages."

He spoke with a touch of newfound, flinty-eyed determination. "The same work that earned them five drachmas in our village would earn them fifty drachmas in Chora or Athens. And after the war, people wanted education for their children, but we had no school here. That meant a life of hard labor for the sons, and if our daughters were lucky, landing a job as a housekeeper in Athens. They all wanted better lives and more modern things. Education was the only way, so they moved. Even my grandson is looking for better opportunities."

Junior smiled. "He's off this morning on a college interview."

Yianni smiled and slapped him on the back. "Congratulations, you must be very proud."

Junior kept smiling. "We are, thank you."

"Who broke the plaque?" said Andreas.

"I can answer that," said Junior. "Some idiot in a rental car backed into it."

"So," said Yianni, "now that we've resolved that mystery, perhaps you can help us with this one." Yianni showed him a page from his notebook listing the six sets of initials.

The grandfather stared at the page for a moment, then waggled a finger in the air. "I've seen these initials before, but I can't quite place where."

Yianni gave him a bit more time to study the page. "Perhaps they relate to your work with antiquities?"

The grandfather moved his stare to the ground. "Yes, that could be it." He shut his eyes and again began to gently rock from side to side. "When I worked at that hotel site, I remember a very large woman in her sixties. I met with her many times. She always wanted to know what new things we'd found. We'd describe them, and then they'd disappear."

"Did she take them?"

"I don't know, but no one ever questioned where they'd gone."

"I can't recall ever seeing someone like that on the site," said Tassos.

"She only met with us who dug and her project manager who'd hired us. And we always met with her away from where we worked."

"What was her name?" said Tassos.

"I never heard it."

"What about the initials?" said Andreas.

"She had six children but never spoke of them by name, only initials."

"What would she say about them?" asked Yianni.

The grandfather opened his eyes. "Something like, 'These are right for BZ' or 'This should go to AS.'"

Tassos stared at Andreas. "Sounds like we've come across a dynasty of antiquities plunderers."

Yianni leaned into the old man. "Sir, can you think of anything at all that might help us identify the woman?"

"No, but her project manager would know all about her." The grandfather paused.

The cops perked up.

"But he's dead. Died in a car accident here on Naxos twenty-five years ago."

Tassos looked at Andreas. "At about the same time as Honeyman went into the antiquities storage business."

———

"Where to now, Chief?" said Yianni as Andreas made a U-turn, headed south, toward the village of Moni.

"I want to stop at the police station in Filoti. There must be someone around who can identify that woman. From the way the grandfather spoke of her, she spent a lot of time on the island and likely came from money. A big woman with six children? She shouldn't be that difficult to identify."

"Then what?" said Tassos.

"Not sure yet, but at least we'll know we're barking up the right family tree."

Yianni grimaced. "That was really bad."

Andreas smiled. "I happened to like it. And speaking of liking,

I really liked the way you handled the grandfather. Where did you learn to do that?"

"Too much personal family experience." Yianni paused. "The key to dealing with folks with teetering memories is to keep yourself calm, not to push them, and to do what you can to make them feel comfortable. Start with what they know or once knew well, and only when you sense they've regained some confidence in their memories do you risk probing gently."

"I'll try to remember that," said Andreas.

"On the subject of remaining calm," Tassos said to Yianni, "I'm all for the good cop, bad cop routine, but when you, with your two broken ribs and bandages, launched in on Junior over that long, hard shovel in his hands, I wondered if you'd taken into account the size of the man you were trying to stand down."

"Yes, I had."

"And what was your plan if he'd swung?"

"To keep ducking until one of you shot him."

"Great plan."

Ring, ring.

"Now what?" said Andreas, grappling for his phone with one hand and driving with the other. He looked at the screen. "It's the minister. Here, Yianni, answer and put us on speakerphone."

"Hello, Andreas?"

"Yes, Minister. Hello."

"Where are you?"

"Naxos, on our way to the police station in Filoti."

"How goes the investigation into the missing reporter?" The minister spoke in a measured tone, unusual for him.

"We've got some good leads on some bad folks, and once we locate them, we should be in a better position to find her."

"In other words, you have no fucking idea where she is."

So much for measured tones. "I guess some cynics might describe it that way."

"This is not a joke, Kaldis."

"Let's cut to the chase, Minister. Who's beating down your door on this?"

"I just received a letter delivered by hand from the reporter's publisher, charging you with gross dereliction of duty in your handling of her disappearance and threatening to wipe you and me off the face of the earth if I don't immediately fire you. He also accused you of making 'extortionate threats' if he sought the help of the public to find her."

Andreas answered calmly. "And what reason did he offer for my conduct?"

"To quote him, 'Kaldis's megalomaniacal ego and psychotic obsession for control endangers the very citizens he's sworn to protect.'"

"So, what's his bottom line?"

"If you're not fired by the end of today, he's going public with his charges."

"Good."

"*Good?* What the hell does *that* mean?"

"I told him to give me until midnight to find the reporter. He's obviously agreed."

"Maybe you are insane."

"I'll take that to mean I still have my job. At least until midnight."

"I'll fax a copy of the letter to you at the Filoti station. Once you've read it, tell me how you want to handle it. This man wants your head. Decide whether you want to resign or be dismissed."

"Is there another choice?"

"Yes, find his reporter before midnight."

The line went dead.

"Didn't we discuss this possibility when you decided to

threaten the head of the most powerful publishing family in Greece?" said Tassos.

"Is this an I-told-you-so moment?" said Andreas.

"No, more of a looks-like-now-you'll-have-more-time-to-spend-with-the-family moment."

Andreas glanced at Yianni, "Thank you for your help on that call."

"What are you talking about? All I did was hold the phone."

"No, for your advice on how to deal with the senile. It also seems to apply to bureaucrats. Stay calm, make them feel comfortable, and then pounce."

"Gentlemen, we only have until midnight," said Yianni. "What do you suggest we do?"

"I want to call Dimitri and see who he thinks can help us identify that woman and her children. No reason to waste time in Filoti if he can give us leads himself."

"But what about the letter?"

"Screw it. I know what it says. I don't have to see it in print. All it will do is cause me to lose my newfound *fucking calm* at that asshole publisher." He banged away on the steering wheel.

———

Lila, Maggie, and Toni left the house by nine, but appealing distractions along the way led them first to the Temple of Demeter and then on to a slew of historical sites, churches, and monasteries before they made it to Halki. They found the artist's gallery tucked away on a lane off the main road, but by then it was early afternoon and the gallery was closed. They stood staring in through display windows, wondering where to go next, when a woman's voice yelled out to them from a *kafenio* across the lane. "Sisters, I'm over here."

Artist sat at a café table, waving for the others to join her. "I never thought you meant it when you said you'd visit my gallery. I thought you were just being courteous."

"If you knew us better, you wouldn't say that," said Toni.

"I'll keep that in mind." Artist exchanged cheek kisses with her visitors and waved to a woman standing in the doorway. "Three more wineglasses and another carafe of white, please. And don't forget the meze."

Once they'd been seated, Artist whispered, "I ordered some things to nibble on, but if you're looking to have lunch, this isn't the place."

"The whole town has such a wonderful neoclassical atmosphere. I love it," said Lila.

"Thanks. I prefer calling it neohippie classical. At one time Halki was the capital of Naxos, and a few of us have done our best to revitalize the village. The trouble is, as soon as a new shop opens with a unique concept or product, others spring up copying the original idea and charging half the price for one quarter the quality."

"Welcome to today's universal business model," said Lila.

Artist glanced inside the *kafenio*. "Oh, no, she's on her phone. Probably with her boyfriend. Who knows when she'll bring our order. Come, I'll show you my gallery while we wait."

As soon as she stepped inside the gallery and saw the artist's work, Lila asked Artist to allow her to make an introduction to one of Athens's leading gallery owners. "I know her personally, and I can assure you she would love to represent you. That is, if you're interested."

"I thought you were some kind of psychologist?"

Lila nodded. "Believe me, I am, but art is my passion and I know what's good. If you're interested, let me know."

"Your drinks are on the table" came trilling across the road from the *kafenio*'s doorway.

"If you're serious, of course I'm interested. Thank you."

"As I said before we don't say things just out of courtesy, especially not this one," said Toni, pointing at Lila.

"I said the drinks are on the table."

"She must have had a fight with her boyfriend. Let's get back to the table before she explodes. Her voice could shatter my windows."

Over the ensuing hour, they finished off the carafe of wine; nibbled away at the bits of cucumber, cheese, and sausage offered as meze; discovered common interests; and elicited Artist's promise to hook Lila and Toni up with her friend on Naxos, who, like them, worked with abused and trafficked young girls.

"Usually, I don't have to say this," said Maggie, "because Tassos does it for me, but where do you suggest we have lunch?"

"Where are you headed?"

"No plans. We thought we'd stop by Eggares to see your friend," said Lila.

"She's not there today. Maybe tomorrow."

"Then we're wide open to suggestions."

Artist paused. "If you're up for it, a wondrous ten-kilometer drive from here gets you to a mountain village with a great taverna. A girl who used to work here now works there. She moved to Halki to be closer to her boyfriend, but when that fell through she went back home to work in her family's taverna. It sits on the edge of a mountainside."

"Sound's great. What's the village?"

"Apeiranthos."

"What's it like?" asked Toni.

"It's built between two valleys on the slopes of a mountain range. Some call it the *marble village* because marble's used everywhere, from the squares used to pave its streets to the construction of its houses. The village is dominated by two seventeenth-century Venetian stone towers, and for more than half a millennium, its people have mined emery, raised livestock, and grown wine grapes. Today, it's popular with tourists looking to explore the more remote parts of the island."

Maggie smiled. "That's a very good Chamber of Commerce presentation, but aren't you leaving out a few details?"

"Like what?" asked Toni.

"Shall I tell them, or will you?" Maggie asked Artist.

"I assume you're referring to the village's tough mountainfolk reputation."

"In body as well as mind," added Maggie.

Artist nodded. "I'm not an anthropologist, but I'd venture to guess much of that comes from their Cretan roots. To this day they speak in a distinctly Cretan dialect and know how to make it through hard times by being quick-witted and doing whatever's necessary to survive."

Lila said, "I have friends with Apeiranthos roots. Those same qualities have served them well in fashioning highly successful and distinguished lives around the world."

"It's also a place where vendetta is still practiced," said Maggie.

"I'm not so sure about that," said Artist, "but just to be on the safe side, I'd say don't offend someone from Apeiranthos."

They all laughed.

Lila called for the check, but Artist insisted that in *her* village, she paid.

Before saying goodbye, they exchanged phone numbers, and Artist promised she'd call her friend at the mountainside taverna to tell her to expect them.

As they walked back to the SUV, Artist yelled out to the three from her doorway, "Safe travels."

Toni looked at Lila. "Should we take that as a warning?"

Lila smiled. "Unlike us, I think she's just being courteous."

———

Dimitri told Andreas he had no idea who the large woman with six children might have been. He said, assuming she was an off-islander keeping a low-key presence in what back then was the isolated, undeveloped southern end of the island, she might have remained virtually anonymous to all but her neighbors. Then, too, she might have stayed on a boat, making her even less likely to mingle with locals. Still, he would reach out to old-timers from the area who might recall her or know of someone who would, but from how carefully she avoided being seen on the hotel site—and the suspicious death of the project manager who could identify her—he did not hold out much hope at getting an ID on her or her children.

On his own, Andreas reached out to the five locals he'd met with the day before on the off chance one of them, or their friends or relatives, might have known of the woman.

Chef said he'd check, but as she'd be well over a hundred by now, he doubted any local contemporary of hers would still be alive, although perhaps one of their children might know of her.

Shepherd said he knew little about that part of the island and nothing about the woman, but he'd ask around.

Andreas received similar responses from Farmer, Bookseller, and Artist, except Artist asked that he please tell Lila to let her know how she liked her restaurant recommendation. Andreas promised he would.

Finished with his calls, Andreas sat quietly staring out the cruiser's front window at the line of mountains rolling north, one off into the next. Yianni and Tassos stood a few meters to the left of the front of the car, likely talking football. He'd pulled over to make his calls, and they'd gotten out to stretch their legs.

Andreas liked being a cop. Make that, *loved* being a cop. Mostly the camaraderie. He hoped his bravado performance with the minister wouldn't prove to be his swan song on the force. But from the way things were shaping up, the odds weren't in his favor.

Worse, how am I going to tell Lila that, come midnight, I'll likely be hers, 24/7?

Chapter Seventeen

Artist's directions had them following a twisting mountain road into the heart of Apeiranthos, where they found parking across from the Panagia Aperathitissa, one of the oldest and most impressive churches on the island. Artist had recommended they visit the church as well as a small gem of an archaeological museum, one of several such museums in the village. But at this moment their minds were on lunch.

They strolled west toward a broad, marble-paved lane running south through the heart of the village at the eastern border with one of its two embracing valleys. *Kafenia,* tavernas, and tourist shops lined the lane's uphill side. Across the lane, tables offered parklike views out across a schoolyard and down into the valley, while farther on, tavernas and a few private homes claimed the more spectacular views.

Groups of three and four hard-looking men of broadly ranging ages sat scattered at well-worn tables on both sides of the lane, sipping *tsipouro* or beer, smoking one cigarette after another, and commenting among themselves on all who passed by. The men's eyes locked on to the women as they approached and did not shift away as they passed, but they said not a word to the women.

"Anyone care to guess what's on their minds?" said Lila.

"Bet it's not hard," said Toni.

"That's not what I asked." Lila winked.

"Hey, you made a joke," said Toni. "But whatever they're thinking, at least they're keeping it to themselves. On Mykonos, by now I'd have heard a dozen not so interesting proposals yelled out in a remarkable variety of languages."

"Amazing isn't it, how men have the same thing on their minds no matter where they come from?" said Lila. "Though I must say, these men have been respectful, aside from where they fixed their eyes."

"I'm past the age where I need worry about that sort of thing," said Maggie. "But before you get too enamored of their gentlemanly behavior, allow me to remind you that vendetta is very much part of this village's heritage. We're strangers to these men, so until they're sure we're not somehow related to one of their neighbors, they wouldn't dare insult us."

"Oh well, I guess that's a good side to vendetta," said Lila.

"Until the shooting starts."

"Wow, look at that," said Toni, staring up at a looming fieldstone tower surrounded by matching stone terraces and verandas. It sat anchored above the west side of the lane on a base of solid rock, framed at the level of the lane in complementing stone arches and the limbs of a massive plane tree.

"It looks like a fortress," said Maggie.

"I think the taverna we're looking for is named after that tower."

"I wouldn't mind living up there," said Toni. "It's only two stories, but the view must be terrific."

"Yeah, but just think of the heating bills," quipped Maggie.

"I'd only use it in summer."

"I think we've found lunch." Lila stopped in front of a taverna bearing a sign with an image of the tower. "Yep, this is it."

The place wasn't crowded and Lila told the lone waitress they had a reservation. She showed them to a table at the edge of a long veranda spanning the rear of the taverna that overlooked a valley dappled gray-green from the shadows of passing clouds. "I'm the one who took your reservation. Welcome to my village."

Toni stared down into the valley. "It's beautiful. I can't get over how green this island is compared to Mykonos."

"I can't get over how hungry I am," said Maggie.

"Don't worry, ladies. When my friend called to make the reservation, she said to treat you like family. And my family likes to eat. So, unless you'd prefer to order from the menu, I can start the food coming and keep it coming until you say stop."

Three hungry women exchanged shrugs. Maggie said, "Go for it."

"What about wine? We have wonderful local wines."

"Why not?" said Maggie.

"But only two glasses," said Lila. "I'm driving, and these roads and wine don't mix."

The waitress nodded. "There are far too many memorials along these roads attesting to the wisdom of your thinking."

"I will take a ginger beer, though. Nonalcoholic, please."

"Done."

She left, headed to the kitchen, and returned with a liter carafe of wine, a bottle of ginger beer, a bottle of water, and glasses. "Enjoy."

"I like this place," said Toni, looking around. "Not old, not modern, just right."

"Let's face it, in places like this it's all about the view," said Maggie.

"And, we hope, the food," added Lila.

Five minutes later the waiter arrived with platters of *taramasalata*, tzatziki, *melitzanosalata*, Greek salad, grilled octopus, shrimp *saganaki*, zucchini fritters, and pita bread. "How's this for starters?"

"Starters?" said Lila. "This is enough for lunch, dinner, *and* tomorrow's breakfast."

"Well, save room. The goat and lamb are in the oven."

By the time the main courses arrived, they'd insisted the waitress join them at their table, and soon had her sharing tales about the village and the wild and crazy people who lived there.

"I've heard it said that living and working in the mountains is what makes us crazy," she said. "If you're a fisherman, you're surrounded by the sea, and that's calming. But the wildness of all this," she waved her hand at the vista, "takes hold of your spirit and makes you just as untamed."

"I don't know if I wholeheartedly agree," said Toni. "At least insofar as this village goes. Frankly, I'm picking up a distinctly melancholy vibe. From what I can see, many of its magnificent homes look neglected, and as lovely as this view is down into the valley, it's an eastern-facing village, meaning no sunsets. Over time, that must play on the villagers' minds as a disappointment, for there's no visible, sensual closure to the day."

The waitress stared at Toni. "Where'd you learn to think like that? I mean, reading people so well."

Toni shrugged. "I guess from playing piano for tips in a gay bar."

"Perhaps that melancholy is why so few people live here year-round," said Sofia. "Most come only for the summer, and once they're gone, there's very few of us left to deal with the winter."

"Which I assume puts more stress on you?"

"You learn to deal with it. Life is hard."

"Let's change the subject," said Lila. "What can you tell us about that fortress across the lane?"

"The Tower? It's been in the same family since our Greek Revolution in 1821, but a Venetian family built it in the seventeenth century and the symbol of Venice still stands above the entrance."

"What is it with coats of arms?" said Toni. "Europeans seemed obsessed with them."

"Coats of arms and all that heraldry stuff is beyond me," said Lila. "All I know about them is that long before any of that became fashionable, ancient Greek Hoplite soldiers individualized their shields. Perhaps that explains why some modern Greeks create their own coats of arms."

"To me, all that's nothing more than another ego trip, this time to create a corporate logo for a family." Maggie lifted her glass of wine. "To pretensions, long may they perish."

"More wine?" said the waiter.

"Thank you, but I think not," said Lila. "My friends must stay awake on our ride home in order to keep me awake."

"Nicely played, Lila," said Maggie, waving her glass in salute. "Instead of saying 'cut her off,' you said help her save a life."

Lila laughed.

"Does anyone live in that tower?" asked Toni.

"If you're seriously thinking of living there, you *definitely* had too much to drink," said Maggie.

"I'm just curious."

"Yes, the heirs of the family come for a month in the summer."

"And the rest of the time it's empty?" said Lila.

"Sort of."

"What's that mean?" asked Toni, sipping from her water glass.

"The man who looks after it makes special arrangements for villager friends, and friends of friends, who wish to stay there."

"For a price?" said Maggie.

"Of course," smiled the waitress. "Everything is for a price."

"Could we possibly get in to see it?" asked Toni.

"I'm afraid not. It's rented at the moment."

"Oh well, just a thought."

"What sort of services does it offer?" asked Lila.

"Don't tell me you're interested too," said Maggie.

"Just asking."

"Whatever the client wants. The one in there now orders every meal from us. Doesn't even squeeze her own orange juice."

"I'd like that kind of life," said Maggie.

"I wouldn't," said the waitress. "She never leaves the tower, and every time I suggest she walk across the road to our place for a meal, she gives me the same answer: 'Why should I? My view's better than yours.'"

"That sounds like behavior symptomatic of a melancholic mind," said Maggie.

"More like clinical depression," said Lila.

The waitress gestured no. "I don't think so. I think it's more a function of her work."

Toni put down her glass. "What kind of work?"

"Writing away on a computer."

"What is she writing?" said Lila.

"A biography."

"Who is she writing about?" said Toni.

"I don't know. She doesn't like to talk about it. The most she ever said to me was that her book is about someone she met here."

Maggie picked up her nearly empty wine glass. "Is she a famous writer?"

"She looks vaguely familiar, but unless she were a TV, movie, or music video star, I wouldn't have a clue to her name. I try not to pay attention to what else is happening in the world. It keeps me from getting aggravated."

"Not a bad plan," said Toni.

"What *do* you know?" said Lila.

"I saw the title once."

"What is it?"

"A crazy-sounding one."

"How crazy could a biography title be?" asked Maggie, finishing off her wine.

"You tell me. It's titled *The Life and Times of My Black Hat Protector.*"

———

When Andreas saw the caller was Lila, he almost didn't take it. He sensed she'd know something was bothering him, but by the fifth ring he answered.

"Hi, my love."

"Hey, where are you?"

"In Moni, sitting under a big pine tree, breathing in the sharp, fresh scents of wild mountain herbs as we wait for our lunch to come."

"You've got to get over to Apeiranthos immediately."

Andreas sat up. "What's wrong? Are you okay?"

Lila repeated what the waitress had told them about the mysterious female guest in the tower. "And she's been here since last Thursday."

"Tell me again the name."

"*The Life and Times of My Black Hat Protector.* Nikoletta's hacker calls himself a 'black hat.'"

"I know, but what I missed was the name of the taverna you're in."

She told him.

"Don't move an inch. We'll be there in twenty minutes."

"Please drive safely; we don't need another accident."

Andreas smiled. "Yes, dear."

He pushed back from the table and stood. "Let's go. We've got a lot of ground to cover in the next twenty minutes."

Yianni raised his eyebrows.

"What are you talking about? We just ordered," said Tassos.

"Lila said they think they may have found Nikoletta holed up in Apeiranthos. I'll tell you all about it on the way, but it's on the other side of the mountains from where we are, so we've got to hustle." He canceled the order, left a twenty-euro tip on the table, and raced out the door, followed by Yianni and Tassos.

They drove south past Halki and through Filoti before turning north, lights flashing all the way until a kilometer before Apeiranthos. Andreas parked in the plaza next to Lila's SUV.

"The taverna's just past the tower. Let's try to look casual so as not to spook the townsfolk."

"Spook them over what?" asked Yianni.

"No idea," said Andreas, "but in this village I'm sure there are more than enough guilty consciences to get some folks thinking *raid* anytime they see a cop, let alone three."

The men sitting at the tables lining the cops' way to the taverna turned away as the trio passed by.

"What do you think?" said Andreas.

"I smell lookouts," said Tassos.

"For what?" asked Yianni.

"I guess we'll find out soon enough." Andreas pointed ahead to the left. "There's the taverna."

As they entered, Lila jumped up from her table and waved for them to come out onto the veranda. Maggie and Toni remained seated, talking to a young woman Andreas assumed was the waitress who'd set off their mad dash across the mountains.

Andreas smiled and extended his hand to the woman, "Hi, I'm Andreas, Lila's husband."

The woman stood and shook his hand. "A pleasure to meet you." She waved to Tassos and Yianni. "And you, too. Please, come sit, we'll pull together another table."

Andreas motioned for her to sit down. "No reason to bother. We won't be staying long."

She looked surprised. "I don't understand."

Andreas sat. "I'm a chief inspector with the Greek police, and these gentlemen are also with the police."

Her face blanched but she said nothing.

"Don't worry; you did nothing wrong, and we're not here to arrest anyone. We're here to find a missing woman."

"What missing woman?"

Andreas reached into his pocket, pulled out a photo of Nikoletta, and showed it to her. His eyes fixed on hers, searching for any sign of emotion.

She jerked back in her chair. "Oh, my. It's the woman in the tower."

Andreas didn't bother to wonder what emotion his face betrayed at hearing those words. His rapidly beating heart had answered that question.

"What is your name, Miss?"

"Sofia."

"Ah, a beautiful name, the same as our daughter's. There are a few things I need to know that perhaps you can help me with. First of all, is there anyone else in the tower besides the woman?"

"No, not that I've noticed. That is, aside from Christina, who's the housekeeper. But she's only there in the mornings."

"Have you seen anyone other than Christina in the tower since the woman arrived?"

"No."

"Have you noticed any strangers hanging around the tower?"

"No."

"Are you certain."

"Ye-es." She strung out the word oddly, or so it seemed to Andreas.

He glanced at Yianni, who nodded.

"When do you usually deliver dinner to the woman?"

"Before we get busy, which would be around now."

"Do you have a key or does she let you in?"

"I press a button at the terrace door, she asks who it is, I tell her, and usually she comes down to open the door for me. Sometimes she just buzzes me in."

"I need you to go with us to the tower. When she asks who it is, don't tell her we're with you. As soon as she opens the door, get out of the way. We'll take it from there."

She looked around the table. "Really? You're making me worry."

"There's no need, Sofia. We're being cautious for the sake of the woman, just in case there's someone with her you don't know about."

"Don't worry, I'll be with you," said Toni, patting Sofia's hand.

"The hell you will," said Yianni.

"Don't mind him. That's my overprotective boyfriend, worried that I'll somehow mess up this very simple food delivery. Isn't that right, Chief Inspector?"

Andreas spoke through a clenched jaw. "Does that work for you, Sofia?"

She nodded yes and squeezed Toni's hand.

Andreas sighed and looked to Yianni. "Then I guess that's how we'll do it."

"What about video surveillance?" said Tassos. "Security's a big concern among homeowners these days."

"It wasn't so different four hundred years ago," said Maggie. "Why do you think they built this tower like a fortress?"

"And pirates still found their way in," said Sofia.

Andreas nodded. "I'm sure we will too."

Chapter Eighteen

A group of three couples armed with maps and snapping photos with their phones wound their way up beside a tower along a twisting path of marble steps. The steps led to a pair of bronze-clad doors framed in marble and crowned by the emblem of Venice carved in stone. The women stopped a few paces before the doors to snap photographs of the valley below, while the men argued over where to visit next. The group seemed oblivious to the young woman carrying a tray of food up the steps behind them.

As the arguing intensified, the three women turned away and started back down the steps, yelling back at the men that they'd be waiting at the car for them to make up their minds. The men kept up with their argument but slowly followed the women, stopping every step or so to accentuate a point.

The young woman with the tray pressed a button next to the doors and stood watching the men argue.

One of the doors swung open wide and a smiling, dark-haired woman appeared. "Good evening, Sofia."

"Evening, *keria*." As Sofia stepped inside, the three arguing men sprinted for the doorway.

Panic spread across the woman's face, and she tried to slam the door shut, but Sofia and her tray blocked the woman just long enough for the men to grab the door and force their way inside.

The woman screamed for help.

"Relax, Nikoletta, we're the police," said Andreas, pulling his ID out from beneath his shirt.

Yianni and Tassos did the same.

"You scared the bloody hell out of me," said Nikoletta.

"Are you alone in here?"

"Yes."

He turned to Yianni and Tassos. "Make sure that she is."

Yianni and Tassos headed into the tower, guns drawn.

"Is everything okay in here?" said Toni, stepping through the doorway.

"Seems to be," said Andreas.

"Who is she?" asked Nikoletta.

"More like who are *they*?" said Lila coming up behind Toni with Maggie.

"Don't I know you?" asked Nikoletta.

"I'm Lila Vardi."

"The socialite," she turned to face Andreas, as Lila frowned at the description, "married to Andreas Kaldis, chief of Special Crimes."

Andreas bowed. "At your service."

"I'm flattered by all this attention."

"Your newspaper is very worried about you."

"I bet. I'm sure they can't wait to hear my story."

"Personally, I can't wait to hear it myself. Why don't we start with a basic question: Where is your kidnapper?"

"Kidnapper? I've not been kidnapped. I've been protected."

"By whom and from whom?"

"I truly wish I knew. Why don't we go inside where we can sit down? I can try to answer your questions, and perhaps you can answer some of mine?"

"Sounds good to me."

Nikoletta turned to Sofia. "Please bring the tray inside."

"I'm sorry, ma'am. I had no choice. They are the police."

"Don't worry. I know you were only trying to help me." Nikoletta paused and looked at Andreas. "Are you expecting any others to join us?"

Yianni came out of the tower, followed by Tassos, caught Andreas's eye, and flashed him a thumbs-up.

He turned back to Nikoletta. "None of the invited sort."

——

Nikoletta led them to a second-floor library that could have passed for a museum dedicated to seventeenth-century baroque furniture. A large rectangular table fitted with marble inserts and adorned in elaborately carved cupids and shells dominated the center of the room. Bold scrolls embellished the table's legs and the legs and arms of twelve matching chairs. A comparably carved gilded writing desk sat to the side between two windows. An open laptop computer atop the desk served as the room's only visible sign of the modern age.

Nikoletta sat in a chair on the side of the table closest to the desk. She pointed at the computer. "I assume you know I'm working on a book about this experience."

Andreas smiled as he sat directly across from her. "We'd prefer not having to wait until it's published to learn what happened."

Yianni and Tassos sat next to Andreas, while Lila, Toni, and Maggie sat at the end of the table farthest away from the others.

"I'm sure you have a lot of questions for me, but before we get to them, I have one that's been gnawing at me since the night I disappeared from the hotel."

"What is it?" asked Andreas.

"Why hasn't a single word appeared anywhere in the media about my disappearance? Not even in my own newspaper."

"If you're able to answer my questions as easily as I can answer yours, I'll be a very happy cop." Andreas told her that keeping a lid on her disappearance was all his doing, and he'd done so out of concern that if she had been kidnapped, the inevitable avalanche of publicity might cause her abductor to panic and harm her. He emphasized that her publisher did not agree with his strategy.

"Thank you. I feel better knowing there were people out there who cared." She took a sip of water from a plastic bottle. "Where do you want me to start?"

"How about with what happened the night you disappeared."

Nikoletta shut her eyes, took a deep breath, opened her eyes, and began. "My planned final evening on Naxos had me joining some new friends for dinner in Chora, which in the inevitable Greek way led to way too much drinking and a very late night. I literally staggered out of the taverna, and in my haste to get back to the hotel, I decided to take a shortcut that involved leaving paved roads to climb a very dark, rocky dirt path that ran alongside a steep cliff high above the sea."

She paused. "That's all I know firsthand, because I reached my hotel without incident. The rest of what happened I learned from Soter."

"Who's *Soter*?"

Nikoletta laughed. "Sorry, I've been so immersed in my writing that I only think of my interviewee-turned-protector by the name I created for him in the book. In Greek mythology, Soter represented the male personification of safety and deliverance from harm."

"Do you know his real name?"

"No. I wish I did."

"You're probably better off not knowing," said Tassos.

"What did he tell you?" asked Andreas.

"On the day after my article about him appeared in the paper, he received an offer over the Dark Web to kill me. Obviously, the person making the offer didn't realize he was the man I'd interviewed. Though he turned it down, he knew someone would take the contract because the fee was extremely high. That's when he started following me."

Nikoletta picked up the water bottle. "At the time, he thought I'd been targeted because of his interview. He felt responsible. That his bragging had put me in danger." She took another sip. "The night of my disappearance, he'd been watching me from outside the taverna, and after I left, he followed me on a motorbike. When he saw me stop to stare up the hillside path, he guessed I'd take it, so he parked and made it onto the path some distance ahead of me. As he hurried up the hill, he saw a man crouched in the shadows across and back from the path at its closest point to the cliff edge. He recognized the man as a professional assassin—*definitely not top-drawer*, was how he later described him to me. The man did not recognize Soter or realize he'd been seen and stayed focused on my struggle up the hill. Soter walked by the man as if he hadn't noticed him, then circled back down and around to come up behind him. He knew the man had to be planning to push me off the edge of the cliff to make it appear an 'accidental death.'" Nikoletta used finger quotes for emphasis.

"But, as we all know, it didn't end up that way."

Nikoletta cleared her throat. "I was oblivious to all of that. After I'd safely reached my hotel, Soter made his way down to the rocks and stripped the now-dead would-be assassin of his mobile phone and identification. Once he'd finished with him, he called me on the man's phone and told me to meet him outside my hotel. He'd long before then culled my number from my mobile provider."

"But how did he know the password to unlock the phone?" asked Yianni.

She smiled. "Funny you should ask. I had the same question. He told me he didn't, but he just ran through the five most common passwords and 111111 worked."

"Clever guy," said Toni.

Nikoletta nodded. "When we met, he told me someone was trying to kill me and I had to come with him immediately. I told him my mother hadn't raised a fool, and I wasn't about to go off in the middle of the night with a nearly total stranger, especially one who'd recently bragged to me about being a master criminal. He told me my mother was a wise woman, but she wasn't here to protect me, and in a few minutes he wouldn't either. He walked to the edge of the cliff and shone a light down onto the rocks.

"He told me, 'The body down there would have been you if I hadn't intervened.' I looked over the edge and saw the man on the rocks. I almost fainted. 'He was waiting for you on your walk home,' Soter told me. 'Someone tipped him off that you were on your way back to the hotel. You have two choices. Come with me to a safe house I know while I figure out who's after you, or stay here and be a target. You've thirty seconds to make up your mind.'"

She exhaled. "Longest thirty seconds of my life. Obviously, I went with him. We took his motorbike to a parking lot in the harbor, where we switched to a car and drove directly here. When we got to the village, it was still dark, and no one saw us walk from the car to this fortress."

"You must have been frightened," said Lila.

"I believe the technical term is *scared shitless.*"

"What did you two talk about on the ride up from Chora?"

said Tassos. "That was a long trip, especially at night along strange roads."

"He knew the roads. He said he'd hidden out in the tower several times, and the local people knew him. He said this time he wouldn't stay in the village but had arranged for some locals to keep an eye on me. He didn't say, but I got the impression locals knew what he did and might even have used his services."

"Why do you think that?" said Tassos.

"Because when I asked if the locals who'd be keeping an eye on me could be trusted, he said, 'They know what would happen to all of them and their families should any one of them ever break his word to me.'"

"That's quite a reputation," said Andreas.

"You said something before that piqued my curiosity," said Maggie.

"What's that?"

"You said, '*At the time*' Soter thought you'd been targeted because of the story about him. Did his thinking change?"

"The second day I was here he called to say that he didn't think our interview was the cause."

"Why did he say that?" asked Andreas.

"He said there was still a contract out on me, but a new contract had just gone up, offering even more money for anyone who immediately took out another target on Naxos, this time an Athens cop. That contract was attracting a lot of attention from a low-end crowd of thugs, indicating a state of panic on the part of whoever had put out those contracts. Soter's clients would never use such unprofessional types, nor would they have hired the inept one who intended to kill me outside my hotel.

"Besides, it made no sense for someone afraid of what Soter might say to go after the person to whom he'd told his story. He could tell his story to any number of journalists. The only way to keep more stories like it out of the press was to kill Soter, not the writer. All of which led him to believe there must be another motive behind why someone was after me."

"Any idea what that motive might be?" said Andreas.

"That's the kind of 'step back and think out of the box' approach I'm never good at when it comes to looking at myself."

"As the cop whose contract kill price topped yours, permit me to offer a possible answer." Yianni leaned in across the table. "You kept a sixth notebook. I've seen five of them. What's in the sixth?"

She appeared surprised. "I had the idea for another article I wanted to write after finishing the tourism piece. It's based upon a strange local character I came across purely by chance, selling honey from the back of a pickup truck." She took a sip of water. "He was a true fast-talker, and in the traditional style of Greek men, tried to impress me by claiming his honey-selling operation was just a hobby to keep himself in touch with local common folk. His real money-generating operation was in artifacts. I tested him with my slight knowledge of the subject and must admit he impressed me with what he knew. But not enough to buy his honey.

"Later on, in my interviews with locals, I'd ask if they knew Honeyman, and everyone had a story about him. Usually it involved the term 'con man,' and some had very sharp words to say. Most suspected he was involved in the illicit antiquities trade. But what really got my attention was when some said he'd approached them as the representative of different companies seeking to assemble vast parcels of beachfront land. I smelled a great story in this but didn't want to get into any of that in my tourism piece. I wanted to save it for a special article. So I put anything relating to his story into notebook number six, and as far as I know, no one knows about my plans for that story, except my editor and publisher."

"Did Honeyman know?" asked Yianni.

"No."

"But you did ask a lot of people about Honeyman?"

She nodded. "True, but if he knew, I doubt he would have showed up at my farewell party the night that man tried to kill me."

"He was there?" said Andreas.

"Yes, I was surprised too. I'd invited everyone who'd helped me with the piece, including Honeyman. I couldn't risk slighting him and losing his cooperation on my story about him. Frankly, I didn't think he'd fit in with the crowd, but he stayed to the bitter end."

Andreas looked at Yianni. "Well, now we know who the *someone* was who tipped off the killer that Nikoletta was on her way back to the hotel."

"And why the killer had a phone," said Yianni. "Honeyman must've called him when Nikoletta left the bar."

Andreas decided not to tell Nikoletta that Honeyman was dead. No reason to alarm her further.

"You said Soter calls you?" said Yianni.

"Yes."

"Do you ever call him?"

"Sometimes."

"Do you have his number?"

"It's on speed dial on the phone he gave me when he brought me here."

"May I see it, please?"

"Sure, but it's locked." She smiled, "and not with one of those top five passwords." She punched in a code and, as she was about to pass the phone to Yianni, said, "I've got a new message from him."

She read the message and shook her head with a grin. "Wait until you hear this. 'Hi, Nikoletta. Now that you're safely in the hands of the police I can rest easy and go back to simply being a fan of your columns who's heading off into blissful retirement. Stay safe. By the way, these phones will get the police nowhere, and I'm dumping mine now.'"

Andreas nodded. "I guess the locals watching out for you are doing a good job of keeping him informed. Well, let's pack up and get you back to Chora and on to Athens."

"I don't want to go."

"What do you mean? You could still be in danger."

"As you said, the locals are keeping a close watch on me, and how will I be any safer walking Athens's streets or in my apartment than I am here? Until you find whoever's behind this, I think this is the better place to be. Besides, I've been remarkably productive with my writing here."

Andreas looked her straight in the eye. "Honeyman and two others involved with him have been murdered. This is real, Nikoletta."

She blanched. "Wow." She shook her head. "Wow, wow, wow." She shook her head again. "Where do you plan on keeping me?"

"I don't know yet. For the time being, at police headquarters in Chora."

She gestured no. "Despite what happened to those men, with all due respect, I feel safer here than in 'don't know yet.'"

"I don't think your newspaper is going to be happy about this. Your publisher has convinced my minister to fire me if I don't find you by midnight."

"You never told me that," said Lila.

Nikoletta looked at her phone. "We've got time left before midnight, so why don't you come around to this side of the table?"

"What for?" asked Andreas.

"For a selfie we can send to my paper and your minister. Proof of life, as they say. Proof you found me."

"You do have style," said Andreas.

"And it beats a sketch," said Yianni.

"For sure."

"May I see your sketchbook?"

"It's next to the computer."

Yianni went to look for the sketchbook while Nikoletta and Andreas posed for their selfie.

"Why do I have the distinct feeling that I'm going to regret this?" said Andreas.

"Because having salt rubbed into your wounds is painful and inspires a desire for retribution," said Tassos.

Andreas settled on what he considered a non-gloating photo, and after adding all the necessary recipients' email addresses, watched Nikoletta hit send.

"Excuse me, Nikoletta," said Yianni, holding the open sketchbook. "Does Soter know about your sketchbook?"

"I don't think so."

"You're very good. I recognize many of the faces." Yianni put the book down in front of her and pointed to a face. "Who's this?"

She bit at her lip. "I don't know."

"I know him. In fact, I believe we both met him at the same place."

"I don't recognize him." Now she was chewing her lip.

"Well, what about this one?" He pointed to another sketch of the same face, "Or this one?" turning to another page. "How many more pages showing this face do you want me to turn to before you tell me what we both know?"

She lowered her head. "He saved my life. And I protect my sources. I promised myself I'd destroy those sketches, but they were my only companions here. They made me feel safe."

Andreas and Tassos came around the table and looked at the sketches.

"So this is Soter?" asked Andreas.

"Yes," Nikoletta murmured.

"Where did you meet him?" Andreas asked Yianni.

"At the bar where she first met him. That snug little place down from the Kastro, where this guy kindly made me a pizza my first night in town."

Andreas pressed his finger on the sketchbook. "You mean Soter's the owner of the bar?"

"That's what he told me."

"Is that true, Nikoletta?"

"He never said anything like that to me, and he didn't act like the owner when we were there."

Andreas turned to Lila. "Ladies, it looks as if our night is just beginning. I suggest the three of you head on home and not wait up for us."

"Why do you have to do that?" said Nikoletta. "It's very late, the roads are tricky, you've had too much to drink, and this place has a zillion bedrooms. Please, ladies, stay here, at least until it's light out."

"I don't like that idea," said Yianni.

"Don't bother to tell us why; we already know," said Toni. "You're afraid an assassin will show up tonight and do us all in."

"It's not a joke."

"I didn't mean it as one," Toni said.

Maggie jumped in. "Why don't you get Dimitri to send a couple of cops to watch over us until morning? He's going to owe you big-time for all the great publicity his department will get for finding Nikoletta. Besides, this is a fortress."

"I'm not going to get involved in a losing battle trying to convince you otherwise, my love," said Tassos, reaching into his waistband. "But here, keep this." He handed Maggie his pistol and kissed her on the cheek. "I know you know how to use it."

"Isn't that overkill?" said Nikoletta.

"Only until you need it," said Maggie. "Now get out of here, guys, so we can get some sleep."

"What do you think we should do?" said Yianni looking at his partners.

Tassos smiled. "My vote is for leaving, because from what I've heard so far, I'd say we've likely got a better chance of winning the lottery than convincing these ladies that they need us keen-minded men to protect them from the bad guys."

Yianni glared at Tassos, "Soter, where are you when I need you?"

"With any luck," said Andreas, "we just might get your question answered tonight."

Chapter Nineteen

Andreas, Yianni, and Tassos made it to the bar by one a.m. The place was packed, with most of its customers focused on a guitarist playing a mix of American folk songs and old French chansons.

As their eyes scanned the room, Tassos said, "I can see why Nikoletta called this place Bohemian."

"Do you see him?" said Andreas.

"No."

"Me neither," said Yianni. "Let me ask the bartender."

Yianni made his way through to the bar and waved for the bartender.

"Yes, sir."

"Is Stelios here tonight?"

"Stelios? Stelios who?"

"The owner."

"The owner's name is Aris. And he's standing over by the door."

Yianni turned to see a short, pudgy clean-shaven man with long white hair wearing an "I adore Edith" T-shirt, rocking side-to-side in time with the music.

"I was in here a few nights ago, just after the kitchen closed, you were working at the bar, and a guy named Stelios told me he'd make me a pizza. I thought he was the owner. Maybe he was the manager?"

The bartender frowned, then smiled. "Oh, that guy. Yeah, I remember him. He tipped me big-time to let him make the pizza. Also a salad and fruit, right? Nice guy, but he's not the owner. Or the manager."

"You're new here, aren't you?"

"If five years behind this bar six nights a week is new, then I'm new."

"I'm sorry, sir. I must be confused, but tell me, did you ever see the man who called himself Stelios here before the night he made that pizza?"

"Yeah, maybe a week before. He'd tipped a waiter to invite a woman passing by to come inside for a drink. He struck up a conversation with her, and they spent hours together talking at a table by a window. He tipped me big that night too."

Yianni exhaled, shook his head, and took out his phone. "By chance, is this the man who tipped you?" Yianni showed him a photo of one of Nikoletta's sketches.

"Yeah, that's him. Is he someone famous or something?"

"You could say that." Yianni skimmed through until he came to another photograph. "Have you ever seen this guy in here?"

The bartender stared at the photo. "No, can't say that I have."

"That night, Stelios, or whatever his name is, told me when he was at the table with the woman, this man sat at the bar practically the whole time, watching them in the mirror."

"No way he'd have been here that long and I wouldn't have noticed. That was a very slow night, not like tonight. I'd have noticed him for sure. Is he famous too?"

"In some circles, yes."

"Who is he?"

"Peter Zagori."

"Never heard of him."

Yianni nodded, took ten euros out of his pocket, and handed it to the bartender.

"What's this for?"

"I should have tipped you for dinner the night I was in here. I thought Stelios had taken care of me."

Come to think of it, he did, and quite effectively.

———

Yianni sat outside the bar, telling Tassos and Andreas of his conversation with the bartender.

"What a con artist that guy is," said Tassos.

"Smooth as they come," said Yianni. "He had me thinking I was suckering him into giving up information, when all the while he was picking my brain and doing what he could to throw me off the scent. Peter Zagori wasn't even in Greece the night Nikoletta first met Soter, and though he never directly said the guy at the bar was Zagori, he tossed out just enough cop catnip to get me thinking there might be a new angle to what went down. He made it all up about the man in the mirror just to slow us down."

"Well, I think it's safe to say we're no longer slowed down," said Tassos. "We're at what I'd call a dead stop."

"There's another way to look at why Soter mentioned Zagori," said Andreas. "He might have made all that up to steer us toward investigating Zagori. Soter knew that Zagori wasn't in Greece the night he met Nikoletta, but he also knew that sometime after her article about Soter was published Zagori was hired to kill her. Investigating Zagori might have led us to who wanted her dead."

"That Soter guy grows more impressive every moment," said Tassos.

"But how did he know I was a cop investigating Nikoletta's disappearance?"

"You didn't exactly arrive undercover," said Andreas. "The morning after her disappearance, you were met at the airport by the chief of police and driven by him straight to where a body had been found on the rocks below Nikoletta's hotel. You questioned the hotel's night manager about her disappearance and spent time searching her room. The island gossip mill wouldn't have had to churn too hard to figure out there's a new cop in town. He might have started tailing you at the hotel, or just waited around the bar until you showed up. After all, the logical thing for police to do in a kidnapping is retrace the victim's steps, and for sure you'd be expected to check out the bar where she first met Soter."

"Damn. Four dead, two kill contracts still out there, and us without a clue as to who's behind them," muttered Tassos, slapping the table.

"We do know who killed Zagori," said Yianni.

"Only because the killer admitted that to a reporter," said Andreas.

"But we did find the reporter," insisted Yianni.

"Correction. Maggie, Lila, and Toni found the reporter." Andreas shook his head. "All we've found are a bunch of phony beehives, broken pottery, and an alphabet soup of initials."

"There has to be an explanation, a key we're missing that ties everything together," said Tassos.

"And what is *everything*?" asked Yianni.

"I don't know if it's a network, a pyramid, a sewing circle, or a lone crazy, but something's triggered a rash of violence unlike anything this island's seen in modern times. And whatever that trigger is, Nikoletta pulled it."

"Agreed," said Andreas. "I also agree with Nikoletta's point that anyone afraid of what Soter might have told her had to know it would do no good to eliminate her while he remained alive to tell his tales to others. Bottom line, I don't see her story as the trigger."

"Then what is?"

"My money's on something connected to that sixth notebook and those damn initials."

———

Andreas's phone rang at nine a.m. He struggled to find it on the nightstand next to the bed. "Hello."

"Good morning, my love."

"Morning. How's it going up in the tower?"

"You make it sound like I'm a Greek version of Anne Boleyn. Actually, it's lovely. We had breakfast on the terrace. Sofia joined us. She brought a nice young policeman from Filoti to watch over us."

"Terrific. When are you coming back to the beach house?"

"I thought you were busy."

"That's a relative term."

"I assume that means no luck at finding Soter."

"Or figuring out anything, really. Plus, we didn't get to bed until after three."

"I'm just calling to make sure you saw my email."

"The only email I saw before going to sleep was a two-word response from the minister to my selfie with Nikoletta. 'Got it,' was all he wrote. I'm not sure if he was disappointed or elated."

"A true politician."

"At least he's not corrupt; otherwise he'd have gotten rid of me long ago. So, what's your email to me about?"

"The policeman brought a letter with him. The minister faxed it to his office in Filoti for delivery to you. It's from Nikoletta's publisher, addressed to the minister."

"What's the letter say?"

"I took a photo of it and emailed it to you. It's demanding that you be fired by midnight yesterday."

"Oh, I know what's in that letter. I never bothered to pick it up in Filoti, but it's what triggered my race to find Nikoletta by midnight. Thanks anyway. Let me know once you and your merry band decide what you're doing today."

"Will do. Kisses. Bye."

Andreas lay in bed staring up at the ceiling. He missed his wife. She somehow always knew when something was bothering him. Even when he didn't know it himself. That's a rare quality to have in a partner.

He listened for the sounds of children. Not a stir, not a murmur. Or a scream. Yes, he missed even that. But not as much as he did his wife.

I'm one lucky guy.

His mind was waking up. He didn't want it to, quite yet. He'd have preferred sleeping but knew his preference was losing the battle to duty. He rarely slept this late, and even though he had no idea what to do next, he was awake. He picked up his phone and skimmed through a string of utterly useless email offerings, until he came to the one from Lila. He opened it and clicked on the attachment.

Andreas looked at the letter without bothering to read it. He didn't want to read it, for it would only remind him of how his father had been blackballed from the police force by another powerful man. One who'd set Andreas's father up to suffer a public shaming for something he had not done, ending with eight-year-old Andreas losing his father to suicide.

The letter was typed single spaced on the publisher's personal stationery, with a blue-and-gold coat of arms emblazoned across the top of the page. Andreas rolled his eyes at the crest.

Of course he *has one.* He looked at the coat of arms more closely, trying to discern what the publisher's family had chosen to portray about its history to the world. On one side stood a ship honoring the fortune his family had made at sea. On the other side, a printing press paid homage to the family's current financial engine. And in the central place of honor, the goddess Athena stood upon the pedestal of an open book. He wondered what the book represented and tried to make out what was written on its pages.

He casually tinkered with enlarging the words the family had thought important enough for Athena to stand upon.

One page of the book read,

JSS

GTS

AKS

Its facing page read,

KSM

RIM

BZ

Andreas bolted out of bed, yelling, *"Yianni, Tassos, wake up. The world as we know it is over."*

———

"I can't believe this," said Yianni, staring at the coat of arms on Andreas's phone.

Tassos sighed. "We've either hit upon a one-in-a-zillion coincidence or an explanation that ties everything together."

"Not quite everything, but a hell of a lot," said Andreas. "I asked Lila if she knew whose initials they might be. She said she'd ask her mother, the source of all knowledge about old-line Greek society."

"If the publisher's tied into this, he's involved in at least three murders."

"Plus two attempted murders," added Yianni. "Make that three, if you count Zagori's terminally unsuccessful plans for Nikoletta."

"It also explains how Nikoletta and you became targets. The day after her editor forwarded Nikoletta's sixth notebook to the publisher, Zagori showed up on Naxos to kill her. When that failed and you began retracing her steps, someone panicked, likely over your potentially discovering what she'd learned, and put out a casting call for local bad guys to take you down immediately."

"In the notebook covering her meeting with the hacker, Nikoletta wrote down the names of some persons who'd used his services," said Yianni. "But I don't recall any name fitting those initials, and certainly not the publisher's name."

"So that notebook isn't likely what set this off."

"Something in the sixth notebook is what did it," said Tassos. "And if those initials represent the members of some sort of cabal, there are at least six involved in this."

"But none of those initials is the publisher's," said Yianni.

"Which means it could be more than six. I know it looks like a perfect match to us, but with all the powerful players potentially implicated, we can't afford the slightest misstep. That's another reason I asked Lila for help."

"I don't mean to rain on anyone's parade," said Tassos, "but as the resident cynic in this trio of cops, do you think it even matters what we prove? Whoever's behind this undoubtedly has both the money and the power to *literally* get away with murder."

"As I see it," said Andreas, looking at Tassos while motioning for Yianni to give him back his phone, "my job is to chase down bad guys. After that, it's up to prosecutors and courts to seek whatever justice is called for. If I started thinking about what actually happens to so many of the bad guys I bust my ass to catch, I'd go crazy."

"Thanks for the pep talk, Chief," said Yianni, handing Andreas the phone.

"Hmm," said Tassos. "It makes you wonder whether the corruption among our brethren on the force is the cause of this sort of thing or the consequence."

"A bit of both, I suspect," said Andreas. He felt the phone vibrate in his hand and put the incoming call on speakerphone. "Hi, darling. We're all gathered around the phone to hear the results of your research."

"You mean my *socialite* efforts?"

"I knew you didn't like it when Nikoletta called you that, but I very much admired your self-control."

"I've since explained my feelings on that subject to her, and all is now fine in the fortress. She's even offered to do a feature on our Fresh Start initiative."

"That's great." He paused. "But could you please explain to us what those initials represent?"

"My mother's a better search engine than Google."

"No argument here."

"Okay. Let's start with the matriarch of the family. Her name was Athena."

"Well, that explains her namesake's presence on the coat of arms," said Yianni.

"Her father was a very rich and powerful foreign shipowner with vast investments in land across Greece, and one of the first twentieth-century off-islanders to invest in Naxos. He married a Greek who passed away when Athena was born, and he never remarried. He raised Athena to share his penchant for acquiring land—and his passion for collecting antiquities. When he died between World Wars I and II, she was in her twenties and inherited everything he owned.

"She had six children by three different husbands, and the initials are those of her children. All are male, except for RIM and BZ."

"But how does the publisher tie into this?" said Yianni. "His last name begins with none of those initials."

"His mother was BZ, and she took her husband's last name when they married."

"So, what are the names of these folks?" asked Tassos.

Lila slowly recited the names, including those of their spouses and children.

"Oh. My. God," said Tassos.

"You can say that again," said Andreas. "That's a veritable Who's Who of Greek politics, real estate development, shipping, and society. Not to mention publishing."

"And just to spice up your lives a bit, Mother said that for as long as she can remember there've been rumors of the family illegally trading in antiquities to finance their projects. Part of that comes from the family's uncanny success at gaining permission to develop real estate in areas where others were forbidden to even sink a shovel. 'Mining antiquities to finance modern development' is what Mother said should be written across that family crest."

"Oh," said Andreas, a look of dejection spreading across his face.

"What's wrong?" said Tassos. "We've got the bad guys in our sights and a motive."

"But if all of Athens already knows about their operation, why would they panic if a reporter threatens to do a story on it? Surely it can't be the first time. They'll just have their lawyers and friends in Parliament deal with it and continue on with their lives as if nothing happened. To that extent I agree with our resident cynic."

"Are you saying the publisher wasn't involved in trying to kill me and Popi?"

"No. I'm saying there must be a different motive. Something that the publisher and his network saw as so potentially explosive in that sixth notebook that they had to resort to murder to keep it from going public."

"And what, pray tell, could that be?"

"If I knew, Yianni, you'd be the first I'd tell. All I can say is that I don't think it's anything linked to what we know so far."

Tassos shook his head. "You have a unique ability for plunging us from a state of utter euphoria into abject frustration in a heartbeat."

"Now, now, that's my husband you're talking about."

"Then you know that even better than we do," chirped Yianni.

"Enough, guys. The answer lies in Nikoletta's sixth notebook. Somehow we have to get a copy of it." Andreas heard a muffled conversation on Lila's side of the phone. "Is everything okay?"

"Yes. I was just asking Nikoletta again whether she might have a copy of the notebook, perhaps photos of the pages taken with her camera."

"And?"

"She said no. She was so pressed to get it to her editor in a hurry that she didn't think to make a copy."

"Put her on the phone, please." Andreas sat so that his right elbow was on the table, with his right thumb against his cheek and fingers against his forehead. He held the phone out in front of him in his left hand.

"Hello?"

"Hi, Nikoletta, it's Andreas."

"Tassos."

"And Yianni."

"You must be as stunned by the news as we are," said Andreas.

"*Stunned* is an understatement. My own publisher trying to kill me? Utterly unbelievable. Made even more so by the fact it has to be true. It explains why he's been so desperate to let the world know I disappeared. He needed to find me to kill me. And for the literal life of me, I can't figure out what could possibly have made me his target."

"That's precisely where I need your help. You're the only one besides your publisher who knows what's in your sixth notebook. I'm convinced the answer's in there. The fact that you can't put your finger on what that is means it's only obvious to someone who knows the risk it presents. I'd like you to concentrate on any possible reference or thought you put in that notebook that conceivably could have triggered such a violent reaction in a guilty mind."

"Honestly, I've been trying all morning, ever since Lila told me about the initials."

"Forget about the initials. Forget about the real estate projects, forget about the antiquities smuggling. What else did you mention in your notebook?"

For thirty seconds, only the sound of slow and deliberate breathing came through the phone.

"I can't think of a thing."

"Empty your mind and start again."

This time it was a sigh, followed by more calm breathing, but as the silence went on, the breathing intensified until a rushed voice said, "I thought of something."

"What is it?" Andreas's voice was now as intense as Nikoletta's, his right hand pressed hard against the tabletop.

"At some point I read in a guidebook or brochure that the extraordinary library, furnishings, and priceless archives once housed in the former School of Commerce that is now the Naxos Archaeological Museum were completely destroyed by occupying forces during World War II. That struck me as strange, because those forces were well known for pillaging, not destroying.

Indeed, in the case of Germany, occupying forces were often under orders to send such treasures back to the homeland. I made a note to myself in that notebook to look into how many other Greek libraries, museums, and similar repositories were *destroyed* as opposed to pillaged. And I put a star next to it along with the words, 'Could be great story.'"

Andreas looked at his buddies. "Start your engines, folks. We're back in the race."

Chapter Twenty

Andreas dispatched Maggie to reach out to her army of contacts developed through shared lifetimes of service in the trenches of Greek bureaucracy. Her network ran deep, into all ministries of government, fueled by a camaraderie and transcending loyalty to one another born of knowing that they, not those blown in and out by shifting political winds, kept their ministries running. He wanted any information on valuables destroyed by occupying forces during World War II and any mention of the publisher's family in connection with those valuables or their destruction.

Maggie suggested they also ask for similar reports involving the opposing sides in the Greek Civil War that had followed.

Andreas asked Lila to dig up whatever other information she or her mother could find on Athena, matriarch of the publisher's family.

He called Dimitri for the twenty-five-year-old police records of the car accident that took the life of the project manager.

Andreas sensed they'd discovered the skeletal frame of a time line tying everything together. Athena, assisted by her project manager, had shepherded the family's business dealings through

World War II (1940–45), Greece's Civil War (1946–49), and the Junta Years (1967–74). At some later time, she turned over control to her publisher grandson, and on the project manager's death in the mid-1990s, Honeyman replaced him. All Andreas had to do now was flesh out the frame. Whether the result would be an angel, a devil, or something in between remained to be seen.

Andreas looked at Yianni and Tassos. "Anything else you can think of?"

"Yeah," said Tassos. "Start carrying a bigger gun. Like a howitzer. You do realize that by putting all this out there, word will undoubtedly get back to the publisher, and in his state of advanced paranoia, I don't see him missing where you're headed with this."

Andreas nodded.

"Seriously. The guy could be unstable enough to come after you."

"He could be."

"Or your family," said Yianni.

Andreas nodded again. "I'm sure he can justify that to himself, what with me going after his family." Andreas leaned back and stretched. "Years ago, I decided that anyone who threatens my family gets no quarter. Should he decide to take that route, he damn well better not miss."

"You're starting to sound like those vendetta guys up in Apeiranthos," Tassos said with a smile.

"They're not always wrong."

"Chief, your phone's vibrating."

"My mind's elsewhere. I still haven't switched it to ring." He picked it up off the table. "Hello."

"Hi, it's Dimitri. I found that file and took a look through it."

"Anything interesting?"

"Not *in* the file."

"What's that mean?" said Andreas, picking up a pencil.

"It's a routine report, describing the cause as excessive speed into a sharp turn on a treacherous mountain road and a subsequent loss of control sending car and driver on a terminal roll down the mountain."

"What about *outside* the file?"

"The person making the report was a detective at the time, and that wasn't the sort of thing detectives generally did. More significantly, he left the force under a cloud."

"What kind of cloud?"

"He was notoriously corrupt."

Andreas began tapping his pencil on the tabletop. "When did he leave the force?"

"Fifteen years ago."

"Where's he now?"

"He lives over by where you're staying. In a house almost as nice as yours."

"I guess police pensions are better on Naxos."

"For him, at least."

"Do you have an address? I'd like to pay him a visit." Andreas gestured to Yianni for a piece of paper.

"Would you like me to come along?"

"If you think it would help."

"He hates me."

"Perfect. That way you get to play bad cop. Can you pick me up?"

"I'll be there in twenty minutes. Bye."

Andreas hung up. "What do you think?"

"At the pace you're going," said Tassos, "I'm changing my firepower recommendation to a howitzer and a Sherman tank."

———

The ex-cop lived in a neatly maintained beach house on a wide and deep, bamboo-ringed parcel of land about a kilometer due north of where Andreas was staying. A white late-model BMW SUV sat on the gravel driveway connecting the house to a public dirt road running alongside the property.

Dimitri parked beside the BMW. "I think we should sit in the car for a few minutes, so Bear has time to notice we're here."

"Bear?"

"That's his nickname."

"And just what do you think he'll do if we show up at his front door unannounced?"

"With this guy, there's no telling."

"Well, in that case…" Andreas leaned over and pounded on the horn.

Ten seconds later, a gray-haired bear of a man, wearing nothing but khaki shorts draped beneath a huge belly, came charging out the front door headed directly for the marked police car.

"I see why they call him Bear." Andreas got out of the car and walked toward the man.

Bear stopped a pace in front of Andreas, stuck his finger in Andreas's face, and shouted, "Who the fuck do you think you are, asshole?"

Andreas fixed his eyes on Bear's and grinned. "Dimitri, why don't you make the introductions?"

Dimitri came around to the front of the car. "Permit me to introduce you to Chief Inspector Andreas Kaldis, head of GADA's Special Crimes Unit."

"I don't care if you're the damn archbishop; neither of you are welcome on my property. So get the hell out of here."

"Would you care to get dressed?" asked Andreas calmly.

Bear hesitated. "I said get off my property."

"Then I assume you're willing to come with us dressed as you are."

"I'm not going anywhere."

Andreas shook his head. "You're an ex-cop. Do I have to tell you the potential consequences of resisting arrest?"

"Arrest?"

"Why do you think we're here? I'm sure you're a fun guy to hang out with, but we're not here on a social call. So play nice, turn around, and put your hands behind your back." Andreas stepped back a pace, uncrossed his arms, and reached behind his back for handcuffs.

Veins popped on the man's forehead and he lunged for Andreas. Andreas sidestepped the charge, dropped his left shoulder, and thrust the heel of his left hand hard up against the side of the man's head. Bear stumbled for an instant, then spun around, looking for Andreas. But Andreas found him first, or rather the hard heel of Andreas's shoe found the exposed top of the man's bare foot.

A roar of pain, followed by a fall to the ground, had the man cursing but no longer fighting. "You miserable bastard, you broke my foot."

"We'll take you to the hospital for an X-ray on the way to booking you."

"For what?"

"For starters, how about assaulting a police officer?"

"That's a Mickey Mouse charge."

Andreas crouched down by the man's head. "You know what amazes me about so many ex-cops, especially dirty ex-cops? It's how they think that once they hit their pension years, they're home free and nothing from their past will ever come back to haunt them." Andreas fixed his eyes on Bear's. "Well, guess what? After that little macho performance of yours, permit me to introduce myself differently. I'm the man who's going to haunt your past, present, and future days for the rest of your life." Andreas stood up. "Get the fuck up and turn around. *Now*."

"Chief, we came here hoping not to arrest him," said Dimitri.

"I've changed my mind." Andreas's eyes never left Bear. "I said *get up*."

Bear got to his feet. "You guys are wasting your time with this good cop, bad cop routine. I practically invented it."

"You don't understand," said Andreas. "I'm the good cop in all this. You two don't get along at all, so I came here hoping to find a way to avoid charging you as an accessory to murder, but from the way you're behaving I think you've just become my primary suspect."

"What murder?"

"Turn around."

Bear hesitated but turned. Andreas cuffed him and spun him so they were face-to-face.

"What murder, you say? Have you been involved in so many you can't remember?"

"Stop the bullshit."

"Sure." Andreas said Project Manager's name. "And if that name doesn't jog your memory, how about this one?" He recited Athena's full name, including her maiden name and the last names of her three husbands.

Bear's eyes began to blink and he bit at his lip. "I don't know any of those names or anything about any murder."

"Of course you do. You conducted the investigation into Project Manager's death." Andreas paused, wondering whether to trust his gut and take a wild-ass leap into the unknown. "And for your efforts in that regard, you've been handsomely compensated ever since." Andreas pointed to the car and the house.

"I don't know what you're talking about."

"Permit me to describe your current situation more clearly. At present, you've got two things going for you. One, you're not who I'm after, and I don't even need your testimony. All I need is for you to tell me who was involved in that bogus report and why."

"I've nothing to say."

"Slow down. You haven't heard the second thing, which is: no one besides the three of us knows we're having this conversation. Once we take you in, the whole island will know. And when word gets back to you-know-who, how long do you think it will be before you end up wearing a marble necktie like your buddy Honeyman?" Andreas patted Bear on the shoulder. "You may be gone from the force, but you're certainly not forgotten by those who fear what you know. Talk to us so that we can get to them before they get to you. It's your choice."

A moment passed before Bear spoke. "Can we go inside? I have neighbors, and I don't want them to see me like this."

Andreas looked at Dimitri, who nodded, and the two followed Bear as he limped into his house. It was much bigger inside than it looked from the outside. Bear led them down to a room dominated by a wide-screen TV.

"Is this okay?"

"Yes," said Andreas.

"Could you take off the cuffs?"

"Not yet, talk first."

Bear dropped onto a sofa with fitted pillows. Andreas stepped forward and pulled Bear to his feet.

"What are you doing?" said Bear.

"Sit over there on that chair."

"But it's uncomfortable."

"Sit."

Bear sat on the chair, and Andreas took Bear's former place on the sofa.

"Now talk."

Bear exhaled. "You got it all wrong. Sure I've been getting paid by some folks for things I did for them, but nothing like murder. I wrote that report like I saw it, a simple accident. I only got paid to do what had to be done to keep certain people's names out of the report."

"Which people?"

"The old lady's family."

"Athena?"

"Yes."

"But she was dead by then," said Andreas.

"Yes, but the family was worried something might come out about her history with the man."

"What history?"

"He did things for her."

Dimitri jumped in. "Bear, I know when you're stalling. So get to the point or, so help me, on top of whatever other grief you're heading for, I'll have the buildings department all over your ass for all the illegal things you did building this house."

Bear shut his eyes. "He coordinated her antiquities smuggling. Had been doing it for years."

"How many years?" said Andreas.

"Since before the war."

"How old was he?" Andreas put his hands behind him and fidgeted on the sofa.

"In his seventies when he died in the mid-1990s."

"Did he have a pension like yours?"

"I never got a thing directly from the family. I got a percentage of what Honeyman made off of them."

"How'd Honeyman figure in this?"

"He's the one who had me keep their name out of the accident report. The project manager was driving a car registered to one of the family's companies when it happened."

"And Honeyman has been paying you ever since?" Andreas shifted again on the sofa.

"I was a cop then. He needed me, for a lot of things, and after I retired I agreed to take less."

"How noble of you," said Dimitri.

"No need to be a pig. I didn't want to risk ending up like the manager."

"Whoa," said Andreas, leaning forward, his hands still behind his back. "I thought you said you saw it as a simple accident?"

"I never found any evidence to the contrary, but over the years Honeyman told me things that made me wonder."

"What sort of things?"

"Honeyman had worked as a laborer for him for a couple of years before the accident, and he'd told Honeyman that Athena was a tough and controlling woman who thought her children weak and arrogant. Her grandchildren even more so. She worried how they'd behave after she was gone, so she made a contract with the manager, employing him for life to manage all the nasty projects that could come back to harm the family name."

"I assume that detail didn't make it into your accident report?"

Bear cleared his throat. "I didn't know about it back then."

"So, looking back, what do you think happened?"

Bear coughed. "No idea."

"What were the chances Honeyman arranged for the accident so that he could step into the project manager's shoes?" asked Dimitri.

Bear gestured no. "No way Honeyman could do what that guy did. Honeyman was a fast-talking laborer, and he knew his limitations. He was happy just making what he did off the deal. Besides, he liked the guy and complained that the person he had to deal with after the manager's death was an arrogant, privileged prick who ordered Honeyman around like he owned him."

Andreas nodded. "Perhaps he thought he did. What was this new guy's name?"

"I don't know; he just told me he was one of the old lady's grandsons. I never met him."

Andreas and Dimitri spent another half hour interrogating

Bear but came up with nothing new. Andreas led Bear back up the stairs and undid the handcuffs at the front door.

"No hard feelings, Chief," said Bear.

"No, none at all," said Andreas.

The men did not shake hands.

"Until the next time then," said Bear.

"For sure."

Andreas and Dimitri walked to the car, and once inside, Andreas said, "Hurry up and get us out of here."

Dimitri started the car and put it in gear. "Why the rush?"

Andreas reached behind his back. "Because, when he realizes why I kept squirming on that sofa, who knows what he'll come hauling through that doorway?"

He brought his hand out from behind his back. "This is what I found between the cushions where he wanted to sit." Andreas dropped a nine-millimeter semiautomatic on the console between them.

Spinning, smoking tires followed immediately.

———

By the time Dimitri dropped Andreas off at his borrowed home, Lila's SUV was parked near the front door.

"The women are back. Come on inside and say hello."

Once inside, they followed the sounds of voices out onto the terrace overlooking the sea.

"Look who's back from playing internal affairs," said Yianni.

"And look who's back from playing Rapunzel," said Dimitri.

"Nikoletta, what a surprise," said Andreas. "I'm so happy you decided to leave the tower."

"Only temporarily. My new girlfriends convinced me to spend the day with them, and I said why not?"

"Why not, indeed," said Lila. "Would you boys like to hang out with us today?"

"We'd love to, but things have just gone from hectic to horrific, so I'm afraid we'll have to pass on the invitation."

Toni waved her hand. "Excuse me, but after that bombshell, do you really expect us to simply say *toodle-oo* and be on our sweet way? Uh-uh. Give us the news, Chief."

Andreas turned to Yianni. "She's tougher to deal with than you are."

"Tell me about it."

"Just tell *us* about it," said Lila.

"Enough," said Andreas, raising his hands in a calming gesture. "Here's what happened."

After he and Dimitri finished describing their encounter with Bear, the first person to speak was Lila. "What do you think he planned on doing with that gun hidden in the sofa?"

"Nothing good."

"And you let him go?" said Toni.

"What could I charge him with? He's authorized to possess a pistol."

"And he *was* handcuffed," said Lila.

"Uh, that I didn't find comforting. With a round racked and ready to go, if he got his handcuffed hands around it, he could have spun around and started firing."

Lila shook her head. "I could have done without knowing that last part."

"Bad guys are always looking for a way to do their worst." He looked at Nikoletta. "And that's why I don't like the thought of you in that tower alone."

Nikoletta nodded. "So, what's your next move?"

Andreas looked at Maggie. "Any word yet from your friends?"

"Not yet, but I impressed upon them that this is a Code Red

Urgent matter, so I expect to start hearing back anytime now. If all my friends in high secretarial and clerical positions do what they've promised, our government ministries could come to a screeching halt over the next few hours."

"Not sure if that's a good or a bad thing," said Tassos.

Maggie shot him a glare. "I thought you were trying to stay in my good graces."

Dimitri grinned. "Remind me to change my vote in the next election."

"It won't matter," said Maggie. "We're everywhere."

Andreas stiffened suddenly and pointed at her. "You know what, Maggie, you're absolutely right. It doesn't matter. You *are* everywhere, and I bet *they're* everywhere."

"What are you talking about?" said Yianni. "Who's they?"

Andreas ignored the question. "Dimitri, I want you to set up a meeting with the mayor and the head of the Hoteliers' Association for later this afternoon. Tell them it's about important information relating to Nikoletta and that she'll be there with us." Andreas looked at Nikoletta. "Assuming that's okay with you."

"Not a chance in the world I'd miss that meeting." She paused. "But what do you plan on us saying?"

Andreas looked out toward the sea. "Good question. I'll let you know as soon as I know."

Chapter Twenty-One

The mayor bitched and moaned, threatened and cajoled, all in an effort to learn the agenda of the meeting in advance, but the presence of the once-missing reporter and attendant possibility of nationwide press coverage ultimately convinced him to attend—provided the meeting be held in his office and photographs be allowed showing him with the reporter.

Marco Sanudos, head of the Naxos Hoteliers' Association, said he was honored by the invitation and would gladly attend.

It remained to be seen which of the two turned out to be the better politician.

Andreas, Yianni, Tassos, and Nikoletta arrived at town hall in the SUV. Dimitri and two of his officers were waiting for them outside the side entrance. Andreas huddled with the two officers and Dimitri for several minutes, the officers nodding as he spoke. When he finished, the two officers left, and Andreas's group of five went inside.

They'd made it as far as the atrium when the mayor came rushing over to Nikoletta.

"Ms. Elia, I'm so happy you're safe. We've been working night and day to find you. All of Naxos rejoices and thanks God for your safe return." He crossed himself three times.

No one missed the film crew and photographer capturing the moment. Nikoletta allowed the mayor his moment of glory by standing next to him, smiling, and nodding.

Through a forced smile, she murmured, "Mr. Mayor, could we please go to your office now? I'm afraid my smile's about to crack into a million pieces."

"Why certainly, my dear. Just a few more photos, please."

Ten minutes later, they made it to the mayor's office. Marco was already there, sitting on the far side of the conference table. He immediately stood to shake hands with Nikoletta and Dimitri and nodded to Yianni, who introduced him to Andreas and Tassos.

"Please sit," said the mayor, taking his seat at the head of the table. "So, to what do I owe the honor of this meeting, aside of course from the rescue of Ms. Elia?"

"We've never met before, Mr. Mayor," said Andreas, "but I've heard wonderful things about you."

The mayor's chest seemed to puff out from beneath his snug suit jacket. "Why, thank you, Chief. As I'm sure you know, it's always rewarding to hear that the sacrifices we make to serve our constituents are appreciated."

Andreas nodded. "That's why I've come to you for your counsel and assistance on a matter of the utmost delicacy."

The mayor's brow furrowed and he leaned in toward Andreas. "Please tell me how I can help."

"Thank you. I knew I could rely on you." Andreas shook his head. "As you know, over the last week, four people have died, three clearly murdered, the fourth most likely as well. In addition, two police officers were the subject of another murder attempt."

"Horrible, horrible. All so unlike anything that's ever happened on our island."

"Yes, I know," said Andreas. "I've come to warn you of a

pernicious evil that's lain dormant on your beloved island for decades but has now come into bloom with a vengeance."

The mayor's furrows grew deeper. "I don't follow."

"Let me be blunt. All those murders and attempted murders are connected. They're tied into one family's efforts at keeping secret something I'm hard-pressed to believe many here on Naxos haven't suspected for years."

"What family?"

"And what secret?" asked Marco.

Andreas spoke Athena's full name.

The mayor leaned back, looking relieved. "That's old news. For a moment I thought you had something. Are you talking about their antiquities dealings?"

"In part, but I think illegal antiquities trafficking is a more accurate description."

The mayor waved his hand dismissively. "If we went after everyone who found and didn't turn in antiquities, we'd lose half our population."

"Even if your numbers were close to accurate, which I doubt, that's an interesting perspective on enforcing the law. It's the sort of attitude that can justify a lot of bad behavior."

The mayor's tone turned aggressive. "Like what?"

"Oh, I don't know; let's start with something simple, like murder."

"Are you accusing me of murder?"

"I didn't realize we were talking about you."

The mayor bit at his lip. "I'm very close to that family. They are big supporters of mine, and I take personal offense at any suggestion that they would be involved in anything like murder."

"I can understand your concern. Since you know the family so well, I assume you also knew the man who used to be their project manager." Andreas spoke his name.

The mayor smirked. "That piece of shit." He turned to Nikoletta. "Excuse me."

She said nothing.

"Why do you call him that?" asked Andreas.

"He was blackmailing Athena for years; everybody knew it."

"Who's everybody?"

"Everybody in the family. When he died, it was good riddance to bad rubbish."

"Wow, I'm impressed at how much you know about the family and its history. We should have come to you first. It would have simplified a lot of things."

"And saved you from wasting a lot of my time," the mayor added.

"The only question I have is, based upon all this knowledge you possess about the family, what secret are they so afraid of that they're prepared to commit murder to conceal?"

"That's just the point. There is nothing to hide. Everything's already out there."

"You know, I thought the same thing. But then I spoke to Nikoletta. And you'll never guess what she's learned through her investigative reporting."

"You mean she's a better investigator than our distinguished Chief of Special Crimes," said the mayor with a slight chuckle.

"Simply amazing, isn't it? Why don't you tell the mayor what you learned from your sources?"

Nikoletta smiled. "As you're well aware, Mr. Mayor, during World War II, Nazis plundered Greece. Much of our patrimony went straight to Germany, but some treasures were reported as destroyed. Take for example your island's School of Commerce, now the Naxos Archaeological Museum."

The mayor nodded.

"Over the years, our Ministry of Culture has documented

those destroyed treasures in connection with our nation's claim for war reparations from Germany."

Nikoletta paused to take a sip of water from a bottle in her bag. "In response, Germany submitted its own documentation contesting their alleged destruction and listing specific items claimed to have been destroyed that still existed."

"Are you going to believe the Germans?" snapped the mayor.

She smiled. "No, but the Germans weren't asking Greece to take their word for it. They provided auction-house records, gallery records, insurance records, private collection records, and other types of reputable third-party documents showing the items to still exist, decades after the war."

The mayor pulled a handkerchief out of his pocket.

"Many of those rebuttal records also reveal the provenance of the items and, lo and behold, guess whose family name, or companies recorded in other Greek ministries as being tied to that family, pop up? Athena's family appears in the provenance of a plethora of items allegedly destroyed in World War II as owning those items *before* the war. If true, that would convey legitimacy upon anyone subsequently acquiring an item through the family. But we know, don't we, Mr. Mayor, that before the war those items were the property of Greek institutions, *not* private individuals or companies?"

The mayor said nothing.

"In some instances, nonfamily members and unrelated companies are listed as participating with the family in ownership of the items." She paused. "Who those participants *are* is particularly interesting."

More silence.

"As I said, the German government went to great pains to demonstrate how claims by the Greek government were inaccurate. In its rebuttal documents, Germany listed military officers of the occupying forces, and persons and entities connected to those officers, found to have participated in transactions involving items previously reported by those same officers as destroyed. In many instances, those records show Athena or her children as participants in those transactions."

"This is insane! How could that be?" shouted the mayor, exploding out of his chair.

"If you're asking from a logistical perspective how such a distinguished Greek family could conspire with Nazi occupiers to steal Greece's national heritage, the answer's *very easily*. The family had both the means and experience necessary for smuggling and disposing of such treasures, and the officers had the incentive. If the Nazis didn't claim the items were destroyed, they'd be ordered to ship them back to Germany to enrich their superiors. Working with the family made sense for both sides." Nikoletta shook her head in disgust. "If you're looking for moral justification for robbing their fellow Greeks, may they find that answer rotting in hell."

Andreas cleared his throat. "Allow me to summarize. I think it's safe to say that this story shatters the image of the family as a stalwart supporter of Greece. After all, how is this going to play out against Nikoletta's publisher's crusade to have Britain return the Parthenon Marbles, when his own family pillaged Greece during its moment of greatest suffering?"

Andreas paused and motioned for the mayor to sit down. "That said, Mr. Mayor, which side of this story of Nazi collaboration and murder do you wish to end up on?"

He sat quietly.

A minute passed.

"Well, say something, already," said Marco. "This is outrageous. It's not even an issue open to discussion. We must cooperate immediately with the police."

Andreas wagged a finger in Marco's direction. "I'm so happy you said that. Because something has been percolating in the back of my mind that never quite sat right. I've heard that Spyros—you probably know him as Honeyman—was acting as the front man in efforts to acquire beachfront properties on behalf of Athena's family."

"Yes, I've heard that too," said Marco.

"But I've also heard that Honeyman knew his limitations, and negotiating those kinds of potentially sophisticated transactions doesn't seem to fit within his skillset. Nor do I think his boss—and I think by now we all know who that is—would trust him to be his man on this island in charge of supervising such significant ventures."

Marco nodded.

"I think the big boss would look for someone familiar with the terrain and the people, someone experienced in business who would know which buttons to push and people to reach out to, even if he didn't do it himself." Andreas stared at Marco. "Can you think of anyone who might fit that description?"

"No."

"Permit me to put it differently. We are investigating murders here. Anyone tied into doing that family's business on this island is a suspect. If you know anyone who might qualify for the role of Honeyman's boss and buffer between him and the big boss, you should encourage him to come forward *now*. The longer he waits, the closer he gets to a murder charge. And I can promise him that, in my experience, he can expect no assistance from the guy at the top of the pyramid. The only words that guy will say are, 'I knew nothing about what my subordinates might have done.'"

Andreas stared at Marco. "In other works, speak up now or be set up later."

Marco looked away. "I didn't do anything wrong. My only

dealings on behalf of the family were in connection with its efforts to acquire the properties. All told, this was a huge project. The biggest the family had ever attempted. Sovereign funds were banking on Naxos becoming bigger than Mykonos and were lined up to invest in the project once we acquired the land. It was my job to manage that, but I had to stay behind the scenes if we hoped to get all the necessary properties."

He paused to swallow. "If locals learned I was involved, they'd know something big was underway, and there'd be instant organized opposition."

Dimitri glared at his friend. "So, *that's* why you picked Honeyman to be the face of your project. Someone so ill-regarded by his neighbors that they wouldn't take him as a serious threat to succeed."

Marco looked down, avoiding Dimitri's eyes. "We needed a low-key, nonthreatening farmer type, but Honeyman was far from my first choice." He swallowed again, still looking down. "I had no say in hiring him. I was ordered to use him."

"Ordered by who?" said Andreas.

"By the head of the family, Nikoletta's publisher."

Andreas shifted his gaze. "Your turn, Mr. Mayor. Who's running the family's operations on the island?"

It was the politician's turn to lower his gaze. "The publisher runs all the family's businesses. The other family members have nothing to do with how he runs them. He treats them all like sheep, paying the six branches of Athena's family tree equal shares to distribute among themselves. They take what he gives them to maintain their lifestyles and ask no questions."

That's why there are no new initials, thought Andreas.

He looked at Marco. "If word got out that the publisher's family had been secretly collaborating with the Nazis against Greece, what effect do you think that would have on the development project?"

"It would kill it. Look, the publisher's potential investors aren't exactly upright citizens of the world, so I'd think the last thing they'd want to be is ensnared in that kind of emotion-charged public mess. They'd certainly still be interested in the project, but not if it involved the publisher's family."

"In other words, if the family's Nazi-collaboration past got out, the publisher would see his family's biggest deal ever disappear. Or, worse yet for a man with his ego, be snapped up by someone else."

Marco nodded. "Yes."

Andreas stood. "Thank you, gentlemen. I suggest you keep our discussion to yourselves. Not because I'm concerned about any of this getting back to the publisher, but because *you* might be concerned if that happens. Thanks for your time."

Andreas led his group from the mayor's office, down the stairs, and out of the building.

Once outside, Andreas turned to Nikoletta. "I'd say you have a pretty big story to write."

"Thanks to you."

"Just do our chief a favor," said Yianni, "and leave out the part where he talked about '*a pernicious evil* that's *come into bloom with a vengeance*.' He'll get razzed about that line for the rest of his life."

Andreas showed Yianni an open hand. "I was setting the mood for that pretentious putz of a mayor." He turned back to Nikoletta. "Do you remember our agreement?"

Nikoletta nodded. "I received all my information through my sources, and I will never reveal a source."

"Perfect. We don't want Maggie and her friends getting fired because of this."

"It shall remain our secret."

"By the way," said Andreas, "you might want to hold off for

a day or so on getting your story out there. I sense there are a couple more shoes to drop."

"No problem. I've got other things to do anyway."

"Like what?" said Yianni.

Nikoletta smiled. "Like finding someone to publish it."

———

"Gray puffy clouds drifting across the western sky transformed by hues of orange and gold into flowers, clowns, and big balloons as they pass across the setting sun." Lila smiled at Nikoletta sitting on a deck chair between Lila and a rattan outdoor couch. "There's nothing like an Aegean sunset, and sharing such a glorious one as this with my closest friends out here in the fresh air inspires me. Though, to be honest, I think I should leave the descriptive efforts to professionals like you."

"No, that was perfect. Besides, I write about crime, not sunsets."

"I never tire of sunsets," said Toni. "Even though they're really nothing more than nature's alarm clock, telling me it's time to get ready to head off to work."

"I wish we could share more sunsets," said Yianni, his head on Toni's lap and facing west, legs stretched out on the couch.

She stroked his hair. "Don't worry; you soon may have the opportunity. I was supposed to be back at my job yesterday."

"I'm sure he'll take you back," said Lila.

"He'd better," said Yianni.

"So you like the thought of me chained to my piano seven nights a week?"

"You got that right."

Toni smacked him lightly on the head.

"What's on the agenda next, Chief?" asked Maggie from a deck chair wedged between the couch and a recliner Tassos had angled toward the house while announcing he'd rather see his friends than another sunset.

"I head back to Athens first thing tomorrow. There's not much more I can do here."

"What about me?" asked Yianni, sitting up.

"Take the rest of the week off."

"I want to go back to Athens to see Popi and her husband. Thank God they won't have to remove her spleen, but I bet it'd make her feel a million times better to hear in person what we've learned so far."

"I can't argue with that," said Andreas.

"Nor can I. As much as I'd like to have you stay with me on Mykonos," said Toni.

SMASH.

"What the hell was that?" asked Tassos.

"Sounds like something broke one of the big windows by the front door," said Maggie.

Andreas stood up from his chair next to Lila and turned to go inside. He took one step toward the doorway and froze.

Bear stood in the doorway to the terrace, a shotgun aimed at Andreas's chest. "Like I said, *asshole,* until next time."

Yianni and Tassos jumped to their feet, and Tassos stepped toward the doorway.

"Don't try to be heroes. This is between me and him."

Andreas motioned with his hand for them to stay back. "Cool it, guys."

"You have something of mine."

"What would that be?"

"Don't play cute. You found it in the sofa. A cool but stupid move."

"Well, if we're speaking frankly, your move is definitely not cool and is seriously stupid."

"Just give me the fucking gun."

"Sorry, no can do."

"You're pretty cocky now, but what if I start shooting up these pretty ladies?"

"I still couldn't give you the gun. I don't have it."

"Who has it? That numbnuts, Dimitri?"

"Nope."

Bear pulled the butt of the shotgun tight against his right shoulder and clenched his teeth. "I'm done talking."

"Well, let's look at the situation. If I had the gun and gave it to you, your smart play would be to leave us alone and at worst face charges surrounding this little performance. So, if I had your gun, why would I risk you killing me and then everyone else in an effort to cover your tracks? Am I getting the general drift of your thinking so far?"

Bear snorted dismissively.

"Good, so let me give you another scenario. Walk away now and all you'll face are charges of owning the gun that killed Honeyman by that marble quarry and his two goons by the airport. With the right friends in high places, you'll likely get away with little if any time served. But if you go through with this, you just might singlehandedly get Greece to reinstate the death penalty."

"You're full of shit." He squeezed the gun tighter against his massive shoulder.

Andreas put up his hand. "Hear me out. There's no way the guy who ordered those three murders would ever risk doing the dirty work himself. What did he offer you? The chance to take over Honeyman's place in the food chain?"

"You've no proof of *any* of that," growled Bear.

"True, and even if the ballistics lab that currently has your gun comes back with a report tying your gun to the bullets dug out of those three dead guys, the *only* provable charge is that you owned the gun. So, do the smart thing and put down the shotgun."

Bear's nerves, plus whatever he'd taken to juice up for this confrontation, had elevated Andreas's own. He raised his hand to his head and begun running his fingers through his hair. "Put the gun down, Bear."

"*FUCK YOU.*"

"This is not going to end well for you."

"For me? I'm the one about to pull this trigger."

"Take a look at your chest."

A red dot twitted about the center of Bear's chest. His eyes jumped to find the source, the barrel of the shotgun drifting in sync with his gaze.

"Drop the gun."

"The hell I will." As he swung the gun back around toward Andreas, Andreas dropped his hand to his side.

Bear's chest imploded a microsecond before the *crack* of the sniper rifle reached the terrace.

Bear nearly toppled, and he struggled to turn his gun on Andreas, but Tassos leaped across the terrace and tore it out of the injured man's hands.

"Call an ambulance!" Andreas yelled to Yianni.

"This guy isn't going to need one," said Tassos. "That bullet took out his heart. He's been running for the last few seconds on pure venom."

"Shit."

"Why are you complaining? This dirtbag was about to kill you and all of us."

"He's the last witness we had who could tie the publisher to the murders."

"Shit."

Five other voices said the same.

———

It was dark by the time the ambulance drove off with Bear's body.

Lila stood with Andreas by the terrace doorway looking down at the bloodstains on the marble. The others sat on the terrace, waiting for local police to complete their investigation.

"How am I ever going to explain to my family's friend what happened in her lovely home?" asked Lila.

Andreas put his arm around her shoulders. "Don't worry; we'll get someone here first thing in the morning to take care of cleaning all this up and to fix the window he smashed to get in."

"How can you be so calm?" She rested her head on Andreas's chest. "I'm still shaking. He was going to *kill* you."

"But he didn't. So I put it all behind me. No reason to dwell on it. Just learn from it."

"And what did you learn?" said Dimitri, stepping out onto the terrace.

"That it pays to go with my instincts."

"What instincts?" asked Lila.

Dimitri answered for him. "He told me to arrange to have two men assigned to watch the house until you all left."

"That's what you were talking about with those two cops outside town hall?" asked Yianni.

"Yeah. Dimitri brought them there so we could meet. He introduced one as a former Greek Special Forces sniper, and I told him to bring along his rifle, just in case."

"Why didn't you tell us?" said Nikoletta.

"I get somewhat paranoid whenever my family is involved, and I didn't want to send everyone else off the deep end based on my hunch."

"How did the sniper know when to shoot?" asked Toni.

"We'd worked out three signals. If I brought one hand up to my head and began running my fingers through my hair, it meant dot him on the chest with his sight. If I brought my other hand up so that both my hands were running through my hair, it meant stand down. But if I had only one hand in my hair and dropped it to my side...well, you know what that meant."

"You do realize," said Dimitri, "that there's no way to keep this from the press. A total of five killings in one week in all of Greece would be front-page news. Five on one island..." He spun his hand in the air.

"Should do wonders for tourism," said Tassos.

"I can already hear the mayor's spin," said Dimitri. "'Through the keen investigative skills and bravery of our Naxos police, our nation has been cleansed of a murderous network responsible for the death of four men.' He'll play that tune long, loud, and often."

"At least you'll get some credit," said Andreas.

"Only because he has no choice."

"Excuse me, but I thought Bear only killed three," said Lila.

"Knowing our mayor," said Dimitri, "he'll add the death of Peter Zagori to his tally rather than leaving open the possibility of the public thinking another killer might still be at large on the island. Besides, it will give him a better excuse than the one he's been using for not keeping his promise to the press to turn over Zagori's name. He's been saying, 'We're waiting to hear back from the Americans.' Now he'll say he didn't want to jeopardize a far more significant investigation."

"Do these guys ever tell the truth?" said Toni.

"Actually, the mayor may be correct in saying Bear killed four," said Andreas. "If not more."

"Who's the fourth?" asked Dimitri.

"The project manager. Bear was Honeyman's natural go-to guy for that kind of thing. If the publisher told Honeyman to get rid of the manager, my money's on Honeyman hiring Bear to do the job. It would have made everyone happy because Bear could arrange to conduct the investigation of his own hit."

"But Bear said Honeyman liked the manager and disliked the publisher," said Dimitri.

"And the mayor said the project manager was a blackmailer," said Yianni.

"Putting aside that Bear was a pathological psychopath and the mayor is a pathological politician, all of that could be true," Andreas paused. "Or not. But my sense of Honeyman is that he was the sort of man who'd be loyal to whoever kept the easy money coming, and that meant the publisher. So, bye-bye, project manager, no matter what he thought of him personally."

"What goes around comes around," said Yianni. "Bear did away with his buddy Honeyman for the same reason."

"And on the orders of the same man," said Maggie.

"For twenty-five years, maybe more, Bear was on easy street, collecting money through Honeyman for doing nothing except possibly listening to Honeyman bitch about his boss."

"Something cops are used to hearing a lot of from their buddies," said Tassos with a smile.

"It wasn't until Honeyman's botched efforts at getting rid of Nikoletta, Popi, and me that the publisher panicked and reached out to Bear directly, offering him Honeyman's gig if he took out Honeyman and the two who'd run Popi and me off the road."

"The publisher must have known Bear killed the manager," said Dimitri.

Andreas nodded. "Bear was unstable. Knowing what Bear knew, I doubt the publisher would have allowed him to live much longer."

"This publisher guy must be a psycho himself," said Dimitri.

"Anything he considers potentially harmful to his family name, he eliminates."

"Precisely why I want Nikoletta to get her story out there ASAP. Once it's published, the harm will be done and he'll no longer have a reason to go after her."

"Except revenge," said Toni.

"I was thinking more about him going after you, Andreas," said Dimitri.

Lila's head jerked away from her husband's chest. Andreas kissed her forehead. "Let's see what happens after Nikoletta's article comes out." He pulled Lila snugly back against his chest. "Then I'll decide what has to be done to protect *my* family."

———

Later that night, before going to bed, Andreas took a walk around the house to make sure all the doors and windows were locked. As he pulled shut the sliding door to the terrace, he heard, "Whoa, there. Is this your way of telling me to go to bed?"

Andreas slid open the door and stepped outside. "Just taking precautions in an effort to limit my run-ins with two-legged madmen to one per day."

"At the risk of raising your count to two, come, sit beside me." Tassos patted the couch.

Andreas slid the door closed behind him, walked to the couch, and dropped next to his friend.

"Tough day, huh?" said Tassos.

"They all are, but when someone comes that close to taking you out..." Andreas shook his head. "Thanks, by the way, for taking the shotgun away from that nutjob."

"It was nothing."

"We both know that's not true. He had the barrel pointed

straight at you when you came at him, and he still had more than enough juice to pull the trigger." Andreas smacked Tassos on the thigh. "You can still move pretty quickly when you have to."

"For an old man."

"Nope, for any man."

Tassos sighed. "We do what we have to do to protect our friends."

"For sure."

"Now, it's my turn to thank you."

"Me?" said Andreas. "For what?"

"I don't know how many more years I have left, and—"

"Stop with that sort of—"

"Just let me finish." Tassos swallowed. "And that's had me wondering recently what really matters anymore. I can't contribute as I once did…so why bother to learn new things, visit new places, make new friends? What's the use? I'm just a relic."

"How much longer do I have to listen to this?"

"Shh, I'm coming to the good part. They say people suffering from deep depression—which I don't see myself as having—can benefit from shock therapy. It literally jolts them back to realizing how beautiful life can be. This afternoon on this terrace with that shotgun in my face, I experienced a sort of shock therapy. Not only did I realize in a matter of seconds that I could still contribute, but also how lost I'd be if I let anything bad happen to those I loved."

Andreas sat quietly for a moment, then thrust a fist into the air. *"Right on."*

Tassos laughed. "I'm serious. I feel…different now. Better, for sure. Like maybe I'm back on track, headed toward some purpose."

"What sort of purpose?"

"Not sure yet, but one will come to me. I'm certain of that."

Andreas smiled. "Look out, bad guys of the Greek Isles, Tassos is back."

Chapter Twenty-Two

Within a week of Andreas's return to Athens, Nikoletta's exposé appeared as a front-page story in the newspaper owned by her publisher's biggest rival.

The publisher countered with stories in his paper accusing Nikoletta of being, on the one hand, a deranged purveyor of libelous fake news and, on the other, a disgruntled employee under exclusive contract to his company, barred from publishing elsewhere. In bold letters across the front page of his paper, he threatened to sue her, the paper that had published her story, and anyone else who "dared to libel his family by repeating Nikoletta Elia's lies."

The trouble was, Nikoletta's story included copies of documents substantiating her claims, and news organizations throughout the EU found them quite convincing. With the Brits having been under siege by her former publisher's paper for years over Lord Elgin and the Parthenon Marbles, the bloodthirsty UK press had a field day, running story after story of how generations of the publisher's family had systematically plundered their own homeland while blaming others. The Germans seized on what they saw as an opportunity to undercut Greece's World

War II reparations claims by, "in the interest of full transparency," releasing a trove of previously unreleased documents listing the current owners and provenance of artifacts and other treasures claimed by Greece to have been destroyed in World War II. Many of those records related to transactions that in no way involved the publisher or his family, but they did name other prominent Greek families, now drawn into the spotlight.

As the publisher's defense of his family grew to ever more vituperative attacks on the European press, CNN got into the act with a special report titled "Has Greece Lost Its Marbles?" The premise of its piece questioned whether the broadening scandal might jeopardize even Greece's legitimate claims for return of its plundered treasures.

Despite all the heat, the publisher showed no sign of backing down. When members of Parliament and prominent citizens urged him to end the battle of words and address his concerns in court, he labeled them "useless, spineless embarrassments to those who know what it means to be Greek."

He used even harsher words to describe his longtime managing editor, Giorgos Pappas, who resigned in protest over his boss's treatment of Nikoletta. Never, though, did the publisher address his critics directly or, for that matter, the substance of Nikoletta's reporting.

Instead, he did what came naturally to him: he berated, bragged, and bullied.

———

Sunday mornings in the Kaldis household generally meant breakfast together, followed by church with the children's grandparents, coffee at a place of the grandparents' choosing, and in summer, a trip to the beach.

This Sunday morning, Andreas only made it to breakfast. Nikoletta's story had galvanized public opinion into demanding the prosecution of the publisher and his family for their crimes. State prosecutors, feeling the intense heat from this red-hot-potato of a case, ducked responsibility for deciding whether sufficient evidence existed to prosecute by kicking the decision back to Andreas and his unit.

Until now, the publisher's link to the murders had not been disclosed to the public. Nikoletta's story focused exclusively on the family's involvement in the illicit antiquities trade. Andreas had no doubt that, once the murders were added to the mix, an already bloody war would turn nuclear, unleashing fevered worldwide media attention upon this modern-day Greek family tragedy and triggering an unimaginable cornered-rat syndrome in the unhinged publisher.

Whether any of that happened would come down to the decision Andreas had to make by the next morning.

Once his family left for church, Andreas retreated to his wife's study to review the evidence, organize his thoughts, and formulate his recommendation.

Thirty minutes later, the building's intercom buzzed. It was a call from the doorman.

"Mr. Kaldis, you have a visitor." He said the name.

Andreas blinked. "Is he alone?"

"Yes. He'd like to see you."

Andreas hesitated. "Okay, send him up."

He put down the phone, left his wife's office, shut the door behind him, and went into their bedroom. Inside his nightstand's bottom drawer, he opened a small gun safe, removed a nine milli-meter, racked the slide, and stuck it in the back of his jeans beneath his untucked shirt.

The doorbell rang as he walked through the rooms leading to

the entrance foyer, wondering what the hell this guy was doing here.

A man in his fifties, wearing an expensive blue suit, white shirt, and red tie, stood outside the apartment's front door. About Andreas's height and build, but decidedly pudgy, with a ruddy complexion and dyed jet-black hair, he reminded Andreas of a Greek version of a former Italian prime minister.

"Thank you for seeing me unannounced, Chief Inspector. May I come in?"

Andreas stepped back from the doorway and gestured for the publisher to enter. "But of course, sir."

He led the man to a sitting room offering a view of the Parthenon. "May I offer you a glass of water? The housekeeper and nanny are off to church, so I'm afraid I can't offer you much more than that."

"No need. I'm fine." Without asking, he sat in the most prominent chair. "You should exercise better control over your staff. No reason why you should be inconvenienced on their behalf."

Andreas forced a smile. "I'll keep that in mind." He dropped onto the sofa across from his visitor. "So, to what do I owe the honor of this visit?"

The man snorted. "No reason to play coy with me, Kaldis. We both know why I'm here."

Andreas raised and dropped his hands. "Sorry, but I can't say that I do."

The publisher leaned in toward Andreas. "It's about that recommendation you're due to submit tomorrow morning."

Andreas showed no reaction.

"And don't bother to ask how I know about it. I know everything."

"You must have friends in high places," said Andreas.

"The highest."

"And the lowest too, I suspect."

"They all have their usefulness."

Andreas wondered how often the man dyed his hair.

"I'm here to ask you what you plan to recommend."

Andreas nodded. "I admire your frankness."

"There's no reason to waste time."

"I agree."

"Well?"

"I haven't made up my mind yet."

The publisher first glared, then softened his look. "That's actually good news. It means perhaps I can convince you to make the right decision."

"I assume I know what you think that would be."

"May I continue to be frank?"

Andreas nodded. "Please."

"One thing you should know, if you don't already, is that in Greece I am all powerful. I know where *every* body is buried, where *every* scandal lies hidden, and where *every* prominent person has a pressure point. That means I can weather this round of unfounded accusations manufactured by my enemies and government peasants. And when all this is forgotten—and believe me, it all shall pass—I shall systematically destroy *anyone* who dared assault my family. Starting with that, that..." he stammered as if running possible adjectives through his mind, "slut Nikoletta Elia."

Andreas yawned.

"Am I boring you?"

"Not at all. Please, go on."

"I don't think you're taking me seriously."

"Oh, believe me when I say that I do. I was just up early with my children."

The publisher glowered at Andreas. "Children are important. I value mine. I'll do anything to protect them."

"I already got that point, sir, so how about getting back to the speaking frankly part?"

The publisher squeezed the arms of the chair, his face approaching beet-red. "If you make the wrong recommendation, I will destroy you and all you hold dear."

"That certainly is frank." Andreas leaned forward. "But what precisely do you think would be the *wrong* recommendation?"

"You have no proof supporting any charges implicating me or my family in any deaths." He smiled. "All potential witnesses to the contrary have sadly passed away."

Andreas smiled back. "If that's what you think, then why are you here?"

"I don't leave anything to chance. That's why."

"You mean you're willing to sit across from one of those government peasants, begging him for mercy."

The publisher yanked himself up to his feet. "I do not beg. I demand. And if you don't do as I say, I will destroy you and your family. And that includes your crooked-cop friend Tassos, who dealt in the same antiquities trading as you accuse my family. And that's just for starters."

Andreas struggled to keep his cool. He'd baited the publisher into revealing what he had in mind to do, and now that he'd heard, there was no reason to allow himself to be baited by his answers.

"Frankly, sir, you're wasting your time. Tassos has no fear of anything you might publish. I'd say you've got an empty quiver."

Spittle flew from the man's mouth as he responded. "And you've got a family to protect. Remember that accidents can happen to anyone, anywhere, anytime." He stabbed a finger at Andreas. "If you know what's good for you, Lila, Tassaki, and Sofia, you damn well know what you'd better do."

Andreas reached behind his back and squeezed the butt of

his gun. "As a matter of fact, I do." Andreas stood. "I think now would be a good time for you to leave."

———

Following his conversation with the publisher, Andreas arranged private security for his family and warned Nikoletta, Tassos, Maggie, Yianni, and Toni, of his threats. Yianni passed along the warning to Popi and her husband, now both back on Naxos.

The day after the publisher paid his visit to Andreas's home, prosecutors charged him and members of his family with crimes relating to their illegal antiquities activities, tax evasion, and fraud. They also announced a continuing investigation by Greece's Special Crimes Unit into five murders potentially linked to the publisher himself. As predicted, the charges set off a second worldwide media explosion and triggered verbal attacks by the publisher on Nikoletta, Tassos, Andreas, and everyone in Andreas's family.

In Nikoletta's new column, granted to her by her new publisher as thanks for his paper's booming boost in sales and growing international reputation as Greece's crusading publication of record, she gave no quarter to her ex-boss, starting with an online column titled, "I Defend My Friends."

When asked by the press for a comment on the war raging all around him, Andreas would only say, "This, too, shall pass."

"So, how do you feel this morning, Mr. Media Star?" said Yianni, sticking his head through the doorway of Andreas's office.

"I'd feel a lot better if we had even the scent of a lead on some way to pin the bastard to one of those murders. There's gotta be *something* out there."

"Hey, guys, turn on the television!" Maggie raced into the

office and straight for the TV remote. She tuned to a news channel, catching a reporter in midsentence. "No explanation yet for what went wrong, but the tragedy couldn't have come at a worse time for the family. Its patriarch has been engaged in a protracted battle to salvage the family's reputation, but now this."

"What the hell is *this*?" yelled Yianni at the TV.

Maggie pointed. "It's there on the chyron running across the bottom of the screen."

PUBLISHER OF LEADING ATHENS NEWSPAPER DIES IN HELICOPTER CRASH.

"Can't be," said Yianni.

Andreas stared at the screen. "I hope no one else died."

"I heard it was just him. He had a helicopter-pilot license."

"Where did it happen?" asked Yianni.

Maggie pointed at the TV as the reporter continued. "We're here with the Naxos chief of police, who's taken personal charge of the investigation. What can you tell us?"

"Hey, it's Dimitri!" said Yianni.

"We know," said Maggie, putting a finger to her lips.

Dimitri spoke directly into the camera. "The matter is currently under investigation by the U.S. military. What we know so far is that a United States drone based on Crete unexpectedly locked on to the victim's helicopter as it flew from Naxos to Crete and launched a missile that destroyed the helicopter in midair. As yet, the United States has offered no explanation for how such a tragic accident could have occurred."

"Seems poetic justice, doesn't it?" snipped Maggie. "Dimitri reporting on the investigation of the publisher's accidental death."

"Turn it off," said Andreas.

"Why? He's not done yet," said Yianni.

Andreas barked, "*I said turn it off.*"

Maggie turned it off. "What's bothering you, Chief? Were

you wishing he'd die, and now that it's happened, you feel guilty?"

"Maybe."

"Or maybe what else?" asked Yianni.

Andreas ran his hands through this hair and ended by rubbing the heels of his hands into his eyes. He looked at them and exhaled. "Maybe I could have prevented this."

"How?"

"I don't know, but with so many people angry at this guy, I should have done something to dampen down their rage."

"Bullshit," said Yianni. "You always took the high road."

"While letting everyone else take the low," mumbled Andreas.

"*STOP*. Enough already," said Maggie. "This guy had more people wanting to kill him than lined up to murder Samuel Ratchett on the *Orient Express*. No way you could have stopped them all."

"Not to mention that one of us would have had to do the job that drone did if that piece of shit had ever tried hurting your family."

Andreas rubbed at his eyes some more.

A message ping came through on Andreas's mobile. He looked at the screen. "It's from Nikoletta. Just after the publisher's death was announced on the news, she received an anonymous comment to one of her online columns. The one titled, 'I Defend My Friends.'" Andreas cleared his throat. "It reads, 'As you see, I also defend my friends. Your fan, Soter.'"

Read on for an excerpt from

Island
of Secrets

Book 10 in the Chief Inspector
Andreas Kaldis Mystery series.

Available now!

Chapter One

He never wondered about the purpose of life or how he turned out as he had. It all just sort of happened. He became a cop because he saw it as the surest way for a kid born into Greece's working class in the tumultuous early 1960s to make a living. He got lucky when, after the fall of the Military Junta in 1974, he joined the youth movement of a left-wing political party that came to power in 1981 and remembered to reward its loyal friends.

As he rose in rank, the more friends and money he made, the more power he amassed. He kept careful track of where the bodies were buried and possessed an uncanny instinct for digging up the ones he needed to achieve his purposes. An effort by the opposition party to paint him as corrupt failed when the prosecution's main witness died in a boating accident. An investigation into the witness's death faded away soon after he announced his decision to retire from the Hellenic Police force with the rank of colonel.

That's when he began to make truly big money, capitalizing on his contacts and former position as head of police for the South Aegean Region, home to Greece's most popular tourist islands for the rich and hard-partying globe-trotting crowd.

Tonight, the Colonel was far away from all that glitz and glamour. He sat in a restaurant in a nondescript, middle-class eastern suburb of Athens, virtually equidistant from downtown Athens, its port town of Rafina, and Venizelos International Airport.

"A convenient place for a meeting," said the one who'd arranged it.

The Colonel leaned back in his chair and yawned. The conversation had been as boring as the meal. Everything about the place was mediocre, from its tired, thirty-year-old decor to the hookers at the bar, and the ruddy-faced, pudgy man sitting across the table from him who had yet to say why their mutual business acquaintance thought they should meet.

"Am I keeping you awake, Colonel?"

"Barely."

Ruddy Face smiled. "How do you like my place?"

The Colonel leaned forward. It was long past time to get down to business. "If this is your joint, why don't you just tell me why you wanted to meet? You sure as hell don't need my services to run this operation."

"You're right, it's a dump." Ruddy Face paused. "But I have plans."

"What sort of plans?"

"I'm buying a club on the islands. It's going to be first-class in every way." He nodded toward the bar. "Including the girls."

"Which island?"

"One you control."

"Control is a mighty big word."

Ruddy Face smiled. "Let's just say, I don't like the idea of getting involved in a business where my investment isn't secure."

"That's prudent of you."

"Can you help me?"

"If you're asking for security, the answer is yes."

"I'm talking about *protection* for *all* aspects of my business."

The Colonel shrugged. "It's all a matter of price. You tell me what you want, and I'll tell you what it will cost you."

"I hear you're pricey."

"You heard right. But I make sure things run smoothly."

"How do you do that?"

"I don't have competitors stirring things up, jockeying for business. I maintain order among the chaos."

"They might see things differently."

"If by *they* you mean competitors, there are no *they* on my island. I'm the only game in town."

"I get your point," said the man. "I'm sure we'll come to terms."

"If you want to open a club where I'm in business, I'm sure we will."

The Colonel declined an offer of coffee, and the two men agreed to talk again once Ruddy Face had a better idea of what he might need from the Colonel.

He walked the Colonel to the front door, shook his hand, thanked him for coming, and wished him safe travels. "*Kalo taxidhi.*"

But the Colonel only made it as far as the front door of his Mercedes.

———

Greece's General Police Headquarters, better known as GADA, sat close by the heart of Athens's bustle, next door to a major hospital, down the block from Greece's Supreme Court, and across the street from the stadium of one of Greece's most popular soccer teams. GADA's Special Crimes Unit, charged with investigating potential corruption and other matters of national concern—at least those that piqued the interest of its Chief

Inspector Andreas Kaldis—occupied the eastern side of the fourth floor.

Andreas had been at his desk since shortly after sunrise. With two early-rising young children at home, it wasn't unusual for him to flee the morning domestic chaos for the relative calm of tracking down bad actors. His wife, Lila, never seemed to mind when he abandoned her to the ruckus, undoubtedly because she rightly considered him an active accessory to their children's early-morning mischief.

It wasn't as if he were leaving his wife alone to deal with their son and daughter; she did have a housekeeper and nanny to help, a decidedly suspicious luxury on an honest cop's salary. But all of that, and more, had come with his marriage to the daughter of one of Greece's most respected and wealthiest families. He appreciated his good fortune and considered himself a lucky man.

Too bad he couldn't say the same thing for the guy plastered all over the morning news headlines: RETIRED POLICE COLONEL STAVROS AKTIPIS ASSASSINATED. That summed up virtually everything the various news stations had to report on the shooting, though they tried their best to spice up their coverage with references to corruption allegations that had haunted the victim.

All the allegations preceded Andreas's time as chief of Special Crimes, but he'd heard the stories and much more about the Colonel. Instinctively, Andreas believed the victim had been corrupt, for the system far too often brought temptations to one in his position. Yet, if Andreas pursued every case of official corruption brought to his attention, he'd need all the offices in the building to house his staff—not to mention an unimaginable number of additional prosecutors.

Compounding all of that, innovative criminal types from around the world kept introducing new schemes and methods into Greece that added to his caseload. Overwhelmed as his unit was, and Greece a decade into a crippling economic crisis, he knew he'd be wasting his time asking for more support from the government. That left Andreas with little choice but to pursue the most egregious offenders, hoping to make an example of them in a manner that discouraged others from doing the same.

What happened last night to the Colonel, he knew, would be headed straight for his desk, in a file marked NASTY in all-red letters. The Colonel had been murdered for a reason, and it wasn't robbery. His wallet, filled with euros, and an expensive watch were untouched. Three quick bullets to the back of his head as he stood at his car door. No witnesses, and no terrorists claiming credit for the killing. At least none so far.

Andreas held a remote in his right hand, surfing through local news coverage on the wall-mounted TV screen to his right, while drumming the fingers of his left hand on his desktop. He looked at his watch. Detective Yianni Kouros should be at the scene by now. Andreas had called him at home as soon as he'd heard the early morning news. Yianni had been his right-hand man since their days together on Mykonos, back when Andreas was the island's police chief and Yianni a brash young bull of a rookie cop.

Andreas bit at his lip. Killing cops, retired or not, wasn't something even the most hardened criminals undertook lightly, especially when the victim was an ex-colonel. He'd been assassinated for a serious reason, most likely with the blessing of serious people. That's why he'd sent Yianni to the scene. He wanted his own people in on the investigation from the start. Screw-ups early on—unintentional or otherwise—haunted investigations, at times serving as a convenient pretext for bad guys getting away with murder. Not this time, though. Not if Andreas could help it.

Yes, this definitely would be a nasty one.

ACKNOWLEDGMENTS

Anastasia Antoniadou; Mihalis, Roz, and Spiros Apostolou; Marios Assimakopoulos; Vassilis Condilis; Diane DiBiase; Andreas, Aleca, Mihalis, and Anna Fiorentinos; Eleftherious Fiorentinos; Flora and Yanni Katsaounis; Panos Kelaidis; Giannis Nikiforou Konstantakis; Bogdan and Martina Kopec; Vicky Koromina; Marine Lascaris; Nikoletta Lianos and Dimitris Lianos; Linda Marshall; Tottie Mitchell; Terrence, Karen, and Rachel McLaughlin; Barbara G. Peters and Robert Rosenwald; Amargyros Protonotarios; Spyros Protonotarios; Dora Rallis; Alexander Reichardt and Katharina Bolesch; Grand Master Mark Shuey (founder of Cane Masters); Jonathan, Jennifer, Azriel, and Gavriella Siger; Ed Stackler; Yiannis Vassilas and Sophia Dimakopoulou; Barbara Zilly.

And, of course, Aikaterini Lalaouni.

ABOUT THE AUTHOR

Photo by Thanasis Krikis

Jeffrey Siger was born and raised in Pittsburgh, Pennsylvania, practiced law at a major Wall Street law firm, and later established his own New York City law firm, where he continued as one of its name partners until giving it all up to write full-time among the people, life, and politics of his beloved Mykonos. *A Deadly Twist* is the eleventh novel in his internationally bestselling and award-nominated Chief Inspector Andreas Kaldis series, following up on *Island of Secrets* (first published as *The Mykonos Mob*), *An Aegean April*, *Santorini Caesars*, *Devil of Delphi*, *Sons of Sparta*, *Mykonos After Midnight*, *Target: Tinos*, *Prey on Patmos*, *Assassins of Athens*, and *Murder in Mykonos*.

The *New York Times* described Jeffrey Siger's novels as "thoughtful police procedurals set in picturesque but not untroubled Greek locales," and named him as Greece's thriller writer of record. The *Greek Press* called his work "prophetic," Eurocrime described him as a "very gifted American author... on par with other American authors such as Joseph Wambaugh or Ed McBain," and the City of San Francisco awarded him its Certificate of Honor citing that his "acclaimed books have not only explored modern Greek society and its ancient roots but have inspired political change in Greece." He now lives in Greece.